Colin Bamford and Susan Grant

Cambridge International AS and A Level

Economics

Coursebook

Third Edition

CAMBRIDGE
UNIVERSITY PRESS

CAMBRIDGE
UNIVERSITY PRESS

University Printing House, Cambridge CB2 8BS, United Kingdom

One Liberty Plaza, 20th Floor, New York, NY 10006, USA

477 Williamstown Road, Port Melbourne, VIC 3207, Australia

314–321, 3rd Floor, Plot 3, Splendor Forum, Jasola District Centre, New Delhi – 110025, India

79 Anson Road, #06–04/06, Singapore 079906

Cambridge University Press is part of the University of Cambridge.

It furthers the University's mission by disseminating knowledge in the pursuit of education, learning and research at the highest international levels of excellence.

www.cambridge.org

First published 2002
Second edition 2010
Third edition 2015
20 19 18 17 16 15 14 13

Printed in Dubai by Oriental Press

A catalogue record for this publication is available from the British Library

ISBN 978-1-107-67951-1 Paperback

Contents

Preface

This third edition of *Cambridge International AS and A Level Economics* has been specifically produced for the Cambridge International Examinations 9708 syllabus for examination from 2016.

The text is divided into two clearly identified sections, Chapters 1 to 5 cover the AS Level content that is examined in Paper 1 and Paper 2; Chapters 6 to 10 cover the additional A Level content examined in Paper 3 and Paper 4. Also, there is an Introduction that contains a breakdown of the skills you will need for the successful study of the Cambridge syllabus and a final chapter that gives valuable guidance on how to use your skills to the best of your abilities in examination.

The key features of the book are stated in the Introduction.

This third edition contains up-to-date statistics and many new self-assessment tasks. Where possible and appropriate, these and the text are specifically set within the geographical context of where students are studying the Cambridge syllabus. There is therefore a strong Asian focus, as well as reference to the other developing economies.

The book is accompanied with an extensive Student CD, which has been produced by the authors. This contains substantial information for students including:

- example examination questions and answers drawn from each chapter
- worksheets with answers to assist students on completion of each chapter
- additional advice on how to revise
- a glossary of key terms.

Although the book has been specifically written for the Cambridge 9708 syllabus, it will be of value to students and teachers of any AS or A Level courses, as well as the IB. It will particularly appeal to international students, as well as UK students seeking contextual knowledge of developing economies.

Finally, we would like to record some thanks. First, to the teachers and students who have sent us comments (invariably complimentary) on the second edition. Secondly, to the various Cambridge University Press staff, especially Elizabeth Walne, for their comments on the text and the student CD. Finally, to our students in Oxfordshire and West Yorkshire, who from time to time have provided an opportunity for us to try out new ideas on how to make studying economics a rewarding experience.

We hope you find the book and CD useful and that they help you achieve success in your Cambridge Economics course.

Colin G. Bamford
Susan Grant
August 2014

The authors

Colin Bamford

Professor Colin Bamford is Associate Dean of the Business School at the University of Huddersfield, UK. He has co-authored various text books with Susan Grant as well as writing in his specialist field of transport economics. He has over 35 years' experience of examining. Colin is a Vice President of the Economics and Business Enterprise Association. He is a regular contributor to local and national print, radio and television media on transport issues.

Susan Grant

Susan Grant is an experienced teacher, trainer, examiner and writer. She conducts training sessions throughout the world. Her publications include more than 20 economics books, a number co-authored with Professor Colin Bamford.

Introduction

The economist's toolkit and the Cambridge syllabus

Learning objectives

On completion of this Introduction you should:

- know the key features of the book
- have a broad idea of what is meant by Economics
- know how economists seek to explain economic phenomena
- be aware of the 'toolkit' of skills required for a study of Economics
- be aware of the requirements of the Cambridge International AS and A Level Economics syllabus.

The key features of the book

This book is written both for students who have taken Cambridge IGCSE® Economics and for those students who are new to the subject. Its key features are:

- Chapters that match the sections of the Cambridge International AS and A Level Economics syllabus.
- Many chapter activities: These are designed to give you practice at applying what you are learning and are mainly based on real world examples.
- Clear diagrams: These should help you to become familiar with the diagrams economists use and should enable you to see how you can use them to analyse economic issues and events.
- Top tips: These are designed to improve your performance and to help you avoid common errors made by students.
- Key concept links: These explain how the key concepts identified in the Cambridge syllabus are linked to the topics covered.
- Past examination questions: These provide you with the opportunity to test your skills of knowledge and understanding, application, analysis and evaluation.

What is Economics?

There are almost as many definitions of Economics as there are economists! Although a definition of the subject is to be expected, it is probably more useful at this stage to set out a few examples of the sort of issues that concern professional economists. These topics occur in an introductory form in the Cambridge syllabus.

Let us take you first of all. Most people find that they want to lead an exciting and full life but unfortunately do not always have the money necessary to buy or to do all they want. So, choices have to be made, or as an economist would say, individuals have to decide how to allocate their scarce resources in the most efficient way.

A body of economic principles and concepts has been developed to explain how people, and also businesses, behave in this situation. This is a typical example of what an economist would refer to as microeconomics.

It is not only individuals and firms who are faced with having to make choices. Governments face many such problems. For example, how does a country's government decide how much to spend on health or social security and how much should go into providing new roads and infrastructure for, say, tourism? This is the same type of problem facing all of us in our daily lives but on a different scale.

Governments also have extensive responsibilities in looking after the well-being of their national economies. The finance ministers, for example, prepare an annual budget for their economies, in which taxation and government expenditure plans are reviewed. It is also an opportunity to 'manage the economy' by seeking to ensure that policy objectives are being met. An economist would say that the finance ministers have to decide:

- how to keep the rate of change of prices (inflation) under control
- how to increase total demand in the economy to increase the number of jobs that are available.

These are typical topics that come under the broad heading of macroeconomics since they relate to the economy as a whole.

As you read through this text you will come across many other economic problems and issues of both a micro and macro nature. You may now find it useful to complete Self-assessment task 1 below.

SELF-ASSESSMENT TASK 1

1 Make a list, in your own words, of some of the economic decisions that:
   - you are facing
   - your family has to take
   - your country has to take.
2 Pick up any quality newspaper or look at any quality news website. Look through it systematically and make a note of the various micro- and macroeconomic problems and issues you find. Did you find it easy to classify problems in this way?

The last part of Self-assessment task 1 was designed to help you to appreciate that many economic problems and issues cannot be satisfactorily classified as micro or macro. In other words, such problems encompass both of the main branches of Economics. For example, an increase in taxation on petrol may reduce the demand for petrol. Depending on the extent of this, there is an effect on the income of individuals and the government and, in turn, this affects the economy as a whole. So, there can be complex interrelationships coming into play. This is one of the reasons that Economics is such an interesting subject to study.

As you read through this text, you will be introduced to concepts, theories and simple models that are used by economists to explain the many economic problems and issues that come within the scope of Economics. In time, you will build up a portfolio of such techniques, from a micro- and macroeconomic perspective. Virtually all have their origin in some sort of practical investigation, i.e., a study of real economic phenomena. Some concepts have their origin centuries ago, others are much more contemporary or may have been refined and revised in the light of the growing complexity of the present-day global economy. Again, this serves to enhance the interesting nature of the study of Economics.

It is appropriate from the outset to attempt to give a clear definition of Economics. For a start, Economics is a social science – it adopts a scientific framework but is particularly concerned with studying the behaviour of humans as consumers, in business or in taking decisions about the economy as a whole. More specifically, *Economics is the study of how scarce resources are or should be allocated.* All of the problems and issues you will come across fit into this broad definition.

Regardless of what you may think about Economics and economists at this stage of your Cambridge studies, few would deny that Economics is a logical subject and that the advice provided by economists is derived from a set of well-established principles relating to the operation of the market economy. Figure 1 shows, in simple terms, how economists think and how they seek to explain real problems and issues like those you will have come across in the first self-assessment task.

At this stage, bear this process in mind and return to it whenever you are learning new concepts as it will help you understand how economists think and operate.

Economists cannot always be certain that what they say is completely accurate or how the advice they provide will affect an economy. Much of the content of this book consists of positive statements that are factual and usually acceptable to all economists. For example:

- the inflation rate in Egypt in 2013 was 2%
- Spain had a budget deficit in 2013.

On other occasions, economists make normative statements involving value judgements. For example:

- the government should cut fuel tax to reduce the rate of inflation
- public sector workers should reduce their demands for higher wages.

These latter statements express an opinion about what ought to happen. Unlike positive statements, where economists can use data and practical evidence, normative statements involve value judgements, which are often drawn from the economist's personal views, political beliefs and ethics. As you study the content of the chapters, keep this important distinction in mind. You will also need to think about it when answering some of the more demanding questions.

It is now appropriate to give a fuller definition of Economics. We have established that Economics is a social science. More specifically, it is the study of how society provides for itself by making the most efficient use of scarce resources so that both private and social welfare may be improved. Economics provides a framework for studying how individuals, households, firms, governments and global organisations behave and take a wide range of decisions.

Interest in Economics has never been stronger than it is at present. In 2008 and part of 2009 the global economy was thrown into the most serious recession of modern times. The effects of the downturn were worldwide. Rich, poor and emerging economies were all affected. In turn, there was a profound impact on the lives and economic well-being of people throughout the world.

In 2010 the global economy started to recover but as the article in Self-assessment task 2 shows, there was still some concern in 2014 that the recovery might not last. Read through the article and see if you can answer some of the questions that follow.

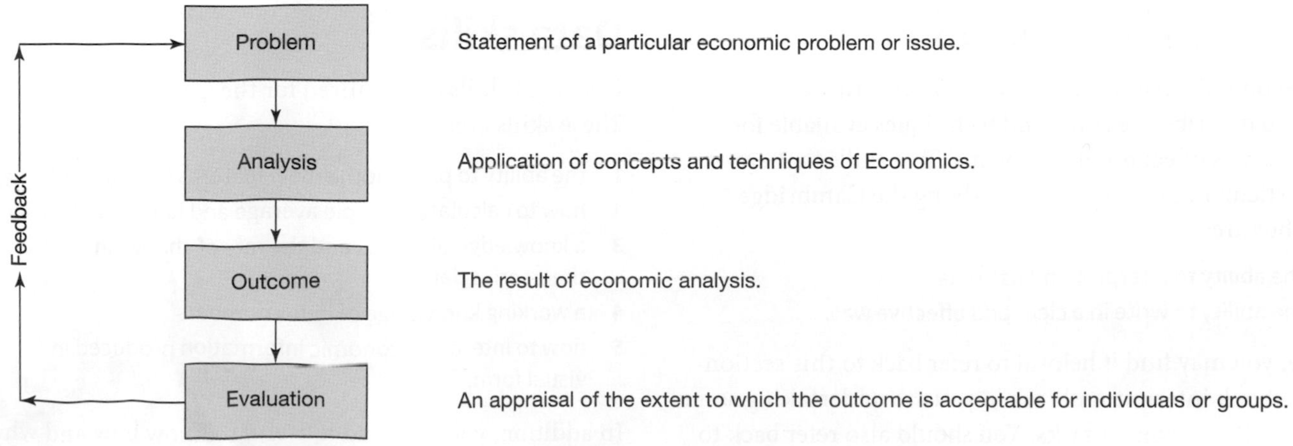
Problem
Statement of a particular economic problem or issue.
Analysis
Application of concepts and techniques of Economics.
Outcome
The result of economic analysis.
Evaluation
An appraisal of the extent to which the outcome is acceptable for individuals or groups.
Feedback

Figure 1 The road to economic explanation

SELF-ASSESSMENT TASK 2

Read the feature below and answer the questions that follow.

Recovery under threat

January 2014 saw a significant fall in share prices on stock markets throughout the world. The fall was particularly significant in the United States of America. The downturn in global share prices combined with a decline in China's economic growth rate led some economists to worry that the recovery from the 2007–2008 recession was under threat.

The US economy had been driving the global recovery but in January 2014 there were some economists who thought that the country's economic performance in 2014 would not be as strong as its 2013 performance. There was some evidence to support this view. Manufacturing and car sales declined at the end of 2013 and start of 2014. Economic activity was disrupted by bad weather at this time with very low temperatures and heavy snowfall.

There were some economists, however, who were more optimistic about future US economic performance. Although consumer confidence had been low in 2013 it was expected to rise in 2014, which it was thought would contribute to a higher economic growth rate in 2014 than in the previous year.

In contrast, there was widespread agreement that China's 2014 economic growth rate would be lower than its 2013 rate. How much China's output increases has a significant impact on a number of other economies, including emerging economies such as Brazil, India and Turkey. In 2013 the Turkish central bank more than doubled the country's interest rates. The European Central Bank and the Central Bank of Japan were, however, seeking to introduce expansionary monetary policy measures, in part to increase the confidence of households and firms in the future economic prospects of their economies.

A rise in optimism about the future could itself contribute to a better economic performance, with higher consumer expenditure and investment increasing output which, in turn, would increase incomes.

1 Which two countries does the article suggest currently have the greatest influence on the world economy?

2 What do you think is meant by bad weather disrupting 'economic activity'?

3 Can you name three stock markets?

4 Explain the effect a rise in interest rates may have on the construction industry.

5 Does the article suggest that expectations influence economic behaviour? Explain your answer.

6 Note down three economic terms from the article you do not currently understand. Using this book and the glossary in the student CD, check on their meaning.

The economist's toolkit

The economist has a varied toolkit, a term that can be used to describe the skills and techniques available for the analysis of economic problems. Two skills that are of particular relevance when studying the Cambridge syllabus are:

- the ability to interpret and use data
- the ability to write in a clear and effective way.

Note: you may find it helpful to refer back to this section of the book intermittently when you are undertaking some of the self-assessment tasks. You should also refer back to this section before you take any examinations.

Data skills

Five main skills are required for the Cambridge syllabus. These skills are:

1 the ability to pick out the main features in a data set
2 how to calculate a simple average and know what it means
3 a knowledge of trends and the rate of change in a set of time-series data
4 a working knowledge of index numbers
5 how to interpret economic information produced in visual form.

In addition, you will find it useful to know how and why economists make forecasts.

It is important that you feel confident in handling data – these simple skills will help you. You will also gain confidence as you become more familiar with economic data and complete the various self-assessment tasks in each chapter.

Economic data are of two main types.

1. **Time-series data:** As the name suggests, the same information is recorded over a period of time, for example a period of years, or months in a year, days in a week and so on.
2. **Cross-sectional data:** The easiest way to imagine this type of data is in terms of a 'snapshot', i.e., a picture taken at a given time.

Another important introductory point concerns the nature of the data itself. Again, two types can be recognised:

1. **Discrete data:** The simplest way to imagine this is in terms of values which are shown as whole numbers, e.g., number of people or number of cars. In this case, there is a distinct jump from one value to another. There cannot be, for example, 2.6 cars.
2. **Continuous data:** Such values can usually be measured in a precise way and are not confined to whole numbers, e.g., income, inflation or economic growth. For example, the inflation rate can be 2.6%.

So, when you are confronted with economic data for the first time, ask yourself:

- Is the data shown a time-series or cross-sectional data?
- Are the values of the data discrete or continuous?

Below are three further matters to consider; these are also important when you come across a data set for the first time, particularly in a time-constrained examination situation.

1. **Title and source of data:** The title should give you a clear guide as to what the data is about. A lot of economic data are from governmental or other official sources such as the World Bank. This should mean that it is accurate, although this may not necessarily be so. If the data has come from other sources, be wary about what it shows – it may have been produced in such a way as to promote a particular viewpoint.
2. **Estimates:** Some data will be an estimate that has been made by the organisation responsible for collecting the data. This is often necessary as there is invariably a time lag in producing more accurate information. In other instances if no data has been collected or it is difficult to collect data then the organisation will produce an estimate.
3. **Forecast:** Economists rely heavily on forecasts in order to take policy decisions (see page 8). Therefore, key economic variables are often forecasted in order to assist this process. Such data is likely to be reasonably accurate but should never be taken to be precise.

Data skill 1 – how to pick out the main features in a data set

Look at the data in Table 1. This gives the average unemployment rates for the 27 countries that were members of the European Union in 2012.

The first skill you need to develop is what is known as 'eyeballing'. All this means is looking at a data set and going down the columns (or across the rows) very quickly to pick out the main features. This is a very useful thing to do, particularly in examinations when it could give you a clue as to what questions might follow.

Looking at Table 1, you can quickly see that there is a wide variation in average unemployment rates for EU members in 2012. Spain had the highest rate at around 25%, whereas unemployment was lowest in Luxembourg at 5.1%.

Data skill 2 – how to calculate a simple average and know what it means

The average is often used to summarise a particular set of data. In the case of Table 1 – where it is shown as 10.5% – it is what is known as a 'weighted average', the weights

Country	Percentage	Country	Percentage
Austria	4.3	Latvia	14.9
Belgium	7.6	Lithuania	13.3
Bulgaria	12.3	Luxembourg	5.1
Cyprus	11.9	Malta	6.4
Czech Republic	7.0	Netherlands	5.3
Denmark	7.5	Poland	10.1
Estonia	10.2	Portugal	15.9
Finland	7.7	Romania	7.0
France	10.2	Slovakia	14.0
Germany	5.5	Slovenia	8.9
Greece	24.3	Spain	25.0
Hungary	10.9	Sweden	8.0
Ireland	14.7	United Kingdom	7.9
Italy	10.7		
Average EU 27	10.5		

Table 1 EU unemployment rates in 2012

Source: Eurostat, February 2014

being the actual numbers of unemployed people in each of the 27 countries listed. The weights are necessary since the populations of the countries are different. If they were all equal, the average would be the sum of all the percentages divided by 27. Twelve countries had unemployment rates above the average and 15 countries had rates below the average.

The average, or mean, can be affected by extreme values. To some extent the use of weighting reduces this problem compared to a situation where all values have an equal weight.

Data skill 3 – how to pick out trends and the rate of change in a data set

Now look at the data in Table 2. This shows the annual percentage change in consumer prices and food and drink prices in Pakistan from 2006 to 2011. (As you will learn later the former is a good measure of inflation in an economy.)

This data set is a time series. You can get an overview of the data by looking at how it has changed on a year-to-year basis over the period.

A closer look at Table 2 shows that:

- the annual percentage change in consumer prices is positive from 2006 to 2011
- the highest rise was in 2009
- food and drink prices are also rising on an annual basis, again with a peak in 2009
- food and drink prices rose more rapidly than the general rise in prices in each year shown.

For time-series data like that in Table 2, you may find it useful to write a '+' or a '–' (plus or minus) sign between each year, so that you can see how the rate of change varies over time. It is conventional to put these signs between the years in question. When you do this, you can see that the rate of change for 'all items' increased slightly more slowly in 2007. It then rose more rapidly in 2008 and 2009. It rose less rapidly in 2010 but the rate of increase again rose in 2011. The annual rate of change for food and drink prices followed a similar pattern except for 2007 when it was positive.

A final word of warning: consumer prices and food and drink prices have increased consistently since 2006. Inflation therefore has persisted, although in some years, such as 2007 and 2010, the annual rate of change has fallen. This does not mean prices have fallen. It simply means that the annual rate of increase has slowed down. Prices have risen but risen more slowly. A common mistake that many students make when considering data like that in Table 2 is to wrongly assume that prices have fallen. This is not so.

	All items	Annual change	Food & drink	Annual change
2006	7.9		6.9	
2007	7.8	–	10.3	+
2008	12.0	+	17.6	+
2009	17.0	+	23.5	+
2010	10.1	–	12.6	–
2011	13.7	+	18.3	+

Table 2 Average annual percentage change in consumer prices for high-income earners in Pakistan, 2006–2011

Source: Adapted from *Pakistan Statistical Yearbook*, 2012

Data skill 4 – a working knowledge of index numbers

With time-series data especially, it is often helpful to show the data in index form, with a base year of 100. Thereafter, data for subsequent years is shown in the form of an index. This avoids some of the difficulties mentioned above when considering the rate of change in time-series data.

To construct an index number:

- Identify a base year. This should be typical and is given an index of 100.
- The next year's figure is then divided by the base year figure and multiplied by 100 to give an index figure. For example, average income in Chile was:
  - US$15,600 in 2008
  - US$16,900 in 2009
  - US$17,400 in 2010
  - US$17,600 in 2011
  - US$18,500 in 2012
  - US$19,100 in 2013.

If 2008 is taken as the base year, the 2009 figure would be converted into an index figure by:

$$\frac{16,900}{15,600} \times 100 = 108.3$$

From this information, it can be seen clearly that income rose by 8.3% between 2008 and 2009.

Similarly the index figure for 2010 can be calculated by:

$$\frac{17,400}{15,600} \times 100 = 111.5$$

Table 3 shows the index figures for all the years given above.

An effective way of considering this form of data is to use a level and trend approach. Level is concerned with the difference between the start year and the final year. Trend refers to the year-to-year changes shown in Table 2 above.

So, the following additional points can now be made:

- Average income rose by 22.4% over the period 2008 to 2013.
- Average income rose most slowly in 2011. It increased by only 1.3 index points or 1.2%.
- Average income rose most rapidly in 2009 at 8.3 index points and 8.3%.
- The second most rapid rise was in 2012 at 5.7 index points or 5.1%.

Data skill 5 – how to interpret economic information produced in a visual form

Increasingly, economic information is produced in a visual form in the media. Figure 2 contains two examples of bar charts. Such representations are particularly effective for mapping out time-series data. The basic principle is that the height of each bar represents the data shown on the vertical scale: in this case, tourist arrivals in Mauritius.

The value of bar charts is that it is possible to see at a glance changes in the level and trend. Figure 2a shows the annual numbers of tourist arrivals over a ten-year period from 2003 to 2012. What is quite clear is that the level of tourist arrivals has increased over this period. A closer examination shows that there was a fall between 2008 and 2009, that just before that there was the most rapid rise and that the numbers were unchanged between 2011 and 2012.

Figure 2b adds a further dimension, namely that for one year, 2012, it shows that there have been monthly variations in tourist arrivals, a point not immediately obvious from the annual data alone. Tourist arrivals peaked in December and were lowest in June. The actual arrivals can easily be read off the vertical scale.

Figure 3 is an example of a pie chart. The basic principle behind its construction is that the respective shares are shown by the relative sizes of the slices of the pie. These shares are determined by allocating 360° for the overall total – the share of each segment is then determined by the following formula:

$$\text{size of each segment} = \frac{\text{number in a given segment}}{\text{overall total}} \times 360^\circ$$

Year	Average income (index figures)
2008	100.0
2009	108.3
2010	111.5
2011	112.8
2012	118.5
2013	122.4

Table 3 Average income in Chile 2008–2013

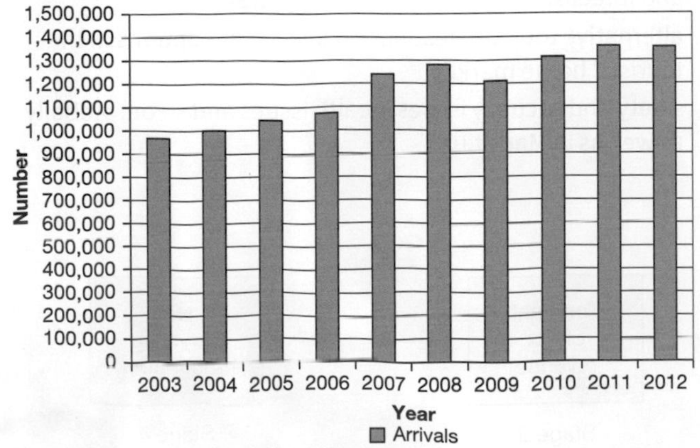

Figure 2a Mauritius: tourist arrivals, 2003–2012

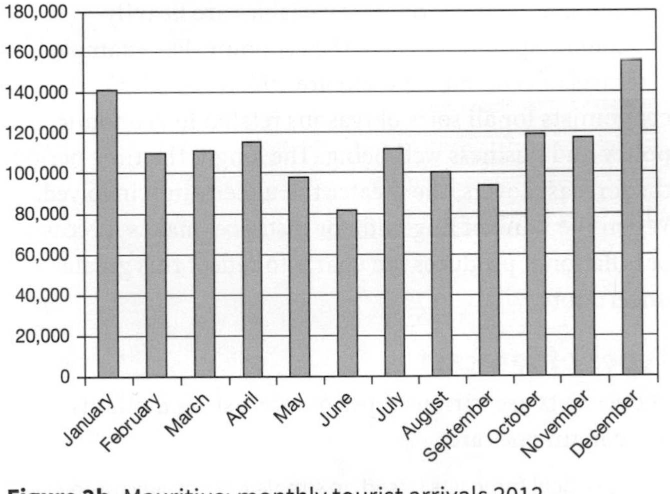

Figure 2b Mauritius: monthly tourist arrivals 2012

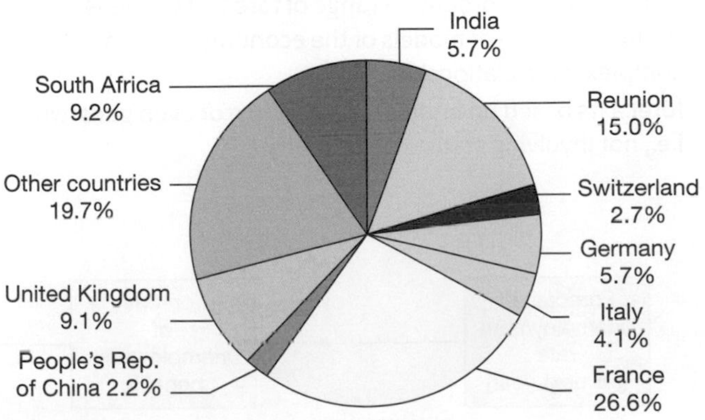

Figure 3 Percentage distribution of tourist arrivals in Mauritius by country of residence, 2012

So, for a total frequency of 200, a segment which has 50 observations in it will be represented by a 90° slice of pie.

Figure 3 shows the country of residence for tourist arrivals in Mauritius in 2012. As this shows, the largest percentage of tourists come from France. Very conveniently, Figure 3 shows the actual percentages in each segment. This is not always the case, but it is possible to make estimates from the relative sizes of each slice of the pie.

Students with access to Microsoft Excel will be able to produce a wide range of bar charts and pie charts with this software.

Newspapers, websites and magazines such as *The Economist* increasingly represent economic information in highly attractive ways, combining various forms of representation.

How and why economists make forecasts

One of the most important tasks of the professional economist, whether in government or private sector employment, is to be able to forecast future economic phenomena. Many economic variables are heavily dependent upon the state of the economy. For example, forecasts of economic growth are widely used by economists for all sorts of reasons related to economic policy and business well-being. The longer the time period the forecast covers, the greater the uncertainty involved. When the Bank of England, for instance, makes forecasts of inflation it produces fan charts to reflect this greater uncertainty.

Types of forecast

Economists use various types of forecasting methods. The three main ones are:

1. statistical forecasts based on simple or complex future extrapolation techniques
2. using models to produce a range of forecasts – this is particularly true of models of the economy involving complex interrelationships
3. forecasts based on intuition, experience or even guesswork, i.e., not involving statistical methods.

Macro- and microeconomic forecasts

Finance ministers and other government officials find it essential to have estimates of projected variables such as the unemployment rate, inflation rate, balance of payments position and economic growth rate. These macroeconomic forecasts are required on a short-term basis (one year or less) or over a longer period of time. In the case of the unemployment rate, the importance of forecasting is shown in Figure 4.

This seems quite simple. In practice, however, the process is much more difficult and at stages 3 and 4 further assumptions are to be made with regard to other sources of revenue and taxation.

Microeconomic forecasts are not quite as obvious, but one example that develops out of Chapter 2 is the need to be able to make forecasts of demand. These are important for future business and economic planning.

Returning to Figures 2a and 2b on page 7, any business in the tourism sector has a need for a forecast of future numbers of tourists. This is by no means easy because of the many factors involved. We can get an idea of some of these from the general determinants of demand that are analysed in Chapter 2. They include:

- the average price of tourism in Mauritius
- the income of tourists
- the price of substitute destinations and the price of complements such as air travel
- a range of non-price factors that might determine whether tourists are attracted to Mauritius.

Looking at each of these factors, it is clear that a whole series of separate forecasts has to be made before an aggregate forecast can be made. These include:

- forecast inflation rates in Mauritius
- forecast economic growth rates in countries generating tourists for Mauritius
- forecasts of the costs of tourism in competing destinations and forecasts of the future cost of air travel
- alternative tourism destination and leisure options in the tourists' home market
- safety and security issues, health issues and so on, globally as well as in Mauritius.

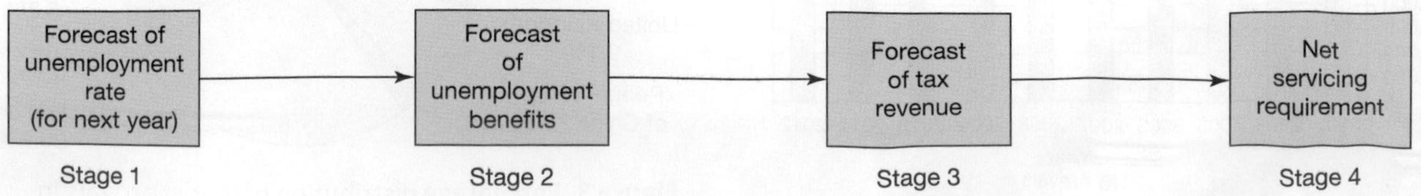

Figure 4 Use of unemployment figures

As you can see, some of these are macroeconomic forecasts. So, in order to obtain what might appear to be a simple future estimate, access to a mass of other statistical information is required. It is for this reason that forecasts may not always be close to what actually occurs.

Forecasting over a longer time period is even more problematic due to the many uncertainties that are involved. An example of this is the forecast made in 2006, which is shown in Figure 5. Global recession in 2008–2009, for example, could not have been foreseen. Revised forecasts would seem necessary. At best Figure 5 should be seen as providing a very broad indication of what might be the case in 2026.

How to write in a clear and effective way

It is beyond the scope of this book to include a lot of material in this part of the toolkit. However, much of the work of economists is communicated in a written manner, in books and newspaper articles in particular. For students, examinations in Economics require ideas to be communicated in a written form. The section on examination skills in Chapter 11 gives you advice on how to write effective answers.

From a more general standpoint, you must always think about what you are writing and how you might

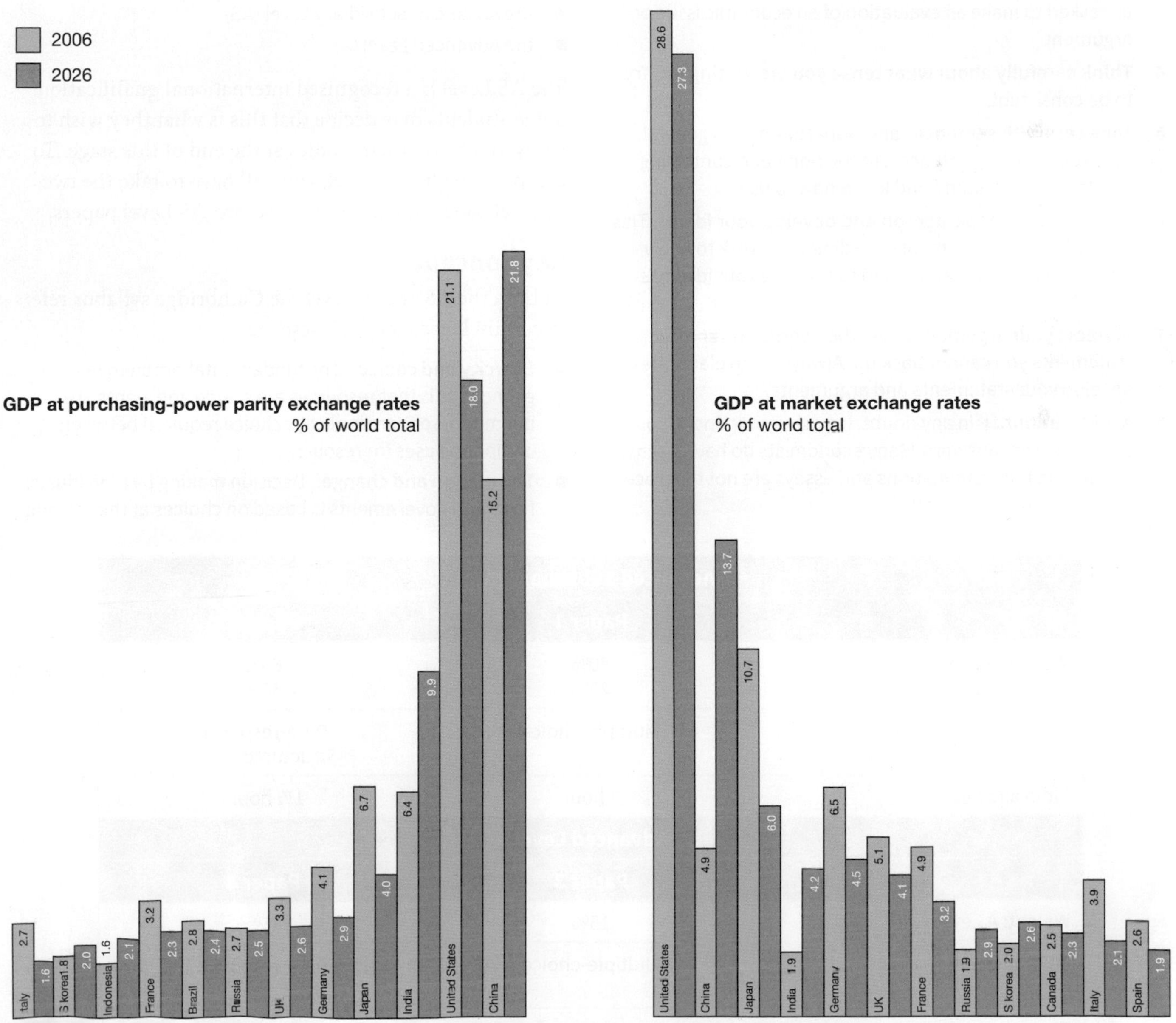

Figure 5 Forecasts of GDP in 2026

Source: Economist Intelligence Unit, 2005

improve your writing skills. You can enhance these skills by reading good newspapers, particularly if you read material that supports your AS/A Level studies.

For the time being, you might like to think about the following ten tips for budding writers:

1 **Be clear and precise in your writing.** Use words you understand and when using technical terms, be specific. This is important because Economics has many terms that are very similar.
2 **Remember to match your writing to your audience.** In most cases this will be your teacher. They will be looking to read material that is written in a relevant way and uses appropriate economic terms and concepts.
3 **Write impersonally.** In other words, do not use 'I' or 'we' in your written essays. This applies particularly when you are asked to make an evaluation of an economic issue or argument.
4 **Think carefully about what tense you are writing in.** Try to be consistent.
5 **Take care with sentences and punctuation.** In general, try to write short sentences, to the point and containing words you understand and know how to use.
6 **Use one idea per paragraph and develop your ideas.** This makes it easier for someone reading your work to know what your answer is about and to see how your idea has been developed.
7 **Support your arguments.** In other words, never make statements you cannot back up. Always try to elaborate or develop your statements and arguments.
8 **Avoid humour.** If in any doubt, leave humour and wit out of your written answers. Many economists do have a sense of humour, but examinations and essays are not the place for it to be demonstrated.
9 **Be professional.** Do not insult or offend, even if you do not agree with what you might have read or with the examination question. There are other ways in which you can make your opinions known.
10 **Keep working at your writing.** Never be satisfied and keep thinking about how you can write in a clear, relevant, authoritative and positive way.

Cambridge International AS and A Level Economics

Overall, the Cambridge International AS and A Level Economics qualification is what is known as a staged qualification. The main features are shown in Table 4. It consists of two stages:

- the Advanced Subsidiary Level (AS)
- the Advanced Level (A).

The AS Level is a recognised international qualification. Some students may decide that this is what they wish to study and finish their studies at the end of this stage. To complete the full A Level, you will have to take the two A Level papers in addition to the two AS Level papers.

Key concepts

At both the AS and A Level the Cambridge syllabus refers to certain key concepts. These are:

- **Scarcity and choice:** The fundamental problem in economics is that resources are scarce and wants are unlimited, so there is always choice required between competing uses for resources.
- **The margin and change:** Decision making by individuals, firms and governments is based on choices at the margin;

Advanced Subsidiary (AS)		
	Paper 1	**Paper 2**
Weight: AS Level A Level	40% 20%	60% 30%
Method of assessment	Multiple-choice	Data-response Structured essay
Time allowed	1 hour	1½ hours
Advanced Level		
	Paper 3	**Paper 4**
Weight: A Level	15%	35%
Method of assessment	Multiple-choice	Data-response Essay
Time allowed	1¼ hour	2¼ hour

Table 4 Cambridge International AS and A Level Economics: qualifications and assessment

that is, once behaviour has been optimised any change will be detrimental as long as conditions remain the same.

- **Equilibrium and efficiency:** Prices are set by markets, are always moving in to and out of equilibrium and can be both efficient and inefficient in different ways and over different time periods.
- **Regulation and equity:** There is a trade-off between, on the one hand, freedom for firms and individuals in unregulated markets and, on the other hand, greater social equality and equity through the government regulation of individuals and markets.
- **Progress and development:** Economics studies how societies can progress in measurable money terms and develop in a more normative sense.

Self-assessment task 3 provides you with an early opportunity to think about these concepts but you will become much more familiar with them as you progress through this book.

Chapter 11 provides important advice on examination skills and how to prepare for examinations. Do study this carefully before you take any examination papers.

As you work systematically through the AS Level and A Level chapters, try to tackle all the self-assessment tasks. In this way you will become increasingly familiar with the content of Economics and the sort of assessments used by Cambridge.

SELF-ASSESSMENT TASK 3

Match each of the following economic issues with a key concept that could be used to examine it. In this activity, you can only use each concept for one issue but note that a particular concept may apply to more than one issue.

Economic issue	Key concept
A supermarket throwing away unsold food.	Equilibrium and equity
A school having to decide whether to build a new sports hall or a chemistry lab.	Progress and development
A government providing free education to children from poor backgrounds.	Regulation and equity
A government introducing a ban on people smoking in private cars.	Scarcity and choice
A car firm reducing its output of a particular model of car.	The margin and change

Table 5 Economic issues and key concepts

Chapter 1: Basic economic ideas and resource allocation
AS Level

Learning objectives

On completion of this chapter you should know:

- what is meant by the fundamental economic problem of limited resources and unlimited wants
- what is meant by scarcity and the inevitability of choices that have to be made by individuals, firms and governments
- what is meant by opportunity cost
- why the basic questions of what, how and for whom production takes place have to be addressed in all economies
- the meaning of the term '*ceteris paribus*'
- what is meant by the margin and decision making at the margin
- the importance of the time dimension in Economics
- the difference between positive and normative statements
- what is meant by factors of production, namely land, labour, capital and enterprise
- what is meant by the division of labour
- how resources are allocated in market, planned and mixed economies
- problems of transition when central planning in an economy is reduced
- the characteristics of a production possibility curve and how opportunity cost can be applied
- the functions and characteristics of money and types of money
- how goods can be classified into free goods, private goods, public goods, merit goods and demerit goods
- the problems associated with information failure.

One economic problem or many?

Economists have to deal with a whole range of economic problems. You may have seen TV programmes about the misery of unemployment and poverty; you may have read about the difficulties caused by inflation or heard politicians discuss exchange rate crises on the evening news. You may also be aware of debates surrounding issues such as the acute shortage of skilled labour, the benefits of greater liberalisation of international trade, the problems of global warming and the population explosion in many developing economies. Despite this extensive range of issues, which economists are trained to consider, they often talk about 'the economic problem'. This is the fundamental problem from which all others arise. This is the fact that we have scarce **resources** to satisfy our unlimited **wants**. As a result of this problem, which is sometimes called the problem of **scarcity**, we have to make a **choice**, and it is the task of the economist to explain and analyse the nature of choice facing economic agents, such as consumers, producers and governments.

KEY TERMS

Resources: inputs available for the production of goods and services.

Wants: needs that are not always realised.

Scarcity: a situation in which wants and needs are in excess of the resources available.

Choice: underpins the concept that resources are scare so choices have to be made by consumers, firms and governments.

TOP TIP

In economics, a need is not the same as a want; consumer wants are not always satisfied because of limited income whereas a need tends to be more important in a scale of priorities.

The fundamental economic problem

The **fundamental economic problem** is: 'scarce resources in relation to unlimited wants'. This problem is summarised in Figure 1.1.

KEY TERM

Fundamental economic problem: scarce resources relative to unlimited wants.

KEY CONCEPT LINK

Scarcity and choice: The fundamental problem in economics is that resources are scarce and wants are unlimited, so there is always a choice required between competing uses for the resources. This is the first of five key concepts that are central to the subject content of the Cambridge International AS Level and A Level Economics syllabus. This concept is a recurring theme, particularly in this first chapter.

Scarce resources

In Economics we categorise the resources available to us into four types. These are known as **factors of production**:

1 **Land:** This factor is the natural resource. It includes the surface of the earth, lakes, rivers and forests. It also includes mineral deposits below the earth and the climate above, as well as the small area of land that makes up a farm or factory. The reward for owning land is the income that is generated.

KEY TERMS

Factors of production: anything that is useful in the production of goods and services.

Land: natural resources in an economy.

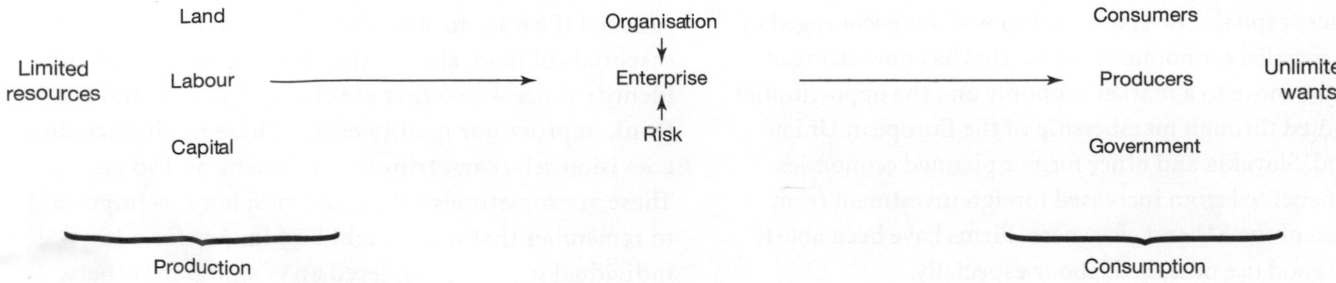

Figure 1.1 Elements of the fundamental economic problem

2 **Labour:** This factor is the human resource, the basic determinant of which is the nation's population. Not all of the population is available to work, because some are above or below the working population age and some choose not to work. The reward for labour is the wage or salary that is paid.

3 **Capital:** This factor is any man-made aid to production. In this category we would include a simple spade and a complex car-assembly plant. Capital goods help land and labour produce more units of output – they improve the output from land and labour. The reward to capital is the rate of return that is earned.

These three factors are organised into units of production by firms.

4 **Entrepreneur:** This factor carries out two functions. First, the enterprise factor organises the other three factors of production. Second, enterprise involves taking the risk of production, which exists in a free enterprise economy. Some firms are small with few resources. The functions of enterprise are undertaken by a single individual, the entrepreneur. In larger, more complex firms the functions are divided, with salaried managers organising the other factors and shareholders taking the risk. The return for enterprise is the profits that are made.

KEY TERMS

Labour: human resources available in an economy.

Capital: a man-made aid to production.

Entrepreneur: organises production and is willing to take risks.

Some economies have a large quantity of high-quality factors of production at their disposal. They can create lots of goods and services to satisfy the wants of their population. They are said to have a good factor endowment. Other economies lack sufficient quantities of one or more of the factors. Developing countries, for example, might have large quantities of land and labour but lack sufficient capital and enterprise. The former planned economies of Eastern Europe, such as Poland and Slovakia, found it difficult to develop because they had few people with entrepreneurial experience as well as a lack of business capital. Entrepreneurship was not encouraged in their socialist economic systems. This has now changed with the move to a market economy and the opportunities presented through membership of the European Union. Poland, Slovakia and other former planned economies have benefited from increased foreign investment from the rest of the EU and elsewhere. Firms have been able to make good use of skilled labour especially.

Car assembly plant in Slovakia

Production and consumption

Resources are combined in the process of **production** to create goods and services. Goods and services have the capacity to satisfy wants. The process through which individuals use up goods and services to satisfy wants is known as **consumption**. Some goods, such as a chocolate bar, are quickly used up to satisfy our wants. Other things satisfy wants over a longer period. These are called consumer durables. Examples of consumer durables include television sets, refrigerators and vehicles.

KEY TERMS

Production: the process of creating goods and services in an economy.

Consumption: the process by which consumers satisfy their wants.

Unlimited wants

We can all identify certain basic needs that must be satisfied if we are to stay alive. These include the obvious essentials of food, shelter and clothing. We might also identify those wants that are clearly less essential but we think improve our quality of life. These might include television sets, cars, trips to the cinema and so on. These are sometimes called luxuries, but it is important to remember that what might be a luxury for one individual may be considered an essential for others.

This is because we all have a scale of preference with our more urgent wants at the top and the less urgent ones at the bottom. Each individual's scale of preference is a product of a complex set of influences, involving culture, upbringing and life experiences. These together influence our likes and dislikes. Unsurprisingly, since we all have different experiences, there is bound to be great variation between any two individuals' scales of preferences. You may find it interesting to conduct a class exercise in which everyone makes a list of ten wants in descending order of priority. When you compare results you may be surprised to find that, although there may be broad agreement on the first few choices, there is likely to be considerable variation as you compare people's choices over the full list. You may also consider how your list would compare to lists compiled by others with very different life experiences, such as your teacher, your grandparents or even a student of Economics in another country. A further point to consider is whether you could imagine any end to your list if you were not limited to ten choices. It is important to remember that our wants are continually expanding, developing and changing.

Some wants expand as we grow up, marry and raise a family. Imagine how our housing needs change as we go through this process or how we change from wanting a small car with two doors to wanting a large, family saloon with four doors. Some of our wants develop and expand when we see others around us enjoying goods and services and we feel the need to keep up. Sometimes our wants change as we have new experiences, for example we might decide to go on a diet because we have seen a TV programme about obesity.

All of this points to the fact that we can never imagine a time when all our wants are satisfied. Our wants are continually expanding and changing. Despite the fact that we are continually finding new, more efficient ways to produce more and more goods and services with the resources available to us, we are still faced with the fundamental economic problem that we have limited resources and unlimited wants. As stated earlier, this is sometimes called the problem of scarcity and as a result we have to make choices.

Choice and opportunity cost

Given limited resources and unlimited wants we have to choose which wants to satisfy. The true cost of any choice we make between alternatives is expressed by economists through the notion of **opportunity cost**. This looks at the cost of our choice in terms of the best alternative forgone. For example, suppose you were given a \$15 gift voucher for your birthday. You could either buy a new DVD that costs \$15 or two paperback books for \$7.50 each. It is clear that you could not have the DVD and the books. The opportunity cost of the DVD, therefore, is the two paperback books. The value of the concept of opportunity cost is that it brings home to us the real cost of our choices. It can be applied in a variety of contexts in Economics and is helpful for economic decision-makers, such as households, firms and governments.

KEY TERM

Opportunity cost: the cost expressed in terms of the best alternative that is forgone.

Basic questions: what to produce, how and for whom?

Because the fundamental economic problem exists, societies need to confront the following three interrelated questions:

1. **What to produce?** Because we cannot produce everything, we need to decide what to produce and in what quantities. We have to choose, for example, whether to produce lots of goods and services, such as food, clothing and vehicles, to improve our standard of living, or whether we need to produce lots of military hardware to improve our defences.
2. **How to produce?** This question arises since resources are scarce in relation to unlimited wants; we need to consider how resources are used so that the best outcome arises. We need to consider how we can get the maximum use out of the resources available to us. It should be noted, however, that other issues besides purely economic concerns should be considered when deciding how to produce. It may be true, for example, that through cheap labour we could produce more goods and services in an economy, but there is a moral objection to such arrangements. Similarly, crop yields could be increased through the introduction of genetically modified plants but this may lead to damage to the ecosystem. The decision to maximise output and satisfy more wants would need to consider the full impact on the environment and any potential long-term health risks.
3. **For whom to produce?** Because we cannot satisfy all the wants of all the population, decisions have to be taken concerning how many of each person's wants are to be satisfied. On a broad level we need to decide whether everyone is going to have a more or less equal share of what

is produced or whether some will have more than others. In some economies there are deliberate attempts to create a more egalitarian society through policies that redistribute wealth and income from the rich to the poor. This could be achieved through progressive taxation systems. In other economies there are no such policies and inequalities of income and wealth, often based upon inheritance, remain extreme. As an issue, it has become very significant in most emerging economies with a widening gap between rich and poor.

Meaning of the term '*ceteris paribus*'

This Latin term is widely used by economists to refer to a situation where 'other things remain equal'. The idea behind this is to be able to simplify an actual situation by assuming that apart from a single change of circumstances, everything else is unchanged. In this way, economists can model one change at a time.

SELF-ASSESSMENT TASK 1.1

Read the feature below and then answer the questions that follow.

Food versus fuel – a classic application of opportunity cost

World food prices have been rising since 2007. The rises have been particularly strong for vegetable oil, wheat and corn. This has resulted in civil unrest and riots in many poor countries. In response, for example in India, exports of grain products have been banned in order to maintain supplies in the home market. China has also taken steps to quell the rise in the price of cooking oil.

One factor that has been driving up world food prices has been the increased demand for biofuels which are produced from agricultural crops traditionally used for food and animal feed. The most important biofuel is ethanol which is produced from corn and sugar cane. These crops are very important sources of biofuel production in the USA, Brazil and India.

As global oil prices increase, there is a growing need for the increased agricultural production of corn, soya beans and sugar cane for conversion into biofuels. This may be good news for farmers producing these products and indeed, for users of biofuels. It is not good news for livestock farmers who experience increased feed prices or for consumers who experience rising grain and meat prices.

Source: Adapted from S. Sexton et al, *Agricultural and Resource Economics*, Vol 12, No 1, 2008.

1 Use the information above to show how the concept of opportunity cost might be used to explain the trade-offs as they affect:
- governments
- farmers
- consumers.

2 Outline the likely costs and benefits of the increased global demand for biofuels.

SELF-ASSESSMENT TASK 1.2

Read the feature below and then answer the questions that follow.

China: the challenges of an ageing population

An ageing population is one usually associated with developed economies. Falling birth rates and increased life expectancy in many European countries and Japan has created a situation in which younger generations are facing the prospect of caring for an ageing population.

This demographic situation is now a major problem in China. The origin lies in China's one-child policy which has restricted the number of children that most urban families could have and was originally designed to reduce the rate of growth of a booming population. There have been positive outcomes from this policy. At present more than 70% of the population are able to work and produce goods – fuelling China's high level of economic growth.

Fewer new workers are now joining the labour force and many of those who are do not want to take on the low paid, unskilled jobs of the previous generation. In addition, China is facing a substantial increase in the number of old people, resulting in additional pressures on health and social care facilities.

Projections suggest that the impact of demographic change could have an even more adverse effect on the economy. Historically, production in China has exceeded consumption, resulting in substantial trade surpluses with the rest of the world. In contrast, over the next few decades consumption may exceed production; what is certain is that by 2050 China will have far more elderly people than any other country, 26% of the total population.

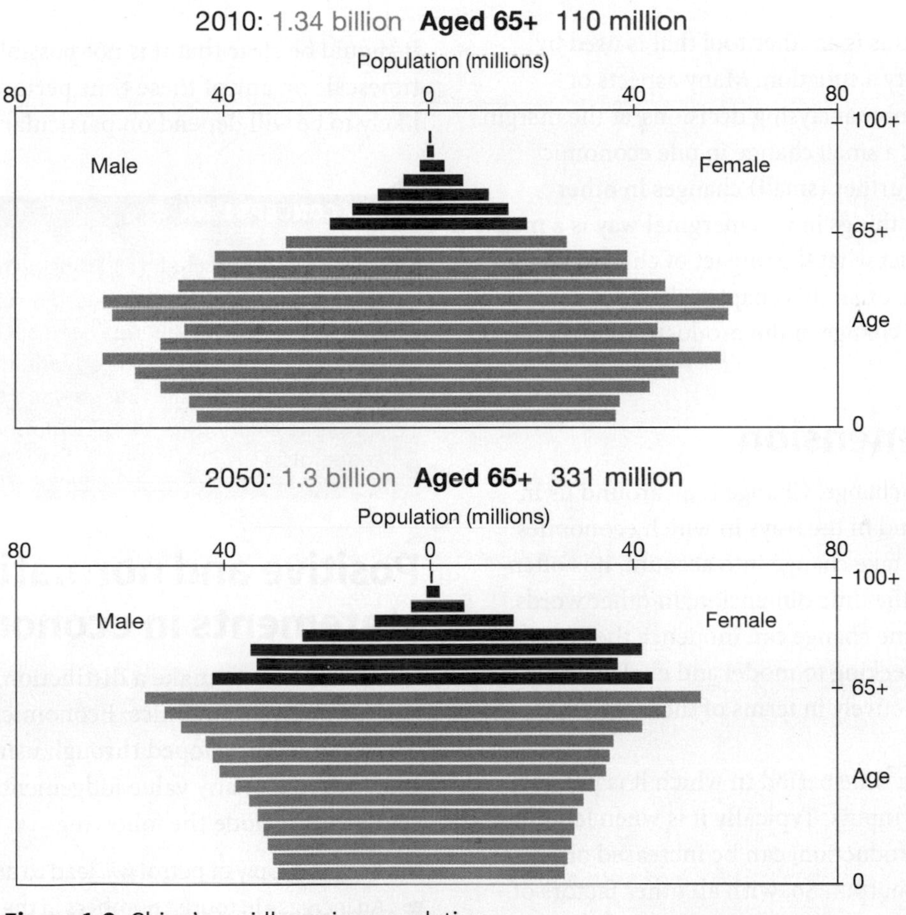

Figure 1.2 China's rapidly ageing population

Source: 'China's rapidly ageing population', Carnegie Europe, 5 July 2013; 'Ageing China', BBC News, 20 September 2012.

1 Summarise the main projected changes in the age composition of China's population between 2010 and 2050.

2 Suggest the likely effects of these changes on decisions concerning:

a what to produce

b how to produce

c for whom to produce.

KEY CONCEPT LINK

Scarcity and choice: It should now be clear tha[t] China is facing a serious economic problem br[ought] about by an ageing population. Serious choi[ces] have to be made. There are competing use[s of] scarce resources since even in China, no[t] can be met.

Over the course of studying Economics at AS and at A Level there will be many occasions where this concept is used to further understanding of the otherwise complex processes that are operating. For example, in the next chapter, a change in the price of a good is analysed on the assumption that all other things that affect the quantity demanded remain the same, i.e., *ceteris paribus*. This is clearly a simplification, since in practice there are many things as well as price that determine how much of a good is purchased when its price falls.

The margin

Like *ceteris paribus*, this is another tool that is used by economists to simplify a situation. Many aspects of microeconomics involve analysing decisions 'at the margin'. By this we mean that a small change in one economic variable will lead to further (small) changes in other variables. Looking at things in this marginal way is a means of being able to predict what the impact of change might be. For example, later on in this chapter, this idea is used to assess the effects of a change in the production possibilities for an economy.

The time dimension

We live in a world of change. Change is all around us in our lives, our work and in the ways in which economies function. In order to take change into account, it is often necessary to specify the time dimension; in other words, to assess how over time change can influence the concepts that economists are seeking to model and explain. This can be done very effectively in terms of the factors of production.

The **short run** is a time period in which it is possible to change only some inputs. Typically it is when labour, a variable factor of production, can be increased or decreased to change output. So, with all other factors of production remaining the same (*ceteris paribus*), a firm taking on more workers may be able to increase its output.

In the **long run**, it is possible for all factors of production or resources to change. So, in the long run, a firm may improve the quality and quantity of its capital by building a new factory to increase its output. This will usually allow it to be more efficient since the firm has had time to evaluate how best this can be done successfully and efficiently. The **very long run** is where not only are all factors of production variable, but all other key inputs are also variable. These key inputs can include technology, government regulations and social considerations.

KEY TERMS

Short run: time period when a firm can only change some and not all factor inputs.

Long run: time period when all factors of production are variable.

KEY TERM

Very long run: time period when all key inputs into production are variable.

It should be clear that it is not possible to put an exact timescale on any of these time periods. Just what they are likely to be will depend on particular circumstances.

KEY CONCEPT LINK

The margin and change: Decision making by individuals, firms and governments is based on choices at the margin; that is, once behaviour has been optimised, any change will be detrimental as long as conditions remain the same. This concept – like the first one, scarcity and choice – can be applied in many different situations that are studied by economists.

Positive and normative statements in economics

It is useful now to make a distinction between positive and normative economics. Economics is a social science. As such it has developed through using positive analysis that is devoid of any value judgements. Typical positive statements include the following:

- A fall in supply of petrol *will* lead to an increase in its price…
- An increase in tourist numbers in the Maldives *will* create more employment…
- An increase in taxation on cars *will* result in fewer cars being sold…

These are statements of what will happen, based on empirical evidence, and are referred to as **positive statements**. No value judgements are involved. When values or opinions come into the analysis, then this is

KEY TERM

Positive statement: one that is based on empirical or actual evidence.

the realm of normative economics. Here an opinion or value judgement is being made. The above statements can become **normative statements**, for example, by adding:

- … and this *should* be beneficial for the environment.
- … and therefore the government of the Republic of Maldives *should* do everything it can to help promote this industry.
- … and this *should* reduce traffic congestion.

KEY TERM

Normative statement: one that is subjective about what should happen.

Positive statements are particularly important in AS and A Level Economics. They are widely used to describe something that can be measured, such as the output of a firm or the rate of unemployment in the economy. Another use is in the construction and explanation of theories and concepts that have been developed over the years to explain how consumers, firms and governments operate. Normative statements are less certain, yet form the basis of policy-making by firms and governments in attempting to solve economic problems. While both types of statement are distinctive, they invariably work together since the normative view is usually based on some positive conceptual basis.

Specialisation and exchange

One of the ways in which more goods and services can be produced in the economy is through the process of **specialisation**. This refers to a situation where individuals and firms, regions and nations concentrate on producing some goods and services rather than others. This can be clearly illustrated at the individual level. Within the family there may be some specialisation in the performance of household tasks, with one person doing the ironing and gardening while another does the shopping and cooking. In the workplace, of course, the fact that some people are labourers or lorry drivers while others have office jobs is also a reflection of specialisation. At this level, specialisation allows individuals to concentrate upon what they are best at, meaning more goods and services will be produced. With specialisation, however, although more is produced, no one is self-sufficient. It becomes necessary to exchange or trade goods and services. As an individual specialises, they will produce a surplus beyond their needs, which they can exchange for the surpluses of others.

KEY TERM

Specialisation: the process by which individuals, firms and economies concentrate on producing those goods and services where they have an advantage over others.

With the expansion of trade and the development of **markets**, the benefits of regional and national specialisation became apparent. Surpluses produced by regions and countries were bought and sold, allowing world living standards to rise. Just as individuals concentrated on what they were best at, so did regions and countries.

KEY TERM

Market: where buyers and sellers get together to trade.

Specialisation has clearly resulted in a massive expansion in world living standards, but there are dangers too. Given the pace of technological change in modern society, there is always the possibility that the specialist skills and accumulated experience that any individual has acquired may become redundant as the economy develops. Individuals need to be flexible and multi-skilled and to be able to move between occupations. At regional and national levels, changes in consumers' wants can sometimes mean that the goods and services produced in a region or country are no longer required in the same quantity, so unemployment can result. Policies then have to be adopted to deal with the economic and social problems that will arise.

The division of labour

With the technical advances of the last few hundred years, production of goods and services has taken place on a much bigger scale. The concentration of large numbers of workers within very large production units allowed the process of production to be broken down into a series of tasks. This is called the **division of labour**. For example, Adam Smith, writing at the end of the eighteenth century, showed how the production of pins would benefit from the application of the division of labour in a factory. He suggested that pin making could be divided into 18 distinct operations and that, if each employee undertook only one of the operations, production would rise to 5,000 pins per employee per day.

KEY TERM

Division of labour: where a manufacturing process is split into a sequence of individual tasks.

This was compared to his estimate that each employee would be able to produce only a few dozen each day if they produced pins individually.

Modern manufacturing processes are usually split up into a number of tasks. A typical example is in a garment factory where each operative produces one part of an item of clothing such as a shirt sleeve or button holes. This division of labour is usually quicker and cheaper than having one person complete each garment on their own. It also allows workers to become more specialised and can lead to an increase in productivity and an improvement in the quality of the finished product.

In the United States the division of labour was taken a stage further in the 1920s when Henry Ford introduced conveyor belt production into the car industry. Ford's method of car production provided the model for much of manufacturing production in the twentieth century with 'Just in Time' processes being widely applied in many types of business. With relevant planning, it is possible to keep production underway with minimal levels of parts or stock.

Although the division of labour raises output, it often creates dissatisfaction among the workforce as they become deskilled and bored with the monotonous nature of their work. In modern developed economies the dehumanising impact of production techniques, such as using a conveyor belt and robots, has been acknowledged and procedures introduced to counteract boredom such as multi-skilling and moving workers around the production plant.

KEY CONCEPT LINK

Scarcity and choice: Through specialisation and the division of labour, resources that are available can be used to increase what is being produced, so meeting more wants.

Resource allocation in different economic systems and issues of transition

Economic structure

The term **economic structure** refers to the way in which an economy consists of various sectors. It is used to show the balance of economic activity, usually measured in terms of the value of total output, between these sectors. The following sectors are recognised:

- Primary sector: This consists of agriculture, fishing and activities such as mining and oil extraction.
- Secondary sector: This term is used to describe the wide range of manufacturing activities that are found in an economy. Typical examples are: food processing, textiles and clothing, iron and steel production, vehicle manufacturing, and electronics.
- Tertiary sector: This is the service sector and covers a range of diverse activities such as retailing, transport, logistics, banking, insurance and education.
- Quaternary sector: A relatively new term to denote the knowledge-based part of the economy, especially the provision of information. Typical examples are scientific research and product development, computing and ICT.

As economies develop their economic structure changes and there is a progression from primary to secondary to tertiary activities. In developed economies, the tertiary sector tends to be the principal employer. In the UK, for example, in 2012 around four out of every five people in employment were employed in the service sector. This is not the case in less developed economies. In Tanzania and Kenya, by way of contrast, similar proportions of workers are employed in the primary sector alone.

KEY TERM

Economic structure: the way in which an economy is organised in terms of sectors.

Systems of resource allocation

The problem of scarcity, which in turn requires choices to be made, is one that is common to all economies, rich and poor. The choices that are made and which can realistically be made are determined by the **economic system** of a particular country. This term is used to describe the means or allocative mechanism by which its people, businesses and government make choices. Traditionally, economists have recognised three distinct types of economic system – these are the **market economy**, the **command** or **planned economy** and the **mixed economy**. Let us briefly consider each in turn.

KEY TERMS

Economic system: the means by which choices are made in an economy.

Market economy: one where most decisions are taken through market forces.

Command or **planned economy:** one where resource allocation decisions are taken by a central body.

Mixed economy: one where market forces and government, private and public sectors are involved in resource allocation decisions.

KEY CONCEPT LINK

Scarcity and choice: The key concept of scarcity and choice applies in all types of economy. How choices are made depends on the relative importance of the government and the free market mechanism.

The market economy

In a market economy, decisions on how resources are to be allocated are usually taken by millions of households and thousands of firms – the exact number will, of course, depend on the size of economy. The key point is that they interact as buyers and sellers in the market for goods and services. Prices and the operation of the price system underpin this interaction (see Chapter 2); in turn, prices act to indicate the likely market value of particular resources. For example, a commodity in short supply but that has a high demand attached to it will have a high price. Alternatively, one that has a high supply and low demand will have a much lower price attached to it. Prices and the self-interest of people and businesses therefore act as a guide to the decisions that have to be taken.

Economics as a subject has its origin in the notion that prices and the **market mechanism** are the 'best' way of handling economic problems. This notion can

KEY TERM

Market mechanism: where decisions on price and quantity are made on the basis of demand and supply alone.

SELF-ASSESSMENT TASK 1.3

Table 1.1 shows a broad comparison of the economic structures of India and Pakistan in 2012.

	India		Pakistan	
	Total output (%)	Labour force (%)	Total output (%)	Labour force (%)
Agriculture	17	53	21	45
Industry	20	19	22	14
Services	63	28	57	41

Table 1.1 Economic structures of India and Pakistan in 2012

Source: Economy Watch and Pakistan Economic Survey 2012/13.

1 Using the information above, compare the economic structure of Pakistan with that of India.
2 In which country:
   a is agriculture more efficient?
   b are services more efficient?
3 Explain how you have arrived at your answers.
4 Discuss whether countries such as Pakistan and India might be concerned if a large proportion of the labour force got new employment in industry or in the service sector (such as call centres).

A call centre in India

be particularly attributed to the Scottish economist Adam Smith, who is remembered for his reference to an 'invisible hand' (the price system) that brings together private and social interests in a harmonious way. This is the fundamental philosophy underpinning the workings of the market economy.

The government has a very restricted part to play in a market economy. For example, in Smith's view, it should control national defence, act against monopolies, issue money, raise taxes and so on, while protecting the rights of the private sector. It certainly should not try to influence the dealings of individuals in the market or to regulate the workings of that market. Figure 1.3 is a simple representation of these functions.

Before moving on, it must be made clear that the market economy is an ideal that does not exist in today's complex, globalised economy. Arguably, its most important representation is the United States of America, and it should be stressed that here federal and state governments play important roles in the economy and society, as well as in providing defence, law and order and other public services. Hong Kong provides an interesting case of what at one time was a near perfect example of a market economy. Virtually all businesses are privately owned; its public transport services and road tunnels are similarly operated by private companies. There is, however, rather more regulation that is being introduced to control aspects of their operations since the 1997 handover to China.

The planned economy

Like the market economy, the command or planned economy in its purest form exists only in theory. In this second type of economy, the government has a central role in all decisions that are made and, unlike the market economy, the emphasis is on centralisation. Central planning boards and organisations make decisions in enterprises that are state-owned or under state regulation and control. In a market economy, consumer sovereignty influences resource allocation, whereas in a command economy it is central planners who determine the collective preferences of consumers and manufacturing enterprises. The planned economies of the past 50 years or so have their economic logic in the Marxian criticism of the market economy. This particular objection was essentially one of class conflict between the wealthy owners of capital and the poor working classes who provided this wealth through the production process. Marx was also critical of the built-in unemployment arising out of the market system. For example, he had observed the trend to replace labour with machines (capital) and the inability of labour to secure higher wages. Under a planned economy, unemployment is not an issue. Marx was also very concerned about the way in which the market economy fostered the concentration of productive resources in the hands of large monopolistic industrial and commercial organisations. As such he maintained that they corrupted the workings of the market and, if powerful enough, could exert pressure on governments. Retrospectively, and in the light of empirical experience, economists have with some justification concluded that Marx's criticisms were excessive. Nevertheless, his general recommendation that more centralisation should occur and that more emphasis should be placed on economic planning has been applied by those countries that have pursued the notion of a planned economy.

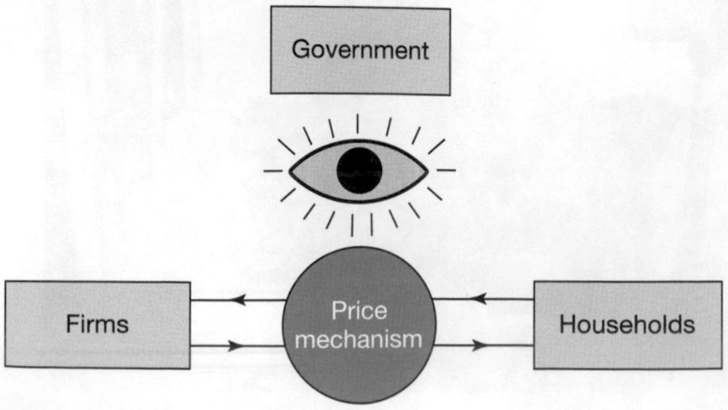

Figure 1.3 The market economy

So, the key features of a planned economy are that central government and its constituent organisations take responsibility for:

- the allocation of resources
- the determination of production targets for all sectors of the economy
- the distribution of income and the determination of wages
- the ownership of most productive resources and property
- planning the long-term growth of the economy.

From a practical standpoint, some of these decisions have to be decentralised, either geographically or by sector, to other government organisations. In certain cases, these bodies have control over the workings of a limited market mechanism. A good example of this is where basic foodstuffs such as bread and meat are heavily subsidised to keep prices at a fixed level and so spare consumers from the price fluctuations that are so commonplace in the market economy. Artificially low prices result in excess demand relative to supply – queuing becomes a way of life. Also from a practical standpoint it is very difficult for all enterprise to be state-owned – there has to be a limited opportunity for the private ownership of small businesses such as shops, restaurants and personal services like hairdressing and cleaning. For more substantive businesses, ownership is often on a shared basis between the state and the private sector. This often involves foreign investors who are keen to exploit the opportunities of an emerging market economy.

Queuing for bread

The outcome of the planned economy is that central planning tends to set goals for the economy that differ from those of the market economy. In particular they have a clear objective of achieving as high a rate of economic growth as possible in order to 'catch up' on the progress being made by much more advanced market economies. The planned economy is more correctly described as one of sacrificing current consumption and standards of living in order to achieve enhanced future well-being. This is the sacrifice that has to be made by the present generation for the benefit of future generations.

It is increasingly difficult to provide examples of truly planned economies. The most obvious cases are North Korea, Venezuela, Cuba and Eritrea. Until recently, Albania would have been prominent on such a list; however, the market is now having much more of an influence on the economy as the country prepares for entry to the European Union.

The mixed economy

It is clear from the brief analysis of market and planned economies that, in the 'pure' sense, these types of economic systems occur in theory and not in reality.

In contrast, the mixed economy is undoubtedly the characteristic form of economic organisation within the global economy. As its name indicates, it involves both private and public sectors in the process of resource allocation. Consequently, decisions on most important economic issues involve some form of planning (by private as well as public enterprises) and interaction between government, businesses and labour through the market mechanism. Private ownership of productive resources operates alongside public ownership in many mixed economies, although, increasingly, the trend is towards the privatisation of certain activities that were once in public sector hands.

The best example of this is undoubtedly the UK economy in the mid-1970s when the public and private sectors were of broadly equal importance. At this time the government was responsible for:

- substantial areas of public expenditure such as health care, social services, education and defence
- the direct operation of nationalised industries, such as coal, iron and steel, railways, gas, water, telephones and electricity
- providing support for large areas of manufacturing, such as vehicle production, aerospace and electronics, in partnership with the private sector.

Over the past 35 years, the strength of the public sector in the UK has been substantially reduced, not only through privatisation and deregulation but also through a policy of non-intervention when private companies experience financial difficulties in their markets. Controversially, successive governments have made little or no attempt to stem the demise of car manufacturing in the UK as, one by one, former British-owned companies have been rationalised by their new owners from the rest of the EU, the USA and South East Asia.

Elsewhere, there have been similar trends. One of the most dramatic has been the restructuring of the economy of the former Soviet Union (*perestroika* as it is sometimes called). Under President Gorbachev's reforms, small private businesses could be set up in the service sector (for example cafés, retail shops, garages and taxi hire) and workers could form their own cooperatives to market and sell surplus production from monolithic state manufacturing companies.

The US economy is also an example of a mixed economy, somewhat contrary to common perception. For example:

- the government at all levels is an important employer and provides basic services, such as education and various types of medical care

- government agencies regulate and control the provision of some essential services, such as energy, telecommunications and transportation
- indirect support is given to various strategically important companies.

These are over and above the expected provision of external defence and internal security services.

It is not easy to explain the importance of a government's role in any particular mixed economy. In most cases the only real explanation is that it is usually a case of differing political philosophies. Figure 1.4 provides a largely normative assessment of where particular economies fall in terms of the relative strengths of market and planned systems of resource allocation. In all cases, except arguably North Korea, countries are moving towards giving the market mechanism an ever-increasing role in their economic structures.

In more recent times, the experience of the newly industrialising countries (NICs) is interesting. In terms of allocative mechanisms, some, such as Singapore and Hong Kong, opted for a strong focus on the market to allocate resources and through this have created an economic situation where enterprise can be encouraged and rewarded. Other South East Asian 'Tigers' have placed more emphasis on central planning, while China's phenomenal growth over the past decade has been based on the controlled management of the economy within a global context and more recent emphasis on freer markets.

The new Baltic Tiger economies of Central Europe – Estonia, Latvia and Lithuania – have re-orientated their economies to foreign investors. In this way, they hope to achieve forecasted growth rates of around 5–7% per annum. These are very much in line with those experienced by their Asian Tiger counterparts, yet significantly higher than those experienced in the past by more developed economies. However, global recession has had a significant impact on these aspirations.

TOP TIP

Virtually all present-day economies are mixed – the role and importance of the market is, however, variable.

Central Hong Kong

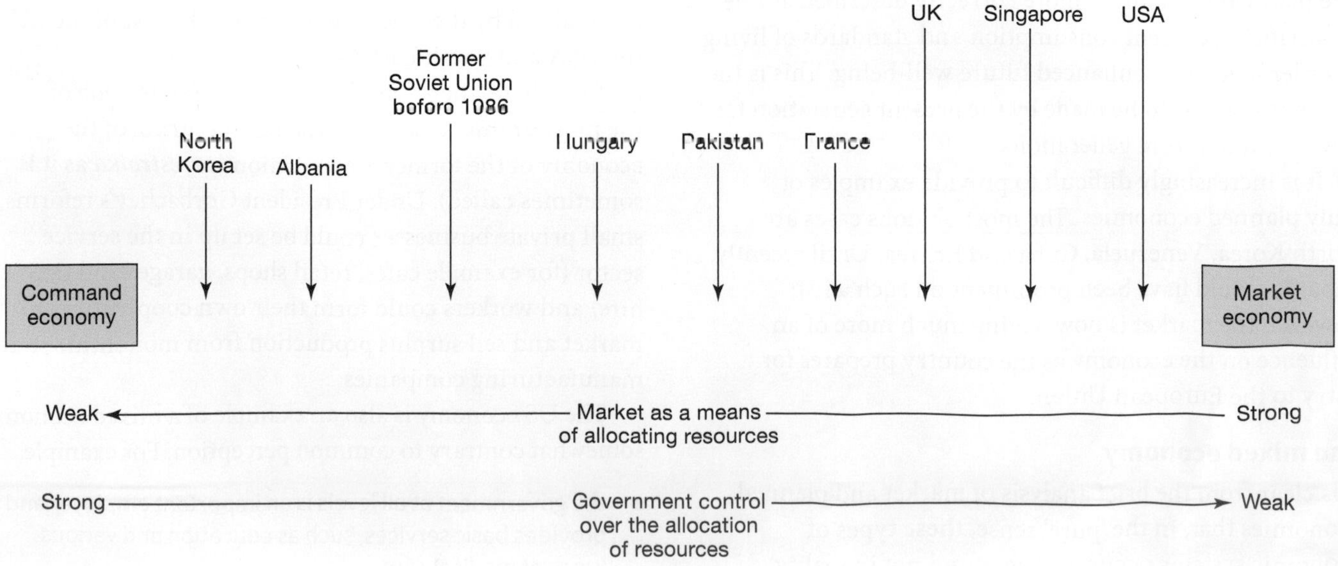

Figure 1.4 Mixed economic systems

SELF-ASSESSMENT TASK 1.4

1 Think carefully about the ways in which your own economy allocates resources. Make a few notes on the ways in which:
- the government
- the market mechanism

are responsible for decision making.

2 Use the above information to insert your own economy into the scale shown in Figure 1.4. How has its relative position changed in recent years?

3 What information might an economist use to quantify the relative importance of the government and the market mechanism within an economy?

Issues of transition when central planning in an economy is reduced

As explained above, most developing economies have a strong foundation based on the model of a planned economy. Over the past 20 years, most have recognised the benefits for the economy when less activity is controlled by the government and when competitive markets and the private sector have an increasing role to play. Internationally, this approach is consistent with that of the World Bank, which – as part of its policy to promote development – encourages such economic reforms. It has also been an essential requirement for those countries of Central and Eastern Europe that have joined the EU.

Figure 1.5 shows two diagrams that represent the general position of a planned economy before reform and the situation once changes have been introduced.

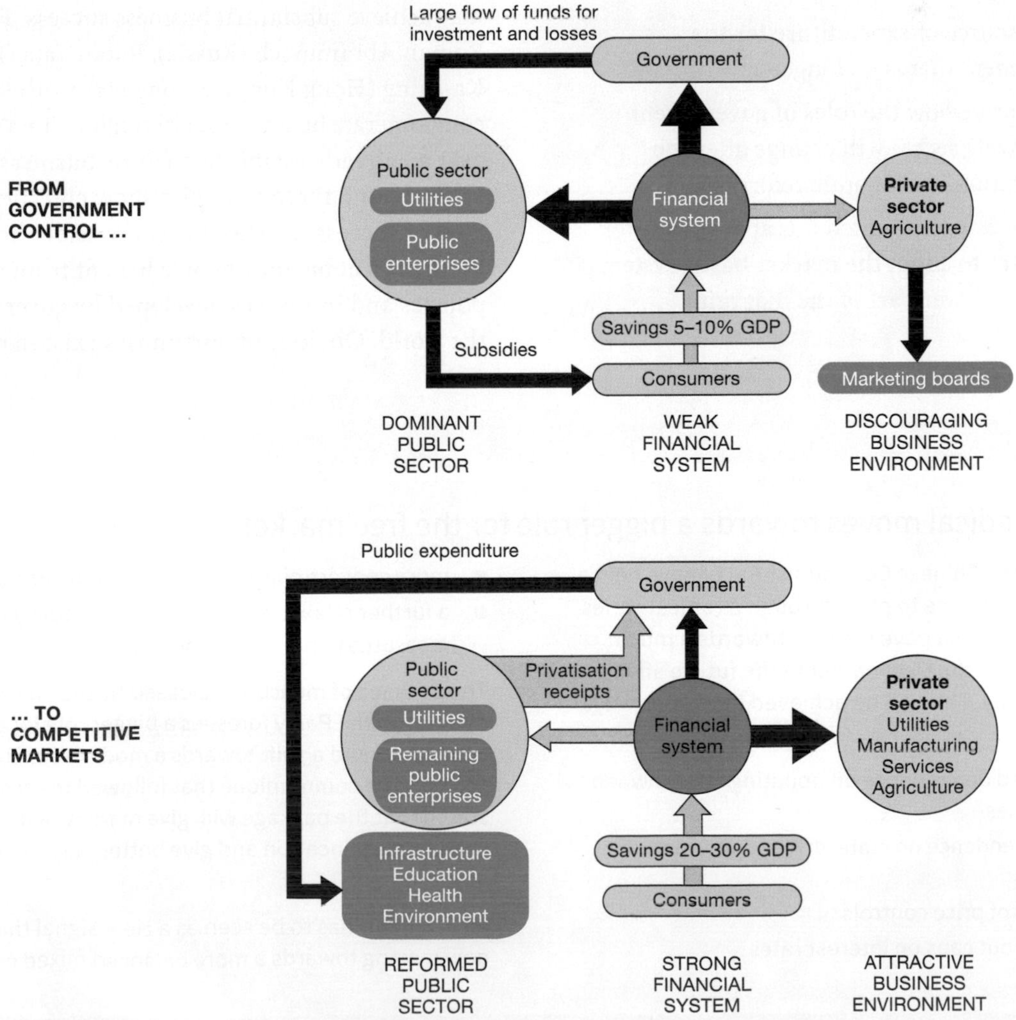

Figure 1.5 The broad process of economic reform
Source: World Bank, 1995 (adapted)

The labels at the bottom of each diagram generally summarise the state of affairs. The direction and relative size of the arrows are important – these show the relationships between the different sectors and the strength of their importance. In promoting economic development and in the allocation of funding, the World Bank seeks to ensure that recipient countries are implementing the processes of economic reform shown in this figure.

SELF-ASSESSMENT TASK 1.5

1 Assume that an economy undergoes the process of reform shown in Figure 1.5.
   a Give an example of an organisation that will disappear with a move to competitive markets.
   b Give an additional source of revenue for the government.
   c Give a source of expenditure for the government that is no longer appropriate.
2 Briefly describe how the roles of government and the private sector will change after the implementation of economic reforms.
3 Discuss the extent to which it is appropriate for your country to adopt the market-based system shown in the lower part of the diagram.

Moving towards a market economy is by no means a painless task, as experience has consistently shown. The restructuring of the economy and the moves to privatise former state-run activities are accompanied with substantial job losses and the need for social reform. It is also essential for there to be a more robust tax regime in place, not least to fund government spending and service the external debt that has had to occur to fund transition. It is by no means a short and trouble-free process. The feature below on China mentions some of the ways in which the world's second largest economy is planning for a greater role for the market in the future.

Role of enterprise in the modern economy

As explained above, the market is performing an ever-increasing role in all types of economy. This has provided opportunities for the development of an enterprise culture whereby people who are prepared to take risks may achieve substantial business success. For example, Roman Abramovich (Russia), Ratan Tata (India) and Li Ka-shing (Hong Kong), among many others, have built up conglomerate businesses, although in Tata's case, he took over an already established family business.

Although these examples show enterprise at its highest level of success, we should also consider how many thousands of businesspeople benefit from enterprise policies and initiatives developed by governments around the world. Obvious opportunities exist in retailing,

China's radical moves towards a bigger role for the free market

Leaders of the Chinese Communist Party have held a four-day conference to push through a radical series of reforms that will pave the way towards a much greater role for the free market in the future affairs of its economy. This will be achieved in various ways including:

- a reduced dependence on polluting state-owned companies
- less dependence on state-driven construction projects
- removal of price controls
- phasing out caps on interest rates
- more convertibility of the yuan on the foreign market
- a further relaxation of the one child policy and measures to help rural communities.

The package of measures released by the Third Plenum meeting of the Party foresees a bigger role for private companies and a shift towards a modern consumer society. The communiqué that followed the meeting stated that the package will 'give markets a decisive role in resource allocation and give better play to the role of government.'

All in all, this has to be seen as a clear signal that China is now moving towards a more balanced mixed economy.

Source: New York Times, 12 November 2013; *Daily Telegraph*, 16 November 2013.

provision of food and drink, personal services such as hairdressing and dentistry, etc. At the same time, many more would-be entrepreneurs have failed to achieve success – they have suffered by not being able to overcome the risks that are involved in competitive markets.

KEY CONCEPT LINK

Scarcity and choice: Just how scarce resources are allocated depends to some extent on the type of economy. Irrespective of this, choices have to be made in all types of economy. Changes to the economic systems and structure of an economy by governments are designed to improve economic well-being.

Production possibility curves

How many goods and services an economy is capable of producing is determined by the quantity and quality of resources available to it, together with the state of technical knowledge. These factors determine an economy's so-called production possibilities.

Take the case of a simple economy which, given its available resources, can produce either military goods or consumer goods or a combination of each. The various possibilities are shown in Table 1.2.

It is sometimes useful to illustrate the choices open to an economy by considering the **production possibility curve**. From the schedule in Table 1.2 we can produce a production possibility curve with military goods plotted on the vertical axis and consumer goods on the horizontal axis.

KEY TERM

Production possibility curve: a simple representation of the maximum level of output that an economy can achieve when using its existing resources in full.

Military goods	Consumer goods
10,000	0
8,000	4,000
6,000	8,000
4,000	12,000
2,000	16,000
0	20,000

Table 1.2 Production possibility schedule 1

Figure 1.6 shows all possible combinations of military goods and consumer goods that could be produced given the existing quantity and quality of resources in our simple economy and the existing state of technical knowledge. At point *a*, only military goods are produced, and at point *d*, only consumer goods are produced, but between these two extremes lie all the other possibilities. The term 'production possibility curve' emphasises that this shows what levels of output an economy can achieve with its existing resources. It can also be used to show what the economy is *not* able to achieve. Point *Y* on the graph represents a combination of military and consumer goods that it is not possible to achieve. It is beyond this economy's production possibilities. Sometimes the curve is called a 'production frontier' because it draws the boundary between what can and cannot be achieved.

Figure 1.6 is also useful in illustrating the real cost to society of unemployed resources. The point *X* on the diagram represents a production of 4,000 military goods and 3,000 consumer goods. This is possible to achieve because it is within the production frontier, but it represents a point where some resources are unemployed or not employed effectively. The economy is capable of moving to point *b* with more military goods and the same number of consumer goods or to point *c*, which would bring more consumer goods and the same quantity of military goods. Alternatively, at a point between *b* and *c*, the economy can have more of both types of goods. Looking at the diagram in this way illustrates the waste from unemployed resources. We are not satisfying as many of our wants as we could if all resources were used.

An alternative name for the production possibility curve is the 'product transformation curve'. This emphasises a further use for the concept in introductory Economics. In Figure 1.6 as the economy moves along

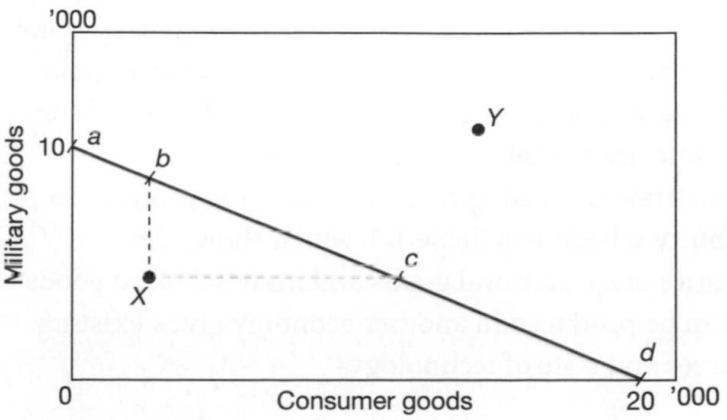

Figure 1.6 A production possibility curve

the curve from point *a* through to point *d* then a different combination of goods is being chosen. More consumer goods are being produced and fewer military goods. This emphasises that the cost of producing more consumer goods is the military goods that have to be sacrificed. Given the figures, we can calculate the opportunity cost of consumer goods in terms of military goods. A move from *b* to *c* on the graph leads to a gain of 8,000 consumer goods but we sacrifice 4,000 military goods. The opportunity cost of one consumer good is therefore half of a military good. This is equivalent to one military good having an opportunity cost of two consumer goods. As we move along the curve, the composition of our output is being transformed. We should also note that for this to happen we need to switch our resources from one use to another. Resources have to be switched from producing military goods to producing consumer goods and vice versa. This is known as the **reallocation of resources** and in the real world, as we decide to change the composition of our output, we need to consider the costs of reallocating resources between uses. These include the costs of retraining the workforce in the skills required to produce different types of goods and services. This might take a long time and might only be possible as new entrants to the labour force are trained in new skills. The extent to which resources can be reallocated from one line of production to another is known as **factor mobility** and, if we want resources to be swiftly allocated to the new use, we have to ensure that factors are as mobile as possible.

KEY TERMS

Reallocation of resources: where resources are deliberately moved from one product to another.

Factor mobility: the ease by which factors of production can be moved around.

It should be noted in our example that the opportunity cost of military goods in terms of consumer goods has not changed because we have chosen different combinations of the two goods. This is in fact quite unrealistic. A more likely outcome is that the production possibility curve will illustrate increasing costs. Consider the production possibility schedule in Table 1.3, which shows the quantities of agricultural goods and manufactured goods that can be produced in another economy given existing resources and state of technology.

Agricultural products	Manufactured products
700	0
660	100
600	200
500	300
300	400
0	500

Table 1.3 Production possibility schedule 2

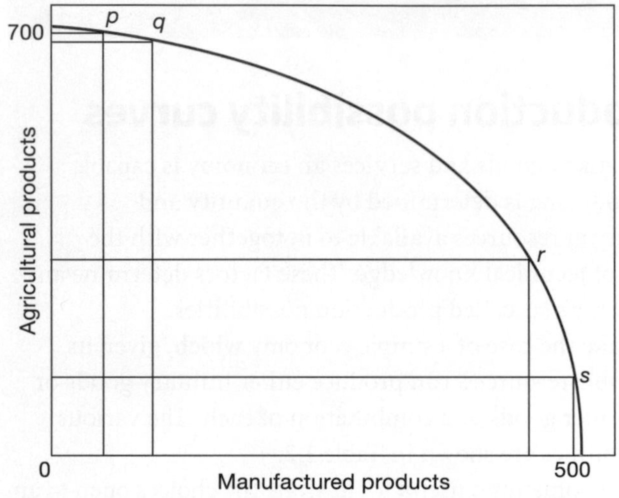

Figure 1.7 A production possibility curve with increasing opportunity costs

Assume that initially the economy is producing at point *p* with 660 agricultural products and 100 manufactured products (see Figure 1.7). Then assume that it is decided to move to point *q* to gain an extra 100 units of manufactured products. Clearly, resources need to be reallocated from agricultural use to manufacturing. At first the least fertile land will be reallocated and only 60 units of agricultural produce will be sacrificed. This means that each extra manufactured good has cost 0.6 of an agricultural good. Now compare this with a movement from *r* to *s*: to gain an extra 100 manufactured goods we have to sacrifice 200 agricultural goods. This means that one extra manufactured good has cost two agricultural goods. The opportunity cost has increased as we have reallocated our resources. This is because at this stage we are switching the more fertile land into manufactured good production so that agricultural output is going to be affected to a much greater extent.

So, the opportunity cost was initially small as resources better suited to the production of manufactured goods move from the production of agricultural goods. Alternatively, if more agricultural goods are produced, then it is necessary to reallocate those resources that are less suited to the production of manufactured goods.

A further case is where opportunity cost is constant. The production possibility curve in this case is a straight line as shown in Figure 1.8. This indicates that every additional unit of agriculture that is produced requires the sacrifice of the same amount of manufactured goods.

Shifts in production possibility curves

A production possibility curve is drawn on the assumption that the quantity and quality of resources and the state of technology are fixed. Through time, of course, economies can gain or lose resources; the quality of resources and the state of technical knowledge can also change. Such changes will shift the production possibility curve to a new position. Figure 1.9 shows the outcomes of changes in the quantity and quality of resources and changes in technology.

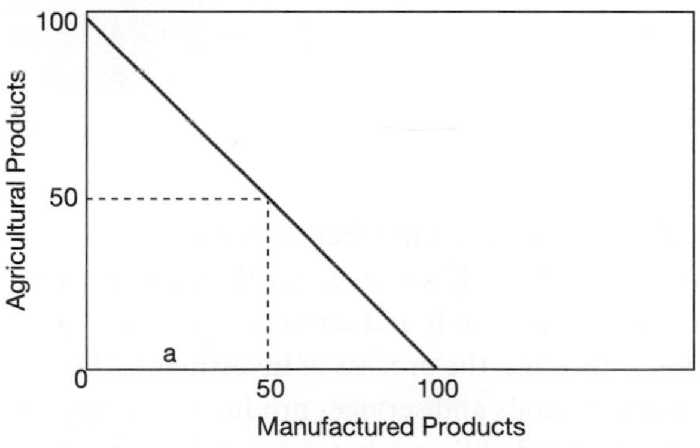

Figure 1.8 A production possibility curve with constant opportunity costs

Figure 1.9a shows a situation in which the production possibilities available to an economy have expanded. This is known as **economic growth**. This could be due to an increase in the quantity and/or the quality of resources available to the economy or an advance in the state of technology. Here the changes have improved the economy's ability to produce both agricultural and manufactured products. In Figure 1.9b, however, only the ability to produce agricultural products has been improved. This could perhaps be because there has been a technological breakthrough in producing agricultural products, which does not apply to the production of manufactured products. Nevertheless, this economy's production possibilities have improved and the curve has shifted outwards from the origin.

KEY TERM

Economic growth: represented by a shift outwards of the production possibility curve.

The production possibilities could also have declined. This could be because in some way the resources available to the economy have declined. Perhaps some of the economy's natural resources have become exhausted or the working population is falling. It might also be because the available technology has changed. An example might be the impact of controls on carbon emissions, which will affect production possibilities as controls become more rigorous.

TOP TIP

With a production possibility curve, the only efficient points are on the production possibility curve itself; a point inside the production possibility curve is inefficient.

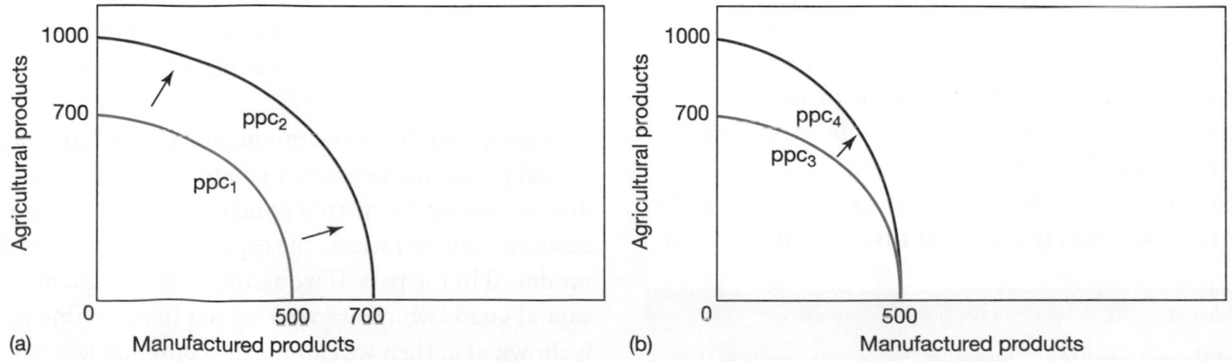

Figure 1.9 Shifts in production possibility curves

SELF-ASSESSMENT TASK 1.6

Read the information below and then answer the questions that follow.

Corn, soya beans or both? Choices facing Brazilian farmers

In recent years there has been a significant increase in the production of biofuels in countries such as Brazil where crops are used to produce ethanol. This alternative clean-burning fuel can be made from corn and soya beans. Table 1.4 shows how production of both crops has increased in Brazil in response to the insatiable demand for fuel that is required by the country's ever-increasing numbers of cars and trucks.

Production (1000 tonnes)	2008	2012
Soybean oil seed	57,800	82,000
Corn	51,000	77,000

Table 1.4 Biofuels in Brazil

Source: US Department of Agriculture.

1 Assume that Brazilian farmers can produce both soya beans and corn. Sketch a production possibility curve to show the choices they might make.

2 On your diagram:
   a show how a reduction in soybean production from 70% to 30% affects the production of corn
   b use the concept of opportunity cost to explain the trade-off.

3 a Use the data above to draw production possibility curves for 2008 and 2012.
   b Suggest some reasons that might explain the difference between these two production possibility curves.

Making use of production possibility curves

We can use production possibility curves to show some of the issues facing economic decision-makers in the real world.

Current consumption or future economic growth?

As stated previously, the production possibilities open to an economy are determined by the quantity and quality of resources available. In the process of production, resources are used up and they need to be replaced if production possibilities are to be maintained. The terms **capital consumption** or depreciation describe the using up of capital goods during the process of production. Some resources need to be devoted to the production of capital goods if production possibilities are to be maintained. The creation of capital goods in the process of production is known as **investment**. This can be defined as 'any production other than for current consumption'. A choice has to be made therefore between producing consumer goods and services or producing capital goods through the process of investment. The more consumer goods and services produced, the higher the current standard of living, but the standard of living might fall in the future if there is a failure to produce sufficient capital goods to replace those worn out in the process of production. In addition, the quality of an economy's capital goods will not be improved and the full benefits of new technology will not be enjoyed if there is a failure to devote sufficient resources to investment.

Figure 1.10 shows the production possibilities between capital goods and consumer goods. These possibilities are determined by the quantity and quality of resources in the economy, which include the capital goods that have been produced in the past. If we assume that the quantity of capital goods which are wearing out in each time period is shown at *a*, then we can see the consequences of our choices. If we fail to produce the quantity at *a* then our capital stock will decline. Production possibilities will diminish and the curve will shift to the left.

KEY TERMS

Capital consumption: the capital required to replace that which is worn out.

Investment: the creation of capital goods.

Hard choices for developing economies

Developing economies are characterised by low standards of living. If they are to grow then they need to increase their capital stock. Like all economies they need to divert resources from current consumption to investment. Some resources must be devoted to consumption, however, to keep their expanding populations alive. The problem they face is sometimes referred to as 'jam today or more jam tomorrow'.

The minimum amount of resources needed is sometimes referred to as the subsistence level of consumption. The difficulty is that in the poorest developing economies almost all their production possibilities need to be devoted to subsistence.

In Figure 1.11, *0–a* represents the capital consumption in a **developing economy** and *0–b* represents the consumer goods required for the subsistence of the population.

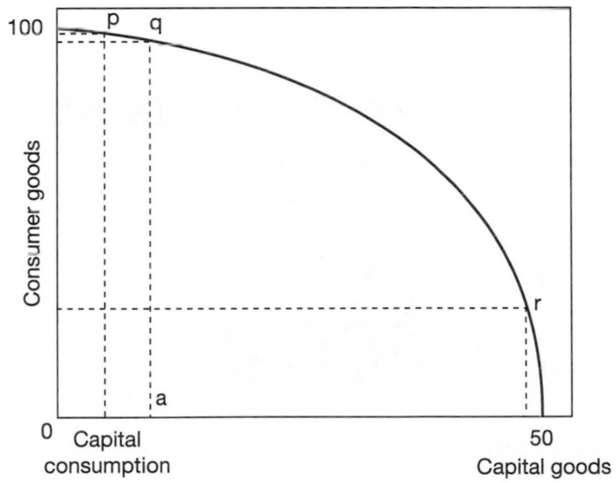

Figure 1.10 The choice between consumer goods and capital goods

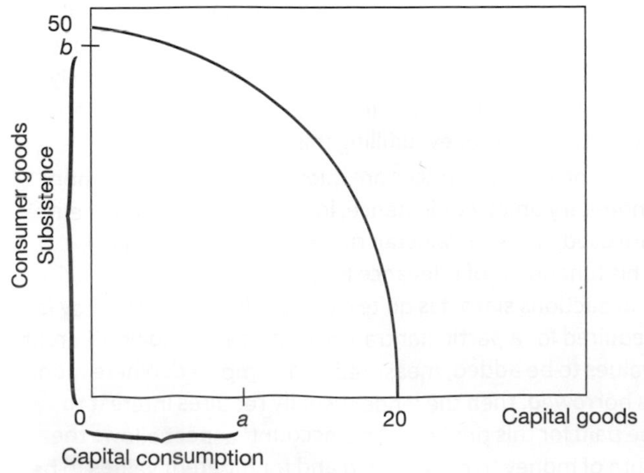

Figure 1.11 Capital consumption in a developing economy

KEY TERM

Developing economy: one that has a low income per head.

SELF-ASSESSMENT TASK 1.7

Explain the choices facing decision-makers for the developing economy shown in Figure 1.11. Discuss the difficulties they face and suggest possible solutions to their problems.

A hydroelectric power station in Africa

KEY CONCEPT LINK

Scarcity and choice: The production possibility curve is a good representation of how choices can be made, *ceteris paribus*. This simple model shows the effects of a decision to change the allocation of productive resources. The production possibility curve can also be used to show how change in the long run affects the resources that are available in an economy.

Money: its functions and characteristics

In some respects **money** is something that virtually all of us take for granted. We need it in order to carry out our daily lives, to pay for things such as riding on a

KEY TERM

Money: anything that is generally acceptable as a means of payment.

bus, purchasing a bottle of water or soft drink, buying lunch and so on. Handing over a few coins or a note is essential if we are to be able to buy what we want to satisfy our day-to-day needs. Larger sums, of course, are required for things such as clothes, shoes, cars and even school fees.

The money that we use for purchases is usually a national currency such as dollars, pounds or rupees (in Mauritius, India and Pakistan for example). For 17 EU member states the euro is their currency and, along with the US dollar, is widely accepted in global markets. The coins and notes have little or no intrinsic value – their value stems directly from the fact that sellers have complete confidence in the money given to them that prompts them to exchange it for the products we want to buy.

So what is money? A simple definition is that it is anything that is regularly used to buy goods and services. Normally, this is cash in the form of coins and notes but the definition also includes bank deposits, cheques, debit cards and credit cards. To be acceptable from a day-to-day practical standpoint, money must also be portable and durable. However, money can also be in the form of a valuable commodity such as gold or platinum. In Russia, for example, oil has been widely exchanged for imports such as buses and trucks from Hungary or agricultural goods from Poland.

Economists also talk about **near money**. This is a term that is used to denote non-cash assets that can be quickly and easily turned into cash. Such assets include foreign currencies, savings accounts, bonds and certificates of deposits. As assets, they contribute to the **liquidity** of banks by providing a supply of cash if this is needed to meet their **liabilities** to depositors.

KEY TERMS

Near money: non-cash assets that can be quickly turned into cash.

Liquidity: the extent to which there is an adequate supply of assets that can be turned into cash.

Liabilities: debt obligations.

Where there is hyperinflation, as in Zimbabwe and Venezuela in recent years, people lose confidence in money. Many farm workers, for instance, have preferred to be paid in produce as this will keep its value and can be easily swapped for other things such as cooking oil, sugar or bread. The direct exchange of one good or service for another in this way is known as barter. Where this is the only way of exchange, then the process of trade and exchange becomes lengthy and difficult. It is also very impractical since there must be a coincidence of wants, whereby both parties in a transaction actually have the goods or services that the other wants. Money is therefore essential if the processes of exchange and trade are to take place.

Zimbabwe's descent into economic catastrophe was a long drawn-out affair. Following a drop in agricultural production after controversial land seizures, exports fell and foreign investors went elsewhere. The government sought to solve its liquidity problems by borrowing from foreign banks, knowing that it could not meet its loan repayments. The government made the situation worse by printing more money, much of which was used to pay the army, police and civil servants. Eventually, inflation reached more than one million per cent and local people lost all confidence in the Zimbabwean dollar. More stability has come about since the country's decision in 2009 to use the South African rand, the Botswana pula, the pound, the euro and the US dollar for all transactions.

Ten billion dollar note from Zimbabwe

Bearing the above in mind, economists recognise the following four essential functions of money:

1 A medium of exchange: Money is the 'medium', or form, that buyers use for purchases; sellers are willing to accept this medium in exchange for these purchases. By handing over money physically, or by transferring money electronically through the banking system, this is a common, automatic acceptance of money fulfilling this function.

2 A unit of account: Prices are quoted in terms of common monetary units. For instance, in the USA dollars and cents are used, while in Pakistan rupees and paise are used. This function is of relevance for current and future transactions since it is quite clear just how much money is required for a particular transaction. It also allows different values to be added, measured and compared. Where money is borrowed, then the lender usually requires interest to be paid for this privilege. The 'account' aspect allows the sum of money to be recorded and for different values to be added or compared.

3 A standard for deferred payment: Not all payments we make are immediate. Some household bills are paid monthly, others may be paid annually. Following on from money as a unit of account, payments can be made in the future once terms have been agreed between the parties involved.

4 A store of wealth: Money can be held or 'stored' for a period of time, usually with a bank or other financial institution, before it is used. This important function means that money is a measure of value over time. Where this value is accumulated, then it represents a source of wealth to its owner. In 2011, the two richest people in the world were both from the USA: Warren Buffet and Bill Gates. Their personal wealth was in a wide range of assets, not just in bank accounts. Money was the common basis on which their wealth was estimated.

These functions of money are vital for the smooth operation of all economies. If any of the functions breaks down – as in the case of Zimbabwe, where money lost all meaning as a store of value or wealth – economic collapse is the inevitable outcome. It is therefore essential that a prudent government puts economic policies in place to ensure that this does not happen.

Classification of goods and services

The fundamental economic problem of scarce resources in relation to unlimited wants only arises in situations where we are dealing with what are known as **private goods**. These are also known as economic goods since they have a cost in terms of the resources used and are scarce. A price must therefore be charged when they are used or consumed.

> **KEY TERM**
>
> **Private goods:** consumed by someone and not available to anyone else.

Private goods are those bought and consumed by individual consumers or firms for their own benefit. Most of the goods we consume on a daily basis are private goods. They have two important characteristics:

1 **Excludability:** It is possible to exclude some people from using a private good. This is normally done through charging a price. If the price is not acceptable, then that good will not be consumed. Once a private good has been purchased by one person it cannot be consumed by others.

> **KEY TERM**
>
> **Excludability:** where it is possible to exclude one from consumption.

2 **Rivalry:** The consumption by one person reduces the availability for others. In some ways it seems obvious that when we purchase food, clothes or a textbook then this means that fewer of these goods are available for purchase by others.

> **KEY TERM**
>
> **Rivalry:** where consumption by one person reduces availability for others.

We can also recognise what are known as free goods. These have zero opportunity cost since consumption is not limited by scarcity. They have no prices – as their name indicates – and in theory, no factors of production are required to produce them. It is not easy to think of examples! In some economies, wild fruit and berries may be gathered or some animals hunted for their meat. The air we breathe could also be seen as a free good along with water in a local river.

Public goods

There are two specific characteristics of a **public good**. These are:

1 It must be **non-excludable**. This means that once the good has been provided for one consumer, it is impossible to stop all other consumers from benefitting from the good.

2 It must also be **non-rival**. As more and more people consume the good, the benefit to those already consuming the product must not be diminished.

> **KEY TERMS**
>
> **Public good:** one that is non-excludable and non-rival and for which it is usually difficult to charge a direct price.
>
> **Non-excludable:** where it is not possible to stop all benefiting from consumption.
>
> **Non-rival:** as more consume, the benefit to those already consuming is not diminished.

There are a number of goods that can be seen as public goods. Take the example of a lighthouse. Once a lighthouse is built to warn one ship at sea away from a dangerous area of rocks, then by its very nature, this service will automatically be provided to all ships that sail within a certain distance of the lighthouse. It is non-excludable. Equally, the fact that other ships see the light given by the lighthouse and are warned away from the dangerous rocks does not reduce the benefit that any one particular ship receives from that warning. It is non-rival. However, very few goods are purely public goods in the sense that they match both of the above characteristics in full. Other typical examples are defence and the police force in virtually all economies.

Quasi-public goods

While there may be some goods that can clearly be defined as 'public' in nature, there are others that have the essential characteristics but only in part. Such goods are referred to as **quasi-public goods**. They are like public goods without truly being public goods.

KEY TERM

Quasi-public good: goods that have some but not all of the characteristics of public goods.

In practice, it is not possible to classify all products as being either 'public' or 'private'. Many products lie somewhere in between these two extremes.

A good example might be a sandy seaside beach. Such a beach is available to all those who wish to use it. It appears non-excludable. However, it is possible to think of ways of excluding consumers. Privately owned beaches do this. Equally, the beach is non-rival up to a point. If you are the first person on a pleasant beach on a warm sunny day, it does very little to diminish your enjoyment of that beach as a few more people arrive to enjoy the benefits themselves. However, there may well come a point at which that is no longer the case. As the beach becomes crowded, space limited and other people's conversations and music become ever more audible, enjoyment may perceptibly reduce. Thus the beach has something of the characteristic of non-rivalry, but not the full characteristic. It is a quasi-public good.

The problem caused by public goods

The problem that may be caused in a free market by the existence of public goods is a serious one: the market may not produce them. There may be a consumer demand for such products (consumers are willing and able, in principle, to pay for the product's services), but the free market may not have a mechanism for guaranteeing their production.

This problem is referred to as the **free rider** issue. Some consumers attempt to gain a 'free ride' on the back of other consumers' purchasing the public good. It is entirely reasonable that they may attempt to do this. One of the key characteristics of public goods is that they are non-excludable. This implies that once one consumer has purchased the product, all other consumers cannot be prevented from benefiting from that product. Take again the example of the lighthouse. Once one particular fisherman has provided a lighthouse close to some dangerous rocks for his own benefit, then all other fishermen in the area will benefit equally from the lighthouse. Their advantage, however, is that they do not have to pay for this lighthouse: they have received a free ride on the back of someone else's purchase. The logical thing to do, then, would seem to be for all fishermen to sit back and to wait for one fisherman to be foolish enough to provide a lighthouse so that those not purchasing can benefit without paying. Unfortunately, the implication of this is that the lighthouse will never be provided: everyone waits for everyone else to provide it, and nothing happens.

KEY TERM

Free rider: someone who does not pay to use a public good.

It could be argued that a more likely scenario to the one described above is that all fishermen in an area might agree to club together in order to make the purchase and thus the lighthouse would be provided. However, there is still a problem here as it is in the interest of any one fisherman to conceal his desire for the lighthouse, refuse to pay but still to gain the final benefit once it is provided. Again, if all fishermen behave like this, the lighthouse is not provided.

The existence of public goods may mean that scarce resources are not used in a way that would be desirable. People may wish for the provision of such goods, but the demand may never be registered in the market. Private goods, however, can also be rejected if the price is too high or the quality is not what is expected. These seemingly obvious qualities of private goods are useful since they help us understand what is meant by public goods.

SELF-ASSESSMENT TASK 1.8

Explain, for your economy, whether each of the following may be described as a private, a public or a quasi-public good:

- the local police service
- a chocolate bar
- a public park
- a firework display
- a stretch of road
- street lighting
- a public cricket pitch
- a museum.

Merit goods, demerit goods and information failure

A **merit good** is a good that has positive side effects associated with it. Thus, an inoculation against a contagious disease might be seen as a merit good. This is because others who may not now catch the disease from the inoculated person also benefit. A **demerit good**, on the other hand, is seen as any product that has adverse side effects associated with it. Thus, junk food can be seen as a demerit good because overconsumption of fatty foods with few nutrients can be viewed as a cause of ill health.

KEY TERMS

Merit good: one that has positive side effects when consumed.

Demerit good: one that has adverse side effects when consumed.

Governments tend to provide merit goods, since there is likely to be underproduction and underconsumption; with demerit goods there is likely to be overproduction and overconsumption largely because these are goods that are habit-forming, relatively cheap and readily available. To understand these types of good, it is necessary to appreciate that there is **information failure** to the consumer. This arises because consumers do not perceive quite how good or bad a particular product is for them: either they do not have the right information or they simply lack some relevant information. This is why merit goods are provided by the government for those who are deemed to need them.

KEY TERM

Information failure: where people do not have full or complete information.

Merit goods

With this idea of a failure of information, a merit good is defined as a good that is better for a person than the person who may consume the good realises. Given this definition, education is often defined as a merit good. The individuals who make decisions about how much education to receive (or how much to allow their children to receive) do not fully appreciate quite how much benefit will be received through being well-educated. We do not always appreciate how good education is for us. We do not perceive its full benefits at the time of making the decision about how much education to receive.

Demerit goods

Demerit goods, on the other hand, are those products that are worse for the individual consumer than the individual realises. Junk food is a good example here. It is suggested that when a person makes a decision to eat junk food, he or she is not fully in possession of all of the information concerning the harmful effects of junk food. If he or she were in possession of such information, then they would be more reluctant to eat fast foods and more likely to focus on a healthy diet.

Junk food may be classed as demerit goods

Merit goods, demerit goods and value judgements

It may have been noticed in the above definitions that a significant question poses itself with regard to merit and demerit goods. Who is to say what is 'good' or 'bad' for a person? If an individual consumer makes a presumably rational decision to consume a product, what right has the rest of society to say that he or she is making a 'wrong' decision? It seems clear that if this is what is going on, we have entered the area of value judgements. If society is able to say to consumers that they do not fully realise what is good or bad for them, then we are accepting that 'society knows best' and has some right to make such a judgement. In effect, we are allowing **paternalism** and we are saying that it is acceptable for society to judge what is, or is not, good for a person regardless of what that person may believe.

KEY TERM

Paternalism: a situation where society knows best and has some right to make a value judgement.

KEY CONCEPT LINK

Scarcity and choice: Governments face the fundamental problem when deciding how to allocate their limited funds on what seem to be unlimited demands for public goods and merit goods. Choices have to be made as not all wants can be met. Choice should seek to maximise the benefits for all and not just a few people.

TOP TIP
Merit goods are a controversial topic in microeconomics; not all economists recognise them as a type of good, arguing that they are a special case of information failure.

SELF-ASSESSMENT TASK 1.9

Discuss, for your own economy, whether each of the following is a merit or a demerit good:

- compulsory secondary education
- wearing a seat belt
- emergency health services
- chewing gum
- visiting a museum
- playing loud music and shouting at a cricket match.

Moral hazard and adverse selection

There are numerous other examples arising from information failure. In welfare economics two types of situation can be recognised: **moral hazard** and **adverse selection**.

KEY TERMS

Moral hazard: the tendency for people who are insured or otherwise protected to take greater risks.

Adverse selection: where information failure results in someone who is unsuitable obtaining insurance.

Moral hazard can best be explained in the context of the health care market. Why does anyone go to a doctor? The most usual reason is because we are not sure how to deal with a health problem, whether this is something trivial like a sore throat or something more serious. We visit the doctor to get information – in doing this we recognise that the doctor is better informed than we are and that the whole point about making this visit is to accept the advice that is given. Moral hazard is when some person in the market (in this case the doctor) is better informed than those seeking advice. However, if the advice is wrong, we shall have made an undesirable choice of treatment. This will be a misallocation of resources.

Adverse selection is rather different. In this case, the information failure is reversed because information may well be withheld or be inaccurate when it emanates from, say, someone requiring health insurance. This puts the insurer in a position where not all the necessary information is provided for risk to be established. If this happens, then the cost of the health premium will be too low. If this person then requires treatment for an undisclosed problem, the premiums for healthy people will have to rise. In the worst case, if premiums become too expensive, healthy people may no longer seek health insurance as it has become too expensive. This is not good news for the insurer who could be left only with 'bad risk' customers. It might even lead to the collapse of the market through the enforced withdrawal of insurers. Again, there is a misallocation of resources.

SUMMARY

In this chapter it has been shown that:

- All economies face the so-called fundamental economic problem of limited resources and unlimited wants.
- Choice is necessary in order to decide what to produce, how to produce and for whom to produce.
- Factors of production (land, labour, capital and enterprise) are essential for the production process.
- Specialisation allows more goods and services to be produced.
- The true cost of choices we have to make is known as opportunity cost.
- A production possibility curve is a representation of what can be produced in an economy and the trade-offs involved in making choices.
- There are various types of economic system for the allocation of resources; the mixed economy is typical.
- There are problems of transition when former centrally planned economics move to mixed economies.
- Money includes a range of cash and non-cash items; it has four functions that are essential for the smooth operation of any economy.
- Economists classify goods in various ways: private goods, free goods, public goods, merit goods, demerit goods.

Exam-style questions

1 a Using a production possibility curve, explain how opportunity cost can be used to show the trade-offs involved. **[8]**

b Discuss some of the problems when a planned economy makes the transition to a market economy. **[12]**

2 a Using examples, explain the characteristics of public goods and merit goods. **[8]**

b Discuss why in many countries certain types of education and health care are provided as private goods and not as merit goods. **[12]**

3 a Explain what you understand by 'information failure'. **[5]**

b Explain why it is necessary to know what this means when classifying goods as merit or demerit goods. **[10]**

Chapter 2: The price system and the microeconomy AS Level

Learning objectives

On completion of this chapter you should know:

- what is a market and effective demand in a market
- what is meant by demand and supply
- what is meant by individual and market demand and supply and how demand and supply curves can be derived
- what factors influence demand and supply
- the meaning of elasticity
- price, income and cross elasticity of demand – what each means, how they are calculated, what factors affect them and the implications for revenue and business decisions
- price elasticity of supply – what it means, how it is calculated, the factors affecting it and the implications of how businesses react to changed market conditions
- what is meant by equilibrium and disequilibrium in a market
- how the interaction of demand and supply leads to equilibrium in a market
- how changes in demand and supply affect the equilibrium price and quantity and how this analysis can be applied
- the difference between movements along and shifts of demand and supply curves
- the meaning of joint demand and joint supply
- how the price mechanism works with respect to rationing, signalling and the transmission of preferences
- what is meant by consumer surplus and producer surplus and their significance
- how these are affected by changes in equilibrium price and quantity.

Introduction

Consider these newspaper headlines:

'Cotton hits 10 month high on global demand expectations' (Reuters, 6 March 2013)

'Damage to rice crops sparks price rise fears in Pakistan' (*Express Tribune*, 5 September 2013)

'Coffee prices may rise 15% on supply woes' (*Business Standard*, India, 3 July 2013)

'Crash of tea market takes fortunes with it' (International Herald Tribune, 10–11 January 2009)

The **price mechanism** underpins each of these particular events. It does so within the context of a **market**. In terms of these headlines, the markets involved are:

- the global market for cotton
- the market for rice in Pakistan
- the market for imported instant coffee in India
- a specialist tea market in a region of China.

KEY TERMS

Price mechanism: the means of allocating resources in a market economy.

Market: where buyers and sellers get together to trade.

These are just a few examples of markets. In practice there are many thousands covering not just products, but also a whole range of services, currencies, metals, stocks and shares.

To many people a market is something that happens in a town or city centre once or twice a week. This market is made up of a number of trading stalls selling a range of products: food – such as fruit, vegetables, meat and fish; clothing; and a wide selection of other items. Economists, however, take a broader view of the word 'market'. The core of any market is trade – somebody has something to sell and somebody else has to want to buy the product that is offered. So, whenever people come together for the purposes of exchange or trade, we have a market.

For example, economists talk about the housing market, where people rent, buy and sell houses. Look in the newspapers or in the windows of property agents' offices and you will see evidence of this market. They also refer to the labour market, where individuals' services are 'bought and sold' – anyone who has a part-time or full-time job participates in the labour market as a seller of labour.

Television newsreaders often refer to the stock market, where shares are bought and sold, and the foreign exchange market, where currencies are bought and sold. A very interesting example of a market is that of the Internet. A huge range of products are traded by companies and individuals and unlike many other markets, individual buyers are in a strong position because they can search the Internet to compare prices and get the best price for the goods they want.

These examples indicate to an economist that a market does not have to have a physical presence as the typical town or street market might have. It is simply a term used to describe the process through which products that are similar are bought and sold.

SELF-ASSESSMENT TASK 2.1

1 How do you participate in the following markets?
   - the fast food market.
   - the telecommunications market.
   - the transport market.

2 For each, say how important price is in your decisions to consume.

KEY CONCEPT LINK

Equilibrium and efficiency: Prices are set by markets, are always moving into and out of equilibrium, and can be both efficient and inefficient in different ways and over different time periods. This key concept is central to the content of this chapter and other microeconomic chapters. It recognises that equilibrium in a market depends upon both demand and supply influences, both of which can change over time.

Demand

To an economist, **demand** refers to the *quantity of a product that purchasers are willing and able to buy at various prices per period of time,* all other things being equal.

Definitions are of critical importance in Economics, so let us break this definition down to understand in some depth what it means.

- Quantity: This refers to the numerical quantity of a product that is being demanded.
- Product: This is a general term that simply refers to the item that is being traded. It can be used for goods or services. We could also stretch this to include tradable items like money or other financial assets such as shares.

KEY TERM

Demand: the quantity of a product that consumers are willing and able to buy at different prices.

- Purchasers: These are the buyers of the product and are often referred to as 'consumers', although they may simply be intermediaries in the supply chain, e.g., Nestlé purchasing large amounts of cocoa to be used in the production of chocolate for sale to the final consumer. We can consider an individual's demand for a product or, more usefully, we can aggregate this to look at the demand for the market as a whole.
- Willing to buy: Purchasers must want a product if they are going to enter into the market with the intention of buying it.
- Able to buy: To an economist, the **notional demand** for a product, which emerges from wanting it, must be backed by purchasing power if the demand is to become an **effective demand**. Sellers are only willing to sell a product if the purchaser has the money to pay for the product. It is this effective demand that is of particular importance for economists.
- Various prices: Prices are crucial to the functioning of a market. Although many things influence demand for a product, it is at the time of purchase, when we have to hand over our money and pay the price that we really judge whether the product is value for money – in other words, whether we really are willing and able to buy it. As the price goes up, and provided no other changes have occurred, more and more people will judge the product to be less worthwhile.
- Per period of time: Demand must be time related. It is of no use to say that the local McDonald's sold 20 Big Macs to consumers unless you specify the time period over which the sales occurred. If that was per minute then demand is high, but if that was per week then this would show there is little demand for Big Macs in this particular market.
- Other things being equal: There are numerous potential influences on the demand for a product. Understanding the connections between the various influences is very difficult if many of these elements are changing simultaneously. This is why it is necessary to apply the *ceteris paribus* assumption referred to in Chapter 1.

KEY TERMS

Notional demand: this demand is speculative and not always backed up by the ability to pay.

Effective demand: demand that is supported by the ability to pay.

The demand curve

The definition of demand can be represented by what is called a **demand curve**. The example shown in Figure 2.1 is based on the overall **market demand** for computers (PCs). Let us assume that we can identify a typical PC, i.e., one with a set of standard specifications We can also assume that we have collected statistical data about consumers' preferences and that the quantity of PCs that people are willing and able to buy at various prices per period of time, other things being equal, can be represented by the data in Table 2.1. This data set is known as a **demand schedule**. We can now plot the market demand curve on a graph to see how the quantity demanded of PCs relates to variations in price. This market demand curve therefore represents the aggregation of many individual demand curves. Figure 2.1 shows the market demand curve for the data in Table 2.1.

KEY TERMS

Demand curve: represents the relationship between the quantity demanded and price of a product.

Market demand: the total amount demanded by consumers.

Demand schedule: the data from which a demand curve is drawn.

Price of a 'standard' PC (US$)	Quantity demanded per week – demand curve D_0
2,000	1,000
1,800	2,000
1,600	3,000
1,400	4,000
1,200	5,000
1,000	6,000
800	7,000

Table 2.1 Market demand schedule for PCs

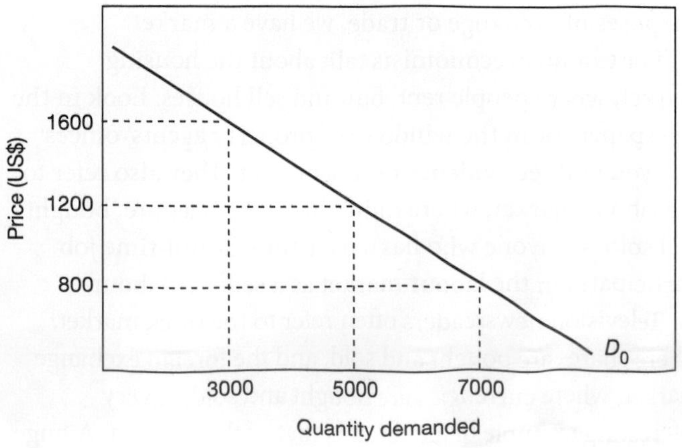

Figure 2.1 The market demand curve for PCs

The market demand curve in Figure 2.1 shows:

- An inverse or negative relationship between price and quantity demanded. In other words:
  - when price goes up, there is a *decrease* in *quantity demanded*
  - when price goes down, there is an *increase* in *quantity demanded.*

Changes in price cause a *change in quantity demanded* and we show this by movements up and down the demand curve.

- A linear relationship – this demand curve has been drawn as a straight line. However, it is perfectly acceptable for price and quantity demanded to be related in a non-linear manner in the form of a type of curve.
- A continuous relationship – we could look at the diagram and find out at what price consumers would be willing and able to buy 1,259 PCs.
- A time-based relationship – the time period here is weekly.
- Other things being equal, *ceteris paribus*.

Figure 2.1 allows us to see the complex relationship of demand. It allows us to estimate how much consumers may spend when buying PCs or, conversely, how much revenue companies may receive from selling PCs. If the price of each PC is $1,800 and the information provided is accurate, then consumers will buy 2,000 units and their total spending will be equal to $3,600,000 – the revenue that companies receive from selling this quantity of the product.

SELF-ASSESSMENT TASK 2.2

Using Figure 2.1 and Table 2.1, answer the following questions:

1. How many PCs per week are people willing and able to buy if the price is $1,100?
2. What price will persuade people to buy 1,350 PCs per week?
3. What assumptions are you making when you answer these questions?

SELF-ASSESSMENT TASK 2.3

Using Figure 2.1, explain how the area under the demand curve could be used to show the total consumer expenditure/total revenue of the firms selling PCs.

PCs have a consistent market demand

Factors influencing demand

The price of a good or service is not the only factor that influences demand. There are others including:

- Income: The ability to pay is vital when considering the importance of effective demand. For any individual, the demand for goods and services invariably depends upon income. (Usually this is taken to mean what a person has left after tax has been deducted). In terms of market demand, it refers to the income of all consumers and is invariably related to the state of the macroeconomy.

  In general, there is a positive relationship between income and demand. An increase in the ability to pay usually leads to an increase in demand. Conversely, if the ability to pay falls then less is demanded. Goods and services that are characterised by this relationship are called **normal goods**. Most products are like this and include things like cars, restaurant meals, quality clothing, etc.

  For some products, however, there is a negative relationship, with less being purchased as income rises. These are called **inferior goods**. Typical examples are poor quality foodstuffs; as consumers become better-off, they are more likely to buy less of these and, instead, purchase more fish, meat and premium priced foods with their increased income.
- Price and availability of related products: Two particular categories can be identified. First, **substitutes**, which are alternative goods and can satisfy the same want or need. Typical examples are Coca-Cola and Pepsi, both well-known brands of cola. A change in the price of one is likely to have

KEY TERMS

Normal goods: one whose demand increases as income increases.

Inferior goods: one whose demand decreases as income increases.

Substitute: an alternative good.

an impact on the demand for the other and on any other similar cola products. The extent of the change in demand depends on the degree of substitutability. Coca-Cola and Pepsi are very close substitutes; Sprite, Fanta and Lipton Iced Tea are also substitute soft drinks but not as close.

Second, there are **complements**. These goods have a **joint demand** as they enhance the satisfaction that consumers derive from another product. Typical examples are cars and petrol, cricket bats and balls, and headphones and electronic devices for playing music. A change in the price or availability of either one of these products will have an effect on the demand for a complementary good. For example, a rise in the price of petrol usually results in a fall in the use of cars for non-essential reasons. Alternatively, a fall in the price of petrol is likely to result in the increased use of cars.

- Fashion, taste and attitudes: These factors are more difficult to explain since they are largely a matter of individual behaviour. As consumers, we are unique and have our particular likes and dislikes. Some of us may like a piece of KFC, others may not for all sorts of reasons relating to personal taste or culture. For some products, our attitude might have been built up over time or it could have been influenced by what we have read or what advertisers would like us to believe about their product.

KEY TERMS

Complement: a good consumed with another.

Joint demand: when two goods are consumed together.

Whether or not we would eat food from KFC is influenced by many factors

TOP TIP

A change in the price of a product is shown by a movement along the demand curve. The assumption is that all other factors affecting demand remain unchanged.

TOP TIP

A good for someone on a high income can be an inferior good whilst for someone on a low income, it can be a normal good.

Supply

To an economist, **supply** refers to the *quantities of a product that suppliers are willing and able to sell at various prices per period of time, other things being equal.*

KEY TERM

Supply: the quantity of a product that producers are willing and able to sell at different prices.

Note the similarities below with the earlier definition of demand:

- Quantities: Economists often deal with numerical values and very often try to represent information in a quantitative way.
- Product: As with demand we are using the term to refer to any item that is being traded. It can be used for goods or services. We could also stretch this to include tradable items like money or financial assets such as shares.
- Suppliers: These are the sellers of the product and are often referred to as 'producers', although they may not be manufacturers of the product, they may simply be an intermediary in the chain or selling services. We could look at an individual company's supply of a product or, more usefully, we can aggregate to look at the supply for an overall market.
- Willing and able to sell at various prices: In a market economy, companies must gain from selling their products. They are also in the fortunate position that in many cases they can withhold supply if the price is too low. When price rises in the markets, it is assumed companies will be more willing and able to supply more to the market.
- Per period of time: Supply must also be time related. It is of no use to say that Acer supplied 200 computers unless you specify the relevant time period. Clearly this needs to be consistent with the time period being used for demand.
- Other things being equal: There are numerous potential influences on the supply of a product. Analysing the connections between the various elements is very difficult if lots of these elements are changing simultaneously. So, we assume these other factors affecting supply remain unchanged, i.e., *ceteris paribus*.

The supply curve

Using the above information on supply, we can construct a **supply curve**. This can be done for an individual firm selling PCs or, by aggregating each company's supply curves, to

KEY TERM

Supply curve: represents the relationship between the quantity supplied and the price of the product.

get the industry or market supply curve for PCs. Assuming we have collected statistical data about companies' selling intentions – represented by Table 2.2 (a market **supply schedule**) – we can plot this supply schedule to see how the quantity of PCs depends upon variations in price. Figure 2.2 shows the supply curve (S_0) for the data in this table.

The supply curve in Figure 2.2 shows:

- A positive or direct relationship between price and quantity supplied. This means that:
  - when price goes up there is an *increase* in *quantity supplied*
  - when price goes down there is a *decrease* in *quantity supplied.*
- Changes in price cause changes in the quantity supplied. This is represented by movements up and down the supply curve.
- A causal relationship – price changes cause the change in quantity supplied.
- A linear relationship – the supply curve has been drawn for simplicity as a straight line. There is no reason why the supply curve should not be represented in a non-linear way, e.g., in the form of an upward sloping curve.
- A continuous relationship – look at the curve to find out how many PCs companies would plan to supply at a price of $1,150.
- A time-based relationship – the time period again is weekly.

Note we are also assuming other things being equal – any other factor influencing supply is assumed to be unchanged.

KEY TERM

Supply schedule: the data from which a supply curve is drawn.

Price of a 'standard' PC (US$)	Quantity supplied per week – supply curve S_0
800	1,000
1,000	2,000
1,200	3,000
1,400	4,000
1,600	5,000
1,800	6,000
2,000	7,000

Table 2.2 Market supply schedule for PCs

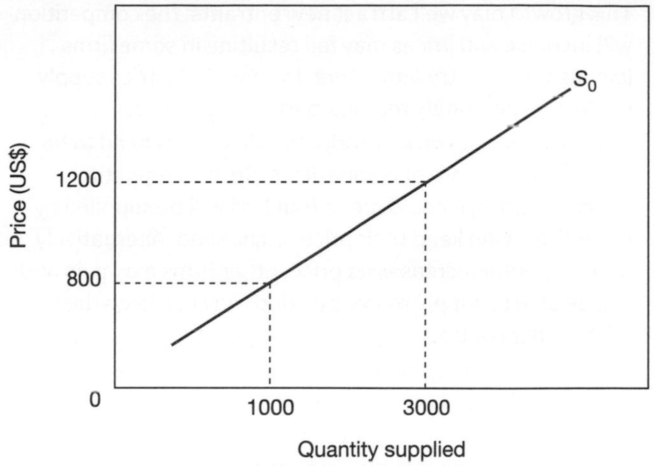

Figure 2.2 The market supply curve for PCs

TOP TIP

A change in the price of a product is shown by a movement along the supply curve. The assumption is that all other factors affecting supply are *ceteris paribus.*

SELF-ASSESSMENT TASK 2.4

1 Using Figure 2.2, how many PCs per week are companies planning to supply if the price is $1,100? What price would persuade companies to supply 1,350 PCs?

2 What assumptions are you making when you answer these questions?

3 What might be the advantages and disadvantages of using a diagram like Figure 2.2 to represent supply?

Factors influencing supply

The price of a good or service is not the only factor influencing its supply in the market. In practice there are many considerations. The main factors include:

- Costs: Supply decisions taken by companies are invariably driven by the costs of producing and distributing their products to customers. For many types of business, labour costs are an important item. In others, the cost of energy or transport may be more important, or the productivity of workers can have a huge impact on costs. This is particularly the case in motor vehicle production and assembly.
- Size and nature of the industry: If an industry is growing in size, then more will be supplied to the market.

This growth may well attract new entrants, the competition will increase and prices may fall resulting in some firms leaving the industry altogether. In some industries supply could be deliberately restricted to keep up prices.

- Change in price of other products: Most firms need to be continuously aware of competitors. So, if a competitor lowers its price, it could mean that less will be supplied by other firms who keep their price unchanged. Alternatively, if a competitor increases its price, other firms may gain and will be able to supply more provided they can keep their costs under control.
- Government policy: Governments influence companies and their supply of products in many ways. A new tax on a product will result in a reduction in supply; a **subsidy** will usually result in an increase in supply.
- Other factors: In agricultural markets, supply is invariably affected by uncertain weather conditions. Storms or frost may affect the supply of coffee or grapes; drought affects cereal crop yields whereas good weather can lead to bumper harvests of corn and wheat.

The factors affecting supply are many. Their particular significance depends on each industry or service.

KEY TERM

Subsidy: a payment made by government to producers to reduce the market price.

The concept of elasticity

In the analysis of demand and supply so far, the focus has been on understanding the general direction of any change in price and its effect on the quantity demanded or supplied. To add greater meaning to this explanation, it is necessary to look at the *extent* of any change in price and its effect on the quantity demanded and supplied.

A few simple examples will show why this is necessary. For some products – e.g., rice – a small change in price is likely to have only a modest impact on the quantity demanded. For other food products, particularly where there are close substitutes, for example different brands of tea, a small change in price may have a much larger effect on the quantity demanded. Similarly, if there is a change in income, there may be little effect on the demand for some products and a much greater effect on demand for others. For example, an increase in income may lead to an increase in demand for restaurant meals yet result in little or no change in demand for eating at local cafés or street stalls.

The concept that explains these variations is referred to in Economics as **elasticity**. This term can be applied to the supply side as well as the demand side of the market. It is defined as 'a numerical measure of responsiveness of one variable following a change in another variable, *ceteris paribus*'.

The extent of any change is important, particularly from a business standpoint. Where a small change in price, for example, produces a bigger change in the quantity demanded, then the relationship is said to be **elastic**. Alternatively, if a large change in the price produces only a small change in the quantity demanded, then the relationship is **inelastic**. The distinction is very important as it can be used to explain how businesses respond to a range of changing circumstances in their markets.

KEY TERMS

Elasticity: a numerical measure of responsiveness of one variable following a change in another variable, *ceteris paribus*.

Elastic: where the relative change in demand or supply is greater than the change in price.

Inelastic: where the relative change in demand or supply is less than the change in price.

Price elasticity of demand

Price elasticity of demand (PED) is a numerical measure of the responsiveness of the quantity demanded for a product following a change in the price of that product. If demand is elastic, then a small change in price will result in a relatively larger change in quantity demanded. On the other hand, if there is a large change in price and a far lesser change in quantity demanded, then demand is price inelastic. A numerical example helps to clarify this. A way of expressing PED in a numerical form is:

$$\text{PED} = \frac{\%\text{ change in quantity demanded of a product}}{\%\text{ change in price of that product}}$$

Using two specific examples of price changes for two general products called product A and product B (see Figure 2.3) assume that both of these unrelated products are currently priced at $100 and demand for them is 1,000 units per month. Consider what might happen to the demand for A and B if the price rises to $105. The quantity demanded of product A only falls

KEY TERM

Price elasticity of demand (PED): a numerical measure of the responsiveness of the quantity demanded to a change in price of a product.

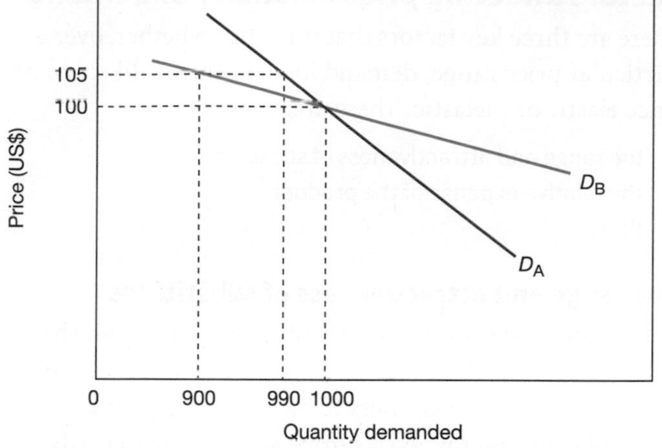

Figure 2.3 Price inelastic and price elastic demand curves

from 1,000 to 990, whereas the quantity demanded of product B falls from 1,000 to 900. By putting these values into the PED equation we can calculate the price elasticity of demand.

$$\text{Product A} \quad \frac{\%\ \text{change in quantity demanded of A}}{\%\ \text{change in price of A}}$$

$$= \frac{-1\%}{+5\%} = (-)0.2$$

$$\text{Product B} \quad \frac{\%\ \text{change in quantity demanded of B}}{\%\text{change in price of B}}$$

$$= \frac{-10\%}{+5\%} = (-)2.0$$

Notice that in both cases a negative figure is given. This is because of the negative (or inverse) relationship between price and quantity demanded; as the price goes up, the quantity demanded goes down. Economists conventionally refer to PED in absolute terms by ignoring the negative sign.

In the case of product A, because the numerical value (0.2) is less than 1, we say that the demand for this product is relatively inelastic or unresponsive to price changes. Over this particular range of prices, the 5% increase has resulted in a much smaller change in quantity demanded.

In the case of product B, because the numerical value (2.0) is greater than 1, we say that the demand for this product is relatively elastic or responsive to price changes. Over this particular range of prices, the same 5% price change has caused a much bigger change in quantity demanded.

TOP TIP

It is accepted practice to ignore the minus sign when considering estimates of price elasticity of demand.

Some special PED values

It is important to realise that mathematically PED values can range from 0 to infinity. These values need explanation. Consider, for example the demand curve shown in Figure 2.4. Irrespective of the price charged, consumers are willing and able to buy the same amount – in this case demand would be said to be **perfectly inelastic.** Look at the PED calculation for an increase in price from $10 to $11.

$$\text{PED} = \frac{\%\ \text{change in quantity demanded}}{\%\ \text{change in price}} = \frac{0\%}{+10\%} = 0$$

When the PED = 0, demand is perfectly inelastic; it is completely unresponsive to price changes.

Consider the demand curve in Figure 2.5. At a price of $10 per unit consumers are not prepared to buy any of this product; however, if price falls to $9, they will buy all that is available. The relative change in quantity demanded here is infinite, since the original demand was zero. So:

$$\text{PED} = \frac{\%\ \text{change in quantity demanded}}{\%\ \text{change in price}} = \frac{\infty}{-10\%} = (-)\infty$$

In this case, demand is **perfectly elastic.**

KEY TERMS

Perfectly inelastic: where a change in price has no effect on the quantity demanded.

Perfectly elastic: where all that is produced is sold at a given price.

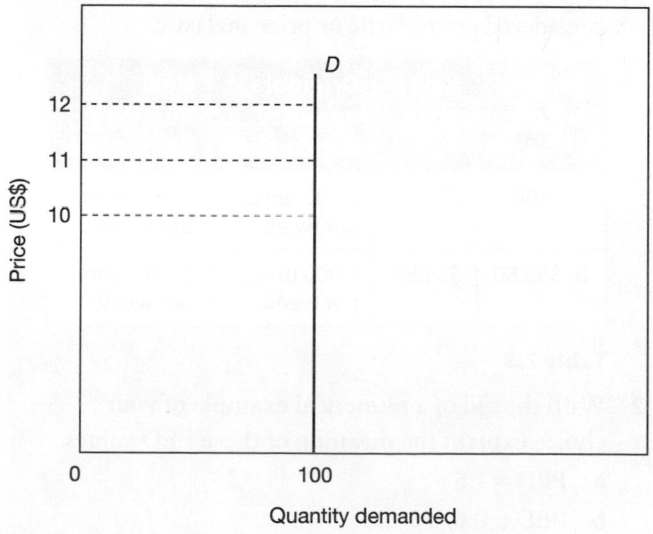

Figure 2.4 A perfectly inelastic demand curve

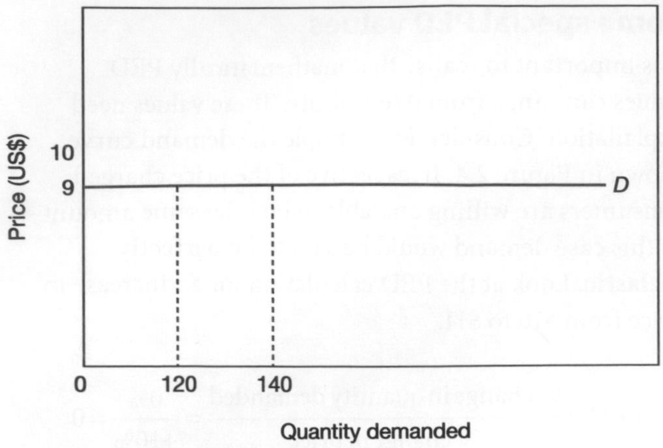

Figure 2.5 A perfectly elastic demand curve

Unitary elasticity

If the relative increase in price is exactly matched by the relative fall in quantity demanded, then the PED value will be (–)1. Demand will be said to have **unit elasticity** over that particular price range. For example, if the price of a product goes from $1,000 to $1,050 and the quantity demanded decreases from 10,000 to 9,500, then the PED will equal (–)1 over this particular range of prices.

KEY TERM

Unit elasticity: where the change in price is relatively the same as the change in quantity demanded giving a numerical value of 1.

SELF-ASSESSMENT TASK 2.5

1 Calculate the PEDs in each of the cases shown in Table 2.3 and explain whether demand would be considered price elastic or price inelastic.

Original price	New price	Original quantity demanded	New quantity demanded
a $100	$102	2,000 units per week	1,950 units per week
b $55.50	$54.95	5,000 units per week	6,000 units per week

Table 2.3

2 With the aid of a numerical example of your choice explain the meaning of these PED values:

a PED = 1.5

b PED = 0.6.

Factors affecting price elasticity of demand

There are three key factors that influence whether, over a particular price range, demand for a product is likely to be price elastic or inelastic. These are:

1 the range and attractiveness of substitutes
2 the relative expense of the product
3 time.

The range and attractiveness of substitutes

The greater the number of substitute products and the more closely substitutable those products are, the more we would expect consumers to switch away from a particular product when its price goes up (or towards that product if its price falls). A good example would be in the case of canned drinks where there are many types of cola, iced tea and fruit juice so a small change in price could see quite large changes in what consumers purchase.

It is important, however, to distinguish between the substitutability of products within the same group of products and substitutability with goods from other product groupings. For example, different types of orange juice are a group of products in their own right; they are also part of a larger group of fruit juices and part of the even bigger category of products that we could label as 'drinks'. If we are concerned with the price elasticity of demand for a particular type of orange juice produced by a specific manufacturer, then it will probably have a fairly high PED because of the range of substitutes. As we aggregate products into groupings – such as 'fruit juices' or 'all soft drinks' – demand will start to become more price inelastic.

Other substitutability issues to consider include:

- the quality and accessibility of information that consumers have about products that are available to satisfy particular wants and needs
- the degree to which people consider the product to be a necessity
- the addictive properties of the product, i.e., whether the product is habit-forming
- the brand image of the product.

The relative expense of the product

A rise in price will reduce the purchasing power of a person's income and hence the ability to pay. The larger the proportion of income that the price represents, the larger the impact will be on the consumer's income level of a change in the product's price. For example, a 10% increase in the price of a flight to Pakistan will have a bigger impact than a 10% rise in the price of a bus trip into town. The greater the relative proportion of income accounted for by the product, the higher the PED, other things being equal.

SELF-ASSESSMENT TASK 2.6

1 Classify the following products into whether, in your opinion, the PED is likely to be relatively high (elastic) or relatively low (inelastic). Justify your classification.
- Coca-Cola
- Nike trainers
- a particular brand of petrol
- fresh vegetables
- Cadbury's chocolate
- all forms of car fuel
- soft drinks in general
- all sweet/candy products
- wheat flour.

2 A manufacturer has received a market research estimate of PED values for its shirts currently sold in three markets: independent retailers, prestige fashion stores and via mail order. Explain and comment upon the PED values shown in Table 2.4.

Market	Current price	Current sales	PED value
Independent retailers	$8	40,000 p.a.	1.0
Fashion stores	$15	10,000 p.a.	0.2
Mail order	$10	3,000 p.a.	3.0

Table 2.4 PED values

Time

In the short term, perhaps weeks or months, people may find it hard to change their spending patterns. However, if the price of a product goes up and stays up, then over time people will find ways of adapting and adjusting, so the PED is likely to increase over time.

PED and a downward-sloping linear demand curve

So far PED and the slope of a demand curve may appear to be the same – this is, however, incorrect. Self-assessment task 2.7 will help you see the difference.

SELF-ASSESSMENT TASK 2.7

Price of product R (US$/unit)	Quantity demanded of product R (units per week)
10	0
9	1,000
8	2,000
7	3,000
6	4,000
5	5,000
4	6,000
3	7,000
2	8,000
1	9,000
0	10,000

Table 2.5 Demand schedule for product R

Use the information in Table 2.5 to calculate the PED values as prices fall from $10 to $9, from $9 to $8, from $8 to $7 and so on. You should see that the PED value falls as you move down the demand curve. In the top half of the demand curve, PED > 1; in the bottom half of the demand curve, PED < 1. We could show that for very small changes in price, PED = 1 at the mid-point of the demand curve. That is why, in theory, a demand curve with unitary price elasticity throughout can be drawn. Total expenditure (the area beneath this curve) for any price quantity combination is constant in this situation.

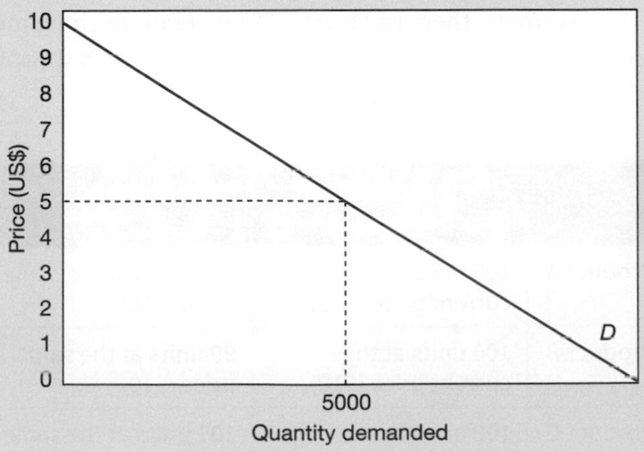

Figure 2.6 The demand curve for product R

Income elasticity of demand

Income elasticity of demand (YED) is defined as a numerical measure of the responsiveness of the quantity demanded following a change in income. All other factors remain unchanged. Once again if demand is responsive, then it is classified as elastic; if unresponsive, it is inelastic.

The formula used in this case is:

$$\text{YED} = \frac{\text{\% change in quantity demanded}}{\text{\% change in income}}$$

KEY TERM

Income elasticity of demand (YED): a numerical measure of the responsiveness of the quantity demanded following a change in income.

It is important to recognise that the relationship between income and demand changes may not always be positive. If an increase in income leads to an increase in the quantity demanded (or a decrease in income leads to a decrease in the quantity demanded), then there is a positive relationship and the product is classified as normal. The YED has a positive value. However, there are some products, inferior goods, which exhibit a negative relationship between income and demand. An increase in income would cause a decrease in the quantity demanded (a decrease in income would cause an increase in the quantity demanded). Here, the YED has a negative value. So the sign that precedes the YED tells you the nature of the relationship between income and the quantity that is demanded; the numerical value tells you the strength of that relationship.

For example, there has been a 2% increase in consumer income and that has led to the changes in demand shown in Table 2.6.

	Original demand (per period of time)	New demand
Product A	100 units at the current price ($10)	103 units at the same price ($10)
Product B	100 units at the current price ($10)	99 units at the same price ($10)
Product C	100 units at the current price ($10)	101 units at the same price ($10)

Table 2.6 Change in demand

$$\text{YED of A} = \frac{\text{3\% increase in demand}}{\text{2\% increase in income}}$$

$$= +1.5 \text{ (normal good – elastic response)}$$

$$\text{YED of B} = \frac{\text{1\% decrease in demand}}{\text{2\% increase in income}}$$

$$= -0.5 \text{ (inferior good – inelastic response)}$$

$$\text{YED of C} = \frac{\text{1\% increase in demand}}{\text{2\% increase in income}}$$

$$= +0.5 \text{ (normal good – inelastic response)}$$

TOP TIP

Knowing whether the estimate of income elasticity of demand is positive or negative is essential.

Cross elasticity of demand

Cross elasticity of demand (XED) is a numerical measure of the responsiveness of the quantity demanded for one product following a change in the price of another related product, *ceteris paribus*.

The formula used is:

$$\text{XED} = \frac{\text{\% change in quantity demanded of product A}}{\text{\% change in the price of product B}}$$

Products that are substitutes for each other (e.g., different types of laptop computer) will have positive values for the XED. If the price of B goes up, then people will begin to turn to product A because of its more favourable relative price. If the price of B falls, then consumers will start to buy B instead of A. Products that are complements (e.g., computers and printers or software) will have negative values of XED. If the price of B goes up, the quantity

KEY TERM

Cross elasticity of demand (XED): a numerical measure of the responsiveness of the quantity demanded for one product following a change in the price of another related product.

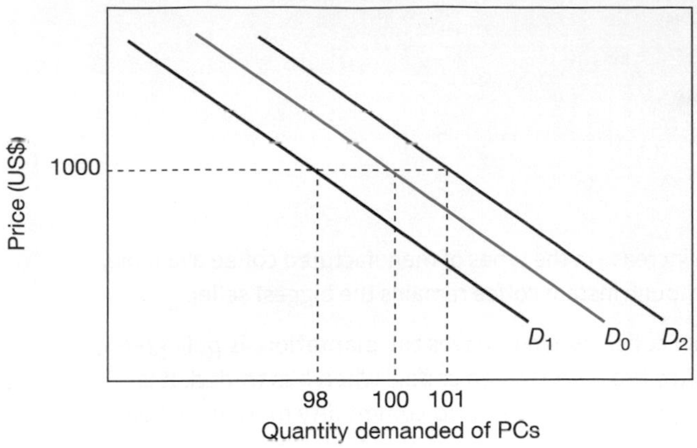

Figure 2.7 A change in the demand for PCs

demanded of B will drop and so will the complementary demand for A.

Assume the current average market price of a standard type of personal computer is $1,000 and current sales are 100 units per day (see Figure 2.7). Consider what might happen if, following a 2% decrease in the price of laptop computers (a substitute product), demand for PCs falls from 100 units to 98 units per day at the original price (D_0 to D_1). Our calculation becomes:

$$\text{XED} = \frac{2\% \text{ fall in demand for PCs}}{2\% \text{ decrease in price of laptops}} = +1$$

The positive sign indicates that the products are substitutes.

SELF-ASSESSMENT TASK 2.8

What would have happened to the demand for PCs if, following the same change in the price of laptops, the XED had been +2? Redraw Figure 2.7 to illustrate this.

Now consider that the average price of software (a complement) falls by 5% – this encourages extra sales of PCs so that demand for PCs rises to 101 per day at the original price and the demand curve shifts from D_0 to D_2.

The cross elasticity calculation is:

$$\text{XED} = \frac{1\% \text{ increase in sales of PCs}}{5\% \text{ fall in price of software}} = -0.2$$

Note that the sign indicates the nature of the relationship (a negative one between complements), and the numerical value indicates the strength of that relationship.

SELF-ASSESSMENT TASK 2.9

1 What would happen if demand for PCs had risen to 110 units per day? Calculate the XED and redraw Figure 2.7 to illustrate what has happened.

2 The owner of a local golf course loans out equipment to non-members who want to play occasional rounds. He estimates that in June and July, if he lowers the hire price of clubs by 10%, the number of non-members playing will increase by 25%. Calculate and comment on the XED. What other factors should the owner consider if he wants to increase demand from non-members?

TOP TIP

When calculating any of the three elasticity estimates, remember that the numerator in the formula is always the % change in quantity demanded.

Business relevance of demand elasticities

Price elasticity of demand

Knowledge of PED is useful to help understand price variations in a market, the impact of changing prices on consumer expenditure, sales revenue and government indirect tax receipts.

A very good example of price variations in a market is the price of tickets to watch a major sporting event. In 2012, the UK hosted the Olympic Games. The price of tickets to watch athletics events ranged from $140 to $650, the cheapest tickets being for the heats of field and track events with the most expensive being for the last day when medals were being awarded for the main events.

Variations in price elasticity of demand can also be used to explain:

- the difference between peak and off peak rail travel in some countries
- why it is usually cheaper to purchase airline tickets a few months rather than a few days ahead of travel
- why restaurant meals are more expensive during religious festivals.

In all of these cases, businesses are using price variations to try to maximise their revenue. They are well aware that there are variations in price elasticity of demand in their markets and therefore trying to exploit the opportunities presented to them.

SELF-ASSESSMENT TASK 2.10

Read the feature below and then answer the questions that follow.

Coffee break

A coffee farm in Kenya

Recent research has shown that 93% of UK households have bought instant coffee in the last year. In addition, coffee as a drink continues to increase in popularity, as consumers try variations such as cappuccino, espresso, mocha and latte. This expansion in demand has also led to an increase in the types of manufactured coffee available, although instant coffee remains the biggest seller.

Raw coffee, when it leaves the plantation, is pale green, hence the name 'green coffee' when it is traded. It is bought and sold on world commodity markets in London and New York. At any one time, the amount to be sold and the quantity that manufacturers and processors wish to purchase are key factors determining its price. Like any product, therefore, the price of raw coffee is determined where market supply and demand are equated.

The final price of raw coffee is very important for the economic well-being of millions of people living in countries such as Costa Rica, Kenya and Colombia, which are heavily dependent on this crop. Typically, farmers in such countries practise small-scale production – their plots of land might be no more than one or two hectares. It is therefore unrealistic for them to sell their product direct to the world market. So they usually sell their crop to a government-controlled agency that in turn releases stocks onto the world market, depending on market conditions.

An alternative approach, practised by major manufacturers such as Nestlé, is for coffee to be bought direct from local farmers. This happens only in countries where Nestlé manufactures locally for export. In such circumstances, Nestlé offers a 'fair price' to farmers to ensure a regular supply of green coffee. This price is widely advertised as the minimum price that will be paid for supplies. It follows that the higher the quality, the higher the price. This arrangement ensures that farmers continue to grow coffee, while providing Nestlé with regular supplies outside the uncertainties of the occasionally volatile world commodity market.

1 a Excluding price, state and explain **two** other factors that determine the demand for raw coffee on world markets.

b Would you expect the price elasticity of demand for instant coffee to be relatively elastic or inelastic?

c Would you expect this estimate to be the same for Nestlé's instant coffee?

2 a Excluding price, state and explain **two** other factors that determine the supply of raw coffee on world markets.

b Would you expect the price elasticity of supply for raw coffee to be relatively elastic or inelastic? Justify your answer.

c Would you expect the price elasticity of supply for instant coffee to be relatively elastic or inelastic? Justify your answer.

Price elastic PED and total expenditure/total revenue

PED can help us understand how total spending by consumers will change as price rises or falls.

Total expenditure = $P \times Q$, where P is price and Q is quantity
= Total revenue for a business or industry

In Figure 2.8, assume there are two products each with the same price ($10) and quantity traded (100 units per day). Total expenditure by consumers per day = $10 × 100 = $1,000 – this is, of course, equal to the revenue received by companies. Now, if the price rises to $11, the differences in PED indicate that consumers respond in different ways, and the total expenditure will change:

- D_e is relatively price elastic over the relevant price range, and quantity falls considerably to 80 units (PED = –2). Total expenditure is now down to $880 per day – the reason, of course, is that the relative fall in sales is greater than the relative increase in price.
- D_i is relatively price inelastic over the relevant price range and the quantity traded only falls slightly to 95 units (PED = – 0.5). Total expenditure actually rises even though less is traded. The reason is that the increase in price exerts a more powerful influence in this case.

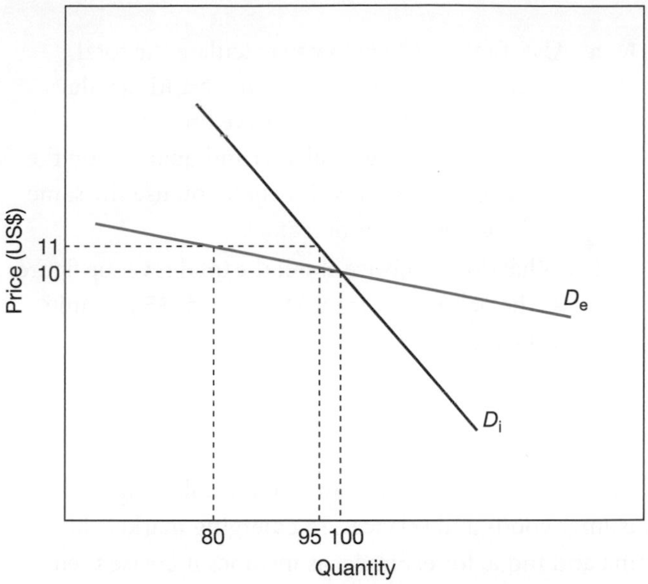

Figure 2.8 Price elastic and price inelastic demand curves

Income elasticity of demand

YED provides information on how the quantity demanded varies with a change in income. It is potentially of great importance for businesses and for governments

SELF-ASSESSMENT TASK 2.11

The market demand schedule in Table 2.7 was previously used to show how the PED varied along the length of a linear demand curve. This demand curve is now shown again in Figure 2.9. (Remember how in the top half PED > 1 whereas in the lower half PED was <1).

Price of product R (US$/unit)	Quantity demanded of product R (units per week)	Total expenditure US$ per week
10	0	
9	1,000	
8	2,000	
7	3,000	
6	4,000	
5	5,000	
4	6,000	
3	7,000	
2	8,000	
1	9,000	
0	10,000	

Table 2.7

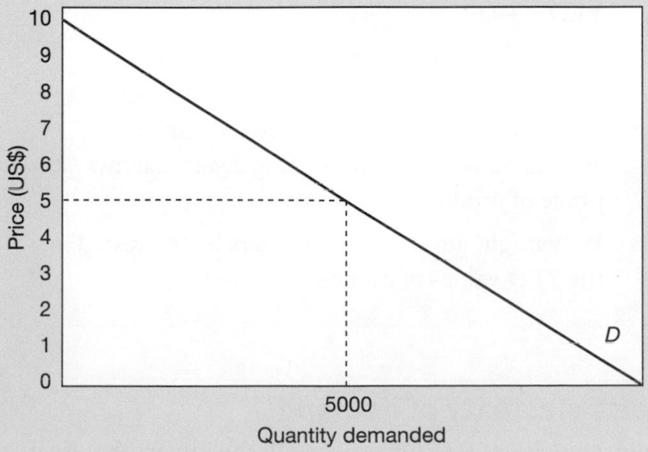

Figure 2.9 The demand curve for product R

1 a Use Table 2.7 to help you calculate the total revenue figures and graph the resulting values underneath the demand curve (put total revenue on the vertical axis and quantity on the horizontal axis – it will help if you use the same scale on the horizontal axis).

b What do you notice about the total revenue figures as the price is cut from $10 towards $5 per unit?

c Why does this happen?

d What do you notice about the total revenue figures as price is raised from $0 to $5?

e Why does this happen?

f Where is total revenue maximised?

2 If a government is interested in raising more revenue from indirect taxes, such as a general sales tax or excise duties, should it tax products that are price elastic or price inelastic? Explain your answer with diagrams and examples drawn from your own country.

in forecasting the future demand for a whole range of consumer goods and services. In emerging markets like China and India, for example, as incomes increase then people demand more cars. Production changes need to occur to satisfy this demand and governments need to build more roads to accommodate the increased demand.

If the YED for a normal good is greater than 1, then demand will be expected to grow more rapidly than consumer incomes. This is usually the case in times of sustained economic growth such as that experienced by China and India in recent years. During a recession, as experienced by many developed economies from 2008, businesses producing these types of product will be extremely vulnerable given the reduced demand.

If YED is negative, in the case of inferior goods, firms that produce these can expect their sales to decline when the economy is doing well; at a time of recession, though, demand for their product is likely to increase.

SELF-ASSESSMENT TASK 2.12

1 What will happen to sales of a product whose YED = +0.6?

2 How could you use YED values to advise a company on how to produce a mix of goods and services that would reduce the risk often associated with only producing a very narrow range of products?

3 Why might government planners be interested in the YED values of different products?

Cross elasticity of demand

Many companies are concerned with the impact that rival pricing strategies will have on the demand for their own product. Remember that substitutes are characterised by a positive XED: the higher the price, the more likely it is that consumers will buy a cheaper substitute. In such cases there is a high degree of interdependence between suppliers, and the dangers of a rival cutting price are likely to be very significant indeed.

Companies are increasingly concerned with trying to get consumers to buy not just one of their products but a whole range of complementary ones, e.g., computer printers and cartridges. XED will identify those products that are most complementary and help a company introduce a pricing structure that generates more revenue. For instance, market research may indicate that families spend most money at restaurants when special deals are offered, even though the PED for meals is low. In this case, for example, the high negative cross elasticity between meal prices and the demand for soft drinks (such as Pepsi Cola and Coca-Cola) means that although the revenue from food sales may fall, the demand for soft drinks may increase. This indicates that the restaurant may need to introduce a more sophisticated pricing structure by looking at the relationships between the demand for all products and services offered.

Cautionary note

We have assumed that calculating demand elasticity values is straightforward. In fact there are enormous practical statistical problems, which mean that elasticity values are best seen as estimates. This is because in all three cases we are trying to measure change in the market and this is by no means easy, as data for two points in time are required. For instance, consider the difficulties of calculating PED values from historical data. Have the price changes only been caused by supply variations? Have there been any non-price demand influences at work? Remember, if we are to calculate the PED value accurately, we need to separate out all the other influences and just measure the impact of the price change alone on quantity demanded. Collecting data from other sources, such as market research reports or surveys (using questionnaires and/or interviews), is costly in terms of time and money and may not be particularly valid or reliable.

Similar problems occur when trying to estimate income elasticity. The data available are likely to be unreliable the longer the time span involved. Over time the products available in the market are subject to tremendous change particularly in technological terms. This makes estimation hazardous. Therefore, many companies may prefer to make rough 'guesstimates' of elasticity values or to work with incomplete data, particularly if they are operating in markets where rapid change means past data cease to be a good indicator of the future.

Price elasticity of supply

Price elasticity of supply (PES) is a numerical measure of the responsiveness of the quantity supplied to a change in the price of the product, *ceteris paribus*. The supply could be that of an individual business or it might refer to the market supply of an industry. It is expressed as:

$$PES = \frac{\%\ \text{change in quantity supplied}}{\%\ \text{change in price}}$$

Since the relationship between the price and quantity supplied is normally a direct one, the PES will tend to take on a positive value. If the numerical value of PES is greater than 1, then we say that supply is relatively price elastic, i.e., supply is responsive to a change in price. If the numerical value of PES is less than 1, then supply is relatively price inelastic, i.e., supply is unresponsive to a change in price.

Figure 2.10 shows five supply curves each with different PES values.

KEY TERM

Price elasticity of supply (PES): a numerical measure of the responsiveness of the quantity supplied to a change in the price of the product.

Factors influencing PES

The key to understanding PES is supply flexibility – if businesses and industries are more flexible in the way they operate, then supply tends to be more elastic. The main influences on PES include the following:

- The ease with which businesses can accumulate or reduce stocks of goods. Stocks allow companies to meet variations in demand through output changes rather than price changes – so the more easily manufacturers can do this, the higher the PES. Companies that provide services are, of course, unable to build up stocks and in most cases, the product is 'perishable'. For example, in the cases of an airline or a hotel, if a seat or room is not sold for a particular flight or night, revenue is lost.
- The ease with which they can increase production. In the short run businesses and industries with spare productive capacity will tend to have a higher PES. However, shortages of critical factor inputs (skilled workers, components, fuel) will often lead to an inelastic PES. This is particularly the case with agricultural products, where it takes time to alter the type of crops produced.
- Over time, of course, companies can increase their productive capacity by investing in more capital equipment, often taking advantage of technological advances. Equally, over time, more businesses can enter or leave an industry and this will increase the flexibility of supply.

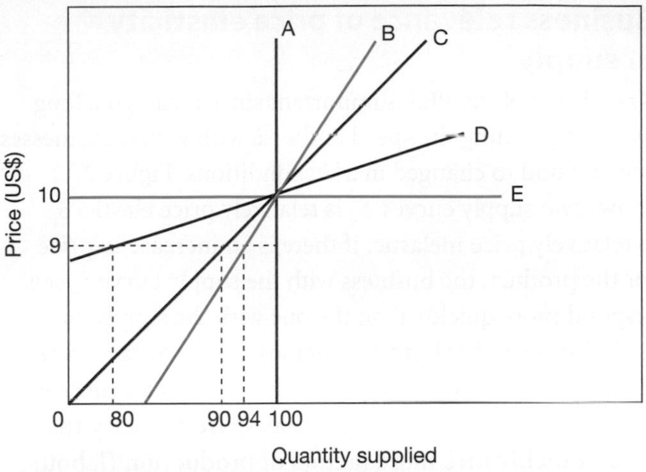

Supply curve	% change in quantity supplied/	/ % change in price	= PES and Description	
A	0	/ 10% decrease	=0	Perfectly inelastic
B	6% decrease	/ 10% decrease	=+0.6	Relatively inelastic
C	10% decrease	/ 10% decrease	=+1.0	Unitary elasticity
D	20% increase	/ 10% increase	=+2.0	Relatively elastic
E	Firms are not prepared to supply any at a price below $10 but will supply as much as they can at $10 (or above!)		=+∞	Perfectly elastic

Figure 2.10 Five different supply curves

Business relevance of price elasticity of supply

Knowledge of the PES is important since it can go a long way to explaining the speed and ease with which businesses can respond to changed market conditions. Figure 2.11 shows two supply curves. S_e is relatively price elastic; S_i is relatively price inelastic. If there is an increase in price for the product, the business with the supply curve S_e can respond more quickly than the one with the supply curve S_i.

Why is this? If both businesses are manufacturers then it relates to the ease with which they can increase production. Where a business has spare capacity then it can quickly hire more factors of production (labour especially) to meet the increased demand. For a business that is at full capacity, it is necessary to expand its scale of operations and this can take time. It can also take time where a business has to diversify into a new

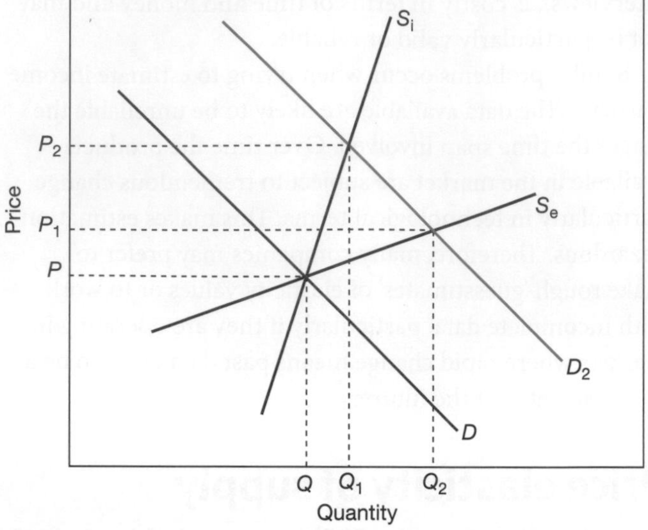

Figure 2.11 Supply curves with different elasticities

SELF-ASSESSMENT TASK 2.13

Read the feature below and then answer the questions that follow.

Damage to rice crop sparks price rise fears

It has been reported that the Rice Exporters Association of Pakistan (REAP) has expressed concerns over damage to rice paddy in the Punjab during recent heavy rains and the effect that these will have on rice prices. In the Punjab, 10% of cultivated rice fields have been damaged and production has been lost. REAP's chairman believes that this is likely to increase domestic prices for Basmati rice by 20%.

Floods and heavy rains have particularly hit Karmoke and Muridke where production is expected to be 50% down. Elsewhere, the crop loss has been less; in Sialkot it is 10–12% down, Pasroor 20% down and in Hafizabad just 5–7% down.

REAP's chairman, Jawed Ali Ghori, has pressed central government to take immediate measures to address the problems faced by growers. He commented that 'Every year we face a disastrous situation' and urged the government 'to take preventative steps to avoid such problems in the future'.

Flooded rice fields in Pakistan

Source: *The Express Tribune*, 5 September 2013.

1 Using the information provided, calculate the likely price elasticity of supply of Basmati rice in the Punjab in 2013. Explain what this means.

2 Explain why the price elasticity of supply might vary between different parts of the Punjab.

3 Comment on whether you feel the data in the feature are accurate.

4 Briefly describe the supply measures that might be used by the Pakistan government 'to avoid such problems in the future'.

product range if it is seen as worthwhile as a result of the price rise.

The PES is particularly relevant in agricultural markets. For valid climatic and geographical reasons, it is often difficult and sometimes impossible for producers to increase crops or switch to more lucrative ones when price rises. Producers may not have the additional land, or conditions may not allow them to grow a crop when price has increased. For example, coffee growers in Brazil or tea growers in Kenya cannot suddenly switch to growing corn, irrespective of the increase in price of corn. Even if they could, it would take time and there would be the added risk that prices may well have fallen.

Interaction of demand and supply– markets in equilibrium and disequilibrium

Earlier in this chapter, each side of the market was analysed separately. We now look at how to put them together. At any point in time, there will be a given set of conditions influencing demand and a given set of conditions influencing supply (see Table 2.8). Using conditions reflected in the demand curve D_0 and the supply curve S_0 previously, these relationships have been combined in Figure 2.12.

The term **equilibrium** refers to a situation of balance where, at least under present circumstances, there is no tendency for change to occur. In this particular situation, equilibrium will exist when the plans of consumers (as represented by the market demand curve) match the plans of suppliers (as represented by the market supply curve).

KEY TERM

Equilibrium: a situation where there is no tendency for change.

Price of a standard PC (US$)	Quantity supplied per week	Quantity demanded per week
800	1,000	7,000
1,000	2,000	6,000
1,200	3,000	5,000
1,400	4,000	4,000
1,600	5,000	3,000
1,800	6,000	2,000
2,000	7,000	1,000

Table 2.8 Market supply and demand schedules for PCs

The market equilibrium will, therefore, be at a price of $1,400 with 4,000 units traded, i.e., bought and sold. These are referred to as **equilibrium price** and **equilibrium quantity**. Total consumer expenditure (and therefore total revenue) will be $5,600,000 per week. Just think about what would happen if for some reason companies thought that consumers were prepared to pay $1,600 and supplied 5,000 units to the market. In this case the market would be in **disequilibrium** (an imbalance where change will happen). At a price of $1,600, under present circumstances, consumers are only planning to buy 3,000 units. As such companies will build up excess stocks at the rate of 2,000 PCs per week. There is disequilibrium due to excess supply. Companies would be irrational to carry on with this unplanned stock building. So how might they react?

KEY TERMS

Equilibrium price: the price where demand and supply are equal, where the market clears.

Equilibrium quantity: the amount that is traded at the equilibrium price.

Disequilibrium: a situation where demand and supply are not equal.

First of all, they could cut prices; they would also probably start to reduce the quantity they supply to the market. Of course, as they cut prices, some consumers who would not have been prepared to pay the higher price are now attracted back into the market – the disequilibrium starts to narrow. Provided there is no change to any of the conditions of supply or demand, and nothing prevented companies adjusting in this way, then eventually, the market price and quantity should move back to equilibrium.

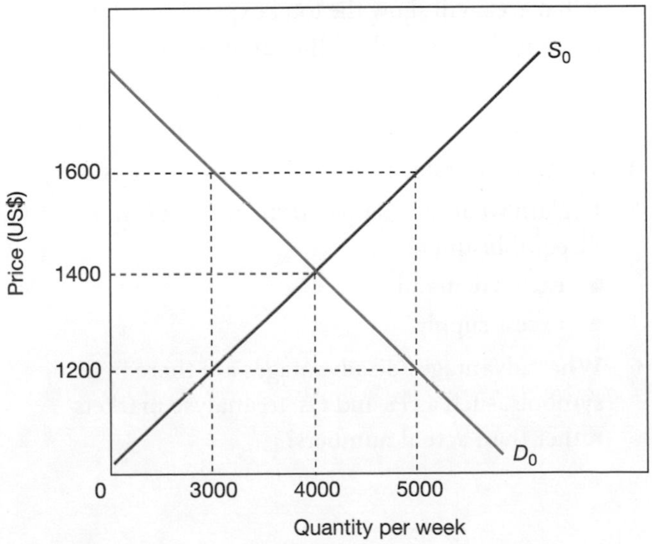

Figure 2.12 Equilibrium price and output in the market for PCs

Consumers can easily compare prices in superstores

Think now what would happen if the price was set at $1,000. Again we have disequilibrium – this time of excess demand. Consumers are now keen to snap up what they consider to be a pretty good deal. However, given the low prices, supplies are fairly low and there are not enough PCs to meet demand – suppliers will run out of stocks far quicker than they had expected, so there are unmet orders. Profit-oriented companies, if they are reasonably sharp, will recognise this and will start to raise the price and increase the number of PCs available for sale. However, as prices rise, some consumers will decide that PCs have become too expensive and the quantity demanded will fall. Once again, the market will adjust back to the equilibrium.

This process of market adjustment may not happen instantly; there will be time lags, perhaps quite lengthy ones if companies cannot react quickly. The point is that there will always be a tendency for the market to move back to its equilibrium position because that is where the underlying motives and plans of consumers and suppliers are driving it. When this position is reached, it is said that the market clears.

KEY CONCEPT LINK

Equilibrium and efficiency, the margin and change: It should now be clear that markets operate in a dynamic way, moving from equilibrium to disequilibrium and back again to equilibrium; the market moves from an efficient position to being inefficient and then adjusts naturally to again being efficient. The causes are many. The time taken for these changes to come about is highly variable. The various elasticity measures provide some answers as to why this is so and how consumers react to change.

SELF-ASSESSMENT TASK 2.14

In Figure 2.13, symbols are used instead of numbers.

1 What is the market equilibrium price and quantity?
2 What area will show the total expenditure by consumers? This will be the same as the total revenue earned by companies.
3 What is the state of the market if the price is at P_1?
4 What is the state of the market if the price is at P_0?
5 Explain what will happen if the market is in a disequilibrium of:
   - excess demand
   - excess supply.
6 What advantages/disadvantages are there in using symbols, such as *P*s and *Q*s, to analyse markets rather than actual numbers?

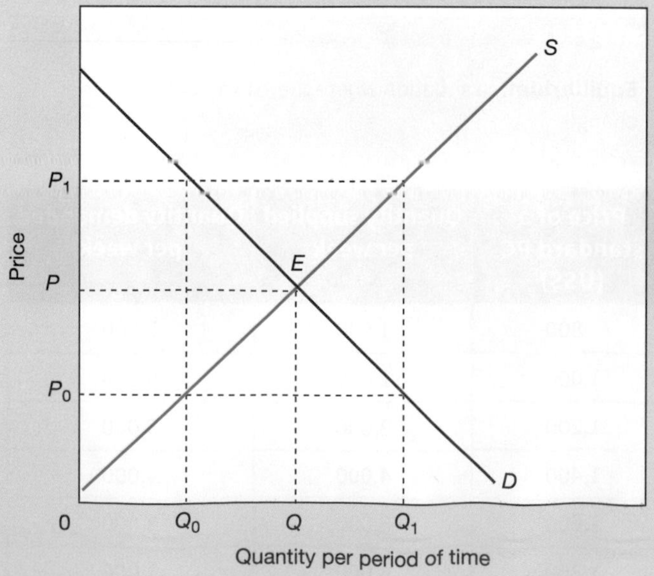

Figure 2.13

Shifts in the market demand curve

Up to now, in looking at the demand curve, we have assumed that price is the only factor that affects the quantity demanded by consumers. While this analysis is very useful, it is clearly limited because the price of a PC, for example, is not the only factor influencing the demand for it – other factors play a part and are not always constant. Changes in these other factors are shown by shifts in the demand curve. A rightward shift indicates an increase in demand; a leftward shift indicates a decrease in demand. Notice how the language changes here when we are talking about a *shift* in the whole curve rather than simply a *movement* along it – a **change in demand** rather than a change in the quantity demanded (see Table 2.9 and Figure 2.14). Figure 2.14 shows:

- Consumers are now willing and able to buy more PCs at each and every price. So, whereas previously as shown in Table 2.8 they had only been prepared to buy 3,000 units per week at $1,600 each, now they are prepared to buy 4,000.
- Consumers previously were prepared to pay $1,600 for 3,000 PCs; now they are prepared to pay $1,800 each for that quantity.

KEY TERM

Change in demand: when there is a shift in the demand curve due to a change in factors other than the price of the particular product.

Causes of shifts in the demand curve

Individuals may differ widely in their attitudes towards products. We could therefore spend a lot of time constructing a very long list of non-price influences.

Price of a 'standard' PC (US$)	Quantity demanded per week – demand curve D_2
2,000	2,000
1,800	3,000
1,600	4,000
1,400	5,000
1,200	6,000
1,000	7,000
800	8,000

Table 2.9 Shifts in the market demand curve

This might be useful in certain circumstances but not in all cases. Economists have identified three key non-price categories that can be used to describe and analyse the factors that influence the demand for most products. They are:

1. the income/ability to pay for the product
2. the price and availability of related products
3. fashion, taste and attitudes.

SELF-ASSESSMENT TASK 2.15

Use the information in Table 2.10 to draw a demand curve and explain what has happened to that demand curve – you are showing a decrease in demand. Draw in demand curve D_0 from Figure 2.14 as well so that you can use it as the basis for your comparison.

Price of a 'standard' PC (US$)	Quantity demanded per week – demand curve D_1
2,000	0
1,800	1,000
1,600	2,000
1,400	3,000
1,200	4,000
1,000	5,000
800	6,000

Table 2.10

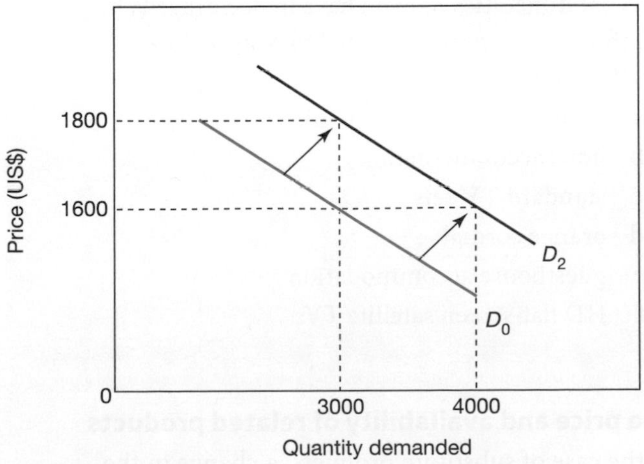

Figure 2.14 A shift to the right in the market demand curve for PCs

Income/the ability to pay

What influences someone's ability to pay for a product? The key things are:

- an individual's income or, more specifically, the purchasing power of their income after taxation
- the availability of loans/credit and the interest rate that must be paid on loans or credit card balances.

In general we expect a positive relationship between the ability to pay and the demand for a product. Such products are called normal goods. So an increase in the purchaser's income generally leads to an increase in demand. This is represented by a rightward shift in the demand curve from D_0 to D_2 in Figure 2.14. A decrease in the ability to pay would lead to a decrease in demand, and this would be represented by a leftward shift in the demand curve from D_2 to D_0. This more unusual case is that for inferior goods.

SELF-ASSESSMENT TASK 2.16

Draw diagrams and briefly explain how you expect changes in the following to influence the position of the demand curve for PCs:

a an increase in interest rates
b a large increase in unemployment
c a sustained rise in earnings from work
d a reduction in income tax.

SELF-ASSESSMENT TASK 2.17

Would you classify the following products as normal goods or inferior goods? In each case draw a diagram to show how a decrease in income will shift the demand curve. Explain your reasoning. What difficulties did you have in deciding? What information would you need to resolve these difficulties?

a premium brand orange juice
b hotel accommodation
c standard TV sets
d orange cordial
e guesthouse accommodation
f HD flat-screen satellite TVs.

The price and availability of related products

In the case of substitute products, a change in the price, availability and even the attractiveness of one product will have an impact on the demand for all substitute goods. If the price rises, then the demand for substitutes will increase as consumers switch their demand to the relatively cheaper products. Equally, a health scare, for example involving chicken, will invariably lead to an increase in demand for a close substitute such as duck or pork. In both of these cases, the demand curve for chicken will shift to the left. It will shift to the right if the price of substitutes increases or if there is a positive report in the media of the health benefits of the product.

For complements, a rise in the price of one product will reduce the quantity demanded for it and its associated product. Conversely, a fall in price will lead to an increase in the quantity demanded and will also lead to an increase in demand for its complement. The outcome for both situations is a shift to the right of the demand curve.

SELF-ASSESSMENT TASK 2.18

1. In each of these cases draw a diagram to show how an increase in the price of the first good will affect the demand for the second good:
   a Lipton tea and Tetley tea
   b Ink cartridges for a PC and computer paper.
2. In each of these cases draw a diagram to show how a fall in the price of the first good will affect the demand for the second good:
   a Duck and chicken
   b Cricket bats and cricket balls.

Fashion, taste and attitudes

We all buy products for a reason: our behaviour is purposefully motivated, at least at the time of purchase! Economists usually consider our behaviour to be a reflection of our tastes and preferences towards different types of goods and services. You may buy a particular type or brand of PC because of its reputation for reliability. You may buy a pair of brand-name trainers because you want to play sport and you genuinely believe them to be of better quality or you may buy them simply because they are fashionable and you want to look cool.

Detailed understanding of the psychological motives that determine our behaviour are beyond our scope here, but clearly we are influenced by our own individual likes and dislikes, by peer pressure and by various forms of advertising and the marketing images that surround us. Nowhere is this more evident than in markets for designer

SELF-ASSESSMENT TASK 2.19

1 Suppose there has been an outbreak of chicken flu in a particular country. Use a diagram to show how this is likely to affect the demand for chicken in that country. Explain your answer.

2 Medical trials have indicated that drinking erh-pur tea from Yunan in China can reduce blood pressure and cholesterol in Europeans. Use a diagram to show how this might affect the demand for this tea. Explain your answer.

Nike trainers – a fashionable designer brand

clothing and accessories, where tastes and preferences can be extremely volatile.

Shifts in the market supply curve

To this point our analysis of supply and the supply curve has assumed that price is the only factor that influences supply. While this is useful, one of the limitations is that companies' supply intentions are influenced by factors other than the price of the product (which is the most tangible expression of consumers' buying intentions). Other things are most certainly not always equal. Changes in these supply conditions can be shown by shifts in the supply curve. A rightward shift indicates an increase in supply; a leftward shift indicates a decrease in supply. Notice again how the language changes when we are talking about a *shift* in the whole curve rather than simply a *movement* along it – a change in supply rather than a change in the quantity supplied (see Table 2.11 and Figure 2.15).

Price of a 'standard' PC (US$)	Quantity supplied per week – supply curve S_2
800	2,000
1,000	3,000
1,200	4,000
1,400	5,000
1,600	6,000
1,800	7,000
2,000	8,000

Table 2.11 An increase in supply

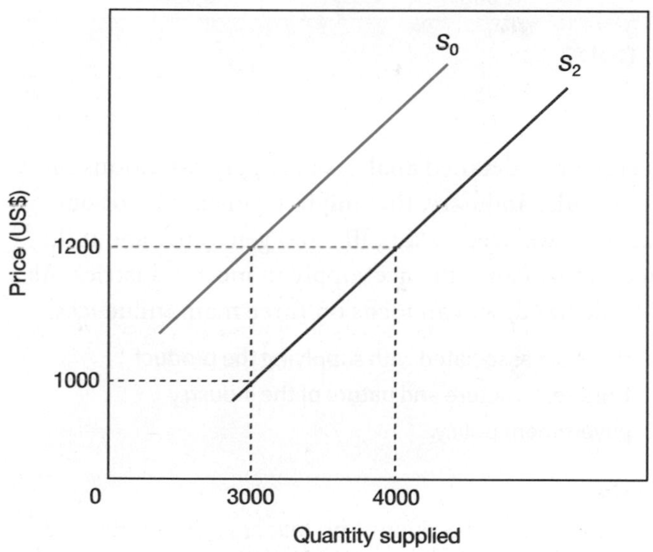

Figure 2.15 A shift to the right in the market supply curve for PCs

Figure 2.15 shows:

- Companies are now more willing and/or more able to supply PCs at each and every price. Previously they had only been prepared to supply 3,000 units per week at $1,200; now they are prepared to supply 4,000.
- Companies previously wanted $1,200 per unit to persuade them to supply 3,000 units per week; now they are prepared to accept $1,000.

Causes of shifts in the supply curve

Companies clearly differ in their willingness and ability to supply products and, as with demand, we could spend a long time building a list of possible factors other than price that will affect supply. If we were required

SELF-ASSESSMENT TASK 2.20

Use the information in Table 2.12 to draw a new supply curve (S_1). Explain what has happened to that supply curve – remember you are showing a decrease in supply. Draw in supply curve S_0 as well so that you can use it as the basis for your comparison.

Price of a 'standard' PC (US$)	Quantity supplied per week – supply curve S_1
1,000	1,000
1,200	2,000
1,400	3,000
1,600	4,000
1,800	5,000
2,000	6,000

Table 2.12

to conduct a detailed analysis of supply conditions in a particular industry, that might be justified. For our purposes we need to simplify and generalise about the factors that can influence supply in most industries. As with demand, we can focus on three main influences:

1. the costs associated with supplying the product
2. the size, structure and nature of the industry
3. government policy.

Costs

In a market-based economy, no business (in the absence of government support) can exist indefinitely if it makes losses, so companies will make supply decisions on the basis of the price they can get for selling the product in relation to the cost of supplying it. What we are interested in is what factors can influence the position of the supply curve – in other words, what factors can cause an increase or a decrease in the costs of supplying each and every unit, since it is likely that this will impact on the price that companies charge per unit. Below are listed some potentially influential factors – if any factor pushes up costs, there is likely to be a leftward shift in the supply curve or a decrease in supply; if the factor lowers costs, there is likely to be an increase in supply:

- wage rates
- worker productivity (output per worker)
- raw material and component prices
- energy costs
- equipment maintenance costs
- transport costs
- the state of technology.

SELF-ASSESSMENT TASK 2.21

Go through each of the following factors: wage rates; worker productivity; raw material prices; energy costs; maintenance costs; transport costs and the state of technology; and work out what sort of change in that factor will cause:

a an increase in supply

b a decrease in supply.

Size and nature of the industry

If it is clear that there is substantial profit to be made by selling a product, then businesses inside and outside the industry are likely to react. Those currently in the industry may invest in capital equipment in an attempt to grow bigger and take advantage of the situation. Businesses outside the industry may try to enter this market and new local competitors may also emerge. If the size of the industry increases, because there are more firms or bigger firms, then it is likely that the supply of the industry will increase. Equally, if firms in the industry start to compete more intensively on price, it is likely that the supply curve will shift to the right as the effects of this price competition start to affect the price that all companies are willing to accept for their products. Of course if a fierce price war breaks out, then consumers, at least temporarily, may enjoy very much lower prices for any given level of supply.

Government policy

Governments influence company decisions in many ways. Legislation designed to protect consumers or workers may impose additional costs on companies and this may affect the supply curve. Governments may also impose a **specific tax** such as excise duties on the output of companies or an ***ad valorem*** **tax** such as a sales tax or value added tax on particular goods and services. The impact of tax is like a cost increase because

KEY TERMS

Specific tax: an indirect tax that is fixed per unit purchased.

***Ad valorem* tax:** a tax that is charged as a given percentage of the price.

companies may seek to pass the tax on to the consumer in the form of higher prices. As such, indirect taxes often result in a decrease in supply. On the other hand, a relaxation of certain types of legislation or government subsidies can increase supply by encouraging firms to reduce prices for any given level of output. Government policy in agriculture may involve the release of stocks to calm the volatility of markets associated with a poor harvest.

SELF-ASSESSMENT TASK 2.22

Refer to the supply curve S_0 in Figure 2.15. What would happen to this curve if the government introduced:

a a tax of $100 per computer?

b a tax of 10% on the pre-tax selling price?

c legislation that raised companies' costs by 20% on average?

Other supply-influencing factors

These are varied and often specific to the particular industry or activity. For example, the supply of agricultural produce is often influenced by weather conditions. Adverse weather can lead to a dramatic reduction in supply; good weather conditions in contrast can result in bumper harvests for producers. Some manufacturers may be able to switch production from one product to another fairly easily, so the relative profitability of alternative product types may be important. In financial markets, such as the stock market or the foreign exchange market, supply may be significantly influenced by expectations of future prices and unanticipated exogenous shocks as a result of a political crisis.

There is also the case of **joint supply**. A good example is soya bean production, where part of the crop is used for human food products while what is left over is used to produce animal feed.

KEY TERM

Joint supply: when two items are produced together.

Changes in the equilibrium

The equilibrium will change if there is a disturbance to the present market conditions – this could come about through a change in supply conditions (the supply curve shifts) or a change in demand conditions (the demand curve shifts).

A change in demand

Look at Figure 2.16 – notice we are using *P* and *Q* symbols again instead of actual numbers – if there is an increase in demand (D_0 to D_2), then, at the original price, there is now a disequilibrium of excess demand equal to $Q_1 - Q_0$. As suppliers begin to recognise this they will start to raise the price and increase the quantity supplied. The rise in price will lead some consumers to decide they do not want to buy the product at the higher price. Although the process may take some time, the market will move back towards the new equilibrium at P^* Q^*, where the market is once more in balance. Note that the new equilibrium is at a higher price with a larger quantity traded than in the original situation.

A change in supply

Look at Figure 2.17 – if there is an increase in supply (from S_0 to S_2) then, at the original price (P_0), there is disequilibrium due to excess supply ($Q_1 - Q_0$). This would, of course, eventually be eliminated as price falls towards its new equilibrium level and the quantity traded in equilibrium rises from Q_0 to Q^* where the plans of consumers and companies once more coincide.

A change in supply and demand

The supply change analysis is useful to deal with simple situations. However, in many situations the conditions

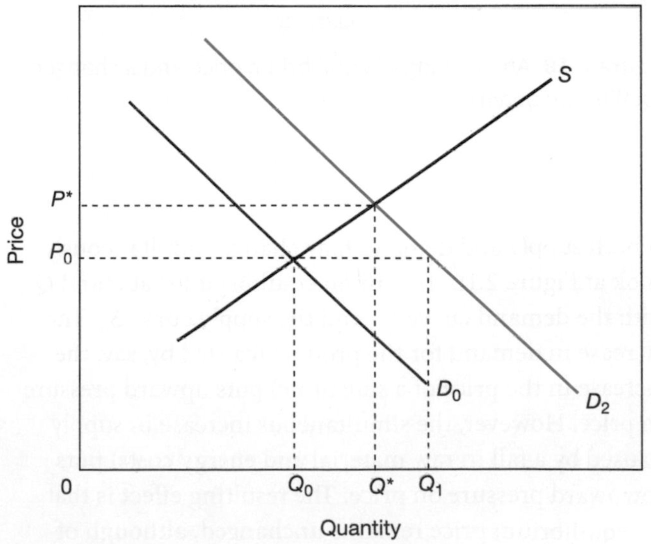

Figure 2.16 The effect of a shift of the demand curve on equilibrium price and quantity

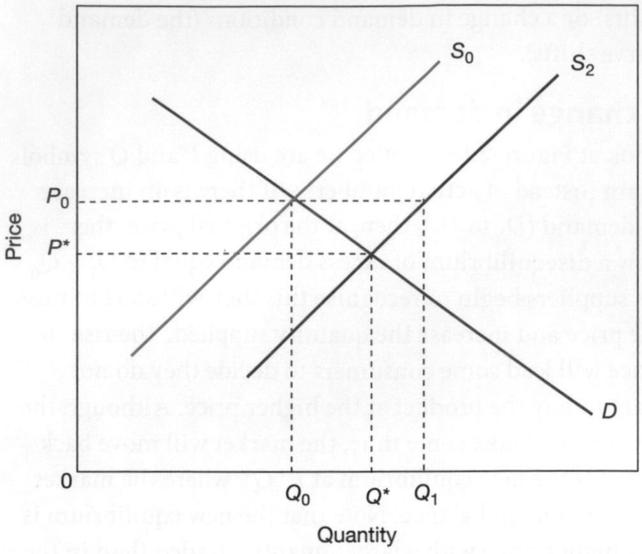

Figure 2.17 The effect of a shift in the supply curve on equilibrium price and quantity

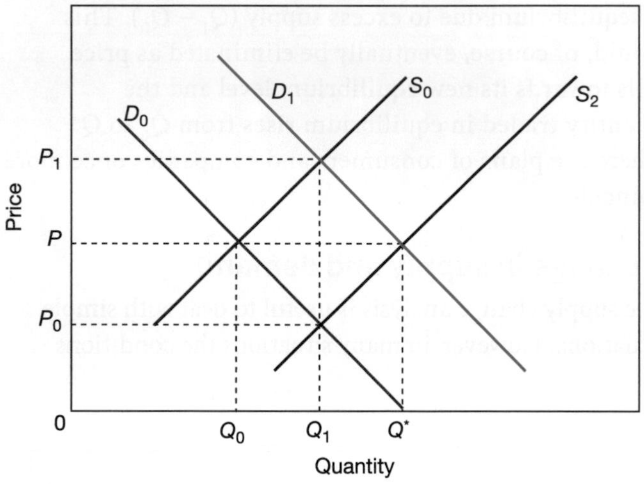

Figure 2.18 An unchanged equilibrium price and a changed equilibrium quantity

of both supply and demand may change simultaneously. Look at Figure 2.18. The initial equilibrium is at *P* and *Q* with the demand curve D_0 and the supply curve S_0. The increase in demand for the product (caused by, say, the increase in the price of a substitute) puts upward pressure on price. However, the simultaneous increase in supply (caused by a fall in raw material and energy costs) puts downward pressure on price. The resulting effect is that the equilibrium price remains unchanged, although of course there is a fairly significant increase in the quantity traded (from Q_0 to Q'').

SELF-ASSESSMENT TASK 2.23

On 1 May 2009, the price of white sugar on the London commodity market reached a two-and-a-half-year high of $441 per tonne. Analysts put this down to an increase in demand from India, the world's largest consumer, and from Russia. A hefty 850,000 tonnes was heading for these two markets in May. With the imminent peak in the Brazilian cane harvest, it was expected that the increase in supply would bring prices down.

1 Using demand and supply diagrams:
   a Show how the increase in demand from India and Russia affected the market.
   b Show how the increased supply of Brazilian sugar might affect the market.
2 What factors might mean that the world price of sugar will continue to increase in the future?

The workings of the price mechanism – final thoughts

It should be clear from this chapter that prices have a very important role in the allocation of resources in the market economy. The price mechanism works automatically: this was referred to by Adam Smith two centuries ago as 'the invisible hand'. The principles behind this process remain good today.

Prices act as a signal to both producers and consumers. A rise in the quantity demanded results in an increase in price, signalling to producers that they should put more of their products onto the market. In turn, if consumers withhold their demand, prices can be expected to fall. This signals that less should be produced. The price mechanism works in such a way that the outcome is a new equilibrium position with consumers' demand equal to producers' supply.

In other situations, the price system can ration products in the market. This process is also automatic. For example, a producer may wish to limit the supply of products to retain their exclusivity in the market. These products are likely to have a high price, as in the case of exclusive jewellery or top of the range sports cars; a form of rationing takes place because of the high price. This limits demand and, in turn, ensures that it is in line with the quantity supplied to the market.

It should be clear that the price mechanism allows the preferences of consumers to be made known to producers. This so-called **transmission of preferences** is again automatic. It is sometimes said that 'consumers vote with their feet'. This means that if consumers do not buy a particular product because it is not liked or it is too expensive, then this message is transmitted back to producers. Their reaction should be one of improving the product, reducing its price or both if they wish to stay in business.

KEY TERM

Transmission of preferences: the automatic way in which the market allows the preferences of consumers to be made known to producers.

There are very valid reasons why governments find it necessary to intervene in the natural workings of the market mechanism. This is invariably because the best allocation of resources is not being achieved when the market mechanism is left free to operate on its own.

KEY CONCEPT LINK

Equilibrium and efficiency: The equilibrium position in a market is affected by a shift in the demand curve, a shift in the supply curve or a combination of both. The outcome is that these changes lead to price changes through the workings of the free market mechanism. When back in equilibrium, resources are being efficiently allocated.

TOP TIP

There is always a time lag involved when market conditions change.

Consumer surplus

The underlying principles behind the demand curve are relatively simple to understand. They are also ones that many of us follow in our daily lives. For instance, when a product is on 'special offer' in a local shop, and its price has been reduced, more will be demanded and purchased.

For any good or service, however, there are always some people who are prepared to pay above the given price to obtain it. Some of the best examples where this happens are in the cases of tickets to popular music concerts or, in England, to watch Premier League football clubs, such as Liverpool or Manchester United, or in India to see a major Test Cricket match where all tickets are sold out. The stated price may well be $40 per ticket, but there will always be some people who are willing to pay more than $40 to obtain a ticket. To the economist, such situations introduce the concept of **consumer surplus**.

KEY TERM

Consumer surplus: the difference between the value a consumer places on units consumed and the payment needed to actually purchase that product.

Consumer surplus arises because some consumers are willing to pay more than the given price for all but the last unit they buy. This is represented in Figure 2.19a where consumer surplus is the shaded area under the demand

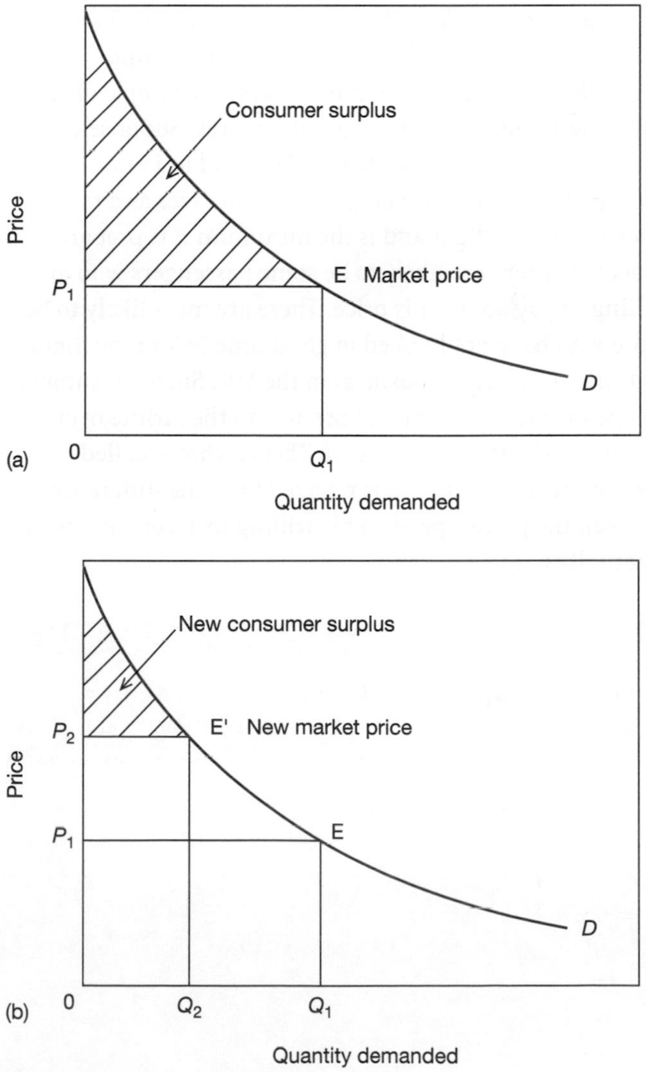

Figure 2.19 Consumer surplus

curve and above the price line. More specifically, it is the difference between the total value consumers place on all the units consumed and the payments they need to make in order to actually purchase that commodity.

When the market price changes, then so does consumer surplus. For example, if the price increases, then consumer surplus is reduced as some consumers are unwilling to pay the higher price. This reduction is shown in Figure 2.19b. The loss of consumer surplus is shown by the area $P_1P_2E\,^1E$. On the other hand, a fall in the market price will lead to an increase in consumer surplus. This is because consumers who were previously willing to pay above the new market price now end up paying less.

Producer surplus

In certain respects, **producer surplus** is a similar concept to consumer surplus. Here, however, we are looking at a situation from the producer's or supplier's perspective. Producers are very keen to supply consumers who are willing to pay a price above that which they would normally be prepared to accept. A typical example of such a situation might be in the case of air fares. Suppose the base-line price for a flight from Islamabad to London is $800. This is what, on average, the airline sees as a fair price for such a flight and is the minimum it is prepared to accept. There are likely to be some passengers who are willing to pay above this price. These are most likely to be those who have not booked in good time before the flight and who have urgent business in the UK. Such consumers will be providing additional revenue to the airline over and above the typical fare level. This is what is called the producer surplus and is referred to as the difference between the price a producer is willing to accept and what is actually paid.

KEY TERM

Producer surplus: the difference between the price a producer is willing to accept and what is actually paid.

Figure 2.20a shows the extent of producer surplus. This is shown by the shaded area above the supply curve but below the price line at P_2. Anything the firm sells below price P_2 is because it is willing to sell to consumers at that price. There is, however, a point P on Figure 2.20a below which the producer is unwilling to supply since it would not be covering the cost of production.

Figure 2.20b shows how producer surplus changes with a change in the quantity supplied. Producers only willing to produce at quantity Q_1 for a price P_1 still receive price P_2. This is their producer surplus, although it is less than if they had been willing to increase their quantity supplied to Q_2.

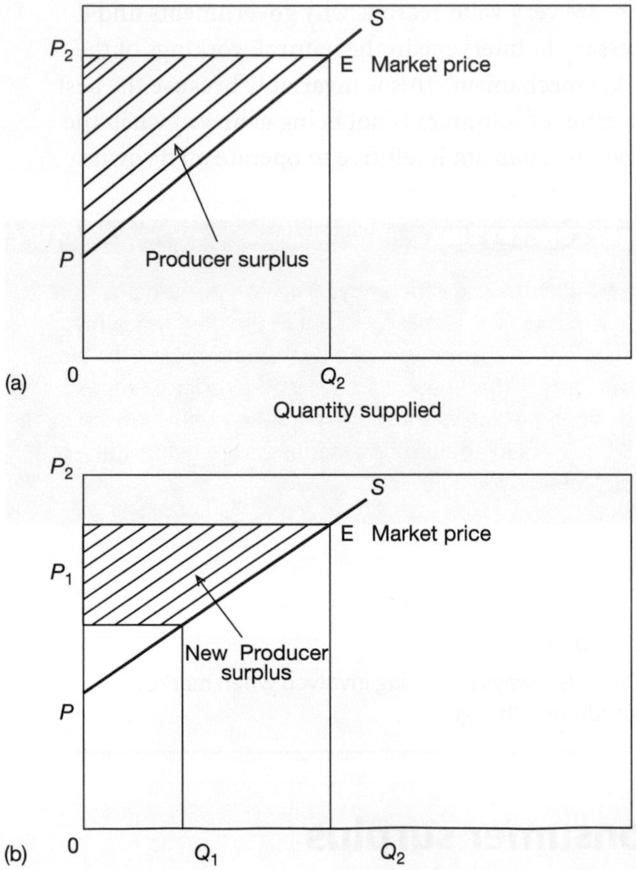

Figure 2.20 Producer surplus

SELF-ASSESSMENT TASK 2.24

The following feature demonstrates how knowledge of demand, supply and the price mechanism can be applied in order to explain the global problem of rising food prices, particularly in the world's poorest economies in Africa and Asia. Read the feature and then answer the questions that follow.

Rising global food prices

In 2009, the World Bank reported that global food prices had almost doubled since 2005 and were forecast to continue to increase. The price of wheat especially had increased at an alarming rate of around 200% from 2008 to the end of 2009. The prices of maize (corn) and rice had also escalated.

In November 2009, the Indian government reported that annual food price inflation was over 21%; the price of pulses had risen by over 30%, as had sugar prices. In Pakistan, food prices had also increased at a record rate amid claims of hoarding by grain processors and retailers.

Normally, price changes for cereals can be attributed to short-term variations in supply caused by disruptive weather conditions. This was not so for the latest set of price increases, which were caused largely by demand-side factors that included:

- the rising demand for meat in the booming economies of China and India; large quantities of grain are needed to feed animals, driving up prices
- a fall in domestic food production by increasingly affluent families in these countries.
- the increased demand for biofuels, especially in the USA and parts of Europe, which has resulted in harvests being diverted from food processing to fuel processing factories, particularly for sugar cane and maize.

Supply side factors have exaggerated price increases and include:

- extreme weather conditions in 2008 and 2009, such as prolonged drought in parts of India, Australia and southern Africa and unexpected frosts in parts of China, which had resulted in poor harvests; Europe's grain harvest was also affected by poor weather
- global stockpiles of grains were at a record low level, meaning that supplies could not be released onto the market to reduce price volatility.

In India, the problems of small farmers have been aggravated by the government's attempts to control prices. When domestic prices are rising, the government restricts export sales; when prices fall, farmers are paid subsidies. These actions seek to protect the interests of consumers and farmers alike. Because of uncertainty, many small sugar farmers abandoned sugar in 2008 when prices fell by 40%. In 2009 and early 2010, sugar prices surged. The obvious response would be for farmers to revert to sugar in the hope that high prices will persist.

Rising food prices have had a heavy impact on the poor in countries such as Bangladesh, India, Pakistan and those in sub-Saharan Africa. For people who have to live on less than $1 a day, the rising price of food is devastating and can affect rural as well as urban communities. There have been riots in West Bengal in protest against subsidised food being sold on the informal market. In Senegal, Mauritania and in other parts of Africa, there have also been protests over rising food prices.

The World Bank has identified 36 countries where there are grave concerns over food security; 21 are in Africa, including Sierra Leone, which lacks access to food from local markets due to its low level of income and the high prices of imported food.

1 Consider the factors that have contributed to rising food prices. Split these into demand factors and supply factors.

2 Using a demand and supply diagram, explain how the following factors have affected the market for food crops:
   a the increased demand for crops for biofuel
   b the increased consumption of meat in China and India.

3 The government of Sierra Leone has announced that it would start to produce its own rice, rather than rely on imports, from 2009. How might this affect the price of rice in Sierra Leone and on the global market?

SUMMARY

In this chapter it has been shown that:

- A market exists whenever people come together for the trade or exchange of goods and services.
- The buying side of the market is referred to by economists as the demand side. It is possible to derive a demand curve for any market – this shows how the quantity demanded varies with the price of a product.
- The selling side of the market is referred to by economists as the supply side. It is possible to derive a supply curve for any market – this shows how the quantity supplied varies with the price of the product.
- Price, income and cross elasticity of demand can be used to explain the extent of a change in the quantity demanded as the price of the good, consumer incomes and the prices of related goods change.
- The price elasticity of supply measures the extent to which the quantity supplied changes with a change in price.
- Equilibrium occurs in the market when there is no tendency to change; the price and the quantity traded match the intentions and plans of consumers and producers.
- The demand curve shifts to the left or right when, *ceteris paribus*, the assumption is changed. Three important causes of this are a change in income, a change in the price of related products and a change in fashion, tastes and attitudes.
- The supply curve shifts when there are changes in the costs of supply, characteristics of the industry and government policy.
- A change to the equilibrium position will produce a new equilibrium price and quantity as a consequence of a change in demand or a change in supply or both.
- The price mechanism acts as a signal, a means of rationing and for the transmission of preferences.
- Consumer surplus arises because some consumers are willing to pay more than the market price for a product; producer surplus arises when consumers are willing to pay a higher price than the minimum sought by producers.

Exam-style questions

1 **a** Explain how an equilibrium price for a product is established in the market and how it may change. **[8]**

b Discuss whether a firm's revenue would increase in response to price and income changes if the price elasticity of demand for its product became highly elastic. **[12]**

Source: Cambridge International AS and A Level Economics 9708 Paper 2 Q2 October/November 2007.

2 Market research has produced the following estimates of cross elasticity of demand.

Branded cola and branded iced tea +1.5
Branded cola and own label cola +0.5

a Explain what these estimates mean and their business significance for sales of branded cola when the price of branded iced tea and own label cola increase by 20%. **[8]**

b Using diagrams, explain how the market is likely to be affected by:

i A substantial cut in the price of branded ice tea.

ii A substantial increase in the price of branded cola. **[12]**

3 Air Passenger Duty (APD) is a flat rate indirect tax on passengers who fly from UK airports. It is collected by the airlines who add the tax onto ticket prices. In 2009, the tax was £5 for economy class passengers travelling on flights within the European Union.

The table below summarises the likely effects of increases in APD on a typical flight.

New tax rate	£10	£15	£25	£35
% change in ticket prices	7%	14%	28%	42%
% change in quantity demanded	–5%	–15%	–40%	–66%

a Calculate the price elasticity of demand for each of the new tax rates. **[4]**

b Explain the meaning of each of the figures you have calculated. **[4]**

c Suppose the UK government wishes to reduce the demand for air travel for environmental reasons. Comment on how it might use the price elasticity of demand estimates to achieve this objective. **[12]**

Chapter 3: Government microeconomic intervention AS Level

Learning objectives

On completion of this chapter you should know:

- why governments may find it necessary to intervene in the workings of the price mechanism
- how maximum and minimum prices work and their effect on the market
- why governments impose taxes
- the difference between direct and indirect taxes, their impact and incidence
- what is meant by specific and *ad valorem* taxes
- the difference between average and marginal rates of taxation
- the meaning of proportional, progressive and regressive taxes
- what is meant by the 'canons of taxation'
- how subsidies impact on the market and their incidence
- what is meant by transfer payments and their effect on the market
- why governments directly provide goods and services and their effect on the market
- what is meant by nationalisation and privatisation and their effect on the market.

Government intervention: introduction

You have only to glance at a newspaper or listen to the news or a political debate for a few minutes to realise that one of the more controversial areas of Economics is concerned with the extent and reasons for government intervention in markets. Governments throughout the world intervene in markets to different extents and the reasons for intervention vary enormously between them.

The justification for intervention is usually where there is **market failure**. We have already seen some examples of market failure at the end of Chapter 1 where it was shown that it was necessary for governments to provide public goods and merit goods as these will be underprovided by the free market mechanism. Demerit goods in contrast would be overprovided. In simple terms, market failure is as the name suggests – a situation where the market fails to make the best use of scarce resources, prompting government intervention. This intervention can take a variety of forms.

Regulations

Governments use different methods of **regulation** as a means of controlling the free market. Legal and other methods are used to control the prices, quality and quantity of goods and services that are produced and consumed. Regulations have been important in combating environmental problems. For example, excessive levels of pollution are prohibited by regulations that apply to the manufacture of vehicles and the production of chemicals. Regulation may also refer to prices. Examples of price controls include minimum wage legislation and maximum price controls.

Financial intervention: use of taxes and subsidies

Financial tools, such as **taxes** and subsidies, are frequently used by governments to influence production and the prices of a wide range of goods and services in the market. For example, demerit goods are usually subject to high rates of indirect taxation. By contrast, subsidies, involving a direct payment by the government to a producer, make the price paid by consumers less than it should be. Typically, subsidies are paid for goods and services that benefit the community and that might not be provided in a free market. These payments can be in the form of a partial subsidy, as in the case of staple food products and public transport, or total, as in the case of free school meals for children from low-income families.

KEY TERMS

Market failure: where the free market does not make the best use of scarce resources.

Regulation: various means by which governments seeks to control production and consumption.

Taxes: charges imposed by governments on incomes, profits and some types of consumer goods and services to fund their expenditure.

Government provision

It is possible for a government to take over the production of a good or service, either in whole or in part. In many countries state-owned industries such as electricity generation, coal mining, water provision and railways are entirely owned and managed by the state and are often referred to as nationalised industries. In some countries, such as the UK, this is no longer the case. This follows a major shift towards privatisation that took place during the 1980s and 1990s when many former state-run industries were sold to new private owners. It is also very common to find that some goods and services are produced by both the state and the private sectors. Education and health care are particularly good examples in many types of economy. State-run hospitals function alongside private hospitals and independent schools operate alongside state schools.

KEY CONCEPT LINK

Regulation and equity: There is a trade-off between, on the one hand, freedom for firms and individuals in unregulated markets and, on the other hand, greater social equality and equity through the government regulation of individuals and markets. The previous chapter concentrated on the workings of unregulated markets. In this chapter, as a consequence of market failure, it will be shown how government regulation can enhance social equality and equity.

Maximum and minimum price controls

Maximum price controls or price ceilings are only valid in markets where the maximum price imposed is *below* the normal equilibrium price as determined in a free market. This means that the price that can be legally charged

KEY TERM

Maximum price: a price that is fixed; the market price must not exceed this price.

by sellers must not be any higher. Governments use legislation to enforce maximum prices for:

- staple foodstuffs, such as bread, rice and cooking oil
- rents in certain types of housing
- services provided by utilities, such as water, gas and electricity
- transport fares especially where a subsidy is being paid.

Figure 3.1 indicates that at the price ceiling of P_1, production is not sufficient to satisfy everyone who wishes to buy the product. Too few resources are being allocated. Consequently, as price cannot rise, the available supply has to be allocated on some other basis. The most likely way is by means of queuing; a much-evidenced form of control in the former planned economies of Central and Eastern Europe. Rationing is another means of restricting demand – but this inevitably leads to an informal or underground market for the products involved, with consumers then having to pay inflated prices well above the ceiling price. Such markets inevitably arise when there are dissatisfied people who have not been able to buy the goods they want because not enough has been produced.

In contrast, there are different circumstances where the government may find it necessary to impose **minimum price** control in a market. This acts as a price floor. These cases are not as common as where maximum price control is imposed. Controls are only valid in markets where the minimum price is set *above* the normal equilibrium price. Governments use legislation to enforce minimum prices for:

- demerit goods such as tobacco products and alcohol
- wages in certain occupations, usually low skilled, to avoid exploitation by employers
- certain types of imported goods where domestically produced close substitutes are available.

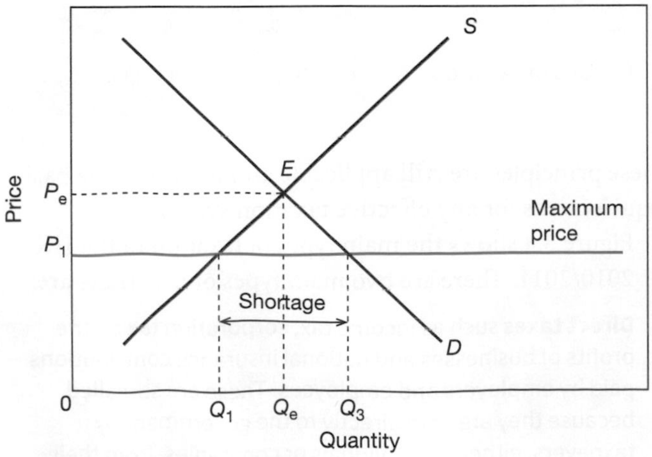

Figure 3.1 The effects of maximum price control

KEY TERM

Minimum price: a price that is fixed; the market price must not go below this price.

Figure 3.2 indicates that at the minimum price, suppliers are willing to supply considerably more products than are demanded by consumers. As price cannot fall, supply is restricted to Q_1 – this is all consumers can afford to buy. A lower quantity is traded than would have occurred at the equilibrium price. It is also the case that producers are likely to be inefficient; firms with high costs have little incentive to reduce these costs since the high minimum price protects them from lower-cost competitors. As with maximum price control, there is a danger that an informal market will develop especially for sought-after products like imported alcohol and cigarettes. Consumers will be more than happy to buy from dealers offering these goods at less than the regulated minimum price.

TOP TIP

To be effective, a maximum price must always be fixed below the equilibrium price; a minimum price must always be fixed above the equilibrium price.

KEY CONCEPT LINK

Regulation and equity: Maximum prices interfere with the unregulated market mechanism largely for reasons of social equity. The prices of essential items are capped to help those who are on low incomes and this goes some way towards a more equal distribution of income. The trade-off is that the free market is distorted and may not bring the full benefits that might be expected.

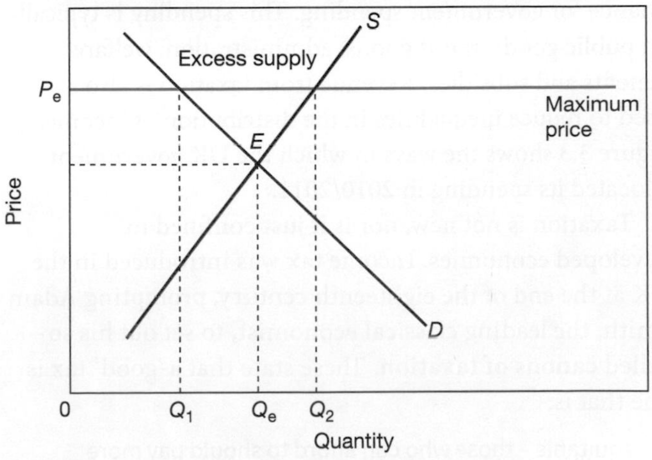

Figure 3.2 The effects of minimum price control

SELF-ASSESSMENT TASK 3.1

Read the feature below and then answer the questions that follow.

Outrage in Kenya as maximum price controls are reintroduced

Kenya's President Mwai Kibaki has signed legislation that will regulate the prices of essential commodities to protect consumers against exorbitant prices charged by unscrupulous traders. The latest move allows the government to control the prices of essential goods such as maize flour, wheat, rice, sugar, paraffin, diesel, cooking oil and petrol in order to secure their availability at reasonable prices. Under this law, the minister may from time to time declare any goods to be essential commodities and determine their maximum prices.

A prominent supporter of the new law, MP Ephraim Maina, said the prime responsibility of the government is to ensure basic commodities are available to the citizens at affordable prices. 'I'm confident that, if the law is applied correctly, Kenyans will get reasonable prices.' He said the new law would deal with large companies in the food, financial, fuel and utility industries, which prevent Kenya from operating as a free market economy. These companies have been charging exorbitant prices for their commodities to exploit consumers. He added that businesspeople should be prepared to cut down on their profits during hard economic times.

But this law has annoyed manufacturers and consumer organisations, which view it as a violation of the free market and a return to the days of a controlled economy. The Kenya Association of Manufacturers (KAM) condemned the new law, saying consumers would not be able to benefit from competitive prices associated with a competitive market environment. It said controlling prices is not a cure for the high cost of living, arguing that commodity prices could only be driven downwards in a free market environment. Meanwhile, the Consumers' Federation of Kenya (Cofek) said immediate implementation of the new law is likely to cause a serious shortage of commodities in the market.

Source: J. Anyanzwa, *The Standard*, Kenya, 17 September 2011.

1 a Using a diagram, explain why 'implementation of the new law is likely to cause a serious shortage of commodities in the market'.

b What other methods might the Kenyan government take 'to protect consumers against exorbitant prices'?

Taxes – direct and indirect

Taxes are charges that are imposed by governments on people and businesses. Their main purpose is to raise finance for government spending. This spending is typically on public goods, merit goods, administration, welfare benefits and subsidies. Revenue from taxation is also used to reduce inequalities in the distribution of income. Figure 3.3 shows the ways in which the UK government allocated its spending in 2010/2011.

Taxation is not new, nor is it just confined to developed economies. Income tax was introduced in the UK at the end of the eighteenth century, prompting Adam Smith, the leading classical economist, to set out his so-called **canons of taxation**. These state that a 'good' tax is one that is:

- equitable – those who can afford to should pay more
- economic – the revenue should be greater than the costs of collection
- transparent – tax payers should know exactly what they are paying
- convenient – it should be easy to pay.

KEY TERM

Canons of taxation: Adam Smith's criteria for a 'good' tax.

These principles are still applicable and underpin the basic requirements for any effective taxation system.

Figure 3.4 shows the main types of taxation in the UK for 2010/2011. There are two main types of tax. These are:

- **Direct taxes** such as income tax, corporation tax on the profits of businesses and national insurance contributions paid by employers and employees. These are so-called because they are paid directly to the government by taxpayers, either as individuals or companies, from their incomes. In 2010/2011, they contributed 57% of total tax revenue.

- **Indirect taxes** such as value-added tax (VAT) on the retail sales of many goods and services, excise duties on fuel, alcohol and tobacco products. This type of tax also includes council tax and business rates that are charged locally on the ownership of houses, apartments and business premises. Indirect taxes are so-called since they are collected for the government by retailers and local government bodies.

KEY TERMS

Direct tax: one that taxes the income of people and firms and cannot be avoided.

Indirect tax: a tax that is levied on goods and services.

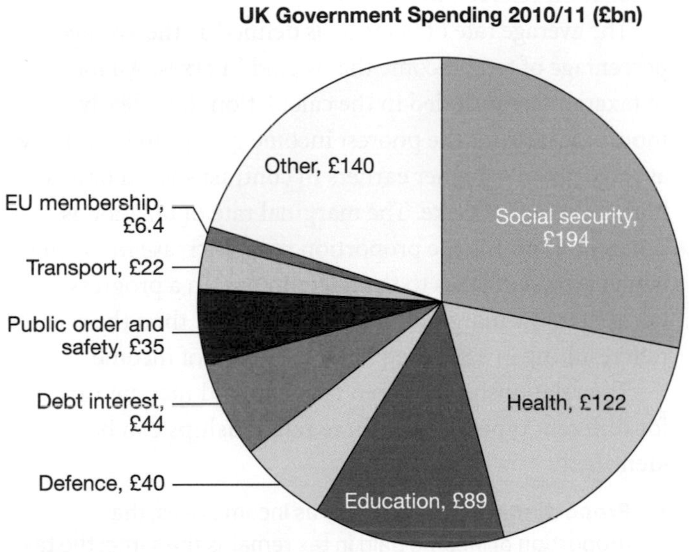

Figure 3.3 UK government spending in 2010/2011

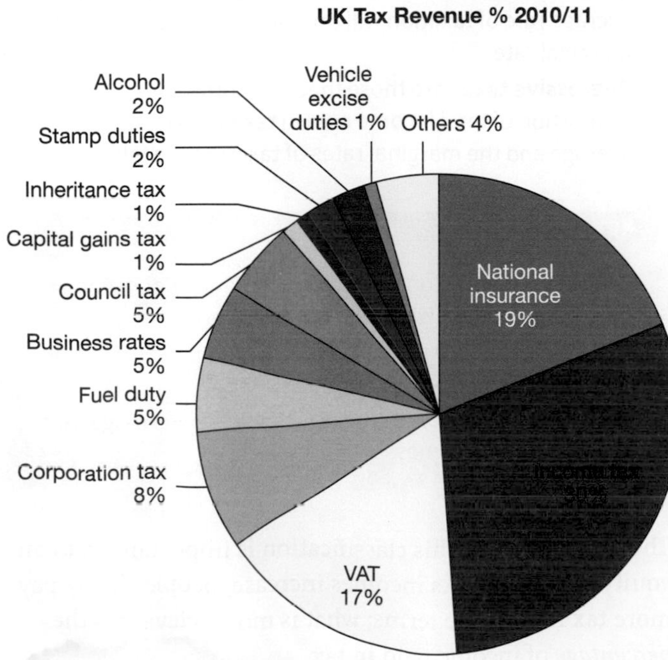

Figure 3.4 UK tax revenue in 2010/2011

In the context of indirect taxes, two main types are recognised. These are:

- *Ad valorem* taxes, which are a proportion or percentage of the price charged by the retailer. VAT in EU countries such as the UK or a general sales tax (GST) as charged in the USA and Canada are typical examples. The final price paid by consumers is inclusive of such taxes. The tax element may be included in the published retail price or, in cases where the GST is on everything, added to the price at the final transaction stage.
- Specific taxes in the form of a fixed amount per unit purchased. These are widely used to tax fuel, cigarettes and alcohol. In all cases the tax is based on a measurable quantity, e.g., per litre or per packet of 20 cigarettes. The final price will incorporate this tax.

When an indirect tax is imposed, this tax must be paid to the government by retailers, wholesalers, manufacturers and other providers of taxable goods and services. This means that the business receives a price that is higher than the original price by the amount of the tax. This is represented by a shift to the left of the supply curve by the amount of the tax.

The revenue from taxation is then used by the government to fund the various types of public spending shown earlier in Figure 3.3.

Indirect taxes are widely used to discourage the production and consumption of demerit goods such as alcoholic drinks and cigarettes. They tend to be passed on to consumers through increased prices in the market, although technically they are imposed on the producer.

Figure 3.5 analyses the effects on the market when an indirect tax is levied by the government. It shows what is known as the **incidence** of an indirect tax.

KEY TERM

Incidence: the extent to which the tax burden is borne by the producer or the consumer or both.

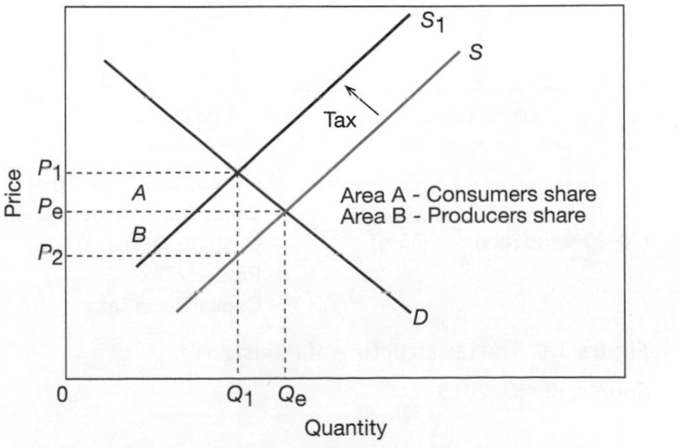

Figure 3.5 The effects of imposing an indirect tax

This is the term used to describe the extent to which the tax burden is borne by the producer, the consumer or both of them. This latter outcome is the case in Figure 3.5 and indicates:

- the market price is higher at P_1 than at the equilibrium price
- the quantity traded is less at Q_1 rather than at Q
- consumers and producers share the burden.

The extent to which the producer is able to pass on the tax by raising the price depends on the price elasticity of demand for the product. The more price inelastic the demand, then the easier it is for the seller to pass on the tax to the consumer in the form of higher prices. This explains why essential products like petrol are heavily taxed in most economies. If demand is price elastic, then consumers will invariably buy less of the product as price rises, resulting in the producer having to absorb a greater part of the indirect tax.

In contrast to the UK, many developing economies struggle to collect tax revenues. Pakistan is typical, with its government anxious to increase its tax revenue to meet the needs of its growing population. In 2012, Pakistan's tax revenue was just 8.5% of its GDP compared to around 39% in the UK. Tax evasion is illegal. It is a major problem, particularly among companies, and one that the Pakistan government is trying to address. One line of approach being pursued is to tax companies on their revenue rather than on their profits. A second approach is to tackle corruption in the disclosure of personal incomes and the evasion of sales taxes by small retail businesses.

SELF-ASSESSMENT TASK 3.2

1 Consider the information in Figure 3.6. Describe how the tax structure of Pakistan compares to that of the UK as shown in Figure 3.4.

2 Draw two diagrams to show how (i) an *ad valorem* tax and (ii) a *specific tax* affect the supply curve for a product.

3 Redraw Figure 3.5 to show how the tax burden of consumers and producers changes when the demand curve becomes more price inelastic.

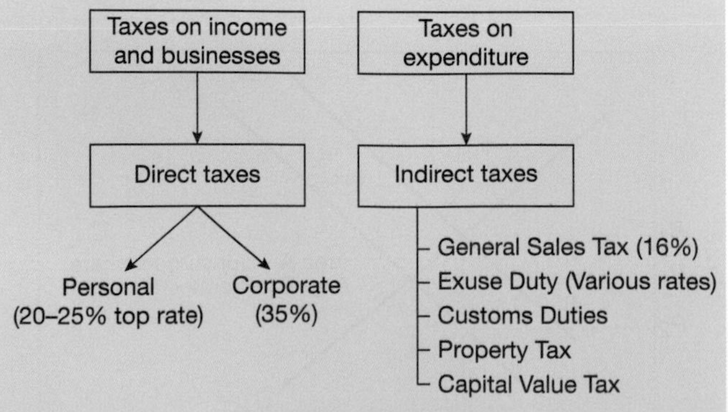

Figure 3.6 The tax structure of Pakistan

Source: KPMG, 2013

Other taxation issues

In collecting taxes and in the development of taxation systems, governments should be very aware of the impact a tax has on the various income groups in the economy. This is entirely consistent with the equity aspect of the canons of taxation referred to earlier.

The average rate of taxation is defined as the average percentage of total income that is paid in taxes. All forms of taxation are included in the calculation. It is clearly more equitable for the poorest income groups to have a low average tax rate; higher earners in contrast should have a higher average tax rate. The marginal rate of taxation is different. It means the proportion of an increase in income which is paid in taxes to the government. In a progressive tax system the marginal rate will be greater than the average rate resulting in a more equal distribution of income.

The relationship between taxation and income varies for different types of tax. Three relationships can be identified:

1. **Proportional taxes,** whereby as income rises, the proportion of income paid in tax remains the same; the tax rate is therefore constant.
2. **Progressive taxes** are those that when income rises, the proportion of the total paid in taxes increases; the average rate of taxation will therefore be lower than the marginal rate.
3. **Regressive taxes** are those that as income rises, the proportion of total income paid in tax falls. Hence, the average and the marginal rates of taxation are falling.

KEY TERMS

Proportional tax: one that takes the same proportion or percentage from all who have to pay it.

Progressive tax: a tax that takes a higher percentage from those with higher incomes.

Regressive tax: a tax that takes a greater percentage from those on lower incomes.

The significance of this classification is important from an equity standpoint. As incomes increase, people clearly pay more tax in absolute terms; what is more relevant is the *percentage* of income paid in tax.

The best example of a progressive tax is income tax. Low-paid workers are usually given allowances that mean that they pay little or even no tax at all. The tax rate may start at 10%, rising in stages to 50% or even 90% in some tax regimes. As the rate increases there is likely to be some disincentive to work on the part of high-earners. There may even be an exodus of such earners to low-tax countries if the rate is too punitive.

Typical regressive taxes are VAT and GST. These sales taxes are widely applied in virtually all types of economy. Both are flat-rate sales taxes paid at standard rates of 10, 13, 15 or 20%. This means that the price of a Big Mac or a can of Coca-Cola is the same for someone on a low wage as it is for a multi-millionaire. As consumer spending does not increase at the same rate as an increase in income, these taxes are regressive. They hit the poor relatively more than the rich.

Governments have decisions to take about their tax regimes, the most important being achieving the right balance between direct and indirect taxes. A trend in many economies has been to collect increasing revenues from indirect taxes on expenditure since these can usually be collected quickly, are less liable to evasion and corruption and do not interfere with the work incentive problem. Those economies that are compliant with this strategy are therefore supporting a regressive tax system, one that will not be well-liked by low- and middle-income earners. This is particularly the case in developing and emerging economies, where it is rather easier to levy indirect rather than direct taxes as a means of establishing a secure tax regime.

Subsidies

Another form of government intervention in the market is through the provision of subsidies. These are direct payments made by governments to the producers of goods and services. When paid to a producer, a subsidy has the opposite effect of an indirect tax – it is the equivalent of a fall in costs for the producer and results in a rightward shift in the market supply curve. This is shown in Figure 3.7. A reduction in a subsidy payment will lead to a shift to the left in the supply curve.

Figure 3.7 shows that introducing a subsidy in the market results in a fall in price from P to P_1 and an increase in the quantity traded from Q to Q_1. This is the usual effect on the market when governments pay money to producers and may be done for many reasons including:

- to keep down the market prices of essential goods
- to encourage greater consumption of merit goods
- to contribute to a more equitable distribution of income
- to provide services that would not be provided by the free market
- to raise producers' income, especially in the case of farmers
- to provide an opportunity for exporters to sell more goods
- to reduce dependence on imports by paying subsidies to domestic producers of close substitutes.

Allocating subsidies from limited government revenue is a controversial issue. It is not only interfering with the workings of the market mechanism but has opportunity cost implications. Another problem is that subsidies are so-called 'blanket' or lump sum payments and, unlike taxes on consumers, cannot easily be linked to incomes and the ability to pay. It is therefore necessary to assess who benefits from a particular subsidy. This is illustrated by the following examples:

- Staple foods like rice, bread and cooking oil are subsidised in some developing economies. As world food prices continue to rise, the case for subsidy is a strong one, mainly to provide relief for the poorest groups in the economy. Subsidised prices, however, are paid by all income groups, many of who can afford to pay more. There could also be shortages as in the case of a price ceiling. If the subsidy is paid to producers, there is no incentive for inefficient producers to improve.
- Mass transit (public transport) is heavily subsidised in all parts of the world, especially in cities and large towns. This is done to give low earners access to employment opportunities, to provide social mobility for older people, to reduce road congestion and to reduce the adverse environmental impact of traffic. The benefits are to individuals and to the community as a whole.

TOP TIP

Do not confuse the effects of indirect taxes and subsidies on the prices of goods and services. An indirect tax raises prices, a subsidy reduces prices.

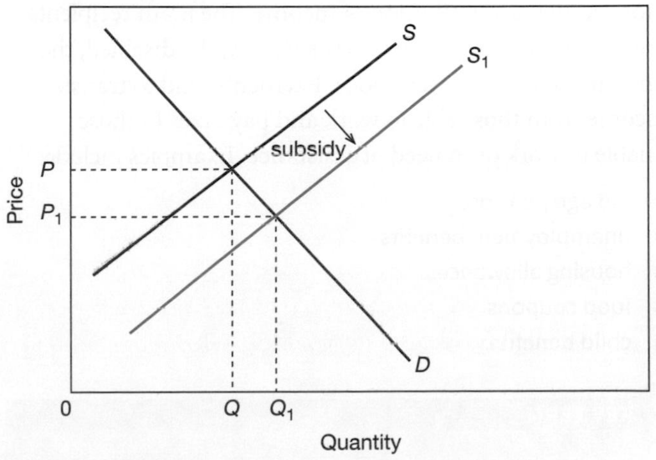

Figure 3.7 The effects of introducing a subsidy

SELF-ASSESSMENT TASK 3.3

1 Using information from your own country where possible, consider the benefits of the government subsidising:
- poultry production
- long-distance rail services
- university education.

2 In August 2013 the *International New York Times* reported a debate on wheat prices in the provincial assembly in Lahore, Pakistan. The main points were:
- flour prices, which are determined by the government, had increased from Rs16 a kilogram in 2008 to Rs45 in 2013
- in the debate, it was stated that 'if the government raised the price, the poor would not be able to buy wheat and if prices were kept down, farmers were unwilling to supply at low rates'
- new subsidies on fertilisers, electricity and petroleum products were demanded.

   a Use a diagram to show how the price of wheat changed from 2008 to 2013.

   b Use diagrams to explain whether you agree with what was stated in the debate.

   c Use a diagram to explain why new subsidies were called for.

Transfer payments

Transfer payments are payments from tax revenue that are received by certain members of the community. They are not made through the market, as no production takes place. Like a progressive taxation system, their function is to provide a more equitable distribution of income. The main recipients are vulnerable groups such as the elderly, the disabled, the unemployed and the very poor. Payments tend to transfer income from those able to work and pay taxes to those unable to work or in need of assistance. Examples include:

- old age pensions
- unemployment benefits
- housing allowances
- food coupons
- child benefits.

KEY TERM

Transfer payment: a hand-out or payment made by the government to certain members of the community.

The extent to which transfer payments can be paid is heavily dependent on how much tax is collected and how many people have paid tax. In developing economies this is affected by all sorts of problems. Pakistan has a growing elderly population, yet it has a low tax base. Pension and social security coverage is limited to the formal sector and therefore only covers a small percentage of the population. Those who work or who have worked in the informal sector are not covered by these schemes. Similar arrangements apply in India although a higher proportion of the population is eligible for help. In Bangladesh there is little or no provision of assistance – even for government workers.

The effect of transfer payments on the market is a controversial issue. It is clear that in most cases they are necessary to protect the most vulnerable groups in the community. They result in less poverty and provide for a more equitable distribution of income. The counter argument is that unemployment benefits and benefits to the poor can act as a disincentive to accepting work, so increasing the unemployment rate. As a consequence, output in the economy is less than it might be and there is a form of inefficiency.

KEY CONCEPT LINK

Regulation and equity: Direct taxes are imposed on high earners to reduce inequality in the distribution of income and wealth. A trade-off is that if the tax rates are too high then disincentives for high-income earners will arise. Indirect taxes and subsidies apply to all irrespective of income and therefore contribute in this way to social equality. Some transfer payments aim to promote a more equitable distribution of income.

Direct provision of goods and services

A further way of reducing inequalities in society is for the government to provide certain important services free of charge to the user. Such services are financed through the tax system. If such services are used equally by all citizens, then those on lowest incomes gain most as a percentage of their income – thereby lowering inequality.

The two most common examples of such free provision in many economies are merit goods, such as health care and education. These markets are subject to various market failures. However, these failures do not, according to standard economic theory, justify free provision to the consumer. The justification must be on the grounds of equity. The view is that everyone should have access to a certain level of health care and education regardless of income. Thus, where these services are provided universally free, they are the material equivalent of monetary universal benefits.

As with transfer payments, there are substantial differences in the direct provision of goods and services between economies. These differences are seen between developed economies as well as between developed and developing economies. Health care provision is particularly variable. The UK has had a National Health Service almost free to all for over 60 years; in contrast, free health care in the USA is limited. Those who can afford to pay are obliged to take out Medicare insurance. In most low-income countries, Cuba being a notable exception, a charge is usually made for most types of health care provision. This is especially the case in many countries in sub-Saharan Africa, where only a very basic system of health care is provided free of charge.

The direct provision of goods and services is also a controversial issue. The main criticism is that the market overprovides especially where no direct charge is made. Resources are not allocated efficiently. If a charge is made or introduced, demand is likely to fall. It can also be argued that many consumers could afford to pay a charge, so reducing the tax burden or allowing the funding saved in this way to be put to alternative uses.

TOP TIP

There are wide variations between economies in their taxation and benefits systems. It is therefore not easy to make generalisations.

Nationalisation and privatisation

Nationalisation is the process by which governments take a private business into public ownership. In the UK, the period 1947–51 saw the extensive nationalisation of transport, fuel, power and the iron and steel industries. Some manufacturing businesses – such as shipbuilding, aerospace, vehicle production and sugar beet processing – followed this trend. Many countries in the world have nationalised their railways, airlines, mining, electricity and water industries as well as, more recently, banks and financial services.

KEY TERM

Nationalisation: when governments take over a private sector business and transfer it to the public sector.

The case for nationalisation

There are some very relevant economic arguments to support nationalisation. These include:

- It makes sense for certain strategic services and activities to be in the hands of the public sector. This is particularly true of railways, bus services, airports and electrical and water supplies.
- There is also a long-standing socialist view that such services are for the benefit of the public and should therefore be in the public sector.
- There is little sense in duplicating certain services like railways and water supplies, largely because of the high costs of establishing that provision.
- Any profits made will be returned to the business and reinvested for the benefit of the public.
- Employees feel a sense of ownership and work hard to ensure financial viability.
- Nationalised industries will be more likely to provide loss-making services for social reasons.

These are powerful arguments that have been accepted and applied in many economies. Nationalisation takes the activity outside the market mechanism. Decisions on prices, the scale of operation and investment are taken by bodies set up by, and responsible to, governments.

Nationalisation in Pakistan has been eventful. In 1972, the government nationalised all major metal industries, heavy engineering, electrical goods, vehicle manufacturing, petrochemicals, cement and public utilities in a major change of economic policy. Banks, insurance, food and cotton processing followed two years later. It is commonly believed that this sudden and extensive programme had an adverse effect on business investment, both by local entrepreneurs and outside companies. Privatisation followed earlier this century. In 2011, however, due to ailing finances, steel, railways and the national airline, PIA, were nationalised. Elsewhere, as in the UK banking system, governments have had no alternative other than nationalisation as a response to the US-induced global financial crisis from 2008.

Privatisation

In a simple sense, **privatisation** refers to a change in ownership of an activity from the public sector to the private sector. In many instances – as in the UK, parts of Central and Eastern Europe and elsewhere – reprivatisation has returned activities that had previously been nationalised to new private owners. In a modern

KEY TERM

Privatisation: the sale of a state-owned public sector business to the private sector.

sense, privatisation means more than this and is now recognised to include:

- The direct sale of government-owned and operated activities to the private sector. The nature of the sale can be diverse and includes offering shares to the public, management and worker buyouts, the direct sale to new owners and, in some cases, a partial sale with the government retaining some share in the new business.
- Deregulation through the removal of barriers to entry, which had protected the public sector from outside competition.
- Franchising to give a new private sector owner the right to operate a particular service or activity for a given length of time. In some cases, the franchise might be an exclusive one; in other cases, some competition may be experienced.
- Contracting out of services previously provided in-house by public sector organisations. Normally, this involves activities that are deemed not to be core to those organisations. In some cases, contracting out allows public sector-based organisations to openly compete with private sector businesses for a particular contract.

TOP TIP

In many economies, deregulation has occurred at the same time as privatisation; it is, however, feasible that deregulation can produce a situation where the public and private sectors compete with each other.

By any measure, privatisation in the UK economy since 1979 (when a right-wing Conservative government led by Margaret Thatcher was elected) has been substantial. In 1979, the nationalised industries accounted for about 9% of GDP and 7% of employment. By 2000, these statistics were just 2% in each case. Table 3.1 shows the extent of privatisation in this period.

As this table shows, the principal privatisations were in the fuel and power and transport sectors. Both were nationalised in the late 1940s and, under government ownership, both relied heavily on various forms of subsidy to cover their losses. Under public ownership, it was also recognised that the government was unable to fund the extensive investment programmes needed to enable them to compete in a rapidly changing UK economy. The table also shows how the government withdrew its support from a wide range of manufacturing activities. In many cases, this support had been essential in order to keep 'lame duck' companies – those that are not properly able to function – solvent and in turn safeguard employment. In many respects, the UK has led the way when it comes to privatisation. Other economies, developing as well as developed, have drawn upon the UK's experience to pursue their own privatisation policies.

The case for privatisation

Taking the UK economy as a particular example, it is possible to recognise various reasons for the extensive privatisation shown in Table 3.1. Some are economic, others much more concerned with political motivation. For example:

- a deliberate commitment to reduce government involvement in the economy
- to widen share ownership among the population and among the employees of the privatised companies
- benefits for consumers in the form of lower prices, wider choice and a better quality product or service
- the sale of nationalised industries has generated substantial income for the UK government over a long period of time. This has been estimated to be £70–80 billion
- privatised companies can be successful in raising capital, lowering prices and cutting out waste; they are more efficient than state-owned operations.

Fuel and power
National electricity generation and regional supply
National gas production and regional supply
Coal production
Nuclear power production
Transport
Railways: passengers and freight
Local and national bus services
Some major airports
British Airways, the national airline
Some road freight services
Some ferry services and ports
Other
Water supply
Telephones and telecommunications
Various manufacturing companies including British Steel, British Aerospace, British Petroleum, British Sugar Corporation, Rover Group, British Shipbuilders

Table 3.1 Privatisation in the UK economy between 1979 and 2000

SELF-ASSESSMENT TASK 3.4

Read the feature below and then answer the questions that follow.

Myanmar to privatise railways

Myanmar's government is planning to privatise some of the state-owned railway lines soon, including the Yangon circular railway system, according to the Ministry of Rail Transportation.

The privatisation will include the Yangon circular train, a Yangon–Mandalay train and a Yangon–Myitkyina train. The privatisation plan is now underway and the Yangon–Myitkyina rail line will be prioritised, the ministry said.

Many changes have been made in Myanmar's railway sector since 2011. The Yangon–Mandalay railroad and the Yangon circular railway system are currently undergoing upgrades. Buildings under the ministry have been rented out to private companies, and a plan to renovate the Yangon Central railway station is also underway.

The ministry said that only a few of the more than 400 train lines under its management across the country can be described as money-makers.

Rail train in Yangon

Source: Asia News Network, 3 January 2014.

1 Explain the likely benefits of rail privatisation for Myanmar.

2 Comment on why some countries have continued to rely on the state to operate their national rail networks.

SELF-ASSESSMENT TASK 3.5

For your own country, consider each of these activities:

- water supply
- rail transport
- telephone services.

a Establish whether these activities are operated by the government or private sector businesses.

b If government-owned, how might the private sector help to improve the economic efficiency of these activities?

c Why in your country might the government not wish to pursue a policy of privatisation?

KEY CONCEPT LINK

Regulation and equality: Privatisation can include the deregulation of markets; experience has shown that the benefits of privatisation may not always be equally distributed. A valid reason for nationalisation is to promote greater social equality by operating services for the benefit of all.

SELF-ASSESSMENT TASK 3.6

Water privatisation in sub-Saharan Africa

Water privatisation, either by direct sale or through public–private partnerships, is now the favoured way forward for tackling Africa's serious problems of water provision. This may seem a little odd, given that the supply of water is best provided by a monopoly to avoid any problems of wasteful duplication.

Most countries in sub-Saharan Africa have a lack of clean water and adequate sanitation. As a consequence, water-borne diseases such as cholera and dysentery are rife and result in high infant and child mortality rates. The problems are acute in rural areas and in the teeming shanty towns in most of the large cities.

The push for privatisation is now required by the International Monetary Fund as a condition for countries receiving loans. It is a further requirement that a market price for water supplies must be established. The UK's Department for International Development took a similar line before giving funding for water privatisation in Ghana, West Africa.

The effects on local populations have been particularly controversial. The problem is that water tariffs have to be set by private companies at a market price that is often far beyond the means of most poor families. As a consequence, many cases of water-borne disease occur, not because of a lack of infrastructure, but because those in most need lack the meagre finances to be able to pay for this life-saving facility.

Queuing for water at a communal tap

1 Discuss the case for and against the privatisation of water supplies in sub-Saharan Africa.

2 Comment on whether water should be provided free of charge to poor communities in sub-Saharan Africa.

SUMMARY

In this chapter it has been shown that:

- Markets do not always operate as suggested by economic theory. There are various reasons why markets fail, necessitating government intervention.
- Government intervention can take various forms including regulations, financial intervention and direct provision of goods and services.
- Financial intervention in the form of indirect taxes and subsidies is widely applied as a means of intervention in the normal workings of the market.
- Transfer payments can have a beneficial effect on the distribution of income.
- Nationalisation occurs when governments take control of the production of goods and services.
- Privatisation has taken place in many economies in recent years, resulting in less government intervention in the market.

Exam-style questions

Read the feature below and then answer the questions that follow:

India leads with bans on plastic bags

On June 20 2014, the Times of India reported that Agra was the latest city to ban the use of most types of plastic bags. The reasons here as elsewhere are to curb pollution. The issue with plastic bags is that their irresponsible disposal causes many problems. Plastic bags block drains and the sewage system; they litter streets and public facilities such as parks and cause a health risk to cows and bulls that roam the streets, foraging for food in waste dumps. When disposed of in rivers, the inks used to promote retailers often contain toxic lead which can work its way into drinking water supplies. Their manufacture also poses environmental issues due to the release of toxic fumes into the atmosphere.

Six years earlier, the authorities in the capital, Delhi, had led the way by passing a regulation banning plastic bags. For various reasons, this regulation was never properly implemented. So, amidst growing fears over problems of their disposal, any retailer giving out plastic bags could be fined up to 100,000 rupees or five years in jail.

Interestingly, a recent survey carried out in Pune showed that around 80% of respondents favoured a complete ban on plastic bags, blaming their production and disposal as a contributor to climate change. This view though is not shared by the many manufacturers of plastic bags. There are over 400 such businesses in Delhi alone and they claim that many thousands of jobs will be lost if the ban is properly enforced. They also argue that using recyclable products like paper, cotton and jute to make bags is not always as environmentally acceptable as it might appear to be. Furthermore, they claim that there is a desperate need for Indian consumers to be made more aware of the damage caused by plastic bags. This, rather than a ban or an indirect tax, should become the focus of how the community wants to control the use of plastic bags in the future.

India appears to be taking the lead on bans on plastic bags. Other cities including Mumbai, Karwar, Tirumala, Vasco and Rajasthan all have a ban in place. The problem, as typified by Delhi, is that any ban will only reduce pollution if it is effectively applied.

1 Explain why a plastic bag in many Indian cities is seen as a demerit good. [4]

2 Using a diagram, explain the effects on the market of an indirect tax on the use of plastic bags. [8]

3 Comment on the case for introducing an indirect tax on plastic bags compared with that of banning their use in many Indian cities. [8]

Chapter 4: The macroeconomy

AS Level

Learning objectives

On completion of this chapter you should know:

- the determinants of aggregate demand and aggregate supply and the shapes of their curves
- how changes in the price level are measured; money values and real values
- the causes and consequences of inflation, deflation and disinflation
- the components of the balance of payments
- the distinction between a balance of payments equilibrium and disequilibrium
- the causes and consequences of balance of payments disequilibrium
- definitions of different types of exchange rate
- the determination of different exchange rates in different exchange rate systems
- the causes and consequences of exchange rate changes
- what is meant by the terms of trade and how the terms of trade can be estimated
- the causes and consequences of changes in the terms of trade
- the distinction between absolute and comparative advantage
- the benefits of free trade
- the main characteristics of free trade areas, customs unions and economic unions
- the methods of and arguments in favour of protectionism.

The macroeconomy

The level of activity in an economy is determined by the interaction of aggregate demand and aggregate supply. Demand for an economy's products comes from households, firms and the government within the country and from households, firms and governments in other countries. An economy's output of products is made by producers in the country. Some of these will be in the private sector and some will be in the public sector.

KEY TERM

Macroeconomy: the economy as a whole.

Changes in the demand for and supply of the economy's products influence prices in the country and the international competitiveness of the products made.

There are a number of benefits that may be gained from those in one country being able to buy from and sell to those in other countries without any restrictions. There are, however, also arguments for protecting domestic firms from competition.

Central to an understanding of changes in economic activity is the key concept of equilibrium. In considering absolute advantage and comparative advantage the key concepts of scarcity, choice and efficiency are also relevant.

Aggregate demand

Aggregate demand (*AD*) consists of four components:

1 Consumption (C): This is also known as consumer expenditure. It consists of spending by households on goods and services.
2 Investment (I): This is spending by private sector firms on capital goods.
3 Government spending (G): This covers government spending on goods and services.
4 Net exports (X–M): This is the difference between the value of exports of goods and services and the value of imports of goods and services.

KEY TERM

Aggregate demand (*AD*): the total spending on an economy's goods and services at a given price level in a given time period.

The aggregate demand curve

The aggregate demand curve shows the different quantities of total demand for the economy's products

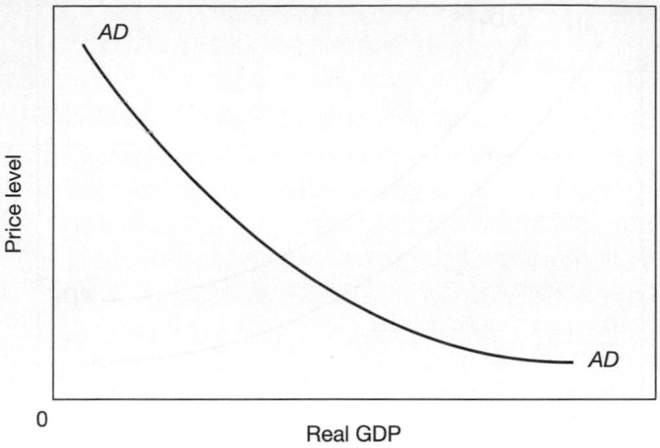

Figure 4.1 The aggregate demand curve

at different prices. A rise in the price level will cause a contraction in aggregate demand and a fall in the price level will result in an extension in aggregate demand. The downward sloping nature of the *AD* curve is shown in Figure 4.1.

The relationship between aggregate demand and the price level might seem similar to the relationship shown in the demand curve for an individual product. There is, however, a significant difference. A demand curve for a product shows the relationship between a change in the relative price of a product and the quantity demanded. The price of the product is changing but it is assumed that the prices of other products have not changed. More of the product is purchased when the price falls, in part because people switch away from rival products. In contrast, in the case of the *AD* curve, the prices of most products are changing in the same direction.

So why does aggregate demand fall when the price level rises and vice versa? There are three reasons:

1 The wealth effect: A rise in the price level will reduce the amount of goods and services that people's wealth can buy. The purchasing power of savings held in the form of bank accounts and other financial assets will fall.
2 The international effect: A rise in the price level will reduce demand for net exports as exports will become less price competitive while imports will become more price competitive.
3 The interest rate effect: A rise in the price level will increase demand for money to pay the higher prices. This, in turn, will increase the interest rate. A higher interest rate usually results in a reduction in consumption and investment.

Shifts in the aggregate demand curve

Whilst a change in the price level causes a movement along the *AD* curve, if any non-price level influence

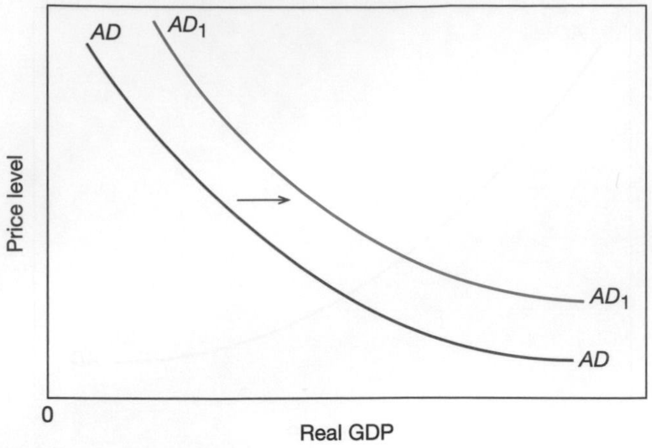

Figure 4.2 An increase in aggregate demand

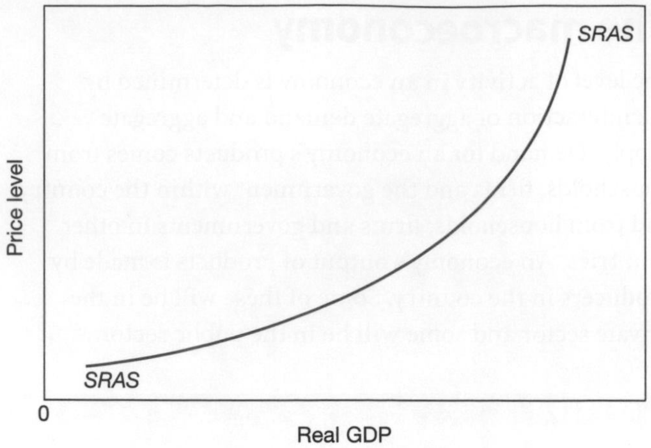

Figure 4.3 The short-run aggregate supply curve

causes aggregate demand to change, then the whole *AD* curve will shift. A shift to the left indicates a decrease in aggregate demand while a shift to the right shows an increase in aggregate demand, as shown in Figure 4.2.

A change in any non-price level influence on consumption, investment, government spending and net exports will shift the *AD* curve. Examples that would cause an increase in aggregate demand include:

- consumption – a rise in consumer confidence, a cut in income tax, an increase in wealth, a rise in the money supply, an increase in population
- investment – a rise in business confidence, a cut in corporation tax, advances in technology
- government spending – a desire to stimulate economic activity, a desire to win political support
- net exports – a fall in the exchange rate, a rise in the quality of domestically produced products, an increase in incomes abroad.

Aggregate supply

Regarding **aggregate supply (*AS*)**, economists sometimes distinguish between **short-run aggregate supply (*SRAS*)** and **long-run aggregate supply (*LRAS*)**. Short-run aggregate supply is the output that will be supplied in a period of time when the prices of factors of production (inputs, resources) have not had time to adjust to changes in aggregate demand and the price level. In contrast, long-run aggregate supply is the output that will be supplied in the time period when the prices of factors of production have fully adjusted to changes in aggregate demand and the price level.

KEY TERMS

Aggregate supply (*AS*): the total output (real GDP) that producers in an economy are willing and able to supply at a given price level in a given time period.

Short-run aggregate supply (*SRAS*): the total output of an economy that will be supplied when there has not been enough time for the prices of factors of production to change.

Long-run aggregate supply (*LRAS*): the total output of a country supplied in the period when prices of factors of production have fully adjusted.

The short-run aggregate supply curve

The short-run aggregate supply curve slopes up from left to right as shown in Figure 4.3.

As the price level rises, producers are willing and able to supply more goods and services. There are three possible reasons for this positive relationship:

1. The profit effect: As the price level (that is, the price of goods and services) increases, the price of factors of production such as wages do not change. So the price level rises, the gap between output and input prices widens and the amount of profit increases.
2. The cost effect: Although the wage rates and raw material costs remain unchanged in the short run, average costs may rise as output increases. This is because, for example, overtime payments may have to be paid and costs will be involved in recruiting more members. To cover any extra costs that may be involved in producing a higher output, producers will require higher prices.

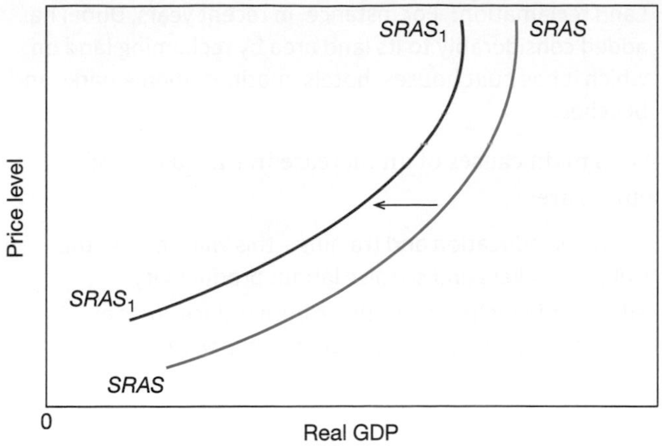

Figure 4.4 A decrease in short-run aggregate supply

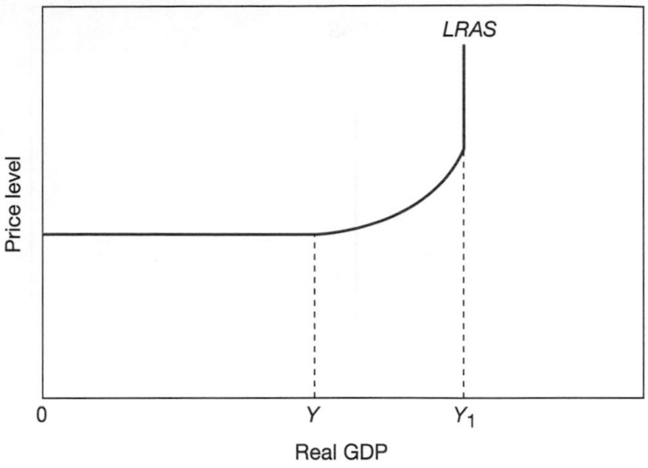

Figure 4.5 The Keynesian long-run aggregate supply curve

3 The misinterpretation effect: Producers may confuse changes in the price level with changes in relative prices. They may think that a rise in the price they receive for their products indicates that their own product is becoming more popular. As a result they may be encouraged to produce more.

Shifts in the short-run aggregate supply curve

While a change in the price level will cause a movement along the short-run aggregate supply curve, there are four main causes of a shift in the *SRAS* curve. These are:

1 A change in the price of factors of production: A rise in wage rates, not matched by an increase in labour productivity, and raw material costs will cause a decrease in *SRAS*, shifting the curve to the left as illustrated in Figure 4.4.
2 A change in taxes on firms: A reduction in corporation tax or indirect taxes will cause an increase in *SRAS*.
3 A change in factor productivity/quality of resources: A rise in labour productivity and/or capital productivity will cause an increase in aggregate supply both in the short and long run.
4 A change in the quantity of resources: In the short run the supply of inputs may be influenced by supply side shocks including natural disasters. These shocks may not have a significant impact on productive potential in the long run. The factors that will cause an increase in the quantity of resources in the long run will also increase *SRAS*.

The shape of the long-run aggregate supply curve

The long-run aggregate supply curve shows the relationship between real GDP and changes in the price level when there has been time for input prices to adjust to changes in aggregate demand.

Keynesians often represent the *LRAS* curve as perfectly elastic at low rates of output, then upward sloping over a range of output and finally perfectly inelastic. This is to emphasise their view that, in the long run, an economy can operate at any level of output and not necessarily at full capacity. Figure 4.5 shows that from 0 to *Y*, output can be raised without increasing the price level.

When output and hence employment are low, firms can attract more resources without raising their prices. There is time for input prices to change but, due to the low level of aggregate demand, they do not. For example, when unemployment is high, the offer of a job may be sufficient to attract new workers.

As output rises from *Y* to Y_1, firms begin to experience shortages of inputs and bid up wages, raw material prices and the price of capital equipment. When output reaches Y_1, the economy is producing the maximum output it can make with existing resources.

Another group of economists, called **new classical economists**, illustrate the *LRAS* curve as a vertical line. This is because they think that in the long run the

KEY TERMS

Keynesians: followers of the economist John Maynard Keynes who maintain that government intervention is needed to achieve full employment.

New classical economists: economists who think that the *LRAS* curve is vertical and that the economy will move towards full employment without government intervention.

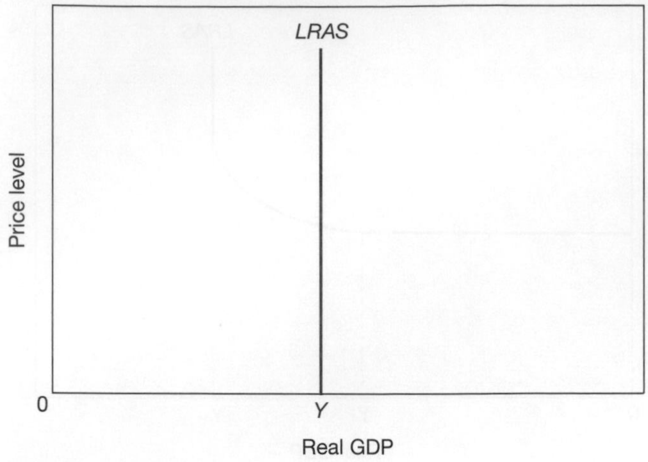

Figure 4.6 The new classical long-run aggregate supply curve

economy will operate at full capacity. This version of the *LRAS* curve is shown in Figure 4.6.

> **TOP TIP**
> The distinction between the Keynesian and new classical school versions of the shape of the *LRAS* curve can be used as an evaluative point in a answering a number of questions; e.g., 'discuss whether a rise in aggregate demand will cause inflation'.

Shifts in the *LRAS* curve

Both Keynesian and new classical economists agree that the causes of a shift in the *LRAS* curve are a change in the quantity and/or quality of resources (factor productivity). Both of these will increase the productive potential of an economy.

The causes of an increase in the quantity of resources in the long run are:

- Net immigration: If the immigrants are of working age, this will increase the size of the labour force.
- An increase in the retirement age: This will increase the size of the labour force. A number of countries have raised the age at which people can receive a state pension and some of these plan to raise it even further in the future as life expectancy increases.
- More women entering the labour force: The proportion of women who work varies from country to country. For example, in 2013 only 15% of women of working age were in the labour force in Saudi Arabia, while 75% of women in Norway were in the labour force.
- Net investment: If gross investment (total investment) exceeds depreciation (capital goods that have to be replaced because they have become worn out or become out of date) there will be additions to the capital stock.
- Discovery of new resources: The discovery of, for instance, new oil fields or gold mines can increase a country's productive potential.
- Land reclamation: For instance, in recent years, Dubai has added considerably to its land area by reclaiming land on which it has built houses, hotels, marinas, theme parks and beaches.

The two main causes of an increase in the quality of resources are:

1 improved education and training – this will increase the skills of workers and so raise labour productivity
2 advances in technology – these both reduce costs of production and increase productive capacity.

> **TOP TIP**
> Be very careful not to confuse aggregate demand and aggregate supply diagrams with demand and supply curves. Take care to include macro-labelling on *AD*/*AS* diagrams.

Interaction of aggregate demand and aggregate supply

The equilibrium level of output and the price level are determined where aggregate demand is equal to aggregate supply. The **macroeconomic equilibrium** is illustrated by the point where the *AD* and *AS* curves intersect, as shown in Figure 4.7.

If the price level was initially below *P*, the excess demand would push the price level back up to the equilibrium level. If the price level was above *P*, some goods and services would not be sold and firms would have to cut their prices.

> **KEY TERM**
> **Macroeconomic equilibrium:** the output and price level achieved where *AD* equals *AS*.

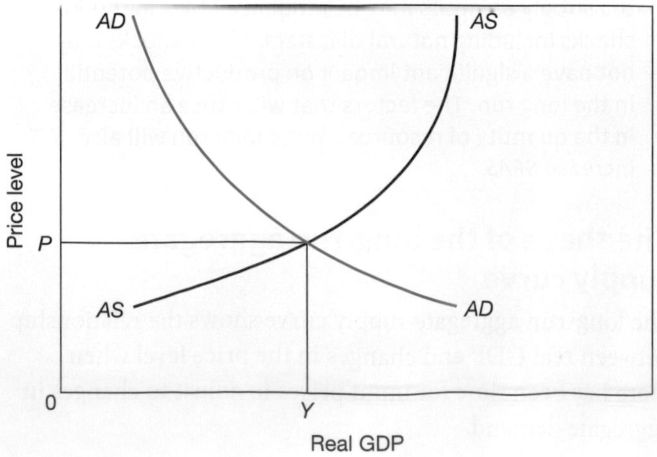

Figure 4.7 Macroeconomic equilibrium

Changes in aggregate demand and aggregate supply will move the economy to a new macroeconomic position. Where that position will be will depend on the direction of the change, the size of the change and the initial level of economic activity.

TOP TIP

Remember that changes in some variables, including investment, net immigration and government spending on education may shift both the aggregate demand curve and the aggregate supply curve.

In assessing many questions on macroeconomics, it is useful to include *AD*/*AS* diagrams.

KEY CONCEPT LINK

Equilibrium and efficiency: The section above refers to macroeconomic equilibrium. Economists study what the current macroeconomic equilibrium is, why it has changed in recent times and what the desired level of macroeconomic equilibrium would be.

SELF-ASSESSMENT TASK 4.1

Identify the effects of the following on aggregate demand, aggregate supply, output and the price level:

- a reduction in the rate of interest
- an increase in government spending on health care
- advances in information technology
- net emigration
- a cut in income tax
- an increase in wealth.

TOP TIP

To analyse macroeconomic issues, it is often useful to draw an aggregate supply curve in the shape shown in Figure 4.5. This enables you to make comments about the effect on output and the price level of changes in *AD*.

SELF-ASSESSMENT TASK 4.2

Read the feature below and then answer the questions that follow.

Changes in Ireland's economic performance

In 2010, Ireland got into considerable financial difficulties and had to be helped out by the European Union. Irish workers experienced significant pay cuts and increases in income tax.

By 2013 its economic performance had started to improve. Its unemployment rate had fallen from 14.7% to 12.5% with 50,000 jobs being created. Its output, instead of falling, started to rise with both aggregate demand and aggregate supply increasing.

a Using a Keynesian *LRAS* curve, explain at what point on the curve the Irish economy was operating in 2013.

b Explain what probably happened to consumer expenditure in Ireland in 2010.

Inflation

Inflation does not mean that every price is rising or that they are rising at the same rate. What it does mean is that, on average, prices are rising at a particular rate. For instance, an inflation rate of 6% would mean that, on average, prices are 6% higher than in the previous period. When the price level increases, the value of money falls and its purchasing power declines. Each unit of the currency, e.g. each dollar note, will buy less.

> **KEY TERM**
>
> **Inflation:** a sustained increase in an economy's price level.

Degrees of inflation

A low and stable rate, of for instance 2%, is generally regarded not to be a problem. Indeed, seeing a low and steady rise in prices may encourage firms to produce more. Such a rate of inflation is sometimes known as **creeping inflation**. In contrast to a low rate of inflation is **hyperinflation**. This is often taken to be an inflation rate that exceeds 50% but it can go much higher. At the start of the twenty-first century, Zimbabwe experienced an inflation rate so high that economists had difficulty measuring it. It has been estimated that it reached in 2008 anywhere between 200 million per cent and 89 sextrillion per cent. Hyperinflation occurs when inflation gets out of control and sometimes results in people resorting to barter. In such cases the currency usually has to be replaced by a new currency unit.

> **KEY TERMS**
>
> **Creeping inflation:** a low rate of inflation.
>
> **Hyperinflation:** an exceptionally high rate of inflation, which may result in people losing confidence in the currency.

Measurement of inflation

A country's price level indicates how much it costs to live in that country. A rise in the price level means that the cost of living has increased. To assess changes in the cost of living, governments construct consumer price indices. There are a number of stages in doing this:

- Selecting a base year: This is usually a relatively standard year in which nothing unusual has occurred. It is given a value of 100. The base year is changed on a regular basis.
- Carrying out a survey to find people's spending patterns: A sample of the population's households are asked to keep a record of what they buy. The products purchased are placed into categories such as food and clothing and footwear.
- Attaching weights to the different categories: Weights are based on the proportion of total expenditure spent on the different categories. For instance, if on average households spend $500 of their total expenditure of $2,000 on food, the category will be given a weight of ¼ or 25%.
- Finding out price changes: Prices in a range of retail outlets and from a number of other sources such as gas companies and train companies are recorded.
- Multiplying weights by price changes: The total will give the change in the **consumer price index**.

Table 4.1 shows an adaption of the consumer price index for Mauritius for the period December 2011 to December 2012. It stood at 130.4 at the start of this period; by December 2012 it was 134.38, a net increase of 3.05%.

> **KEY TERM**
>
> **Consumer price index:** an index that shows the average change in the prices of a representative basket of products purchased by households.

The distinction between money values and real values

Money values or nominal values are the values at the prices operating at the time. In contrast, real values have been adjusted for inflation. To convert money values into **real values**, the figures are multiplied by the price index in the current year and divided by the price index in the base year. For example, a worker's wages may rise from $5,000 in 2015 to $6,000 in 2016. The worker may think he has received a 20% pay rise. He has in money terms but not in real terms if inflation has occurred. If the consumer price index was 100 in 2015 and 125 in 2016, his wages in real terms would have changed to:

$$\$6{,}000 \times 100/125 = \$4{,}800.$$

So in real terms, his income has fallen by 4%. With an inflation rate of 25%, a 20% pay rise will mean that the worker will be able to buy fewer goods and services.

> **KEY TERMS**
>
> **Money values:** values at the prices operating at the time.
>
> **Real values:** values adjusted for inflation.

Category	Weight	% price change	Weighted price change
Food and non-alcoholic beverages	286/1,000	1.5	0.43
Alcoholic beverages and tobacco	92/1,000	10.3	0.95
Clothing and footwear	51/1,000	2.8	0.14
Housing, water, electricity, gas and other fuels	131/1,000	4.7	0.62
Furnishings, household equipment and routine household maintenance	64/1,000	3.7	0.24
Health	30/1,000	5.3	0.16
Transport	147/1,000	–0.4	–0.06
Communications	36/1,000	1.8	0.06
Recreation and culture	48/1,000	1.2	0.06
Education	32/1,000	2.4	0.08
Restaurants and hotels	43/1,000	6.0	0.26
Miscellaneous goods and services	40/1,000	2.7	0.11
All items	1,000		3.05

Table 4.1 Consumer price index, Mauritius
Source: http://statsmauritius,gov.mu

The causes of inflation

There are two broad causes of inflation. One is **cost-push inflation**. This occurs when prices are pushed up by increases in the cost of production. Figure 4.8 shows that a decrease in aggregate supply caused by higher costs of production pushes up the price level, causes a contraction in aggregate demand and reduces real GDP.

KEY TERM

Cost-push inflation: inflation caused by increases in costs of production.

There are a number of costs that may rise. For instance, wages may increase more than labour productivity and so result in a rise in labour costs. Indeed, higher wages can cause a wage-price spiral. Workers gain a wage rise, which causes prices to increase, then workers seek higher wages to restore their real value and so on. Increases in real material costs and fuel can also push up prices. In some cases, these increases may be caused by a fall in the exchange rate. For example, if the value of the Indian rupee falls, the price of oil imported into the country will rise. This, in turn, will result in higher transport and production costs, which will lead to higher prices.

The other broad cause of inflation is **demand-pull inflation**. This occurs when prices are pulled up by increases in aggregate demand that are not matched by equivalent increases in aggregate supply. Figure 4.9 shows that an increase in aggregate demand has caused a rise in the price level from P to P_1.

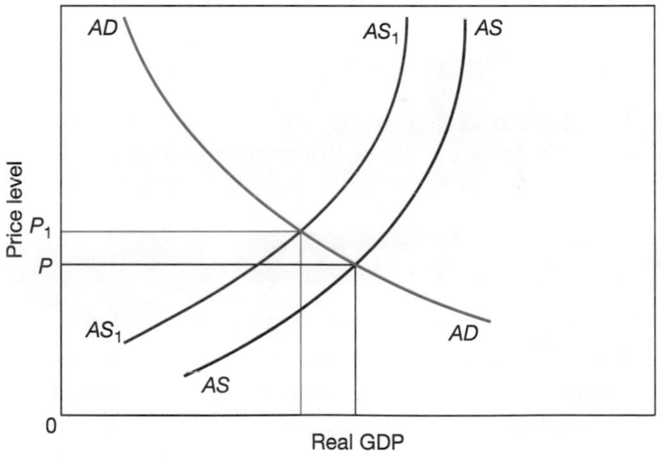

Figure 4.8 Cost-push inflation

A rise in aggregate demand will have a greater impact on the price level, the closer the economy comes to full capacity.

KEY TERM

Demand-pull inflation: inflation caused by increases in aggregate demand not matched by equivalent increases in aggregate supply.

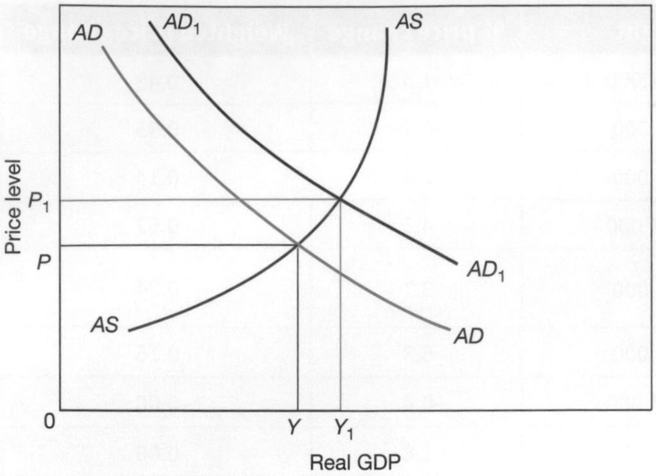

Figure 4.9 Demand-pull inflation

Increases in aggregate demand may result from, for instance, a consumer boom, a rise in government spending, higher business confidence resulting in an increase in investment or an increase in net exports.

Monetarists argue that the key cause of higher aggregate demand is increases in the money supply. They suggest that if the money supply grows more rapidly than output, the greater supply of money will drive up the price level.

KEY TERM

Monetarists: economists who consider that inflation is caused by an excessive growth in the money supply.

SELF-ASSESSMENT TASK 4.3

It is thought that inflation in Argentina exceeded 25% in 2013 at a time when the value of its currency, the peso, was falling. The government had increased its spending by significant amounts. Some of the population lost confidence in the peso and switched to using US dollars in their transactions.

1 Explain why an increase in government spending may cause inflation.
2 Explain what might cause more of the Argentinian population to use their own currency.

TOP TIP

Remember that once inflation is underway, it is difficult to determine its cause. For instance, wages and consumer expenditure may be increasing but it may be hard to tell which occurred first and so whether inflation is the result of demand-pull or cost-push factors.

The consequences of inflation

There are a number of possible costs of inflation but also some potential benefits. The potential costs include:

- A reduction in net exports: Inflation may reduce the international competitiveness of a country's products and so increase import expenditure and lower export revenue. This may result in balance of payments problems.
- An unplanned redistribution of income: Some people may gain and some people may lose as a result of inflation. For instance, if the rate of interest does not rise in line with inflation, borrowers will gain and lenders (savers) will lose. This is because borrowers will pay back less in real terms and lenders will receive less.
- **Menu costs:** These affect firms and are the costs involved in changing prices. For example, catalogues, price tags, bar codes and advertisements have to be changed. This involves staff time and is unpopular with customers.
- **Shoe leather costs**: These are the costs involved in moving money from one financial institution to another in search of the highest rate of interest.
- **Fiscal drag**: This is now sometimes referred to as 'bracket creep'. It occurs when the income levels corresponding to different tax rates are not adjusted in line with inflation. As a result, people and firms are dragged into higher tax brackets. It can be argued, however, that this is a cost of an inefficient tax system rather than a cost of inflation.
- Discouragement of investment: Unanticipated inflation can create uncertainty and so make it more difficult for firms to plan ahead. This may dissuade firms from investing, which will have an adverse effect on economic growth.
- **Inflationary noise**: This is also called 'money illusion'. This arises when inflation causes consumers and firms to confuse price signals. Inflation can make it difficult to assess what is happening to relative prices. A rise in the price of a product may not mean that it has become more expensive relative to other products. Indeed, the product may have risen in price by less than inflation and so may have become relatively cheaper. Inflationary noise can result in consumers and firms making the wrong decisions. For example, firms seeing the price of their products rising may increase output when the higher price is the result of inflation rather than increased demand for their products. This may result in a misallocation of resources.
- Inflation causing inflation: Inflation may generate further inflation as consumers, workers and firms will come to expect prices to rise. As a result, they may act in a way that will cause inflation. For example, workers may press for higher wages, firms may raise prices to cover expected higher costs and consumers may seek to purchase products now before their prices rise further.

KEY TERMS

Menu costs: costs to firms of having to change prices due to inflation.

Shoe leather costs: costs of moving money around in search of the highest interest rate.

Fiscal drag: the income of people and firms being pushed into higher tax brackets as a result of inflation.

Inflationary noise: confusion over relative prices caused by inflation.

The potential benefits include:

- Stimulating output: A low and stable inflation rate caused by increasing demand may make firms feel optimistic about the future. In addition, if prices rise by more than costs, profits will increase, which will provide funds for investment.
- Reduce the burden of debt: Real interest rates may fall due to inflation or may even become negative. This is because nominal interest rates do not tend to rise in line with inflation. As a result, debt burdens may fall. For example, those who have borrowed money to buy a house may experience a fall in their mortgage payments in real terms. A reduction in the debt burden may stimulate consumer expenditure that, in turn, could lead to higher output and employment.
- Prevent some unemployment: Firms in difficulties may have to reduce their costs to survive. For many firms, wages form a significant proportion of their total costs. With zero inflation, firms may have to cut their labour force. However, inflation would enable them to reduce the real costs of labour by either keeping nominal (money) wages constant or by not raising them in line with inflation. During inflation, workers with strong bargaining power are more likely to be able to resist cuts in their real wages than workers who lack bargaining power.

Factors affecting the consequences of inflation

The effects of inflation depend on:

- the cause of inflation
- its rate
- whether the rate is accelerating or stable
- whether the rate is the one that has been expected
- how the rate compares with that of other countries.

Demand-pull inflation is likely to be less harmful than cost-push inflation. This is because demand-pull inflation is associated with rising output whereas cost-push inflation is associated with falling output.

A high rate of inflation is likely to cause more damage than a low rate especially if the high rate develops into hyperinflation. Indeed, hyperinflation can lead to households and firms losing faith in the currency and may bring down a government.

An accelerating inflation rate, and indeed even a fluctuating inflation rate, will cause uncertainty and may discourage firms from undertaking investment. The need to devote more time and effort to establishing future inflation will increase costs.

Unanticipated inflation, which occurs when the inflation rate was different from that expected, can also create uncertainty and so can discourage some consumer expenditure and investment. In contrast, if households, firms and the government have correctly anticipated inflation, they can take measures to adapt to it and so avoid some of its potentially harmful effects. For instance, firms may have adjusted their prices, nominal interest rates may have been changed to maintain real interest rates and the government may have adjusted tax brackets, raised pensions and public sector wages in line with inflation.

It is possible for a country to have a relatively high rate of inflation but if it is below that of rival trading partners, its products may become more internationally competitive.

TOP TIP

Remember that inflation does not always reduce households' purchasing power. It does *ceteris paribus*, but if wages rise by more than prices, households will be able to purchase more goods and services.

Deflation and disinflation

Deflation is sometimes taken to mean a lower level of economic activity, which might be the result of government policy. Indeed, deflationary policy measures are those designed to reduce aggregate demand. However, deflation is now more commonly taken to refer specifically to a sustained fall in the price level. It results in a rise in the value of money, with each currency unit having greater purchasing power.

Deflation involves a negative inflation rate, for example, –3%. In contrast, **disinflation** occurs when the inflation rate falls but is still positive. For instance, the inflation rate may decline from 8% to 6%. In this case, the price level is still rising but at a slower rate.

KEY TERMS

Deflation: a sustained fall in the price level.

Disinflation: a fall in the inflation rate.

Causes and consequences of deflation

Deflation will increase the burden of debt, may increase the real rate of interest and may result in menu costs. The effects of deflation are, however, heavily influenced by the cause of deflation. Economists refer to good deflation and bad deflation. Good deflation occurs as a result of an increase in aggregate supply. Figure 4.10 shows an increase in aggregate supply resulting in a fall in the price level and a rise in real GDP.

Advances in technology, for instance, may create new methods of production and lower costs of production. As well as output increasing, employment may rise and the international competitiveness of the country's products may increase.

In contrast, bad deflation takes place when the price level is driven down by a fall in aggregate demand as shown in Figure 4.11.

In this case output falls, which may result in higher unemployment. This type of inflation runs the risk of developing into a deflationary spiral. Consumers may delay their purchases, expecting prices to fall further in the future. Firms, seeing lower demand, may not invest and may reduce the number of workers they employ. These measures will reduce demand further and economic activity will decline again.

The balance of payments

Changes in a country's price level can affect its balance of payments position which, in turn, can affect its exchange rate.

A country's **balance of payments** is a record of all the economic transactions between residents of that country and residents in other countries. There is a standard presentation of the balance of payments account that is recommended by the International Monetary Fund (IMF). It consists of the current account, the capital account, the financial account and net errors and omissions (also sometimes known as the balancing item). Money coming into the country creates credit items, which have a positive sign. Money going out of the country gives rise to debit items and is recorded with a negative sign.

KEY TERM

Balance of payments: a record of a country's economic transactions with the rest of the world over a year.

Components of the balance of payments

The current account

The **current account** consists of:

- Trade in goods: As its name suggests, this covers the exports and imports of goods such as cars, TVs and clothing. Exports give rise to credit items while imports give rise to debit items. The trade in goods balance is the revenue earned from exports of goods minus the expenditure on the imports of goods. The trade in goods balance can also be called the balance of trade, the visible balance and the merchandise balance. A trade in goods surplus arises when export revenue is greater than import expenditure.
- Trade in services: This covers the trade in exports and imports of services, which may be referred to as 'invisibles'. Services include shipping, tourism, banking and insurance. A trade in services deficit occurs when revenue from the export of services is less than the expenditure on services bought from other countries.

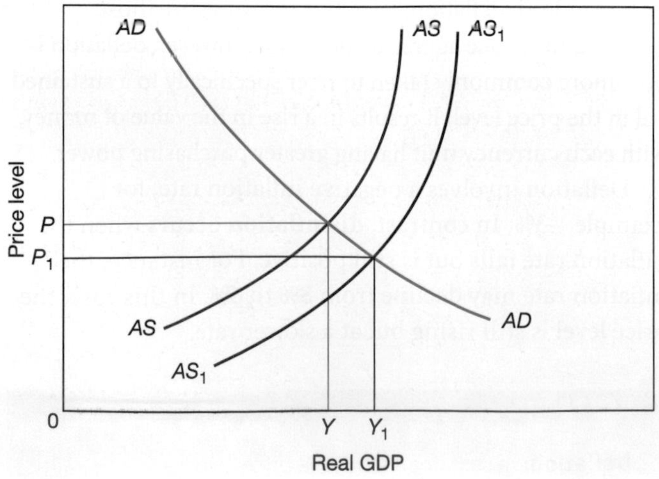

Figure 4.10 Good deflation

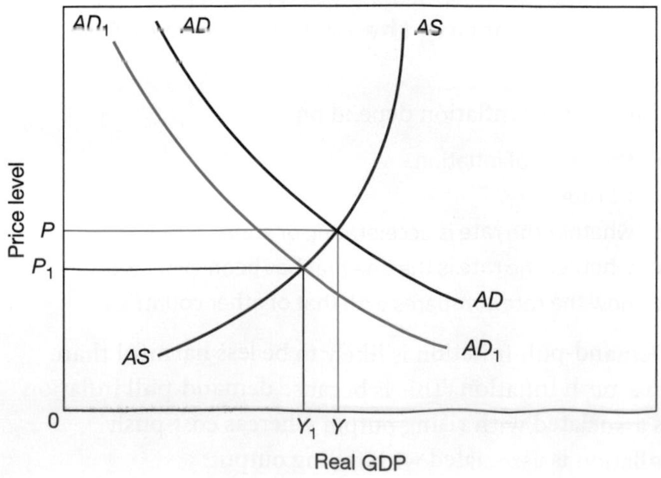

Figure 4.11 Bad deflation

- Income: This includes income in the form of profits, interest and dividends earned on direct investment abroad and foreign earnings on investment in the country. For example, dividends paid on foreign shares by residents in the country appear as credit items, while interest paid to foreigners on bank accounts they hold in the country are debit items.
- Current transfers: These cover payments made and receipts received for which there is no corresponding exchange of an actual good or service. They include government transfers such as payments to and receipts from international organisations and foreign aid. Transfers by private individuals are also included in this part of the current account. One such transfer is workers' remittances. This transfer of money from people working in a foreign country back to their relatives at home forms a large credit item in the case of some countries, for instance the Philippines.

SELF-ASSESSMENT TASK 4.4

Read the feature below and then answer the questions that follow.

Inflation in Latin America

Inflation rates have varied in Latin America in recent years. In May 2013, inflation in Venezuela reached 54%, one of the highest in the world. Prices were driven up largely by higher food prices. Venezuela's population experienced food shortages, lower real wages and a reduction in the value of their savings. The government imposed price controls on a range of products and the president stated these would reverse the rise in prices and might even result in negative inflation.

Higher food prices, along with a falling foreign exchange rate, also caused Brazil's inflation rate to rise in 2013. In April of that year the inflation rate rose to 6.6%, with more than two-thirds of the items in the country's consumer price index rising in price.

Table 4.2 shows the inflation rates in Venezuela, Brazil and Mexico over recent years.

	% change in consumer price index		
Year	Brazil	Mexico	Venezuela
2007	3.5	3.9	18.7
2008	4.7	3.9	28.2
2009	4.7	5.5	30.2
2010	5.3	3.9	32.0
2011	5.0	3.9	32.0
2012	5.3	3.7	25.2
2013	6.3	3.7	36.0

Table 4.2 Inflation rates in Brazil, Mexico and Venezuela 2007–2013

1 Explain in what sense inflation may reduce the value of people's savings.

2 Why might most of the items in a country's consumer price index fall but the consumer price index still increase?

3 Explain why the change in Brazil's foreign exchange rate may have caused cost-push inflation.

4 Using Table 4.2, explain what happened to prices in Brazil between:

a 2008 and 2009

b 2010 and 2011

5 Compare the inflation rates experienced in Mexico and Venezuela over the period shown.

The current account balance is the overall balance of the trade in goods, trade in services, income and current transfers. A current account deficit means that the combined debit items on the four parts exceed the combined credit items on the four parts.

KEY TERM

Current account: within the balance of payments, a record of the trade in goods, trade in services, investment income and current transfers.

Capital account

For most countries, the **capital account** is a relatively small part of the balance of payments. It includes, for instance, government debt forgiveness, money brought into and taken out of the country by migrants, the sales and purchases of copyrights, patents and trademarks.

KEY TERM

Capital account: within the balance of payments, a record of capital transfers and the acquisition and disposal of non-produced, non-financial assets.

Financial account

In contrast to the capital account, the **financial account** is a significant part of many countries' balance of payments, which records large movements of funds into and out of the country. It is made up of four parts:

1 Direct investment: This covers the building of a factory in another country and the takeover of an existing firm in another country (debit items) or the setting up of a new plant or the takeover of a firm in the country by a foreign firm (credit items).
2 Portfolio investment: This includes the purchase and sale of government bonds and shares that do not involve legal control of a firm.
3 Other investments: This part covers shorter-term movements of financial investment including bank loans and inter-government loans.
   Direct, portfolio and other investments generate investment income that appears in the income section of the current account.
4 Reserve assets: These are made up of the government's holdings of gold, foreign exchange reserves, Special Drawing Rights and changes in the country's reserve position in the IMF. Reserves are kept to settle international debts and to influence the value of the foreign exchange rate. Additions to the reserves are shown as debit items, while reductions to the reserves are shown as credit items. This is because, for instance, if the central bank sells some of its foreign currency, it will be gaining its own currency in exchange, so there will be a flow of currency into the country.

KEY TERM

Financial account: within the balance of payments, a record of the transfer of financial assets between the country and the rest of the world.

Net errors and omissions

The balance of payments as a whole must always balance. This is because any credit item has to be matched by a corresponding debit item. For example, if a country sells exports, these exports will be recorded as credit items. To purchase the exports, foreigners would have to obtain the currency of the country they are importing from. They may do this by, for instance, borrowing from the country's banks – a debit item.

A deficit on the current account of the balance of payments should be matched by a surplus of equal value on the capital and financial accounts. In practice, however, with so many transactions involved, it is difficult to keep an accurate record. Some mistakes are likely to be made and some transactions may not be included. To compensate for this, **a net errors and omissions** figure (also sometimes called the balancing item) is included. For example, if the current account plus the capital and financial accounts, add up to minus $2,000 million, this means that $2,000 million more must have come into the country than was recorded. In this case, a net errors and omission figure of plus $2,000 million would be added. By including the net errors and omissions figure, it means that the current account, capital account, financial account and net errors and omissions equal zero.

Over time, more and better quality information is likely to become available and so the size of the net errors and omissions figure usually declines. It is interesting to note that the value of current account deficits experienced by some countries should be matched by the value of the current account surpluses experienced by other countries but again, due to mistakes and items being left out, this is not the case.

KEY TERM

Net errors and omissions: a figure included to ensure the balance of payments balances.

TOP TIP

There is commonly confusion between the items that go in the income part of the current account and those that go in the financial account. The names of the two parts provide clear guidance. Remember that the financial investment goes in the financial account whereas the income that the investment generates goes in the income part.

Balance of payments disequilibria

When economists discuss balance of payments deficits and surpluses they are discussing deficits and surpluses on one or other of the accounts within the balance of payments. Most focus is usually placed on a deficit on the current account of the balance of payments.

Causes of a current account deficit

These include:

- A growing domestic economy: When firms are increasing their output, they may buy more raw materials and capital goods from abroad. As well as import expenditure increasing, export revenue may decline as a result of exports being diverted from the foreign to the domestic market. This cause of a current account deficit is not likely to be considered to be a problem. This is because a growing economy is likely to attract foreign direct investment, which will lead to credit items in the financial account to offset the debit items in the current account. It is also likely to be short-term and to be self-correcting. As the country's firms use the imported raw materials and capital goods to produce more products, they are likely to sell more products both abroad and at home. So export revenue may rise to match the higher import expenditure.
- Declining economic activity in trading partners: If the countries that buy this country's imports experience recessions or slowdowns in economic growth, their import expenditure may fall or rise more slowly.
  A current account deficit that arises from either change in the economic cycle of the domestic economy or the economies of trading partners is sometimes referred to as a cyclical deficit. It is not usually considered to be a problem as, noted above, it will be relatively short-term and is likely to be self-correcting.
- Structural problems: A current account deficit that lasts over the long run is more of a concern. This is because it indicates that domestic firms are not internationally competitive and that the country may have to borrow to finance the surplus spending. There are a number of causes of a lack of international competitiveness. These include an overvalued exchange rate, a relatively high inflation rate, low labour and capital productivity. A structural deficit is a cause of concern as it will not be self-correcting.

TOP TIP

Students often write that a trade deficit arises when imports exceed exports. Remember, however, a trade deficit arises not when the *quantity* of imports is greater than the *quantity* of exports. It occurs when the *value* of imports (price × quantity) is greater than the *value* of imports.

SELF-ASSESSMENT TASK 4.5

The USA's current account deficit in 2005 reached 6.2% of GDP, which suggested the country was living significantly beyond its means. By 2013, it had fallen to 2.5%, a level it could sustain. Import penetration had fallen from 35% of durable goods purchased in 2005 to 31% in 2013.

The deficit had declined partly due to a rising surplus in investment income. The main cause, however, was a reduction in the trade in goods deficit. Output and productivity had risen in the country. There had also been demographic changes, with a rise in the average age of the population. Older people tend to spend more on services, which are mostly produced at home, and less on goods.

1 What is meant by 'import penetration'?
2 Explain what would cause an increase in investment income.
3 Explain **two** reasons why the US's trade in goods balance improved.

A financial account deficit

A financial account deficit is not necessarily a problem, especially as it will give rise to an inflow of profits, interest and dividends in future years. It may also be short-term, resulting from hot money flowing out of the country in search of higher interest rates and in expectation that other currencies may rise in value. It is more of a concern, however, if it results from a long-term lack of confidence in the country's economic prospects. Indeed, such a concern might result in a capital flight. Foreign owners of firms and shares in the country may sell these in large quantities. This movement of firms and funds out of the country reduces tax revenue and employment and may result in the country moving into a recession.

Consequences of a current account deficit and a current account surplus

A current account deficit allows the residents of a country to consume more products than the country produces. This is sometimes referred to as a country living beyond its means. The country will, however, have to finance the deficit by attracting investment into the country or borrowing. This will involve an outflow of money in the future in the form of investment income.

An increase in a current account deficit may also reduce aggregate demand, which may slow down economic growth and may cause unemployment.

It might be thought that a current account surplus is always beneficial as it involves a country saving more than it is spending. It does, however, mean that the country's residents are not enjoying as high a standard of living as possible. The high level of demand, combined with additions to the money supply, may generate inflationary pressure. Those countries experiencing current account deficits may also put pressure on the country to change its policies in order to reduce its surplus.

TOP TIP

The significance of the size of a current account deficit or surplus can be assessed more effectively by considering it as a percentage of the country's gross domestic product (output) than in monetary terms. For example, the USA in 2013 had a current account deficit of US$400 billion whereas South Africa's deficit was only US$22 billion. South Africa's deficit, however, might have been more of a concern as it accounted for 6.5% of the country's GDP whereas the USA's deficit accounted for only 2.5% of its GDP.

SELF-ASSESSMENT TASK 4.6

	Credit	Debit
Trade in goods	24,696	40,461
Trade in services	5,035	8,227
Income	826	4,071
Current transfers	17,686	142

Table 4.3 Pakistan: Current account in US$ millions (2012)

Workers' remittances made a significant contribution to Pakistan's current account position in 2012. Pakistanis working in other countries sent back US$13,186 million to their families in that year.

While the country experienced a current account deficit, it had a surplus on its capital account of US$220 million and a surplus of US$1,312 million on its financial account.

Using the information, calculate:

a Pakistan's current account deficit.

b Pakistan' current account position in the absence of the workers' remittances received.

c Pakistan's net errors and omissions figure.

Definition and measurement of exchange rates

The nominal foreign **exchange rate** is the price of one currency in terms of another currency; that is, the price of the domestic currency in terms of a foreign currency. It is sometimes referred to as a bilateral exchange rate. For example, the price of US$1 may be 50 Indian rupees. This would mean that a 5,000 rupee product would sell in the US for US$100. A rise in India's foreign exchange rate against the US dollar would increase the price of India's exports in terms of US dollars and would lower the price of India's imports in terms of rupees. For example, the value of the rupee might rise to US$1 equals 40 rupees so that a US dollar may be purchased with fewer rupees. Now a 5,000 rupee product would sell in the US for $125. A $20 US import that would have initially sold in India for 1,000 rupees, will now sell in India for 800 rupees.

KEY TERM

Exchange rate: the price of one currency in terms of another currency.

In practice, a country trades with a number of other countries and it is possible that its currency may rise in value against some countries while falling against others. To gain an impression of the general change in a country's foreign exchange rate, economists measure trade weighted exchange rates. A **trade weighted exchange rate** is a measure, in index form, of the value of a currency against a basket of currencies. These are weighted according to the relative importance of the countries in the country's trade. For example, if India undertakes three times as much trade with China as it does with the US, the Chinese renminbi will be given three times as much weight in the calculation as the US dollar. A trade weighted exchange rate is also known as a multinational exchange rate.

As well as trade weighted exchange rates, economists also measure real effective exchange rates. A **real effective exchange rate** takes price changes as well as exchange rate changes into account to assess changes in the competitiveness of a country's products in global markets. A fall in a country's foreign exchange rate would be expected to make its exports more price competitive. If, however, the country is experiencing a relatively high inflation rate, export prices may actually be increasing. A real exchange rate shows the price of domestic products in terms of foreign products:

$$\text{The real exchange rate} = \frac{\text{nominal exchange rate} \times \text{domestic price index}}{\text{foreign exchange rate}}$$

The real exchange rate may rise as a result of an appreciation or an increase in the country's relative inflation rate.

KEY TERMS

Trade weighted exchange rate: the price of one currency against a basket of currencies.

Real effective exchange rate: a currency's value in terms of its real purchasing power.

TOP TIP

Follow changes in your country's exchange rate, noting causes and effects.

Remember there is a difference between the external and internal value of a currency. The exchange rate shows the external value and the price level shows the internal value.

The determination of foreign exchange rates

Floating exchange rates

A **floating exchange rate** is one determined by market forces. Currencies are bought and sold on the foreign exchange market. This market does not exist in a single location but is made up of financial institutions that buy and sell foreign currency on behalf of private and business customers. Large values of currencies are bought and sold on any particular day. The price of the currency is determined by the relative strengths of the demand for and supply of the currency. There are various reasons why currency traders will buy the domestic currency. These include enabling their customers to:

- purchase goods and services from the country
- invest in the country
- speculate on making a profit if the value of the currency should rise in the future. Financial institutions also speculate on future currency movements on their own behalf. The currency will be sold to buy imports, to invest abroad and in expectation that the value of the currency will fall in the future.

Figure 4.12 shows that an increase in the supply of a currency will result in a fall in its value.

A fall in the value of a currency caused by market forces is known as a depreciation. A rise in the value

KEY TERM

Floating exchange rate: an exchange rate that is determined by the market forces of demand and supply.

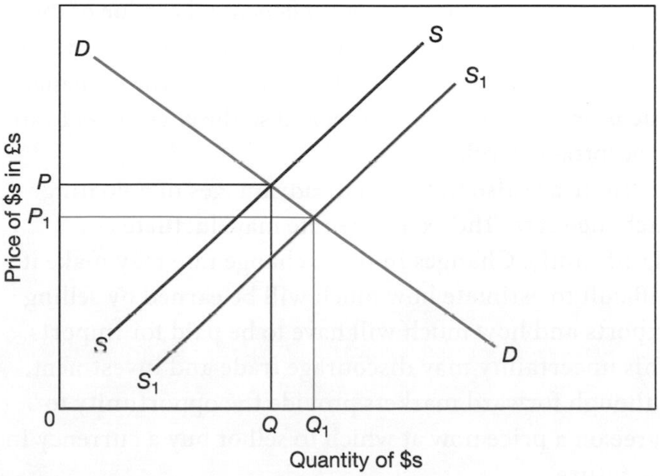

Figure 4.12 The effect of an increase in the supply of currency

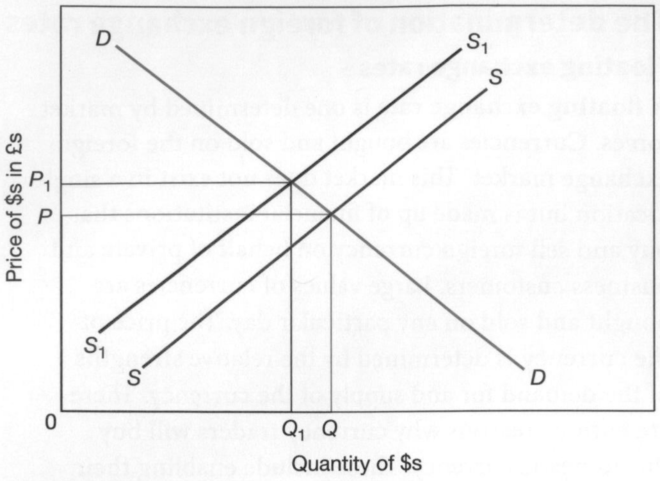

Figure 4.13 The effect on the value of the US dollar of Americans buying fewer UK products

of the currency, caused by an increase in demand and/or a decrease in supply is known as an appreciation. Figure 4.13 shows an appreciation in the value of the pound sterling. This might have been caused by a fall in US demand for UK imports. If Americans are buying fewer UK imports, they will need to sell fewer dollars to purchase pounds sterling.

There are a number of advantages that may be gained from operating a floating exchange rate. One is that the exchange rate should, in theory, move to restore a balance on the current account of the balance of payments. For instance, if a country has a current account deficit, demand for the currency will fall while its supply increases. This will lead to a depreciation, making exports cheaper and imports more expensive. Given elastic demand for exports and imports, this will result in a rise in export revenue and a fall in import expenditure.

With the government not influencing the value of the exchange rate, reserves of foreign currency do not have to be held and can be used for other purposes. The exchange rate is not a government target and so the government can concentrate on other aims.

There are also potential disadvantages of a floating exchange rate. The exchange rate may fluctuate significantly. Changes in the exchange rate may make it difficult to estimate how much will be earned by selling exports and how much will have to be paid for imports. This uncertainty may discourage trade and investment, although forward markets provide the opportunity to agree on a price now at which to sell or buy a currency in the future.

Another potential disadvantage is that a floating rate may remove pressure on the government to maintain price stability. A government may rely on a fall in a floating exchange rate to restore any loss in international competitiveness arising from inflation. There is a risk, however, that a fall in the exchange rate will increase inflationary pressure. This is because the price of imported products will increase. As a result, the cost of imported raw materials will rise, the price of imported finished products will increase and the pressure on domestic firms to restrict their price rises will be reduced.

There is also no guarantee that a floating exchange rate will eliminate a current account surplus or deficit. For instance, the value of an exchange rate may be pushed up despite the country having a current account deficit if speculators are buying the currency expecting it to rise in value.

A fixed exchange rate system

In a **fixed exchange rate** system, the value of the currency is determined by the government. For instance, the value of the UAE's dirham may be fixed at 1 dirham = US$0.25. Its central bank will maintain the rate by intervening in the foreign exchange market and/or changing the rate of interest. If, for instance, there is downward pressure on the exchange rate because the supply of the currency is increasing on the foreign exchange market, the central bank will take action. It may also increase the rate of interest. Such a measure may attract **hot money flows**, with people buying the currency to place into accounts in the country's financial institutions. Figure 4.14 shows that the UAE government fixes its exchange rate at 1 dirham = US$0.25.

If the supply of the currency increases to S_1, the central bank may buy enough of the currency to shift the demand curve to D_1, and maintain the value of the currency at $0.25.

It is easier for a central bank to maintain a fixed exchange rate if that rate is set close to the long-run

KEY TERMS

Fixed exchange rate: an exchange rate set by the government and maintained by the central bank.

Hot money flows: flows of money moved around the world to take advantage of changes in interest rates and exchange rates.

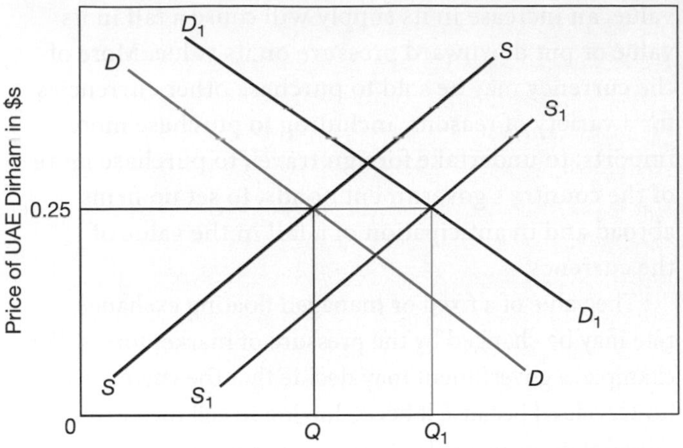

Figure 4.14 Maintaining the value of the UAE dirham

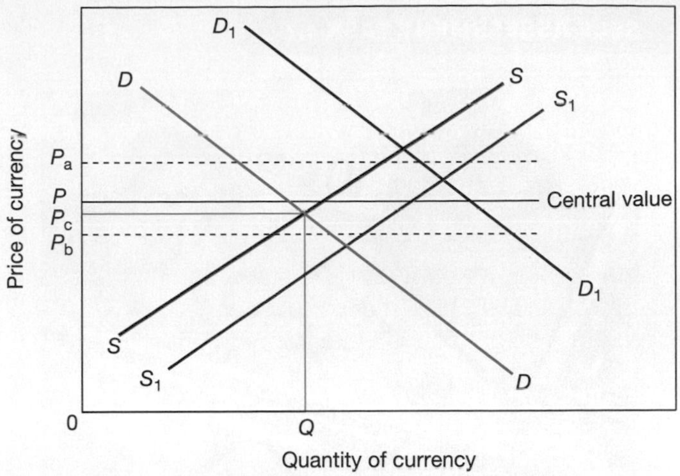

Figure 4.15 A managed float

equilibrium value of the currency. This is because it will only have to offset short-run – and possibly relatively small – fluctuations. If, however, the exchange rate is overvalued, the central bank may be in danger of running out of reserves trying to keep the exchange rate at a level that does not reflect its market value.

Indeed, one of the disadvantages of a fixed exchange rate is the need to keep reserves. This involves an opportunity cost as the foreign exchange or gold, for instance, could be used for other purposes. There is also the risk that a government may sacrifice other policy objectives in order to maintain the fixed exchange rate. For instance, a central bank may raise the interest rate in a bid to keep the exchange rate at the price the government wants maintained. A higher interest rate may, however, reduce aggregate demand and increase unemployment.

Over time, market pressures may mean that the rate at which the currency is fixed may have to be changed. A reduction in the value of a fixed exchange rate to a lower level is known as devaluation. A revaluation occurs when the government raises the exchange rate to a new, higher fixed rate.

A fixed exchange rate does create certainty, which can promote international trade and investment. For instance, a foreign firm may be more willing to set up a branch in the country if it knows how much any revenue it earns will be worth in its own currency.

A fixed exchange rate also imposes discipline on a government to keep inflation low so that a loss of international price competitiveness does not put downward pressure on the exchange rate.

A managed float

A **managed float**, in effect, combines features of a floating exchange rate system and a fixed exchange rate system. It usually involves a government allowing the exchange rate to be determined by market forces within a given band, which has upper and lower limits. Figure 4.15 shows that the government sets a central value of *P*, an upper band of P_a, which it does not want the exchange rate to exceed, and a lower limit of P_b, which it does not want it to fall below.

If the exchange rate is within the limits, for example at P_c, no action will be taken. If, however, demand for the currency were to rise to D_1, the central bank would sell the domestic currency to increase supply to S_1 and so keep the exchange rate within the desired band.

KEY TERM

Managed float: where the exchange rate is influenced by state intervention.

The factors underlying changes in foreign exchange rates

Changes in the demand for and supply of a currency will cause a change in the price of the currency in the case of a floating exchange rate and will put upward or downward pressure on a fixed exchange rate.

Demand for the currency will rise if a higher value of exports is being sold. Foreigners may buy more of the currency if they wish to purchase shares in the country's

SELF-ASSESSMENT TASK 4.7

The Chinese currency, the renminbi, is allowed to change by 1% a day on either side of a rate set each morning by the central bank. In 2013 its nominal rate rose against both the US dollar and the Japanese yen and its real exchange rate rose even more. Its nominal foreign exchange rate rose, in part, because of a higher interest rate in the country than in the US and Japan.

Among the causes of the long-term increase in China's real exchange rate are the country's rapid economic growth and an increasing shortage of workers.

1 What type of exchange rate system does China operate?
2 What does the information suggest about China's inflation rate compared with those of the US and Japan in 2013?
3 Explain why a shortage of workers could result in a rise in a country's real exchange rate.

firms due to the country's economic prospects improving. They may also want to buy more of the currency in order to open accounts in the country's banks because of higher interest rates. Foreign firms may purchase a greater value of the currency in order to set up branches in the country, perhaps because of a rise in labour productivity in the country. Speculation may account for a large proportion of the currency purchased. If it is thought that the value of the currency will rise, people may buy the currency in the hope of making a profit.

While an increase in demand for the currency will push up its price, or at least put upward pressure on its value, an increase in its supply will cause a fall in its value or put downward pressure on its value. More of the currency may be sold to purchase other currencies for a variety of reasons, including to purchase more imports, to undertake foreign travel, to purchase more of the country's government bonds, to set up firms abroad and in anticipation of a fall in the value of the currency.

The value of a fixed or managed floating exchange rate may be changed by the pressure of market forces. For example, a government may decide that the currency is undervalued because it keeps having to sell the currency to maintain its value. In this case, it may decide to revalue the currency.

A government may also decide to alter a fixed exchange rate or influence an exchange rate within a managed float in order to achieve a macroeconomic aim. For instance, a government may devalue its currency, possibly below its long-run equilibrium level, in order to gain a competitive advantage and improve its current account position. Alternatively, a government may set a high exchange rate to reduce inflationary pressure.

The effects of changing foreign exchange rates on the domestic economy and external economy

A depreciation/devaluation

A fall in the value of the exchange rate will make exports cheaper, in terms of foreign currencies, and imports more expensive, in terms of the domestic currency. This may enable domestic firms to sell more products both at home and abroad. Some domestic consumers may now purchase home-made products rather than the now relatively more expensive imports. Some foreigners may now buy the country's exports rather than products produced by firms in other countries.

A rise in net exports will increase aggregate demand. As can be seen in Figure 4.16, this may result in in a rise in output. Higher output may result in lower unemployment.

As the Figure 4.16 shows, the higher aggregate demand that occurs because of a rise in net exports may also give rise to inflationary pressure. As the economy approaches full capacity, resources will become increasingly scarce and their prices will be bid up. In addition, finished imported products that are still purchased will be more expensive and some of these will count in the country's consumer price index. Costs of production will be pushed up because the cost of

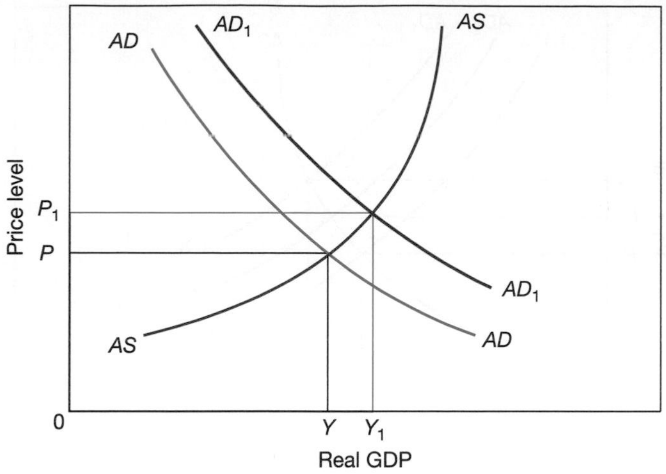

Figure 4.16 The effect of a rise in net exports

imported raw materials will rise. Domestic firms may also feel less competitive pressure to keep costs and prices low.

It is often expected that a lower exchange rate will reduce a current account deficit. This, however, is not always the case. The outcome will depend, in part, on the price elasticities of demand for both exports and imports. If demand for exports is price elastic and demand for imports is price elastic, a fall in the exchange rate will clearly result in a rise in export revenue and a reduction in import expenditure. These changes will reduce a current account deficit. What is sometimes not realised is that if the combined price elasticities of demand for exports and imports are greater than 1, a **depreciation** or **devaluation** will improve the current account position. For instance, PED of exports might be 0 while PED of imports is −1.2. In this case, a fall in the exchange rate will result in export revenue remaining unchanged in terms of the home currency while import expenditure will fall. This requirement for the combined elasticities to exceed 1 for the current account position to be improved by a fall in the exchange rate is known as the **Marshall-Lerner condition**. The box item uses simplified figures to illustrate this condition.

KEY TERMS

Depreciation: a decrease in the international price of a currency caused by market forces.

Devaluation: a decision by the government to lower the international price of the currency.

KEY TERM

Marshall-Lerner condition: the requirement that for a fall in the exchange rate to be successful in reducing a current account deficit, the sum of the price elasticities of demand for exports and imports must be greater than 1.

An illustration of the Marshall-Lerner condition

Initially £1 = US$1.5

- 40 products, which would sell at £10 each in the home market, sell for $15 in the US. Export revenue = £400 ($600).
- 50 imports from the US, which sell in the US at $30, are purchased in the UK at £20 each. Import expenditure = £1,000 ($1,500).
- Deficit = £400 − £1,000 = £600.

Then the pound sterling falls in value to £1 = $1.

- PED for exports = 0. Price in US falls to $10 each. Total export revenue is now 40 × $10 = $400 which is now converted into £400, leaving export revenue in pounds sterling unchanged.
- PED for imports = −1.2. Price of the $30 product will rise to £30, a 50% increase. Demand falls by 60% to 20. Total import expenditure now equals £600.
- The deficit is now £400 − £600 = £200. It has fallen by £400.

The greater the combined PED for exports and imports is, the smaller will be the fall in the exchange rate required to improve the current account position. If the PED is less than 1, a revaluation of the exchange rate would be the more appropriate policy strategy.

The **J-curve effect** is related to the Marshall-Lerner condition. In some cases, a fall in the exchange rate will actually worsen the current account position before it starts to improve it. This is because, in the short term, demand for imports and exports may be relatively inelastic. It takes time to recognise that prices have changed and then to search for alternative products. In the longer term, demand becomes more elastic and current account position may move from deficit into surplus as shown in Figure 4.17.

KEY TERM

J-curve effect: a fall in the exchange rate causing an increase in a current account deficit before it reduces it due to the time it takes for demand to respond.

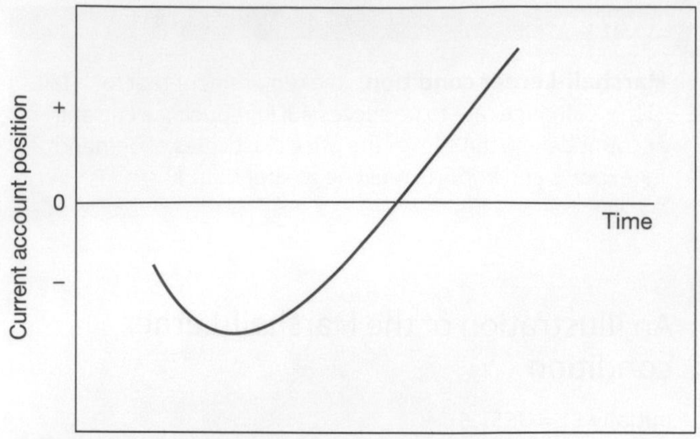

Figure 4.17 The J-curve effect

There are a number of other factors that can influence the effect of a fall in the exchange rate on the current account position. For instance, exports may be cheaper but the impact on the quantity sold may be limited by a low price elasticity of supply, trade restrictions imposed by foreign governments and declines in the relative quality of the products made by the country's firms.

An appreciation/revaluation

An **appreciation** or **revaluation** – a rise in the exchange rate – will make exports more expensive in terms of foreign currencies, and imports cheaper in terms of the domestic currency. Such a change is likely to result in a fall in demand for domestic products. Lower aggregate demand may result in a rise in unemployment and a slowdown in economic growth. Its main impact, however, may be to cause a reduction in inflationary pressure if the economy is operating close to or at maximum capacity. Figure 4.18 shows that in the absence of a rise in the exchange rate, *AD* might increase to AD_1 causing the price level to rise to P_1. A rise in the exchange rate may reduce the growth of *AD* to AD_2 and so the inflation rate would be lower than would be the case if the exchange rate had remained unchanged.

A higher exchange rate may also reduce inflationary pressure by shifting the aggregate supply curve to the right because of lower costs of imported raw materials. The price of imported finished products would also fall and there would be increased competitive pressure on domestic firms to restrict price rises in order to try to maintain their sales at home and abroad.

KEY TERMS

Appreciation: an increase in the international price of a currency caused by market forces.

Revaluation: a decision by the government to raise the international price of its currency.

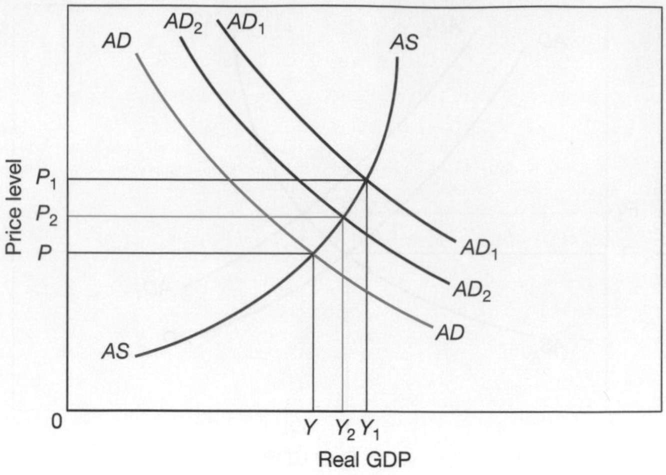

Figure 4.18 A rise in the exchange rate limiting the increase in aggregate demand

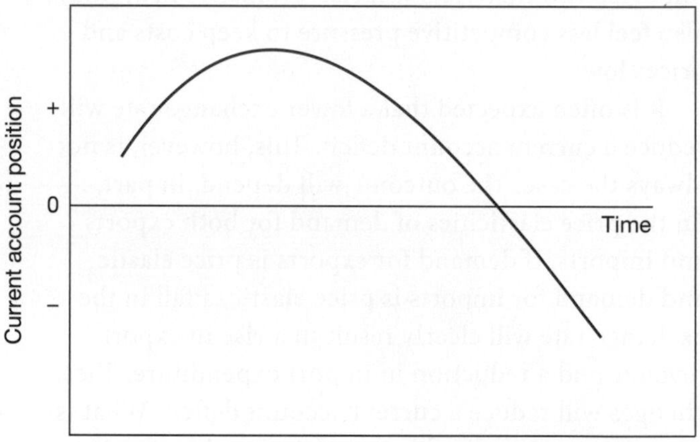

Figure 4.19 The reverse J-curve effect

A higher exchange rate may increase a current account deficit or reduce a current account surplus but the outcome will depend mainly on the price elasticities of demand for exports and imports. The Marshall-Lerner condition and the J-curve work in reverse. So a current account surplus will only be reduced if the sum of the price elasticities of demand for exports and imports is greater than 1. A rise in the exchange rate may increase a current account surplus in the short run before reducing it in the longer run as shown in Figure 4.19.

The terms of trade

A country's current account position is heavily influenced by its relative export and import prices. **The terms of trade** is a measure of the ratio of export prices and import prices.

SELF-ASSESSMENT TASK 4.8

At the end of 2013, the UK's foreign exchange rate rose to its highest level in almost two and a half years. This was despite the country's current account deficit worsening, which might have been expected to have put downward pressure on the value of the pound sterling. The increase did, however, follow favourable predictions for the UK's future economic performance.

The appreciation of the pound sterling was good news for UK tourists but not for UK exporters. Some economists also claimed that the appreciation might threaten the recovery, which was a major reason why it had occurred.

1 Explain why a rise in a country's current account deficit would be expected to reduce its foreign exchange rate.
2 Analyse why a rise in the pound sterling might help UK tourists but harm UK exporters.
3 Discuss whether a rise in a country's foreign exchange rate would always threaten an improvement in its economic performance.

KEY TERM

Terms of trade: a numerical measure of the relationship between export and import prices.

$$\text{Terms of trade index} = \frac{\text{index of export prices}}{\text{index of import prices}} \times 100$$

The ratio is calculated from the average prices of many goods and services that are traded internationally. The prices are weighted by the relative importance of each product traded.

If the index increases, this is described as a favourable movement or an improvement in the terms of trade. It means that fewer exports have to be sold to buy any given quantity of imports. An unfavourable movement or deterioration in the terms of trade means that the index number has fallen. Now more exports will have to be exchanged to gain the same quantity of imports.

Causes of changes in the terms of trade

Essentially what causes a favourable movement in the terms of trade is a rise in export prices relative to import prices. For instance, export prices may rise by more than import prices or import prices may fall while export prices remain unchanged. An unfavourable movement occurs when there is a fall in export prices relative to import prices. In this case, for example, import prices may fall by less than export prices or import prices may rise while export prices may fall.

What leads to changes in export and import prices and so to changes in the terms of trade is changes in demand for and supply of exports and imports, the price level and the exchange rate. An increase in the demand for exports would increase their price and so cause a favourable movement in the terms of trade. A rise in a country's relative inflation rate would also make its export prices higher relative to its import prices. A devaluation is sometimes referred to as a deliberate deterioration of its terms of trade. This is because it is a deliberate attempt to reduce export prices and raise import prices in order to make the country's products more internationally competitive.

The Prebisch-Singer hypothesis suggests that the terms of trade tend to move against primary producing countries. This is based on the view that demand for manufactured goods and for services rises by more than demand for primary products when income increases. In recent years, the relative prices of some agricultural products have fallen but there has been more volatility in commodity prices, with some years witnessing significant rises in the price of, for instance, oil and copper.

The impact of changes in the terms of trade

While a rise in the terms of trade is described as a favourable movement, its impact is not always favourable. This is because its effects will depend on its cause. If the price of exports increases because of a rise in demand then it is likely to be beneficial as more domestic products will be sold. If, however, the cause is a rise in the costs of production, demand for the country's products will fall and export revenue may decline.

An unfavourable movement in the terms of trade may actually reduce a deficit on the current account of the balance of payments. If the Marshall-Lerner condition is met, the fall in export prices relative to import prices should increase export revenue relative to import expenditure.

It is important to remember that the terms of trade is a measure of export and import prices and not export and import values.

Absolute and comparative advantage

Absolute advantage

Some of world trade is explained by **absolute advantage.** A country has an absolute advantage in producing a product if it can produce more of a product with the same quantity of resources than another country. For example, Indonesia has the absolute advantage in producing rice while Brazil has the absolute advantage in producing coffee. Figure 4.20 shows simplified production possibilities for the two countries. This is based on each country devoting half of its resources to each of the products.

If each country specialises in the product in which it has an absolute advantage and then trades, based on opportunity cost ratios, total output will rise and both countries will be able to consume more products. Table 4.4 shows output before and after specialisation.

In this case, the opportunity cost of producing 1 tonne of rice in Indonesia is two-fifths of a tonne of coffee while in Brazil it is 2.5 tonnes of coffee. An exchange rate of 1 tonne of rice for 1.5 tonnes of coffee lies between the opportunity cost ratios and will benefit both countries. Table 4.5 shows the countries' positions after Indonesia has exchanged 300 tonnes of rice for 450 tonnes of coffee.

KEY TERM

Absolute advantage: used in the context of international trade, a situation where, for a given set of resources, one country can produce more of a particular product than another country.

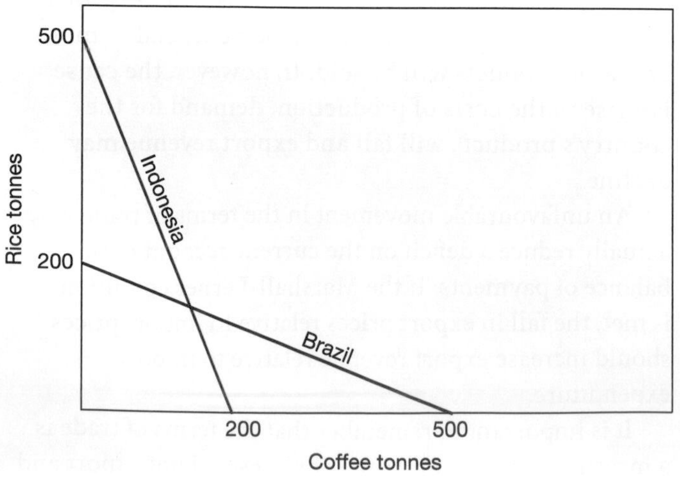

Figure 4.20 Absolute advantage

Comparative advantage

Although absolute advantage explains a small proportion of global trade, more trade is based on **comparative advantage**. Some countries buy products from abroad that their own producers would be capable of producing with fewer resources. This is because it enables its producers to concentrate on producing those products they are even better at producing. For example, the USA may be more efficient than Bangladesh at producing both coats and shirts. Nevertheless, both countries can still benefit from specialising and trading if the USA concentrates on producing the product it is more efficient at producing and Bangladesh specialises in the product it is not so relatively inefficient in producing.

The USA has the comparative advantage in producing coats. It can make four times as many coats as Bangladesh but only one and a quarter as many shirts. It can also be seen that the USA has the comparative advantage as its opportunity cost of producing coats (2½ shirts: 10,000/4,000) is lower than Bangladesh's (8 shirts: 8,000/1,000).

Bangladesh has the comparative advantage in making shirts as it can make them at a lower opportunity cost. In Bangladesh for every shirt produced, one-eighth of

KEY TERM

Comparative advantage: used in the context of international trade, a situation where a country can produce a product at a lower opportunity cost than another country.

	Before specialisation		After specialisation	
	Rice	Coffee	Rice	Coffee
Indonesia	500	200	1,000	
Brazil	200	500		1,000
Total	700	700	1,000	1,000

Table 4.4 Absolute advantage: specialisation

	Rice (tonnes)	Coffee (tonnes)
Indonesia	700	450
Brazil	300	550
Total	1,000	1,000

Table 4.5 Absolute advantage: specialisation and trade

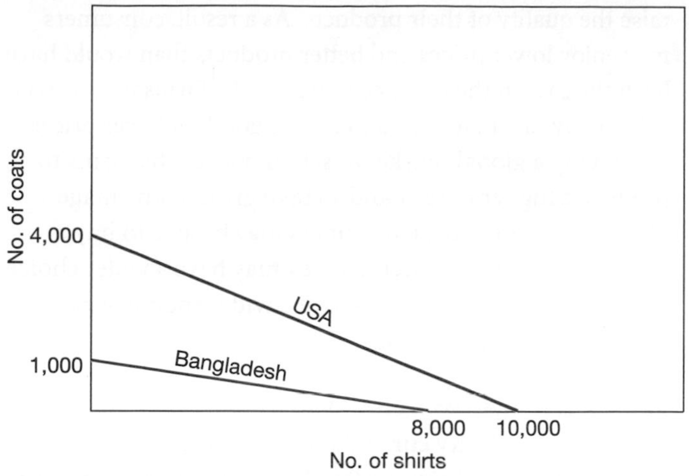

Figure 4.21 Comparative advantage

	Before specialisation		After specialisation	
	Coats	**Shirts**	**Coats**	**Shirts**
USA	4,000	10,000	8,000	
Bangladesh	1,000	8,000		16,000
Total	5,000	18,000	8,000	16,000

Table 4.6 Comparative advantage: the benefits of specialisation

a coat has to be sacrificed, In contrast, in the USA, the opportunity cost of producing a shirt is two-fifths of a coat. Table 4.6 shows how specialisation increases output by 1,000 units.

Despite its importance, comparative advantage does not provide a full explanation of the pattern of global trade. There are a number of reasons for this. Some governments may want to avoid overspecialisation, transport costs may offset the comparative advantage, the exchange rate may not lie between the opportunity cost ratios and other governments may impose trade restrictions.

The theory of comparative advantage also assumes that resources are mobile and that there are constant returns. If the USA did decide to double its output of coats, there is no guarantee that workers and other resources will be able to switch from making shirts to making coats. Even if they are able to do so, it also does not necessarily mean that the extra resources will be as productive as those first employed and so using double the resources may not lead to double the output.

In addition, countries do not always adapt to changes in comparative advantage. For example, over time a country may continue to produce steel despite another country being relatively more efficient at producing it. In such a case, those involved in steel production in the country that has lost the comparative advantage may try to persuade their government to impose trade restrictions on steel imported from the country that has now gained the comparative advantage. In a world with many countries and a vast number of products, it may be difficult to determine where a country's comparative advantage lies.

SELF-ASSESSMENT TASK 4.9

Peru has a strong fishing industry and has a comparative advantage in producing fishmeal, which is used in food for chickens. The country has fertile fishing grounds along its coasts, which benefit from two currents, the Humboldt current and El Nino. Some of the fish caught is used as a raw material in the production of fishmeal.

Peru has a long tradition in producing fishmeal, with its workers well-skilled in the production process. The country is a major producer and exporter of the product. The industry's future prospects and its comparative advantage may be influenced by climate changes and changes in the country's labour costs relative to those in other fishmeal producing countries.

1 Explain **one** reason why Peru has a comparative advantage in producing fishmeal.

2 Explain the difference between a comparative advantage in producing a product and a competitive advantage in producing that product.

TOP TIP

If you are going to include a numerical example to illustrate comparative advantage, keep the example brief and the figures straightforward – e.g., 5,000 rather than 5,136 – and make sure they accurately show comparative advantage. Also do not just rely on an example, but provide a lucid written explanation as well.

KEY CONCEPT LINK

Scarcity and choice, equilibrium and efficiency: In considering what products countries will produce the concepts of scarcity, choice and efficiency are important. Countries have a limited quantity of resources so they cannot produce all they would like to. The concept of comparative advantage can help them decide how to use their resources. It suggests they should concentrate on producing those products they are most efficient at producing.

The benefits of free trade

Free international trade is the exchange of goods and services across national borders without any government restrictions. When free trade exists, firms are free to export and import what they want in the quantities they want. No taxes or limits are imposed on exports and imports, no subsidies are given to distort cost advantages and there is no unnecessary paperwork involved.

Free trade allows an efficient allocation of resources with countries being able to concentrate on producing those products that they have a comparative advantage in. Allowing countries to specialise in those products where their production is most efficient should increase world output and employment and so should raise living standards.

KEY TERM

Free trade: international trade not restricted by tariffs and other protectionist measures.

Factor endowments – that is, the availability and the quality of resources – differ between countries. Free trade permits countries that have, for instance, fertile land and the appropriate climate to concentrate on growing oranges while other countries that have the financial institutions and well-educated workers to concentrate on banking.

The competition that may arise from free trade can put pressure on firms to keep their prices and costs down and raise the quality of their products. As a result, consumers may enjoy lower prices and better products than would have been the case in the absence of free trade. Firms may also be able to buy raw materials and capital goods at lower prices.

Having a global market to sell to may enable firms to produce a higher output and so take greater advantage of economies of scale. Consumers may be able to buy a greater variety of products as they may have a wider choice of products, Firms may also have a wider source of raw materials and capital goods.

Trading possibility curve

A **trading possibility curve** shows how an economy can benefit from specialising and trading. For example, a country may be able to produce a maximum of 50 million units of clothing or 100 million units of food. For every 1 unit of clothing it produces it gives up the opportunity to produce 2 units of food. Engaging in international trade may enable the country to specialise in clothing production and import three units of food for every unit of clothing it exports.

KEY TERM

Trading possibility curve: a diagram showing the effects of a country specialising and trading.

In this case, trading will increase the total quantity of products the country can consume. If the country had initially produced 40 million units of clothing, the maximum output of food it could produce would be 20 million units. If, however, it engages in international trade, it can specialise in clothing production making 50 million units of clothing. It can export 10 million units of clothing in exchange for

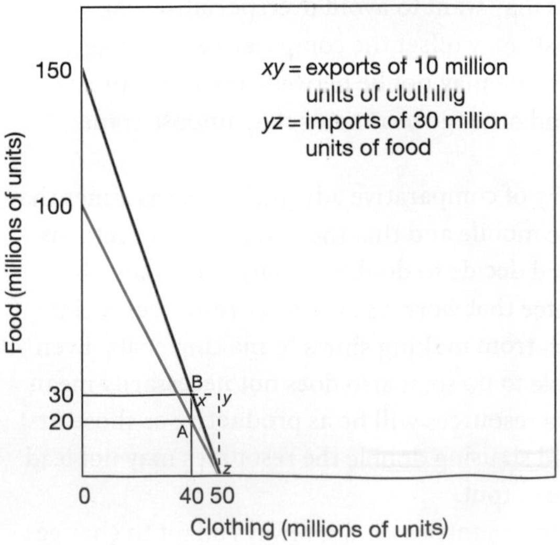

Figure 4.22 Trading possibility curve diagram

30 million units of imported food, enabling it to move from point A to point B and enjoy more products.

Trade blocs

There are a number of **trade blocs**, regional groupings of countries that have preferential trade agreements between member countries.

Free trade areas

In this type of trade bloc, the governments of the member countries agree to remove trade restrictions between each other. The members are allowed to determine their own external trade policies towards non-members. An example of a **free trade area** is the North American Free Trade Agreement (NAFTA). This consists of the USA, Canada and Mexico.

Customs unions

Customs unions go a stage further in terms of economic integration than free trade unions. As well as removing trade restrictions between members, members of a customs union agree to impose a common external tariff

KEY TERMS

Trade bloc: a regional group of countries that have entered into trade agreements.

Free trade area: a trade bloc where member governments agree to remove trade restrictions among themselves.

Customs union: a trade bloc where there is free trade between member countries and a common external tariff on imports from non-members.

SELF-ASSESSMENT TASK 4.10

Read the feature below and answer the questions that follow.

Canada's changing current account position

Canada's international trade is mainly with its neighbour, the USA – 72% of Canada's exports are sold to the USA and the country buys 58% of its imports from the USA.

Canada is a member of a trade bloc, NAFTA. Denmark is also a member of a trade bloc, the European Union.

Denmark's international trade is less reliant on one country. Germany is its main source of imports (supplying 17%) and the main destination of its exports (buying 20%).

Year	Canada's current account position US$bn	Canada's current account position as % of GDP	Denmark's current account position US$bn	Denmark's current account position as % of GDP
2007	21.9	1.6	4.7	2.1
2008	12.5	0	4.4	1.2
2009	−3.9	−1.8	8.5	1.5
2010	40.4	1.9	14.2	2.9
2011	50.0	2.2	18.3	4.6
2012	49.0	2.3	19.7	5.4
2013	67.0	3.5	16.7	4.7

Table 4.7 Canada's and Denmark's current account positions

1 Explain one advantage and one disadvantage of trading mainly with one country.

2 Identify one difference between a free trade area, such as NAFTA, and an economic union, such as the EU.

3 Compare the changes in Canada's and Denmark's current account positions over the period shown.

on trade with non-members. The world's oldest customs union is the Southern Africa Customs Union (SACU). Its members include Botswana, Lesotho, Namibia, South Africa and Swaziland. These countries impose the same tariff on goods being imported from outside the trading bloc. The countries share tariff revenues and coordinate some trading policies.

Economic unions

An **economic union** includes even more economic integration. In this case, restrictions are removed on the movement not only of goods and services, but also capital and labour. Mercosur is a South American trading bloc which has Argentina, Brazil, Paraguay, Uruguay and Venezuela as full members. It is seeking to create a single market across the members. The European Union (EU) is even more integrated. It operates a single market and its members have adopted the same policies on a number of labour market and social issues. Most of the members have adopted the same currency, the euro, and the European Central Bank operates a single interest rate. Figure 4.23 shows the membership of the EU in 2014.

Monetary union involves economies operating the same currency, as the members of the euro area do. Full economic union is the final stage of integration. This involves the

> **KEY TERM**
>
> **Economic union:** a trade bloc where there is free trade between member countries, a common external tariff and some common economic policies, which may include a common currency.

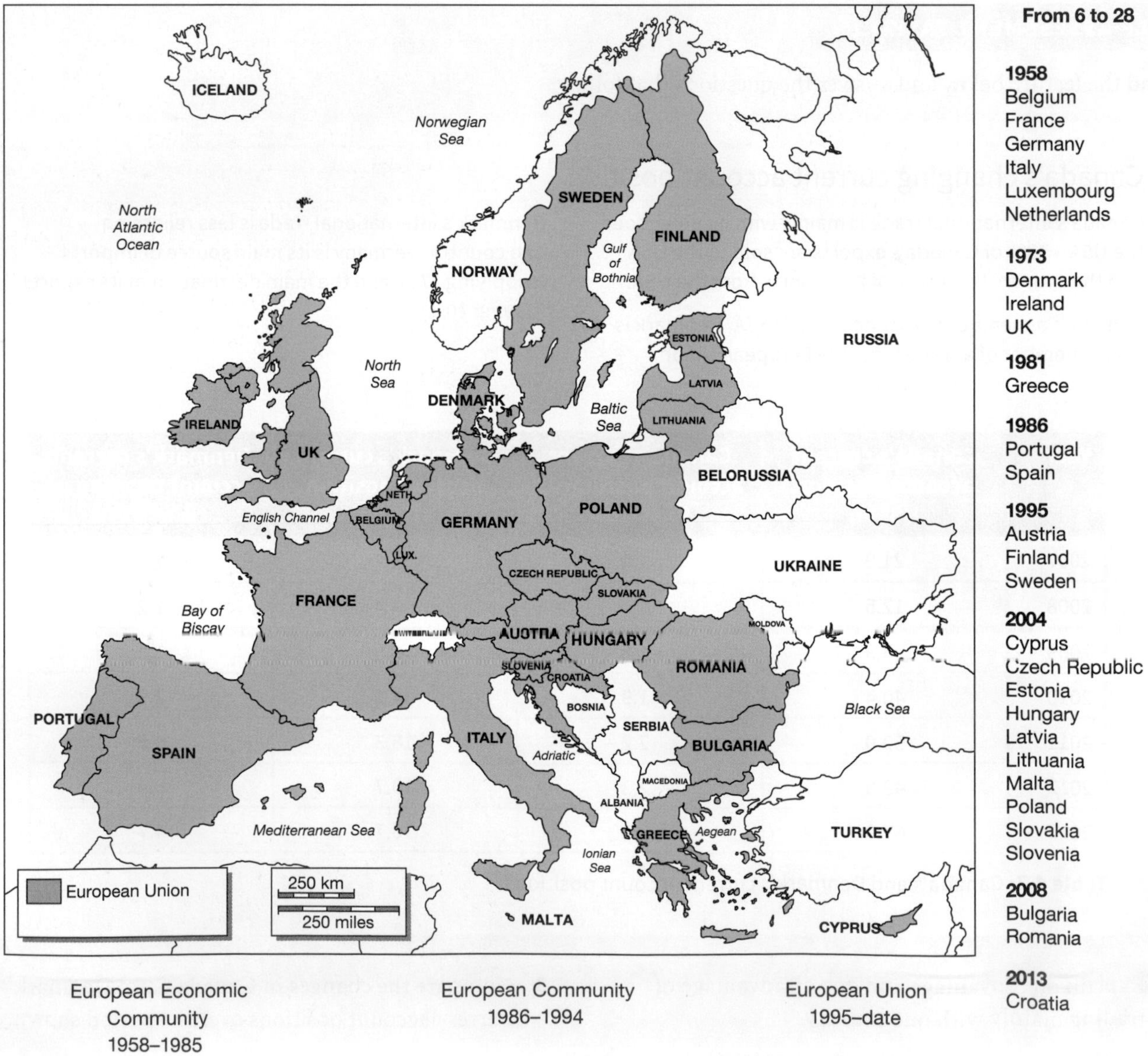

Figure 4.23 The new Europe

members having the same currency and following all the same economic policies. In effect, the different economies become one economy. This occurred when the 13 original states formed the United States of America.

Trade creation and trade diversion

Trade creation

Membership of a trade bloc may give rise to **trade creation.** This occurs when the removal of tariffs allows members to specialise in those products in which they have a comparative advantage. More expensive domestic products can be replaced by imports from another member country that are lower in price. The efficient firms within the trade bloc will be able to sell to a larger market and this may enable them to lower prices even further because they will be able to take greater advantage of economies of scale.

KEY TERM

Trade creation: where high-cost domestic production is replaced by more efficiently produced imports from within the customs union.

Figure 4.24 shows the effect of trade creation. Before joining the trade bloc, the price of the product in the country is *P* and the quantity consumed is *Q*. Of this amount, Q_a is supplied by domestic producers and $Q_a - Q$ amount is imported. When the country joins the trade bloc, it can import the product without paying the tariff. This pushes down the price to P_1 and the amount consumed increases to Q_1. Consumers clearly gain from the lower price and the greater quantity consumed. Domestic producers lose as their sales fall and they gain a lower price. They may, however, be shifting resources to making products that have now become more price competitive relative to those of member countries because of the removal of other tariffs. Indeed, trade creation permits both imports to be purchased more cheaply but also additional exports to be sold as other members lose their tariff protection. The domestic government will lose out on tariff revenue but there is nevertheless a welfare gain. The lower price increases consumer surplus by *a, b, c* and *d* amount. Producer surplus falls by *a* amount and tariff revenue by *c* amount, giving a net gain of *b* and *d* amount.

Trade diversion

Trade diversion occurs when membership of a trade bloc results in a country buying imports from a less efficient country within the trade bloc rather than from a more efficient country outside. This results in a less efficient allocation of resources. Efficient countries outside the trade bloc may lose as they are not now able to trade on equal terms. A country joining the trade bloc may also lose. Figure 4.25 shows that originally the country buys a product from the most efficient country and places a tariff on imports of the product. The price paid is *P*, the quantity consumed is *Q* and the tax revenue earned is *c* + *e*. When the country joins the trade bloc, trade is diverted to a member country. The price to consumers falls to P_1 and the quantity consumed rises to Q_1. Consumer surplus increases again by *a, b, c* and *d* amount. Producer surplus falls by *a* amount but this time, tariff revenue will fall by *c* and *e* amount. Welfare will be reduced if the areas *b* and *d* are smaller than area *e*.

KEY TERM

Trade diversion: where trade with a low-cost country outside a customs union is influenced by higher-cost products supplied from within.

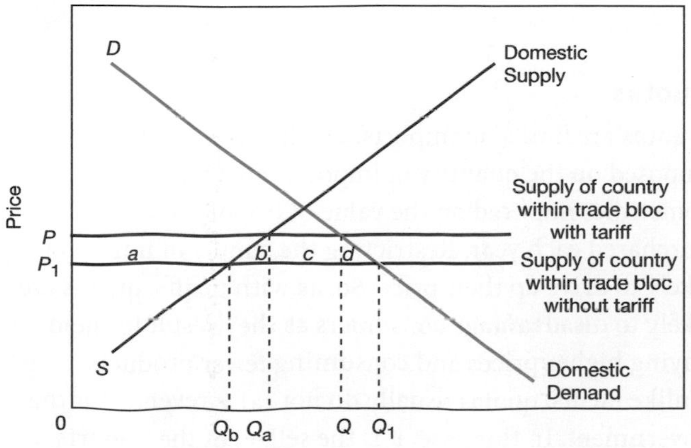

Figure 4.24 Trade creation

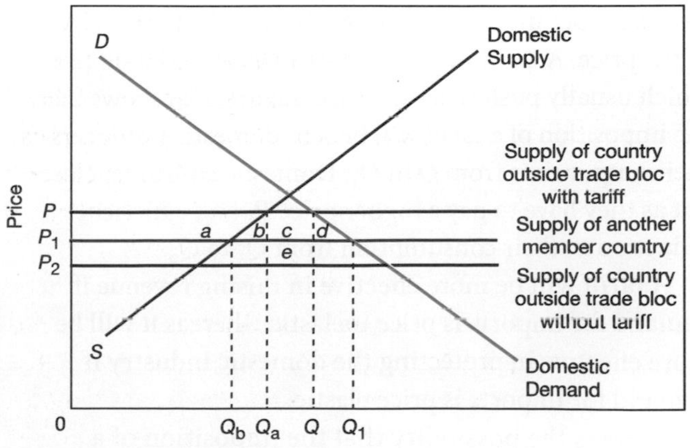

Figure 4.25 Trade diversion

Name	Membership
Association of Southeast Asian Nations (Asean)	Brunei, Burma, Cambodia, Indonesia, Laos, Malaysia, Philippines, Singapore, Thailand, Vietnam
Caribbean Community and Common Market (Caricom)	Anguilla, Antigua and Barbuda, Bahamas, Belize, Dominica, Grenada, Guyana, Haiti, Jamaica, Montserrat, Saint Kitts and Nevis, Saint Lucia, Saint Vincent and the Grenadines, Suriname, Trinidad and Tobago
East African Community (EAC)	Kenya, Rwanda, Tanzania and Uganda
Economic Community of West African States (ECOWAS)	Benin, Burkina Faso, Cape Verde, Gambia, Ghana, Guinea, Guinea-Bissau, Ivory Coast, Liberia, Mali, Niger, Nigeria, Senegal, Sierra Leone, Togo
GCC (Gulf Cooperation Council)	Kuwait, Bahrain, Kuwait, Oman, Qatar, Saudi Arabia, United Arab Emirates

Table 4.8 Examples of trade blocs and their membership

Protectionism

Protectionism involves protecting domestic industries from foreign competition. It restricts free trade and the methods used often seek to increase domestic industries' relative price competitiveness.

KEY TERM

Protectionism: protecting domestic producers from foreign competition.

Methods of protection and their impact

Tariffs

Tariffs are the best known method of protection and are sometimes referred to as customs duties. Tariffs are taxes usually on imports but may also be imposed on exports. There are two key motives behind taxing exports; these are to raise revenue and to increase supply of the product on the domestic market. Revenue raising may also be the reason for taxing imports. The other motive is to discourage consumption of imports. A tariff can be specific, that is a fixed sum per unit, or *ad valorem*, which is a percentage of the price. A tariff imposes an extra cost on the supplier which usually pushes up the price. Figure 4.26 shows that the imposition of a tariff will benefit domestic producers as their output rises from Q to Q_1. Domestic consumers lose out as they have to pay a higher price P_1 and experience a reduction in their consumption from Q_3 to Q_2.

A tariff will be more effective in raising revenue if demand for imports is price inelastic whereas it will be more effective in protecting the domestic industry if demand for imports is price elastic.

There is the possibility that the imposition of a tariff may not make domestic products more price

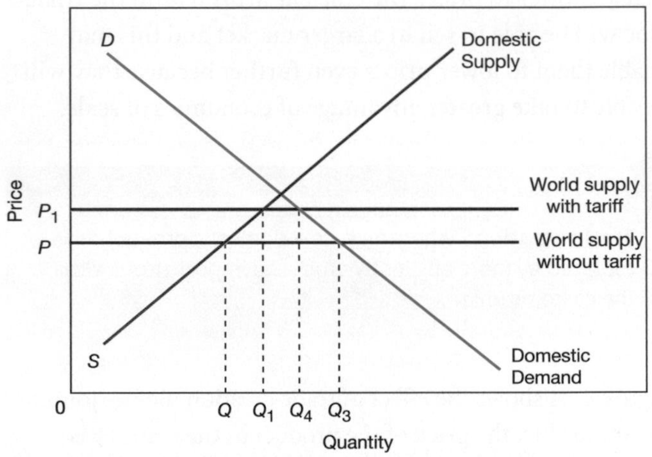

Figure 4.26 The effect of imposing a tariff

competitive. This would be the case if the price of the import plus the tariff is still below the domestic price or if firms selling the imports absorb the tariff and do not raise their prices.

KEY TERM

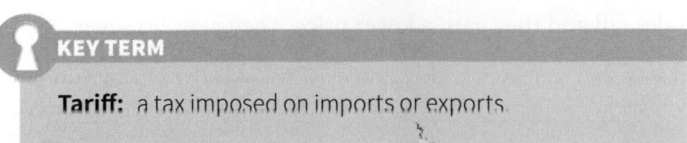

Tariff: a tax imposed on imports or exports.

Quotas

Quotas are limits on imports. The limits are usually imposed on the quantity of imports but are also sometimes imposed on the value of imports that can be purchased each year. Restricting the supply of imports is likely to drive up their price. So, as with tariffs, quotas are likely to disadvantage consumers as they result in them paying higher prices and consuming fewer products. Unlike tariffs, quotas usually do not raise revenue for the government. In this case, it is the sellers of the imports that will receive the extra amount per unit paid by consumers. In some cases, however, licences are sold to foreign firms to sell some allocation of the quota.

KEY TERM

Quota: a limit on imports or exports.

Exchange control

Instead of limiting the imports directly, a government may place limits on the amount of foreign exchange that can be purchased in order to buy imports, travel abroad or invest abroad. This is known as **exchange control**.

KEY TERM

Exchange control: restrictions on the purchases of foreign currency.

Export subsidies

Subsidies may be given to both exporters and to those domestic firms that compete with imports. In both cases domestic firms will, in effect, experience a fall in costs. This will encourage them to increase their output and lower their price. This may enable them to capture more of the markets at home and abroad.

The losers will be the foreign firms and domestic taxpayers. Domestic producers will gain. Consumers will also benefit in the short run. In the long run, however, they may lose if the more efficient foreign firms are driven out of business and the subsidised domestic firms raise their prices.

Embargoes

An **embargo** is a complete ban either on the imports of a particular product or on trade with a particular country. A government may want to ban the import of a product that it regards as harmful, e.g., non-prescription drugs or weapons. A ban on trade with a particular country may arise from political disputes.

KEY TERM

Embargo: a ban on imports and/or exports.

Voluntary export restraints

Voluntary export restraints are sometimes also called voluntary export restrictions. They are an agreement by an exporting country to restrict the amount of a product that it sells to the importing country. The exporting country may be pressured into signing such an agreement or it may agree in return for the importing country also agreeing to limit the exports it sells of another product.

KEY TERM

Voluntary export restraint: a limit placed on imports reached with the agreement of the supplying country.

Economic and administrative burdens ('red tape')

A government may seek to discourage imports by requiring importers to fill out time consuming forms. It may also set artificially high product standards to restrict foreign competition. Such measures restrict consumer choice.

Keeping the exchange rate below its market value

A government may manipulate the country's exchange rate in order to give its producers a competitive advantage. This may lead to other governments lowering their exchange rates.

The arguments in favour of protectionism

Despite the potential advantages of free trade, most countries impose import restrictions. There are a number of arguments that may be put forward for doing this.

To protect infant industries

Firms in a new industry may find it difficult to survive when faced with competition from more established, larger foreign firms. This may be because the foreign firms are taking advantage of economies of scale and benefiting from their names being well-known.

Protecting a new **infant industry** may give it time to grow and so benefit from economies of scale and to gain a global reputation. If the infant (also called sunrise) industry has the potential to develop into an efficient industry in line with comparative advantage, then using trade restrictions may be justified. It is, however, difficult to identify which new industries will develop and gain a comparative advantage. It is, for example, very difficult to estimate the long-run average cost curves of firms in the industry.

There is also the risk that an infant industry may become dependent on protection. Knowing that rival foreign products are being made artificially expensive, it may not feel any pressure to lower its costs.

KEY TERM

Infant industries: new industries that have a low output and a high average cost.

To protect declining industries

If declining (also called sunset) industries, which have lost their comparative advantage, go out of business quickly there may be a sudden and large rise in unemployment. If the industry is granted protection and that protection is gradually removed, unemployment might be avoided. As the industry reduces its output, some workers may retire and some leave for jobs in other industries.

There is again, however, a risk that the industry may resist reductions in the protection it receives. This can lead to considerable inefficiency. For example, a country's steel industry may have lost its comparative advantage while its car industry does have a comparative advantage. If the government imposes tariffs on steel, it will disadvantage its car industry, which will now have to buy more expensive steel from domestic producers. This will raise the car industry's costs of production and so may lose it sales at home and abroad.

To protect strategic industries

Some governments seek to protect industries that produce products they regard as strategic, such as weapons, fuel and food. They may not want to be dependent on foreign supplies of these products. For example, a government may be worried that firms and households in its country would be seriously disadvantaged if fuel was cut off due to a trade dispute or a military conflict. As a result it may protect some home industries even if they are relatively inefficient.

To prevent dumping

There may be an economic justification for imposing trade restrictions in the case of dumping as this practice may be regarded as unfair competition. **Dumping** involves selling products at below their cost price. In the short run, home consumers will benefit from dumping as they will enjoy lower prices. In the long run, however, if the foreign firms drive out the domestic firms, they may gain a monopoly and then raise their prices. Indeed, foreign firms may engage in dumping with the specific intention of gaining control of a market in another country by destroying existing competition and preventing new domestic firms from becoming established.

Foreign firms may be able to engage in dumping by covering losses with previous supernormal profits, by charging high prices in their home markets or because they receive subsidies from their governments.

In practice, it can be difficult to determine if dumping is taking place or whether the foreign firms have gained a comparative advantage.

KEY TERM

Dumping: selling products in a foreign market at below their cost of production.

To improve the terms of trade

If a country purchases a large proportion of another country or countries' exports of a product, it may be able to force down its price. By imposing trade restrictions, it can lower demand and as its demand is significant this may lead to a lower price. This will improve the country's terms of trade and allow it to purchase more imports for the same quantity of exports.

Similarly, if a country accounts for a significant proportion of the world's supply of a product, quotas on its exports may improve its terms of trade. Restricting the supply of exports will drive up their price and so increase the purchasing power of exports.

Of course, such action distorts trade and is likely to reduce global output. It may also provoke retaliation.

To improve the balance of payments

A government may impose trade restrictions in order to improve its current account position. For instance, imposing tariffs may encourage consumers to switch from buying imports to buying domestic products.

This again, however, may provoke retaliation. If foreign governments do retaliate by imposing their own trade restrictions then, while the country's imports may fall, so might its exports. International trade would decline and again global output would fall. In addition, if the country's products are not internationally competitive because of strategic problems, trade restrictions would only provide a short-term boost to the current account.

To provide protection from cheap labour

It is sometimes argued that trade restrictions should be imposed on products from countries where wages are very low. The view is that, in order to compete, wages and so living standards in the country would have to fall. This is not a very strong argument. Low wages do not always mean that a country will be able to produce products more cheaply as labour productivity may be low and so labour costs may actually be relatively high. If low wages are actually linked to low costs, it may indicate that the countries have a comparative advantage.

There may be moral arguments for imposing trade restrictions on products produced using slave or child labour. Even here, however, other approaches may be more appropriate as trade restrictions may drive down wages even further in relatively poor countries.

Other reasons

There are a number of other reasons why a government may impose trade restrictions. Tariffs may be used to raise revenue. This will be successful if demand for imports is inelastic.

A government may also engage in trade restrictions to try to persuade another government to reduce its trade protection. By retaliating against, for instance, another government imposing a quota on its exports, it may persuade the other government to remove its quota. There is, however, a risk that a trade war will develop.

In addition, a government may seek to protect a range of industries to avoid the risks attached to overspecialisation.

TOP TIP

Remember that the arguments for free trade are, in effect, also the arguments against protectionism. Similarly, the arguments for protectionism are the arguments against free trade.

When students are asked to write about the arguments for protectionism, they often just devote too much attention to describing the methods of protectionism. Always consider very carefully what a question is asking.

SELF-ASSESSMENT TASK 4.11

In recent years there has been less use made of tariffs and quotas to protect domestic industries but a rise in the use of other ways of reducing imports and increasing exports. These include government subsidies and the provision of loans on favourable terms from state-owned banks.

In 2012 a trade dispute broke out between China and the USA. The USA imposed tariffs on Chinese solar-panel exporters claiming they were receiving government subsidies to engage in dumping. The Chinese threatened to retaliate by imposing tariffs on a range of American imports. Eventually the dispute was settled with the Chinese producers agreeing to sell the solar panels at an agreed minimum price.

1 Why might favourable loans to exporters be regarded as a form of trade protection?
2 Why is dumping regarded as unfair competition?
3 Explain why government subsidies to exporters may not increase exports.

SUMMARY

In this chapter it has been shown that:

- Aggregate demand is total spending on goods and services produced in an economy at different price levels.
- The aggregate demand curve is downward sloping.
- Aggregate supply is total output in an economy at different price levels.
- One of the causes of a shift to the left of the short-run aggregate supply curve is an increase in costs of production.
- The long-run aggregate supply curve will shift to the right if the quantity and/or quality of resources increases.
- Macroeconomic equilibrium is achieved where the *AD* and *AS* curves intersect.
- The general price level in an economy can be measured by means of a weighted price index.
- Inflation can be caused by increases in aggregate demand (demand-pull inflation) or increases in aggregate supply (cost-push inflation).
- Among the costs of inflation are a loss of international competitiveness, a random redistribution of income, menu costs, shoe leather costs, fiscal drag, discouragement of investment and inflationary noise.
- The benefits of inflation include stimulating output, reducing debt and preventing unemployment.
- Inflation is likely to have more of an adverse effect if it is high, accelerating, unstable and caused by cost-push factors.
- Deflation may be caused by a decrease in aggregate demand or an increase in aggregate supply.
- The balance of payments is a record of a country's international transactions and is composed of the current account, the capital account, the financial account and net errors and omissions.
- A current account deficit may be more serious if it is caused by structural problems as in this case it will not be self-correcting.
- A financial account deficit may be a cause for concern if it is the result of a lack of confidence in the economy.
- Current account disequilibrium can affect economic activity and the exchange rate.
- A floating exchange rate is determined by demand for and supply of the currency whereas a fixed exchange rate is set by the government and a managed float by both market forces and government intervention.
- A floating exchange rate has the potential advantages of eliminating current account deficits, avoids the need for reserves and is not a government target, but it does not provide the certainty of a fixed exchange rate.
- A floating exchange rate may rise if demand for exports increases, demand for imports falls, the country attracts more investment and currency dealers speculate that the value will rise.
- A fixed exchange rate is maintained by the central bank buying and selling the currency and changing the rate of interest.
- A rise in the exchange rate may reduce net exports and aggregate demand and produce a current account surplus.
- The Marshall-Lerner condition states that a fall in the exchange rate will only improve the current account position if the combined price elasticities of demand for exports and imports is greater than 1.
- A rise in the exchange rate can cause a reverse J-curve effect.
- The terms of trade is a measure of the ratio of export and import prices.
- A fall in the exchange rate will worsen the terms of trade.
- Absolute advantage and comparative advantage emphasise the benefits of free trade.
- Free international trade can increase output, lower prices, increase choice, raise employment.
- Countries may form trade blocs, which include free trade unions, customs unions and economic unions.
- Membership of a trade bloc can increase trade or divert trade away from more efficient producers to less efficient producers.
- Among the methods of protection are tariffs, quotas, exchange control, subsidies, embargoes, voluntary export restraints and excessive administrative burdens.
- Among the motives for imposing trade restrictions are to protect trade restrictions, to slow down the decline of sunset industries, to protect strategic industries, to improve the terms of trade and to improve the balance of payments position.

Exam-style questions

1 Explain how an economy may face a deficit in its trade in goods yet have a surplus on its current account of the balance of payments. [8]

Source: Cambridge International AS and A Level Economics 9708 Paper 23 Q4 October/November 2012.

2 Discuss whether a satisfactory balance of payments, a strong exchange rate and a low rate of inflation are likely to be achieved at the same time. [12]

Source: Cambridge International AS and A Level Economics 9708 Paper 23 Q4 October/November 2012.

3 **The price of rice in international trade**

Between January 2002 and July 2008 the world price of rice, a staple food for many people in developing countries, rose by slightly over 300%. As shown in Figure 4.26 the price of rice changed very significantly in the six months to July 2008 and was influenced by the actions of different governments.

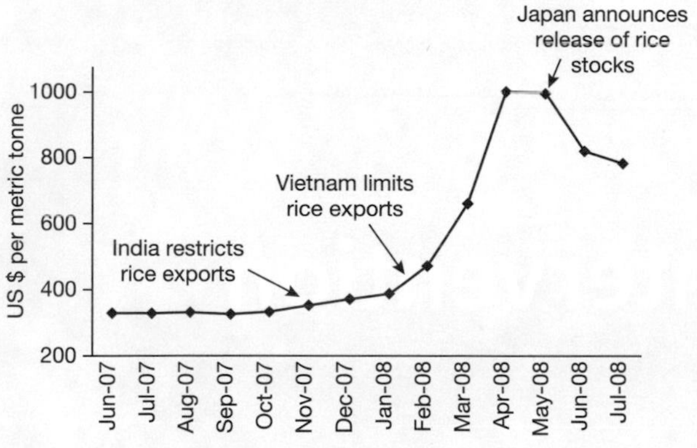

Figure 4.26 Actions of different governments and the world price of rice

The rise in the price of rice was typical of a wide range of commodities. These price rises caused food and fuel riots in developing countries. As a result some governments turned to protectionist trade measures. Vietnam limited rice exports while Cambodia and Egypt banned all rice exports.

The Indian Government replaced the minimum export price that it enforced for non-basmati rice with a complete ban on rice exports. At the same time it placed restrictions on wheat imports for the purpose of disease control.

a Calculate the approximate world price of rice in January 2002. [2]

b With reference to Figure 4.26, analyse the different causes of the price movements of rice from November 2007 to April 2008, and then after May 2008. [4]

c Explain **two** possible economic reasons for India's introduction of export restrictions. [4]

d i How might an effective minimum price for exports have helped India's position? [2]

ii Why might India have changed from the use of a minimum export price to an export ban? [2]

e Discuss the potentially harmful effects of India's protectionist trade policy for both its own economy and that of the rest of the world. [6]

Source: Cambridge International AS and A Level Economics 9708 Paper 22 Q1 October/November 2011.

Chapter 5: Government macro intervention

AS Level

Learning objectives

On completion of this chapter you should know:

- the aims of macroeconomic policy
- what is meant by fiscal, monetary and supply side policies
- the aims and instruments of each policy
- how fiscal, monetary and supply side policies may correct a balance of payments disequilibrium
- the factors that influence the effectiveness of fiscal, monetary and supply side policies to correct a balance of payments disequilibrium
- how fiscal, monetary and supply side policies may correct inflation and deflation
- the factors that influence the effectiveness of fiscal, monetary and supply side policies to correct inflation and deflation.

The aims of macroeconomic policy

The main government macroeconomic policy aims are:

- full employment
- low and stable inflation
- balance of payments equilibrium
- steady and sustained economic growth
- avoidance of exchange rate fluctuations
- sustainable economic development.

At any one time, a government may prioritise one objective. For example, if the inflation rate is at 20% and rising, a government may decide to concentrate on achieving price stability.

The macroeconomic policy aims are examined in more detail in Chapter 10. To achieve macroeconomic policy aims, a government will use a range of policy measures. In examining macroeconomic policy measures, the key concepts of efficiency, equilibrium and progress are important.

Types of policy

Fiscal policy

Fiscal policy is the use of taxation and government spending to manage aggregate demand in order to achieve the government's macroeconomic aims.

Reflationary or expansionary fiscal policy is designed to increase aggregate demand. This can be achieved by a government increasing its spending and/or cutting tax rates or the tax base. In contrast, deflationary or contractionary fiscal policy is intended to lower aggregate demand. This time, the government will reduce its spending and/or increase taxes.

Changes in government spending may be the result of changes in government policy or the result of changes in economic activity. Deliberate changes in government spending and taxation can be referred to as **discretionary fiscal policy.**

A government can also allow **automatic stabilisers** to influence aggregate demand. Automatic stabilisers are forms of government spending and taxation that change, without any deliberate government action, to offset fluctuations in GDP. For example, during a recession, government spending on unemployment benefits automatically rises because there are more unemployed people. Tax revenue from corporation tax, income tax and indirect taxes will fall automatically as profits, incomes and expenditure decline. Figure 5.1 shows how tax revenue and government expenditure change automatically as GDP changes.

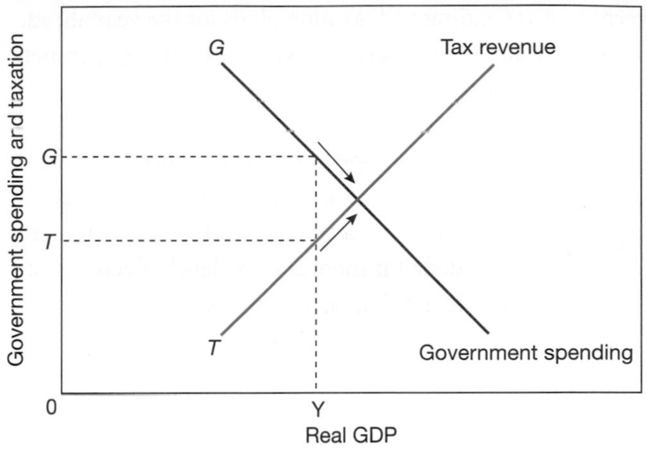

Figure 5.1 The automatic stabilisation process

KEY TERMS

Fiscal policy: the use of taxation and government spending to influence aggregate demand.

Discretionary fiscal policy: deliberate changes in government spending and taxation.

Automatic stabilisers: changes in government spending and taxation that occur to reduce fluctuations in aggregate demand without any alteration in government policy.

Initially, the economy is operating below full employment at Y with a significant gap between government spending and taxation. As GDP rises, government spending on benefits falls while tax revenue rises with more people in employment and so receiving more income.

KEY CONCEPT LINK

Equilibrium and efficiency: Equilibrium and efficiency are important key concepts when assessing an economy's initial macroeconomic position. If an economy is in macroeconomic equilibrium below full capacity, it is not being productively efficient.

The budget position

The annual **budget** is a statement of fiscal policy. It often achieves much media attention as it is an indicator of both fiscal policy intentions and economic performance. In the budget statement, the finance minister outlines the

KEY TERM

Budget: an annual statement in which the government outlines plans for its spending and tax revenue.

government's spending and taxation plans for the year ahead. A budget surplus arises when tax revenue exceeds government spending. In contrast, a budget deficit occurs when government spending exceeds tax revenue and a balanced budget is when government spending matches tax revenue.

Most governments seek to achieve a balanced budget over time. In the short term, a government may aim for, or welcome, a budget deficit if there is a low level of economic activity. A budget deficit that occurs due to automatic stabilisers is known as a **cyclical deficit**. A government is unlikely to be concerned about this as it will move towards a balance as economic activity increases. A government will, however, be concerned about a **structural deficit**. This arises when a government is committed to too much spending relative to its tax revenue. In this case, the deficit will not disappear when GDP increases. In practice, a budget deficit may contain both cyclical and structural elements.

KEY TERMS

Cyclical budget deficit: a budget deficit caused by changes in economic activity.

Structural budget deficit: a budget deficit caused by an imbalance between government spending and taxation.

TOP TIP

Be very careful to avoid confusing a budget deficit and a current account deficit.

Monetary policy

Monetary policy refers to any policy measures or instruments to influence the price or quantity of money. The three instruments of monetary policy are the **interest rate**, the **money supply** and the exchange rate.

Monetary policy, like fiscal policy, seeks to influence aggregate demand. Again reflationary or expansionary monetary policy is intended to increase aggregate demand.

KEY TERMS

Monetary policy: the use of interest rates, direct control of the money supply and the exchange rate to influence aggregate demand.

Interest rate: the price of borrowing money and the reward for saving.

Money supply: the total amount of money in a country.

In this case, this may be achieved by a cut in the interest rate, an increase in the money supply and a reduction in the foreign exchange rate. To reduce aggregate demand, deflationary or contractionary monetary policy may be adopted. This might include a rise in the interest rate, a decrease in the money supply and an increase in the foreign exchange rate.

Monetary policy measures are usually implemented by the central bank of the country or area. In recent years, in a number of countries, changes in interest rates have been the main policy measure used to control inflation and, more recently, to influence economic activity.

A central bank may also target the money supply in the economy as changes in the money supply can influence aggregate demand. Policy measures to change the money supply include those that seek to influence lending by commercial banks. This is because such lending is a major cause of changes in the money supply.

Exchange rate measures include government decisions on what type of exchange rate system to operate and, in the case of a managed and fixed exchange rate, at what rate to set the exchange rate.

The growth of Islamic finance

Financial institutions in more and more countries are offering Islamic finance. Among the most important centres in the Middle East are Iran, Kuwait, the UAE and Saudi Arabia. In Asia, Pakistan, Bangladesh, China, India and Indonesia are leading providers of Islamic finance. In Europe the main centre is in London in the UK.

Islamic finance is finance that complies with sharia, the religious law and moral code of Islam. Sharia bans the charging and payment of interest and excessive risk-taking. Instead, it encourages the sharing of risks between financial institutions and their customers. For instance, mortgages may be given on the basis that those seeking to buy a house pay rent for a period of time. Savings accounts may be paid a proportion of the bank's profits and firms that need finance may pay a proportion of their profits. Investment is permitted in shares in firms that do not produce alcohol, tobacco or pornography.

Supply side policy

Supply side policy measures are designed to increase aggregate supply by improving the workings of product

KEY TERM

Supply side policy: measures designed to increase aggregate supply.

SELF-ASSESSMENT TASK 5.1

Read the feature below and then answer the questions that follow.

Changes in monetary policy

The main monetary policy measure used has traditionally been direct changes in the central bank's interest rate, called bank or repo rate, and such changes have been mainly used to control inflation. In the first decade and start of the second decade of the 2000s, however, the governments of a number of countries – including Japan, the USA and the UK – shifted their priorities to encouraging an increase in economic activity. To achieve this they adopted rather more unorthodox monetary policy measures concerned with changing interest rates more indirectly and with providing details about future plans on interest rates.

One of these measures is what is known as quantitative easing. This involves the central bank printing money in order to buy financial assets, particularly government bonds. This measure indirectly lowers the rate of interest. This is because the higher demand for bonds pushes up their price and enables a lower interest rate to be paid on them. A lower interest rate may increase consumer expenditure and investment.

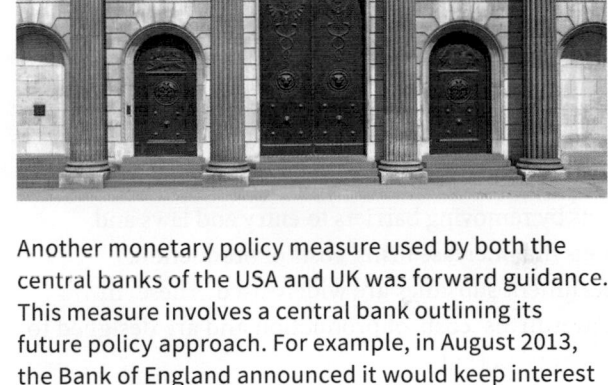

Another monetary policy measure used by both the central banks of the USA and UK was forward guidance. This measure involves a central bank outlining its future policy approach. For example, in August 2013, the Bank of England announced it would keep interest rates unchanged until unemployment had fallen to 7%. The intention of forward guidance is to provide greater certainty and so to encourage investment. It is regarded as a monetary policy measure as it is connected with decisions on the rate of interest.

1 In what circumstance would quantitative easing allow a central bank to move the change in the price level back in line with its inflation target?

2 What effect may quantitative easing have on the price of shares?

3 Explain what could reduce the effectiveness of forward guidance.

and factor markets. They may involve reducing government intervention or, in some cases, increasing it. The measures include cutting corporation tax, cutting income tax, reducing welfare payments, increasing spending on education and training, increasing spending on infrastructure, trade union reform, privatisation, deregulation and provision of government subsidies.

Cutting corporation tax may encourage investment, as firms will have more funds to invest and they will know that they will be able to keep more of any profit earned. More investment will increase both aggregate demand and aggregate supply. Cutting income tax may encourage workers to increase their working hours and accept promotion and greater responsibility. It may also persuade some workers to stay in the labour force for longer and persuade others to enter the labour force.

A reduction in welfare payments may encourage some of the unemployed to put more effort into searching for a job.

Increasing spending on education and training may raise the quality of education and training. If this does occur, workers' skills and productivity may increase as well as their flexibility and mobility. Trade union reform may also increase workers' flexibility and mobility and cut down on the number of days lost through strikes. Increasing spending on infrastructure can reduce firms' transport costs.

SELF-ASSESSMENT TASK 5.2

Decide whether the following are examples of fiscal, monetary or supply side policy measures:

a an increase in unemployment benefit

b an increase in government spending on state pensions

c an increase in the rate of interest

d a reduction in restrictions on bank lending

e a reduction in legal restrictions on firms

f a reduction in the exchange rate.

TOP TIP

Remember supply side policy measures always seek to increase aggregate supply. No government will try to reduce aggregate supply.

In deciding whether a change in income tax, corporation tax or a cut in unemployment benefit is a fiscal or supply side policy measure, think about what the intention is. If the government is trying to influence aggregate demand then it is a fiscal policy measure, whereas if the government is seeking to increase aggregate supply, it is a supply side policy measure.

Many countries in recent years have adopted privatisation programmes in the belief that firms operate more efficiently in the private sector. Some have also deregulated a number of markets by removing barriers to entry and laws and regulations that increase firms' costs of production.

Government subsidies are widely used. These, in effect, lower firms' costs of production and are designed to increase firms' output.

Figure 5.2 compares the three types of policies.

Policies to correct balance of payments disequilibrium

Policy approaches

There are two broad-based policy approaches that can be used to correct an imbalance in the balance of payments. These are expenditure switching and expenditure dampening policies.

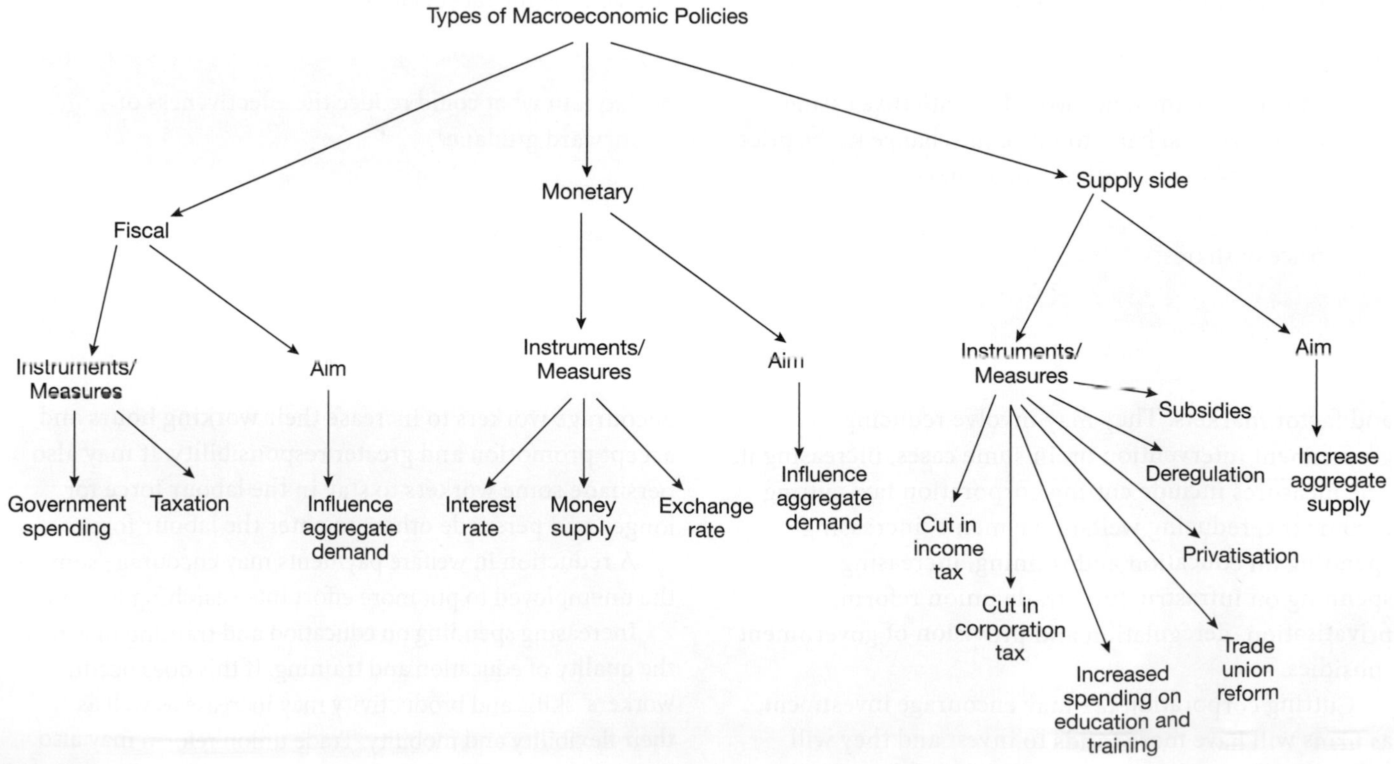

Figure 5.2 Macroeconomic policies

SELF-ASSESSMENT TASK 5.3

Read the feature below and answer the questions that follow.

Brazil aims to be the top spender on education

The Brazilian government is planning to increase its spending on education to 10% of its GDP by 2020, which would be a world record. It already spends a higher proportion, 5.7%, of its GDP on education than most other countries. Many economists, however, argue that Brazil is not getting value for money from its spending. A relatively high proportion of children who leave school without continuing on to higher education have low levels of literacy and numeracy. Teachers are relatively well-paid and many retire in their early 50s on generous pensions.

1 Why is an increase in government spending on education defined as a supply side policy measure?

2 Analyse the effect on aggregate supply of increasing the age at which teachers retire.

Expenditure switching policies

An **expenditure switching policy** is any action taken by a government that is designed to persuade purchasers of goods and services both at home and abroad to buy more of that country's goods and services and less of the goods and services of other countries. Effectively this would include any policy measures designed to persuade domestic households and firms to buy domestically produced goods and services rather than imports. It would also include policy measures designed to persuade foreign households and firms to buy more exports from the domestic economy. These policies are not designed to reduce the total amount of spending in a country but to redirect or 'switch' spending to the country's products rather than those produced in other countries. The intended impact is a fall in import expenditure and a rise in export earnings. The former will lead to a fall in the supply of a country's currency on the foreign exchange market and the latter will lead to a rise in the demand for the country's currency on the market. Both will lead to upward pressure on the exchange rate.

Expenditure dampening policies

An **expenditure dampening or reducing policy** is any action taken by a government that is designed to reduce the total level of spending in an economy. Such a policy has two effects. One is a reduction in spending, which will mean that there will be fewer purchases of imported goods and services. The second is that domestic producers will find that their domestic market is 'dampened'. As a result, they may try to make up for the decrease in domestic sales with an increase in sales abroad. The overall effect, therefore, of an expenditure dampening policy may be a fall in imports and a rise in exports.

KEY TERM

Expenditure switching policy: policy measures designed to encourage people to switch from buying foreign-produced products to buying domestically produced products.

KEY TERM

Expenditure dampening or reducing policy: policy measures designed to reduce imports and increase exports by reducing demand.

KEY CONCEPT LINK

Scarcity and choice: Choice is an important key concept when deciding whether to select expenditure switching or expenditure dampening policies. If, for example, an economy is experiencing high unemployment it is more likely to select expenditure switching rather than expenditure dampening policies.

KEY CONCEPT LINK

Equilibrium and efficiency: In considering how domestic firms respond to being protected from foreign competition it is useful to make use of the key concept of efficiency. Domestic firms may feel less pressure to seek to be productively, allocatively and dynamically efficient if imports become more expensive due to the imposition of tariffs.

Fiscal policy

If a country is experiencing a deficit on the current account of its balance of payments, it may use a variety of fiscal policy measures. To reduce total expenditure, it could increase income tax and reduce government spending. A rise in income tax will reduce disposable income, leaving less income for household to spend on imports as well as domestically produced products. Lower government spending will directly reduce demand for goods and services which, as noted above, may reduce imports and put pressure on domestic firms to increase their exports.

As well as using fiscal policy as an expenditure dampening measure, it can also be used as an expenditure switching measure. To encourage domestic consumers and firms to switch to buying domestic products, a government may impose a tariff or increase an existing tariff on imports. Such a measure works more effectively when high quality, domestically produced substitutes are available.

The effectiveness of fiscal policy

Fiscal policy measures may alter a country's current account position in the short term but are unlikely to be a long-term solution. This is because once the policy measures are stopped, households and firms are likely to go back to spending the same amount on imports relative to the amount of export revenue earned.

Raising taxes may also have adverse side effects. They lower demand, which may increase unemployment and slow economic growth. Higher taxation can also create disincentive effects and so may reduce aggregate supply.

Imposing tariffs against fellow members of a trade bloc is not an option. Imposing or increasing tariffs against other countries involves two risks. One is that it may provoke retaliation and the other is that it may reduce the pressure on domestic firms to become more efficient.

Monetary policy

Reducing the growth of the money supply may be used as an expenditure dampening or an expenditure switching measure. Changing the rate of interest to influence the current account position is a more complex process. If an economy has a low rate of inflation and a current account deficit, its central bank may reduce the interest rate in a bid to put downward pressure on a floating exchange rate. A lower exchange rate may result in the country's products becoming more internationally competitive but there is a risk it may generate inflationary pressure. In contrast, a higher interest rate may act as a dampening policy measure, reducing demand for imports and reducing inflationary pressure. It may, however, raise a floating exchange rate that could reverse the fall in demand for imports.

A government may decide to alter its exchange rate as an expenditure switching measure. If an economy is experiencing a current account surplus and has a fixed exchange rate, the government may decide to revalue its currency. Raising the foreign exchange rate, as mentioned in Chapter 4, will raise export prices and lower import prices. In the case of a current account deficit, a government may consider devaluing the currency. In this case, export prices will fall and import prices will rise.

The effectiveness of monetary policy

In practice, it can be difficult to control the money supply. This is partly because commercial banks have a strong incentive to try to increase their lending and may seek to get round any limits a central bank seeks to impose on the growth of their lending. Trying to control certain forms of money may lead to new forms of money being used.

Using interest rates is also not without problems. There is a time lag between changing interest rates and the full effect being transmitted to the macroeconomy. Some economists have estimated that it can take as long as 18 months for interest rate changes to have their full impact. This is, however, less time than in the case of some fiscal policy measures.

Interest rate changes may be a powerful policy measure but they are also a blunt and uncertain one. Some households and firms are more likely than others to cope with a change in the interest rate. For example, a rise in the rate of interest harms borrowers but benefits savers. A higher interest rate may also have an adverse effect on unemployment and economic growth, as with a deflationary fiscal policy measure.

With increasing mobility of financial expenditure, it can be difficult for a country to operate an interest rate that is significantly different from rival countries. If, for example, the country reduces its rate of interest to a level noticeably lower than that of its rival countries, hot money may flow out of the country.

A rise in the rate of interest may discourage foreign direct investment as it would raise foreign firms' costs and the firms may expect demand to fall in the country.

There are also challenges in using the exchange rate to influence the balance of payments position. For example, lowering the exchange rate will not work if demand for exports and imports is price inelastic or if the relative quality of the country's products falls.

As with fiscal policy measures, most monetary policy measures are not likely to be an effective long-term solution to balance of payments problems. The one exception may be a government deciding to stop maintaining an exchange rate that is set above or below the market value. For example, if a central bank has been keeping an exchange rate above its equilibrium level, the high export prices and low import prices may have led to a current account deficit. In this case, allowing the exchange rate to increase to its market rate may reduce the country's deficit.

TOP TIP

In considering the impact of deflationary fiscal and monetary policy measures, it is useful to consider the initial level of economic activity.

Supply side policy

Supply side policy measures may reduce a current account deficit and a financial account deficit by making domestic products more price competitive and by making domestic markets more attractive to invest in. For instance, deregulation and privatisation may increase

SELF-ASSESSMENT TASK 5.4

Read the feature below and then answer the questions that follow.

The Egyptian Central Bank takes action

Egypt's current account deficit rose significantly in 2013. This contributed to a fall in the country's official reserves and led to a reduction in the value of the Egyptian pound (£E). The depreciation was, in effect, equivalent to a wage cut and reduced living standards, at least in the short run.

Concerns over the growing current account deficit and falling reserves led the central bank to increase its exchange controls. Some economists expressed concern that the exchange controls would discourage foreign direct investment.

1 Why may a current account deficit cause a country's reserves to fall?

2 Explain why a depreciation is 'equivalent to a wage cut' in the short run.

3 Analyse why exchange controls may discourage foreign direct investment.

the competitive pressure on domestic firms to keep costs and prices low, to improve quality and to become more responsive to changes in consumer demand.

Increased spending on education and training and increased investment may also increase exports and encourage foreign direct investment. A more skilled labour force and better capital equipment may reduce the relative price of domestic output and raise its quality. Both of these effects will be likely to increase domestic firms' share of the home market and the global market.

A skilful labour force and good quality capital equipment may also attract foreign multinational companies to set up branches in the country in expectation they will be able to produce good quality products at low cost. Portfolio investment may also increase as the country's economic prospects are likely to improve as a result of higher aggregate supply.

Trade union reform may enable domestic firms to work with more flexibility and so be more responsive to changes in demand. A resulting fall in industrial action may, in addition, make multinational companies more willing to invest in the country.

The effectiveness of supply side policies

Some supply side measures, for example increased spending on education, may not be very effective in the short term as they can take a long time to have an effect. In the long term, however, they have the potential to be very effective. This is because they may directly tackle the problems causing the country's products to lack international competitiveness.

The outcome of supply side policy measures is, however, uncertain. For example, cutting income tax may encourage some people to work fewer hours if they are currently content with their earnings. Providing more education and training may not be very effective if it is not of a high quality or it develops skills that will not be in demand in the longer term.

Privatisation may not result in an increase in efficiency if the privatised industries become monopolies and do not take into account external costs and benefits. Deregulation and trade union reform may also result in increased inefficiency if there is market failure in the product and labour markets, which laws and trade union power initially countered.

Providing subsidies to firms may not always result in lower prices of domestically produced products. This is because the firms may not pass on the subsidies to consumers and the payment of subsidies may make the firms complacent. There is also the risk that subsidies may provoke retaliation as foreign governments may see them as unfair competition.

KEY CONCEPT LINK

Equilibrium and efficiency: Efficiency is an important concept in assessing whether privatisation and deregulation have increased the performance of the firms that have been affected.

SELF-ASSESSMENT TASK 5.5

In 2011 Thailand's government introduced a scheme whereby it agreed to buy rice from Thai farmers at a price significantly above the market price. It was thought that this measure would not only help Thailand's farmers but would also push up the global price of rice. With Thailand being the world's largest producer, the government thought that the reduced supply of Thai rice on the global market would allow it to sell its stockpiles of rice later at a high price. What actually happened was that buyers switched their purchases to other countries. These included Bangladesh, India and Vietnam, which captured a larger share of the global market.

1 How else might the Thai government have used the money it spent on the scheme to increase the country's share of the global rice market?

2 Assess whether the scheme would have increased Thailand's aggregate supply.

Policies to correct demand-pull inflation

To reduce demand-pull inflation, governments employ deflationary fiscal and deflationary monetary policy measures. Income tax rates may be increased, the threshold at which people start paying the tax may be reduced and the tax base may be widened. Governments may cut their own spending and this may be the more favoured option in countries, such as Pakistan, where only a relatively small proportion of the population pay income tax.

In many countries, the main policy used to reduce demand-pull inflation is monetary policy with the focus being on the interest rate. Indeed, many central banks are now given a target rate for inflation and instructed to use interest rate changes to achieve it. If the inflation rate is rising outside its target range, a central bank is likely to raise the rate of interest. This form of deflationary monetary policy may reduce demand-pull inflation for a number of reasons. The cost of borrowing is likely to rise which may discourage large-scale purchases including the purchase of houses and cars. Savings may be increased as the return from saving will rise. The opportunity cost of saving is, of course, spending. A higher interest rate may also attract hot money which may increase the external value of a floating exchange rate. This is likely to put downward pressure on domestic prices as domestic firms will face increased competitive pressure at home and abroad and lower imported raw material costs.

Monetarists argue that the only way to reduce inflationary pressure is to lower the growth of the money supply. If increases in the money supply do not exceed increase in output, they suggest there will be no upward movement of the price level.

To reduce the risk of demand-pull inflation in the longer term, governments use supply side policy measures. Over time aggregate demand tends to increase. If increases in aggregate supply can keep pace with higher aggregate demand, a country can enjoy higher output (higher real GDP) without experiencing inflation. This situation is shown in Figure 5.3.

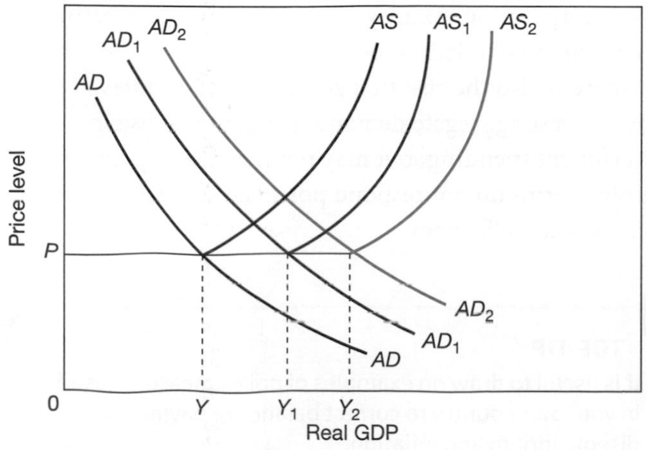

Figure 5.3 Non-inflationary economic growth

SELF-ASSESSMENT TASK 5.6

In 2013 the Mexican government introduced a number of new taxes. These included a value-added tax of 16% on public transport and a tax of 8% on food containing a high number of calories. It also imposed a flat sum tax on soft drinks.

These taxes pushed up the price of food and contributed to a rise in Mexico's inflation rate at a time when poverty was increasing in the country. The top 10% of income earners in Mexico spend less than a quarter of their disposable income on food. This contrasts with the 50% spent by the half of the population with the lowest income.

1 Define a flat sum tax.
2 Explain why imposing a tax on public transport may increase a country's inflation rate.
3 What effect would a reduction in poverty be likely to have on food's weighting in Mexico's consumer price index?
4 Discuss whether imposing a tax on food would increase poverty.

The effectiveness of policies to correct demand-pull inflation

Raising income tax to reduce demand-pull inflation may backfire. This is because workers may seek higher wages to maintain their disposable income. If their wage claims are granted, firms' costs of production may increase. Higher costs can generate cost-push inflation. Higher income tax rates may also, as noted earlier, create disincentive effects. Some workers may respond to a reduction in disposable income by leaving the labour force. This will reduce the economy's productive capacity and so reduce aggregate supply.

There are a number of reasons why a rise in the rate of interest may not discourage consumer expenditure. Commercial banks usually do keep their interest rates in line with the central bank's as it is the rate they will have to pay if they need to borrow from the central bank. There is, however, no guarantee that they will always raise their interest rates when the central bank increases its rate. Even if consumers are faced with higher interest rates, they may not reduce their spending if they are optimistic about the future. (The same applies to a rise in income tax where households may cut their saving rather than their spending if they think their incomes will rise in the future.)

A rise in interest rates may have an adverse effect on investment. This is because it will increase the cost of borrowing funds to invest and will increase the opportunity cost of using profits to invest. If investment falls below depreciation, the capital stock will decline. The resulting decrease in aggregate supply can push up the price level.

Some countries may face constraints on the fiscal and monetary policy measures that they can use to correct inflation. Governments may be worried that if they raise income taxes higher than those operating in rival countries, some of their skilled workers may emigrate. Countries that are members of an economic union may operate the same interest rate and the same exchange rate as other members and the area's central bank may make the decisions on these areas of monetary policy. Another constraint may operate in the case of a country operating a fixed exchange rate. In this case, its central bank may be reluctant to raise the interest rate as it may put upward pressure on the exchange rate.

Supply side policy measures have the potential to benefit all of a government's policy objectives in the long term. They can reduce inflationary pressure, raise economic growth, lower unemployment, stabilise an exchange rate, reduce a current account deficit and promote development. In the short run, however, some supply side policy measures may contribute to inflation. For instance, increased government spending on education and cuts in income tax may increase aggregate demand before they increase aggregate supply.

In addition, as previously mentioned, the effects of supply side policy measures are uncertain. For instance, privatised firms that have considerable market power may raise their prices.

Policies to correct cost-push inflation

In the short term, a government may instruct its central bank to raise the exchange rate in a bid to reduce cost-push inflation. Such a measure may reduce raw material and capital costs and is likely to put pressure on domestic firms to find ways to cut their costs.

Governments may also employ supply side policy measures to correct cost-push inflation. For example, increased spending on training can raise labour productivity and so reduce labour costs or at least reduce the upward pressure on labour costs. Lower corporation tax may encourage firms to buy more efficient capital equipment, which can also put downward pressure on price rises.

SELF-ASSESSMENT TASK 5.7

Between June 2013 and December 2013 the UK's inflation rate, as measured by changes in the consumer price index, fell from 2.9% to 2%. Prices were, nevertheless, rising at more than twice pay increases.

The central bank, the Bank of England, had kept its interest rate unchanged at an all-time low of 0.5% since March 2009. This was despite rising economic growth and falling unemployment.

1 What was happening to UK workers' purchasing power between June and December 2013?
2 Explain why a central bank may keep its interest rate unchanged despite 'rising economic growth and falling unemployment'.

A government may decide to provide subsidies to firms facing, for instance, higher fuel costs, so that they do not have to raise their prices. It may also hope that firms may use some of the subsidies to buy new capital equipment, which may lower prices in the longer term.

The effectiveness of policies to correct cost-push inflation

A rise in the exchange rate may not reduce inflation, if foreign producers decide to keep the price of their exports unchanged in the country's currency. The country's firms may also not respond to the increased competitive pressure to keep down their cost and price rises.

Increased spending on training may be successful in raising the skills of workers but if their pay rises by more than their productivity, costs of production will still rise. Lower corporation tax may not result in more investment if firms are pessimistic about the future.

There is also the risk that government subsidies may increase aggregate demand, through the rise in government spending, but may not increase aggregate supply if firms do not respond positively by using them to increase their efficiency.

TOP TIP

It is useful to draw on examples of policy measures used in your own country to correct balance of payments disequilibrium and inflation.

SELF-ASSESSMENT TASK 5.8

Read the feature below and then answer the questions that follow.

Problems facing the Turkish economy

At the start of 2014 the Turkish economy was facing a number of macroeconomic problems. These included a rising inflation rate and a growing account deficit with declining exports.

The Turkish government had set an inflation target of 5% but in January 2014 the inflation rate was 7%. The Turkish central bank raised the interest rate to 7.75% in a bid to reduce the inflation rate. It was, however, concerned about the effect this move would have on its exchange rate and its current account position.

The economy's current account deficit was largely the result of increases in the price of oil and gas. Turkey was importing 97% of the energy it was consuming, mainly from Russia. The government had signed a deal with a Franco-Japanese consortium to build the country's second nuclear power station. It was also investing more in education, in particular employing more teachers.

1 Explain why a rising inflation rate may contribute to a growing current account deficit.
2 Discuss whether a rise in a country's interest rate would reduce a current account deficit.
3 Assess the effect that Turkey's supply side policy measures may have on the country's imports.

Policies to correct deflation and their effectiveness

A government will not seek to stop good deflation but it will be anxious to correct bad deflation. To reverse a fall in aggregate demand and the price level, governments employ reflationary fiscal and monetary policy measures. For example, a government may increase its spending, cut tax rates, reduce interest rates and/or increase the money supply.

A rise in government spending may be more effective than the latter three policy measures. This is because firms and households may be pessimistic during periods of deflation and so may not spend more even if their disposable incomes rise and it becomes cheaper to borrow.

When interest rates are low it may not be possible to reduce them much further and any cuts may have little effect. For instance, a 2% interest rate is already low so if firms and households are not borrowing, it suggests they are concerned about future economic prospects. So if the interest rate is reduced to 1.5%, it is unlikely to stimulate increased borrowing and spending.

Central banks may increase the money supply, increasing the funds commercial banks have available to lend. The banks, however, may be reluctant to lend because they may think there is an absence of creditworthy borrowers.

TOP TIP

In assessing the effectiveness of one type of policy, it is often useful to compare it with the other two types of policy.

Keep up-to-date with changes in government policy measures.

KEY CONCEPT LINK

Scarcity and choice, progress and development: Choice and progress are key concepts in deciding which policy measures a government should select to achieve a particular macroeconomic objective. In making its choice, a government will consider which policy measure is most likely to result in macroeconomic progress.

SELF-ASSESSMENT TASK 5.9

From the early 1990s Japan experienced periods of deflation and stagnant economic growth. A vicious cycle was created with consumers delaying purchases, firms cutting wages and employment, and consumer expenditure falling further.

In 2012, the new prime minister Shinzo Abe introduced 'Abeconomics'. This was a policy combination of expansionary fiscal and monetary policies designed to encourage households and firms to spend more and so end deflation and stimulate economic growth. The government was increasing its spending, increasing the money supply and encouraging a fall in the foreign exchange rate in a bid to achieve an inflation rate of 2%. It was also urging firms to increase the wages they pay.

1 Explain how an expansionary fiscal policy measure may encourage households and firms to spend more.

2 Assess the influence that expectations may play in breaking a vicious cycle of deflation.

3 Assess what impact a lower exchange rate may have on the domestic price level.

SUMMARY

In this chapter it has been shown that:

- The instruments of fiscal policy are government spending and taxation and the instruments of monetary policy are interest rates, the money supply and the exchange rate.
- Among supply side policy measures are cuts in tax rates, reductions in welfare payments, increased spending on education and training, trade union reform, privatisation, deregulation and government subsidies.
- Governments may use expenditure dampening or expenditure switching measures to reduce a current account deficit. Expenditure dampening measures seek to reduce demand for domestically and foreign produced products, while expenditure switching measures try to encourage households and firms to buy more domestically produced products and less foreign-produced products.
- Fiscal and monetary policy measures may only improve the current account position in the short term and may have adverse side effects on the government's other macroeconomic objectives.
- Supply side policy measures may provide longer-term solutions to a current account deficit and a financial account deficit but the effects of the measures are uncertain and some may take time to have an effect.
- Deflationary fiscal and monetary policies are used to correct demand-pull inflation and supply side policy measures are used to prevent it occurring in the long term.
- There is no guarantee that higher tax rates and higher interest rates will discourage consumer expenditure.
- Among the measures a government may use to reduce cost-push inflation are a rise in the country's foreign exchange rate, increased government spending on training and cuts in corporation tax.
- Foreign firms selling products to the country do not have to allow the price of their products to fall in line with a revaluation of the country's currency, a more skilled labour force may not reduce costs if wages rise by more than output and government subsidies may not always reduce inflationary pressure.
- Reflationary fiscal and monetary policy measures are used to correct deflation but their effectiveness may be limited if households and firms are worried about the country's future economic prospects.

Exam-style questions

1 Explain the causes of an increase in a current account surplus on a country's balance of payments. **[8]**

2 Discuss whether a reduction in the rate of interest will reduce a current account surplus on a country's balance of payments. **[12]**

3 **Inflation Targeting**

Many central banks use 'inflation targeting'. Their principal aim is to achieve a particular annual rate of inflation within an acceptable range. For example, they might aim for a 2% rate of inflation but will accept a rate between 1% and 3%. Some economists claim that inflation targeting will help reduce the actual rate of inflation. The Central Bank of Turkey uses this approach and Table 5.1 shows how well it has worked.

	2003	2004	2005	2006	2007	2008
Target rate	20	12	8	5	4	4
Actual rate	18.4	9.3	7.7	9.7	8.4	10.8

Table 5.1 Inflation in Turkey 2003–2008 (annual % rate)

In 2008 Turkey faced two particular difficulties. The New Turkish Lira (TRY) depreciated by 30% and food prices rose because of drought. Within the Turkish Consumer Price Index, food has a high weighting of 31%.

How successful five countries were in controlling inflation in 2008 is shown in Figure 5.4.

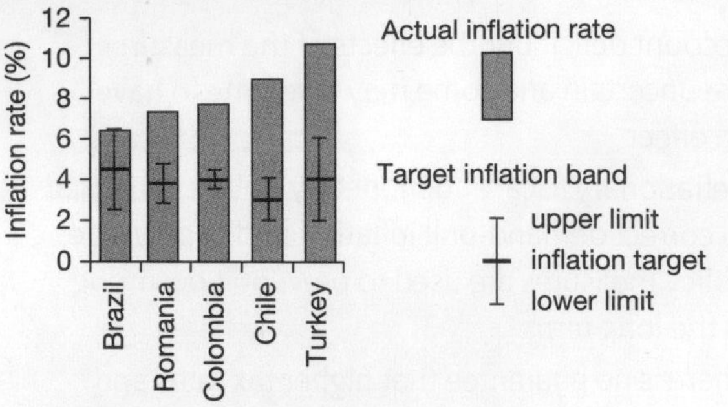

Figure 5.4 Target and actual inflation rates in five countries, 2008

a **i** In which year was Turkey most successful in meeting its inflation target? **[1]**

ii In which year was Turkey least successful in meeting its inflation target? **[1]**

b Explain the likely effect of the depreciation of the New Turkish Lira on Turkey's rate of inflation. **[4]**

c With reference to Figure 5.4, how might differences between the inflation targets and actual inflation rates in Chile and Brazil in 2008 be explained? **[4]**

d How might having a target for inflation affect the causes of inflation? **[4]**

e Discuss the possible problems of constructing an accurate consumer price index. **[6]**

Source: Cambridge International AS and A Level Economics 9708 Paper 21 Q1 May/June 2012.

Chapter 6: Basic economic ideas and resource allocation A Level

Learning objectives

On completion of this chapter you should know:

- what economists mean by an efficient resource allocation and why this is an important microeconomic concept
- what is meant by economic efficiency
- what is meant by productive and allocative efficiency, Pareto optimality and dynamic efficiency
- reasons for market failure
- what is meant by positive and negative externalities and why they lead to an inefficient allocation of resources
- what are private costs, external costs and social costs; private benefits, external benefits and social benefits
- how cost–benefit analysis can be used as an aid to decision making.

Introduction

The fundamental economic problem was considered earlier in Chapter 1. This was explained as the difficulty of having limited or scarce resources with which to do an infinite number of things. In turn, this leads us to having to make choices.

The basic concept of **economic efficiency** stems from this fundamental economic problem. Economic efficiency is said to exist when it could be judged that all of our scarce resources are being used in the 'best' possible way. This means that the greatest possible level of infinite wants is being met with those scarce resources. In agriculture, for example, it is where maximum crop yields result from farming a given area of land, or in manufacturing, where as much output as possible is produced from a given set of inputs. Economic efficiency is a very important concept in Economics. It is something that is always judged to be desirable. It represents the best possible solution to the economic problem. As you will see, it pervades many of the topics that follow, both microeconomic and macroeconomic.

KEY TERM

Economic efficiency: where scarce resources are used in the most efficient way to produce maximum output.

Economic efficiency consists of:

- **Productive efficiency:** This occurs when firms produce at the lowest possible cost. A firm is productively efficient when it is making the best use of resources and producing at the lowest cost possible. For example, it can apply where a car assembly plant is using the most up-to-date technology, minimising the cost of producing each vehicle.
- **Allocative efficiency:** This occurs when firms produce the combination of goods and services that are most wanted by consumers. The implication is that there is no waste and both producers and consumers are satisfied with what is produced. The price that they are willing to pay reflects their preferences and the benefits they derive from consumption. It represents the additional benefit derived from the consumption of one more unit of a particular good. The marginal cost of production is a measure of the opportunity cost of the resources used to produce this unit (see Chapter 7). So, where the price equals the marginal cost, consumers are prepared to pay what it costs to produce it. It is only where this is so that resources are efficiently allocated.

KEY TERMS

Productive efficiency: when a firm is producing at the lowest possible cost.

Allocative efficiency: where price is equal to marginal cost; firms are producing those goods and services most wanted by consumers.

When both these parts of economic efficiency co-exist then it is determined that the best possible use is being made of scarce resources. This, therefore, constitutes a situation of efficient resource allocation. This ideal has particular relevance when evaluating the efficiency of market structures (see Chapter 7).

This notion of economic efficiency can be looked at from a global perspective. Economic efficiency is achieved when economies are using all of the world's resources in the best possible way. We frequently hear concerns that, as a global society, we are failing to do this. This point is very clearly made in Chapter 4 where the use of protectionist trade policies is considered. We have to conclude that global economic efficiency is not being achieved.

A few more simple examples will help to explain the macro nature of economic efficiency:

- Oil: The global supply of oil will one day run out, although just when this will happen is not clear. Consumption continues to increase not only in developed economies but increasingly in developing and emerging economies such as Brazil, China, India and Pakistan. Growing populations, rising living standards and rocketing car ownership levels are just three reasons behind this increase in demand. Here and elsewhere the use of oil is invariably inefficient; much is wasted through traffic congestion, the use of gas-guzzling vehicles and the inefficient use of oil and oil products in manufacturing.
- Timber: The world demand for timber and timber products such as paper and cardboard shows little sign of abating. By the start of this century, only about one-fifth of the world's forests remained intact, with the worst destruction being that of the Amazonian rainforests and other forests in the Congo Basin, Canada and South East Asia. The costs of this destruction are overlooked by the large, powerful global companies who control the sale of timber and pulp on the world market.
- Water: As the global population grows and the effects of climate change become reality, water as a resource will get scarcer and be an even greater political issue. This is already beginning to occur in those countries that share natural water resources such as China and India. Scant attention is often paid in developed countries as to how more efficient use can be made of this essential resource.

> **KEY CONCEPT LINK**
>
> **Equilibrium and efficiency, scarcity and choice:** The above examples and the earlier explanation of different types of efficiency are underpinned by the fundamental problem in economics. Since resources are scarce, it is essential that they are used in the most efficient way in order to maximise what is produced to benefit producers and consumers.

Productive efficiency

For productive efficiency to exist, goods and services must be made using the least possible resources and at the minimum possible cost. Productive efficiency can be shown through a firm's average cost curve as shown in Figure 6.1.

The production possibility curve, which was introduced in Chapter 1, will help to clarify productive efficiency. This curve shows the maximum production points for combinations of any two products (e.g., capital goods and consumer goods produced in an economy). Given this, productive efficiency can only exist when an economy is producing right on the boundary of its production possibility frontier as in Figure 6.2. The problem with point *X* is that more products could be made with the resources available. In other words, the goods are not being produced using the least possible resources: this is productive inefficiency. At point *Y*, it is not possible to produce any more because of the scarce resources that are available to the economy. The minimum possible resources are being used to make the products. This is thus a point of productive efficiency.

Competition can be seen to lead to productive efficiency. In general terms, this is the case as firms are constrained to produce at the lowest possible cost in a competitive market. Firms have the incentive of profit to make their products at the lowest possible cost: the lower the cost, the greater the possible profit. Alternatively, a failure to produce at the lowest possible cost in a competitive market may lead to bankruptcy for a firm. As rivals will produce at lowest cost, the price for the firm that has failed to minimise costs will be too high and thus there will be low demand.

More specifically, it can be seen that perfect competition leads to the necessary conditions for productive efficiency (see Chapter 7 for details of perfect competition), as shown in Figure 6.3.

The point of long-run equilibrium for a perfectly competitive firm is given by price *p* and output *q*. At this point, it can be seen that the firm is producing at the lowest point on its average cost curve. This means that there is productive efficiency. Given that the competition in this market will also constrain firms to be producing at the lowest possible point on their average cost curve, then production at this point is productively efficient.

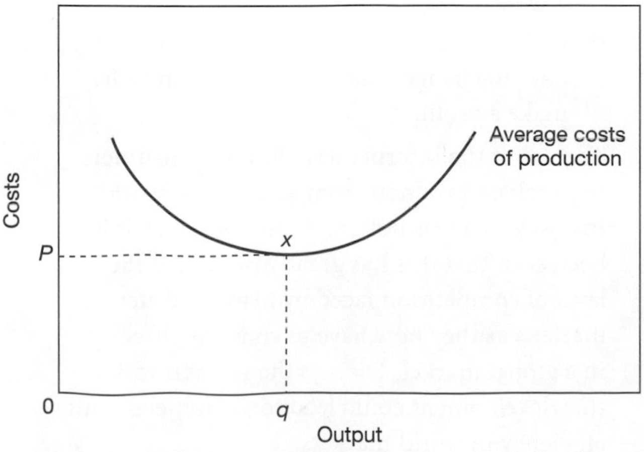

Figure 6.1 Productive efficiency for a firm

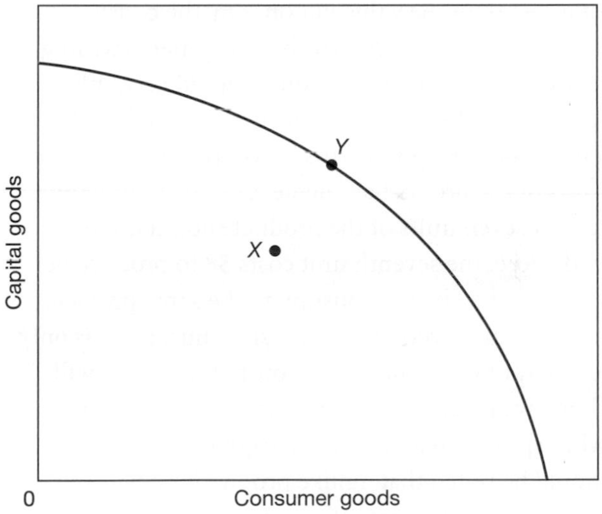

Figure 6.2 Productive efficiency in an economy

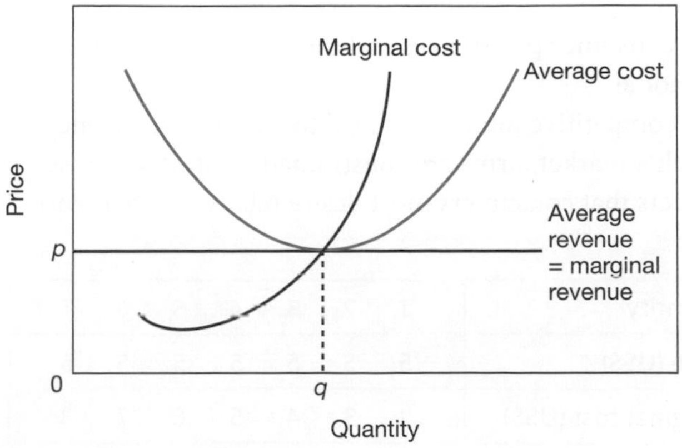

Figure 6.3 Productive efficiency and perfect competition

Allocative efficiency

It is not enough for products to be produced at the lowest possible cost. The right products must also be produced if there is to be economic efficiency. Allocative efficiency is all to do with allocating the right amount of scarce resources to the production of the right products. This means producing the combination of products that will yield the greatest possible level of satisfaction of consumer wants.

As stated earlier, the point of allocative efficiency can be deemed to exist when the price of a product is equal to its marginal cost of production, the cost of producing one more unit of output. In this situation, the price paid by the consumer will represent the true economic cost of producing the last unit of the product. This should ensure that precisely the right amount of the product is produced. This idea can be shown through the simple example in Table 6.1.

For this product, an output of one unit would not be productively efficient. Here, the cost of producing the product is less than the value put on it by the consumer (as represented by the price that the consumer is willing to pay for that product). The product should certainly be produced, but there is scope for further worthwhile production from this point. This is also true when two or three units of the product are made. On the other hand, an output of seven units of the product should not be produced. Here, the seventh unit costs $8 to produce but is only valued at $5 by the consumer. The same problem exists with output levels of five and six. Thus, there is only one ideal output level (that is, one output level that will yield allocative efficiency) and that is an output of four units where price is equal to the marginal cost.

It should be noted that, unlike productive efficiency, it is not possible to illustrate allocative efficiency on the production possibility frontier. Any point on the frontier could potentially be such a point provided price is equal to marginal cost at this point. The exact location will depend upon consumer preferences and these are not part of this model.

A competitive market can lead to allocative efficiency. In such a market, firms are constrained to produce those products that consumers most desire relative to their cost of production. As with productive efficiency, there are two motivations. First, the desire to make the greatest possible profit will drive firms to produce such products and will lead to the highest possible demand and hence the greatest revenue and profits. Second, firms in competitive markets will be forced to produce those products most demanded by consumers as other firms will certainly also do so. A failure to produce such products in this sort of market will force firms to close.

Quantity	1	2	3	4	5	6	7
Price (US$)	5	5	5	5	5	5	5
Marginal cost (US$)	2	3	4	5	6	7	8

Table 6.1

An alternative way to consider how a competitive market will achieve allocative efficiency is through the perfectly competitive diagram as shown earlier in Figure 6.3. It can be seen that the point of equilibrium in this diagram (price p and output q) is a position at which price is equal to marginal cost. This is the requirement for allocative efficiency as explained above.

The suggestion is thus made that in fully (or perfectly) competitive markets there will be economic efficiency. Both productive and allocative efficiency will exist. As will be shown in Chapter 7, this is the only market structure where this is evidenced.

SELF-ASSESSMENT TASK 6.1

1 Explain what type of efficiency each of the following might lead towards.
   - a A firm uses a new machine that costs less than the old one but produces more.
   - b A company swaps production to a different product that sells at the same price but is in greater demand.
   - c A car plant makes 1,000 workers redundant because their jobs can now be done by robots that cost less over a period of time than paying workers' wages.
   - d Following privatisation, firms in an industry have to change what they produce in order to make a profit.

2 The use of the Internet has allowed consumers to purchase products from all over the world in a way that was not previously possible. It has been seen that this has greatly increased the level of competition faced by firms in different markets as they now have to compete directly in a global market. Discuss the ways in which this development could lead to greater economic efficiency in world markets.

Pareto optimality

Pareto optimality occurs when it is impossible to make someone better off without making someone else worse off. It is an optimal situation, with resources allocated in the most efficient way.

KEY TERM

Pareto optimality: where it is impossible to make someone better off without making someone else worse off.

The concept can be simply applied using a production possibility curve (PPC) like that shown in Figure 6.2. When an economy is operating on its PPC, it is not possible to increase the output of capital goods without reducing the output of consumer goods. In contrast, any point within the PPC, for example *X*, would be Pareto inefficient. This is because it is possible to increase the output of either type of goods without reducing the output of the other.

If the allocation of resources is *not* Pareto efficient, then there is scope for improvement; this situation is one where at least one person is made better off without making anyone else worse off. If there are welfare losses at a particular point on the PPC, the reallocation of resources will lead to Pareto improvement. In reality, any improvement in economic efficiency may require some form of compensation to be paid where individuals are worse off. A good example is the case of a new road scheme designed to improve the efficiency of the flow of traffic. Users of the new road benefit because their journey times are shorter and their travel costs are likely to be reduced. Others though, for example those who might lose their homes, will be worse off unless they are paid appropriate compensation. Those living close to the road will be adversely affected by additional noise and fumes and are unlikely to receive compensation. There is, however, an overall efficiency gain.

TOP TIP

The PPC is a relatively simple yet very appropriate way of explaining efficiency.

Dynamic efficiency

Dynamic efficiency is a form of productive efficiency that benefits a firm over time. Resources are reallocated in such a way that output increases relative to the increase in resources. It is achieved when a firm meets the changing needs of its market by introducing new production processes in response to competitive pressures. It can be particularly relevant when analysing how monopolies and oligopolies seek to remain competitive (see Chapter 7). By using their excess profits, such firms are able to engage in research, development and product innovation in order to protect their market share. In turn, this can bring benefits to consumers in the form of new technologies and lower prices while giving the firm a more efficient means of production.

Dynamic efficiency is a longer-term phenomenon. To achieve it requires investment sourced from within or outside of the firm. Initially, it can result in higher costs; the payback comes later yet without investing, a firm may be destined to become less efficient and may be forced to leave the market. Where a firm is dynamically efficient, its long-run average cost curve shifts downwards (see Chapter 7). This is shown in Figure 6.4.

Robots in a car manufacturing plant

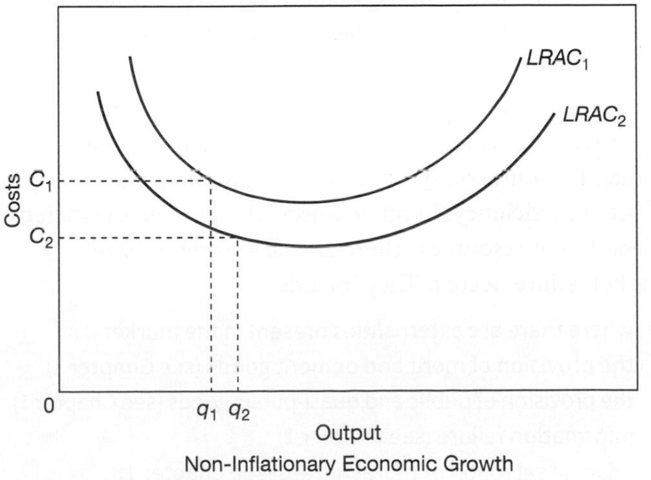

Figure 6.4 Dynamic efficiency

A typical example is that of the motor vehicle manufacturing industry. This is a fiercely competitive industry that has experienced both growth and rationalisation as firms have had to become more efficient to survive. The industry has come a long way since Henry Ford made his factories the most efficient in the USA in the 1920s and 1930s. Innovation and extensive investment have resulted in highly efficient, automated production plants. Computer-aided techniques and robots rather than workers have contributed to increased efficiency and lower production costs per vehicle.

SELF-ASSESSMENT TASK 6.2

Using knowledge from your own country where possible, state in what ways the following might achieve dynamic efficiency:

a the food processing industry

b livestock farming

c postal services.

KEY CONCEPT LINK

Equilibrium and efficiency: Efficiency and inefficiency can be explained in various ways. These are dynamic concepts in so far as over time markets and indeed economies can move from being efficient to being inefficient and back to being efficient.

Market failure

It is stating the obvious to say that market failure exists when a market fails. However, the question needs to be asked: 'Fail at what?' The answer is: 'Fail at delivering economic efficiency.' Market failure exists whenever a free market, left to its own devices and totally free from any form of government intervention, fails to make the optimum use of scarce resources. Using earlier terminology, it is when the interaction of supply and demand in a market does not lead to productive and/or allocative efficiency. In other words, there is *not* an efficient allocation of resources. There are various reasons why market failure occurs. They include:

- where there are externalities present in the market
- the provision of merit and demerit goods (see Chapter 1)
- the provision of public and quasi-public goods (see Chapter 1)
- information failure (see Chapter 1)
- adverse selection or moral hazard (see Chapter 1)
- abuse of monopoly power in the market.

KEY CONCEPT LINK

Equilibrium and efficiency, regulation and equality: Market failure arises because the free market mechanism is not always efficient in the way in which resources are allocated. As will be seen later, this invariably necessitates various types of regulation to make good market failure. This intervention can aid social equality and equity.

Externalities

Defining externality

If the market system is to work well and lead to economic efficiency, it is important that those people who make economic decisions are the same as those who are affected by these decisions. A transaction between a supplier and a consumer for a product needs only to affect the particular supplier and particular consumer involved. As long as this is the case, then both sides will act only so long as both feel that they will benefit from any action – all is well in the market. However, a problem could clearly arise if someone else not party to the economic decision is affected by that decision. This is the concept known as **externality**.

KEY TERM

Externality: where the actions of producers or consumers give rise to side effects on third parties who are not involved in the action; sometimes referred to as spillover effects.

An externality is said to arise if a third party (someone not directly involved) is affected by the decisions and actions of others. The side effects can be negative or positive. A **negative externality** occurs when the side effects have a negative or detrimental impact that involves unexpected costs to third parties. A **positive externality,** which is less common, is where the side effects provide benefits to third parties. In both cases, those who are affected are outsiders to the action that causes the externality to occur.

KEY TERMS

Negative externality: where the side effects have a negative impact and impose costs to third parties.

Positive externality: where the side effects have a positive impact and provide benefits to third parties.

It is further possible to distinguish when the externalities are the result of production or consumption decisions. Typical examples are:

- Negative production externalities: These are spillover effects that occur as a result of production activity. A common case is that of most forms of environmental pollution. Suppose a firm disposes of chemical waste into a river. A production externality occurs because there are additional costs imposed on the community and the river authority who have to clean up the mess, due to the negative consequences of the firm's action. There is little or no cost to the polluting firm.
- Negative consumption externalities: These are created by consumers as a consequence of their use of products that result in harm to others who are not involved in the consumption. A very relevant and topical global example is that of passive smoking. This causes costs to non-smokers in the form of discomfort and respiratory problems where there is extensive exposure. Another example is the increased CO_2 emissions that are generated by coal-fired power stations, aircraft, heavy industry and so on. It is now very clear that these are a cause of global warming.

Coal-fired power station in China

- Positive production externalities: These are benefits to third parties and are created by producers of goods and services. A typical example is when, as a result of medical research, a new drug or vaccine is developed to combat a serious disease. The recipients of the medication obviously benefit; but there are also wider benefits to others and to the economy as a result of the reduced incidence of the disease.
- Positive consumption externalities: Here, the benefits are the spillover effects of consumption of a good or service on others. This is a key argument for the provision of merit goods by a government. In the case of secondary education, those students who receive it clearly benefit from it. Their employment opportunities are greater and they can expect higher pay due to their educational background compared to others who left school earlier. The benefits further extend to their families and to future economic prospects.

KEY CONCEPT LINK

Equilibrium and efficiency: A market is not efficient where there are externalities present; whether a market remains inefficient can be the consequence of the actions taken to combat market failure. These actions are likely to change over time.

TOP TIP

Externalities can arise through the actions of consumers as well as producers; at times the distinction is not always clear.

Externalities and inefficient resource allocation

Private, external and social costs

Another way of understanding a negative externality is to define it as any situation where there is a divergence between the **private costs** and **social costs** of an action. The private costs are those costs that are paid for by someone who produces a good or service. The social costs are the total costs to society of this production. If there is no externality, there is no difference between private costs and social costs and so there is an efficient allocation of resources. When there is a negative externality, the costs borne and paid for by third parties are known as **external costs**.

Therefore, social costs = private costs + external costs.

KEY TERMS

Social costs: the total costs of a particular action.

Private costs: those costs that are incurred by an individual who produces a good or service.

External costs: those costs incurred and paid for by third parties not involved in the action.

It is quite possible that these private and social costs are the same: in other words, all of the costs of an action accrue to the individual or firm. If this is the case, then there are no externalities. However, it is also possible that there will be a difference: private and social costs may not be equal to each other. For example, if you make a decision to take a journey by car, you consider only the costs of the petrol and the time taken.

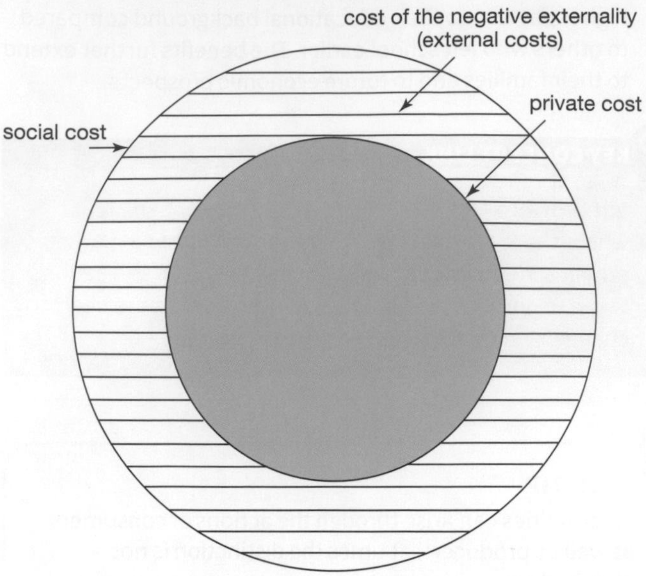

Figure 6.5 A difference between private and social costs

However, you do not consider the further costs that you may be imposing on others in terms of your contribution to road congestion, to atmospheric pollution and to possible car accidents. In this situation, a negative externality exists, the cost of which is an external cost. The situation is illustrated in Figure 6.5. Here, private costs are part of the social costs involved in a decision. However, they do not represent all of the social costs. The difference shown between the two is the external cost or the cost of the negative externality.

Private, external and social benefits

A similar situation can also exist with benefits. The **social benefits** of a decision are all of the benefits that accrue from that decision. The **private benefits** are those that accrue solely to the individual making the action. Again, these may or may not be the same. Any difference between them is the **external benefits**.

Therefore social benefits = private benefits + external benefits

It is possible that the social benefits of a decision may exceed the private benefits. If this is the case, then a positive externality that produces an external benefit is said to exist. For example, if you make a decision to go to the doctor to be inoculated against a particular disease, then clearly you receive the private benefit of not catching that particular disease. However, you may not be the only one to benefit. The fact that you do not get the disease has some possible benefit to all others with whom you come into contact and who will now not catch the disease from you.

KEY TERMS

Social benefits: the total benefits arising from a particular action.

Private benefits: benefits that accrue to individuals who produce or consume a particular good.

External benefits: benefits that that are received by third parties not involved in the action.

Children being vaccinated in Africa

The problem created by externalities

The main problem created by externalities is that where they are present they will lead to an inappropriate amount being produced: the free market will lead either to too much or too little production. This is an inefficient use of resources.

Consider again a firm that produces a chemical. There are costs that the firm will have to meet in producing a certain quantity of this chemical. These would include such things as:

- raw material costs
- labour costs
- energy costs
- distribution costs, etc.

All such costs are termed private costs: they have to be paid for by the decision-maker (the firm). These costs form part of social costs. There are further costs likely to be involved as well. These might include the cost of dumping the chemical waste, perhaps unlawfully, in a local river, which in turn creates clean-up costs for a third party. In addition, any atmospheric pollution created might cause ill health for those living close to the factory and there is likely to be additional road congestion arising from the transportation of the chemicals. These are all negative externalities.

The problem is that only the private costs of producing and distributing the chemical will be taken into account by the firm when making its pricing decisions. The external costs, which are *the costs to society*, will not be taken into account. This will mean that the price will be lower than if all social costs were recognised and taken into account. Consequently demand and production will be higher than if full social costs had been considered. Thus, a negative externality will lead to overproduction. The situation can be seen in Figure 6.6.

The price that will occur in the market will be P_1 where the supply schedule that takes account of the private costs, S_1, is equal to demand. This price is associated with production of Q_1. However, if the supply schedule took into account the social costs, S_2, which are greater than the private costs, then it would result in a price of P_2. This price is associated with a lower production of Q_2. Thus, the negative externality has led to $Q_1 - Q_2$, overproduction. Too many scarce resources are being devoted to the production of this product. The market has failed.

The opposite problem is true of a positive externality. Here, the problem is that too little of the product is being produced. If only the private benefits are considered, there will be underproduction. This situation is shown in Figure 6.7.

This time, the problem is with demand. If only the private benefits are registered, then demand is represented by the demand schedule D_1. This leads to a price of P_1 and an associated production of Q_1. However, if the further extra benefits to society were registered (which they will not be by the private decision-maker), then demand would be greater at D_2. This would lead to a price of P_2 and production of Q_2. Thus there is underproduction of $Q_2 - Q_1$ associated with the positive externality. Insufficient scarce resources are being devoted to the production of this good or service. The market has again failed.

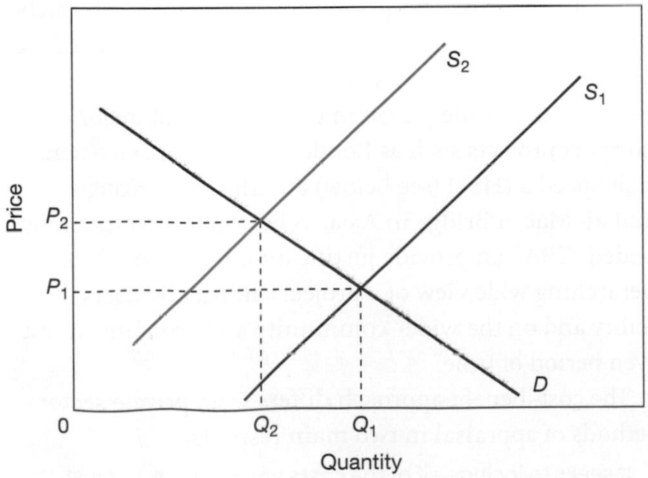

Figure 6.6 Overproduction caused by a negative externality

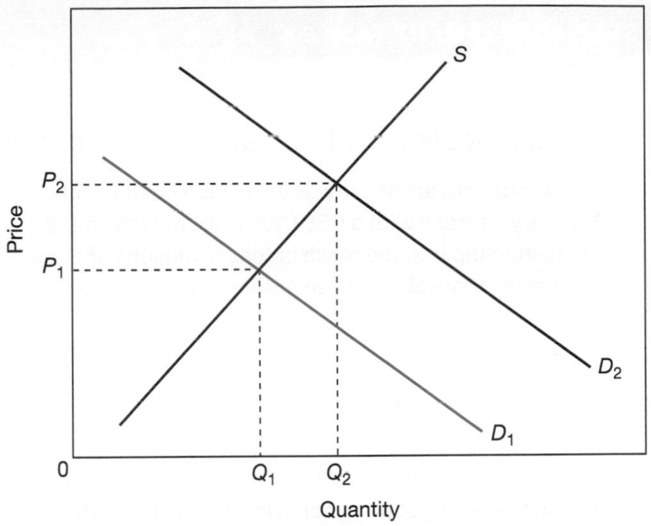

Figure 6.7 Underproduction caused by a positive externality

Externalities are therefore a source of market failure as resources are not allocated in the ideal way: too few or too many resources are likely to be directed to the production of certain products.

SELF-ASSESSMENT TASK 6.3

Identify and explain whether each of the following involves a positive or a negative externality:

- **a** a next-door neighbour playing music loudly
- **b** a person being educated beyond the compulsory school leaving age
- **c** discarding a used battery in the road
- **d** smoking in a public place
- **e** a new, well-designed and pleasant public building
- **f** the use of pesticides in agricultural production.

Use of cost–benefit analysis in decision making

Cost–benefit analysis (CBA) is a widely practised technique that is used to aid decision making, particularly in situations where a conventional financial appraisal would not be entirely appropriate.

KEY TERM

Cost–benefit analysis (CBA): a method for assessing the desirability of a project taking into account the costs and benefits involved.

SELF-ASSESSMENT TASK 6.4

India reveals world's cheapest car – but what are the bigger costs?

The world's cheapest car was unveiled by India's Tata Motors yesterday with a US$2,500 price tag that brings car ownership into the reach of tens of millions of people, prompting fears about its environmental impact.

Critics say the Tata Nano will lead to millions more cars hitting the already clogged up roads in the country's teeming cities. They are concerned that this explosion will add to mounting air and noise pollution problems.

Company chairman Ratan Tata believes that the Nano will be the least polluting car in India and claims that it meets stringent EU emission standards. He also believes that this so-called 'People's Car' will provide India's growing middle classes with the personal mobility and status symbol they long for. For the masses, however, widespread poverty will limit car ownership. For a rickshaw driver in Delhi, earning just over US$2 a day, the so-called People's Car amounts to more than three years' earnings.

The Tata Nano – the world's cheapest car

Source: Adapted from Associated Press/Reuters, *South China Morning Post*, 11 January 2008.

1 Identify and explain:

a a private benefit and an external benefit

b a private cost and an external cost

arising out of Tata's production of the Nano.

2 Discuss whether the production of the Nano is a case of market failure.

It is used by the public sector, for example, in the case of public goods such as a road where no direct charge is made to users. In general terms, CBA takes a long view and a wide view in assessing whether a particular project should be progressed. The long view stems from the nature of most public sector investment. Because of the large sums involved, a project like a new road or rail link is appraised over 30 to 50 years. The wide view stems from the need to take into account the full social costs and social benefits. This is because we are often concerned with situations where major economic projects produce substantial and often controversial side effects, in particular where there are externalities that fall upon people and communities who have no direct connection with the particular project.

There are many situations where CBA can be used to aid decision making. In all types of economy there are numerous examples of environmental pollution that result in external costs being imposed on the local community. These can be far-reaching and substantial. CBA genuinely attempts to quantify the opportunity cost to society of the various possible outcomes or sources of action.

CBA is also widely used in the appraisal of major transport projects such as London's Crossrail extension, High Speed 2 (HS2) (see below) and the Hong Kong–Zhuhai–Macau Bridge in Asia. Where huge investment is needed, CBA can provide justification based on taking an overarching wide view of a project's impact on users of the facility and on the wider community and economy over a given period of time.

The cost–benefit approach differs from private sector methods of appraisal in two main respects:

1 It seeks to include all of the costs and benefits, not just private ones.

2 It often has to impute a **shadow price** on costs and benefits where no market price is available. For example, in the case of transport projects there is a need to value travel time savings. Other situations are how to value the benefit of cleaner air or being able to live in a less noisy environment.

KEY TERM

Shadow price: one that is applied where there is no recognised market price available.

KEY CONCEPT LINK

Scarcity and choice: Cost–benefit analysis is a well-used technique for dealing with the fundamental economic problem in situations where the market mechanism is an inappropriate way of allocating scarce resources. It forms the basis for decision making by governments, especially in the context of public goods.

TOP TIP

CBA is best viewed as a guide to decision making; the final decision invariably will depend on funds that are available in relation to competing alternatives.

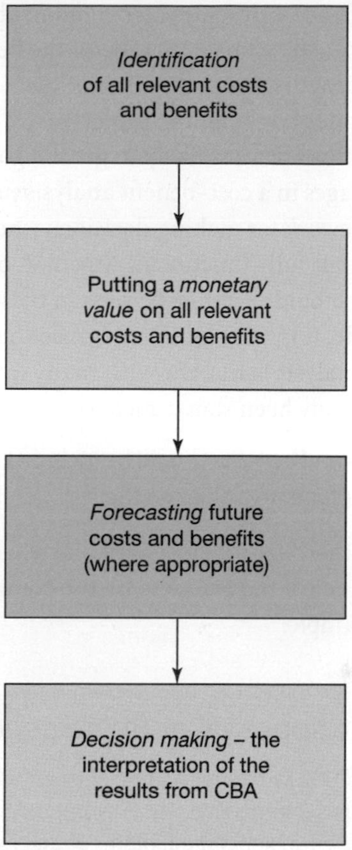

Figure 6.8 Stages in a cost–benefit analysis

The framework of cost–benefit analysis

Whatever the problem under investigation, there are four main stages in the development of a cost–benefit analysis. These are shown in Figure 6.8.

The first stage is to identify all of the relevant costs and benefits arising out of any particular project. This involves establishing what are the private costs, the private benefits, the external costs and the external benefits. On the surface this may seem a relatively simple task. In reality, and with a little more thought, it is not so easy. There are particular problems when it comes to identifying external costs and benefits. These are often controversial, not easy to define in a discrete way and have the added difficulty that it is not always possible to draw the line in terms of a physical or geographical cut-off. The spillover effects of a new retail development or rail route, for example, are wide-reaching and affect people and communities beyond the immediate vicinity of the proposed development.

The second stage involves putting a monetary value on the various costs and benefits. This is relatively straightforward where market prices are available. For example, in the case of a new retail development, a monetary value can be put on the jobs created or the increased profits arising from the development. For other variables, however, a monetary value must be attributed for costs and benefits where no market prices are available. This particular measurement difficulty has occupied economists for thousands of hours over the years. It has also been a very controversial matter in situations where cost–benefit analysis has come under close public scrutiny. A particularly good example of this is the issue of valuation of time, especially travel time savings. Another relevant example is how to put a monetary value on the cost of accidents, particularly where serious injuries or a loss of life is involved.

The third stage applies in situations where projects have longer-term implications that stretch well into the future. Here, economists have to employ statistical forecasting techniques, sometimes of a very crude nature, to estimate costs and benefits over many years. This particularly applies to proposed projects where massive capital expenditure is involved.

The final stage is where the results of the earlier stages are drawn together so that the outcome can be presented in a clear manner in order to aid decision making. The important principle here is that if the value of benefits exceeds the value of the costs, then the particular project is worthwhile since it provides an overall net benefit to the community. An estimate is made of the benefit:cost ratio, the net benefits as a proportion of the net costs of a project. Dependent on funding, projects with the highest benefit:cost ratios are most likely to get the go ahead.

The four stages in a cost–benefit analysis provide a coherent framework for making decisions where the market mechanism is not fully functional. Any cost–benefit study or application should therefore be seen in these terms.

To conclude, it is relevant to recognise that in practice cost–benefit analysis is fraught with many difficulties. Some have already been stated such as:

- which costs and benefits should be included
- how to put monetary values on them.

Additionally, there are others, particularly when it comes to the acceptance of the outcome by the community as a whole. For example:

- CBA does not always satisfactorily reflect the distributional consequences of certain decisions, particularly where public sector investment is involved. In the case of a new retail development, external costs are likely to be highly localised, while external benefits, in terms of employment creation for instance, are likely to be more widely spread.
- Many public sector projects can be very controversial and subject to much local aggravation from pressure groups. This is especially the case with the UK's HS2 project (see below). It may be the case that the outcome of the CBA is rejected for political reasons, with the consequence that the most expedient decision may not be the one recommended by economists. Where this happens, it is easy to dismiss the technique of CBA as irrelevant. This is not a fair conclusion, not least as CBA has at least brought out the issues involved so that a decision can be taken on the basis of all of the information available. CBA is an aid to and not a replacement for decision making.

Economic appraisal of High Speed 2 (HS2)

The planned HS2 rail project is one of the most ambitious infrastructure schemes that has ever been developed in the UK. In short, it is a high-speed, high-capacity rail system that requires the construction of completely new rail track to take trains operating at 225 miles per hour. It is planned in two phases. Phase 1 is 140 miles between London and Birmingham and due for completion in 2026. Phase 2 is in the form of two branches, from Birmingham to Crewe and Manchester on the west side and the eastern leg from Birmingham via the East Midlands and Sheffield to Leeds. The aim is to be carrying passengers here by 2030 (see map).

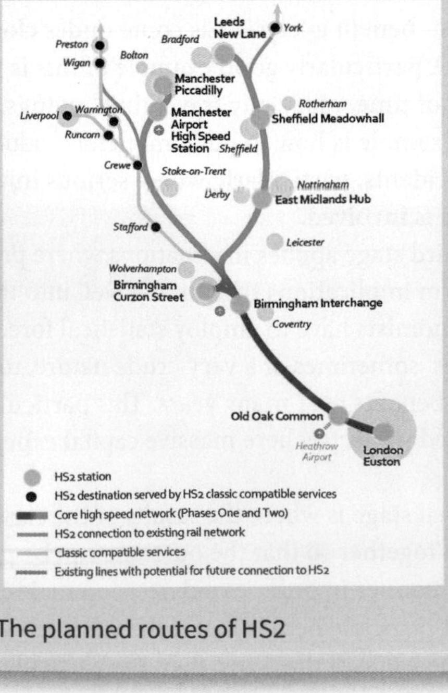

The planned routes of HS2

Though it has important national benefits, it is fair to say that the new north-south rail line is not without controversy. It is backed by the Government, Parliament and city leaders but there is still considerable opposition from people living along the line of the route who may be impacted by the construction and eventual operation of HS2.

Others argue that there is an opportunity cost involved, claiming that the capital would be better spent on improving and updating the current rail network. Another key issue in the debate has been the likely spillover effects of HS2 on London, Birmingham, Manchester and Leeds especially. Here again, opinion is divided.

Some argue that London will be the principal beneficiary and that the other cities will relatively lose out. The opposite view has also prevailed, namely that the biggest cities outside the capital, such as Leeds and Manchester, will benefit from much-needed regeneration and business growth. Table 6.2 is a summary of the government's own cost–benefit analysis. Much of the debate about the project has centred on this and the extent to which it is a true statement of what can be expected. The main features of the cost–benefit analysis are:

- More than half of the benefits come in the form of travel time savings for business users. This 'value of time' benefit is quite normal in transport appraisals and recognises that since less time is spent travelling then the time saved can be put to more effective use. There are also similar benefits for leisure users of HS2, although their hourly value of time used in the appraisal is considerably less than that of business travellers.

- A cost to the government is the loss of indirect taxes that would have been paid by users who would otherwise have travelled by road. These taxes include fuel tax and excise duties on petrol and diesel fuel.
- An attempt has been made to quantify the wider economic benefits that might accrue once the two stretches of line are open. Apart from the many forecasting problems this involves, it is relevant to note that Phase 2 to Leeds and to Manchester should generate a substantial boost to the regional economies in the north of England.
- The capital costs and annual operating costs are normal items in any cost-benefit appraisal.

	BCR Components		Phase 1 (£billion)	Full Network (£billion)
1	Transport user benefits	Business	£16.9	£40.5
		Other	£7.7	£19.3
2	Other quantifiable benefits		£0.4	£0.8
3	Loss to Government of indirect taxes		–£1.2	–£2.9
4	Net transport benefits = 1 + 2 + 3		£23.8	£57.7
5	Wider economic impacts, WEI's		£4.3	£13.3
6	Net benefits including WEI's = 4 + 5		£28.1	£71.0
7	Capital costs		£21.8	£40.5
8	Operating costs		£8.2	£22.1
9	Total costs = 7 + 8		£29.9	£62.6
10	Revenues (from users of HS2)		£13.2	£31.1
11	Net costs to Government = 9 – 10		£16.7	£31.5
12	**BCR without WEIs = 4 / 11**		**1.4**	**1.8**
13	**BCR with WEIs = 6 / 11**		**1.7**	**2.3**

Note: BCR – benefit:cost ratio; WEI – wider economic impact

Table 6.2 Standard case cost-benefit analysis of HS2
Source: Department for Transport (2013)

The benefit:cost ratio, as stated earlier, is crucial in determining whether a project should go ahead. For the full scheme and also phase one, this ratio is greater than 1 indicating that there is a projected benefit. The higher benefit:cost ratios include an estimate of the external benefits. Despite the high costs to the government, the data provide a strong case for the HS2's construction.

High speed rail is well advanced in France, Italy, South Korea and China. Britain developed railways more than 150 years ago. As things stand, HS2 will be progressed. If, however, there is change in political will or a massive increase in costs (as some are predicting), it seems only then that HS2 will be cancelled.

SELF-ASSESSMENT TASK 6.5

Traffic problems in Bangkok

Bangkok, the capital of Thailand, is one of Asia's megacities. For its citizens, and those who visit as tourists or for business reasons, one thing that no one can get away from is its horrendous traffic congestion. The population is increasing at a massive 2% per annum and, as in all parts of Asia, vehicle ownership levels are increasing at a substantial rate as a consequence of economic advancement. This situation means increasing stress levels, deterioration in the quality of life and increasing health problems for its burgeoning population.

A recent government report has estimated that:

- the typical resident spends 44 working days a year stuck in traffic
- peak vehicle speeds have fallen to 6 km per hour
- lost production due to congestion is estimated to be 10% of Thailand's GDP
- much of the energy used to move vehicles is wasted because of the congestion
- one million people a year suffer from diagnosed respiratory diseases linked to the air pollution quality, which has 18 times more CO_2 emissions than the WHO maximum guideline
- there is a high incidence of lung cancer among the adult population and children have unacceptable levels of lead in their blood
- thousands of people a year suffer strain and stress-related illness directly attributable to the severe congestion
- schoolchildren leave home for school at 5am to beat the congestion.

Morning rush hour in Bangkok

Unlike its 'neighbours' such as Kuala Lumpur, Singapore and Hong Kong, Bangkok does not have a rapid transit system, although one has been planned for at least 30 years. The time has surely come when this has to be authorised.

Suppose you have been asked by the authorities in Bangkok to produce a cost–benefit analysis for a new rapid transit system for the city.

1 Using the above information as a guide, what costs and benefits would you include in your analysis?

2 What are some of the measurement problems you might encounter?

3 On what theoretical basis might you:
   - recommend that a new rapid transit system be constructed?
   - recommend that there is no case for a new rapid transit system?

SUMMARY

In this chapter it has been shown that:

- Efficiency is a fundamental concept in microeconomics and is used to assess how well scarce resources are allocated.
- Economic efficiency exists when there is both productive and allocative efficiency in a market; these conditions only occur when there is perfect competition.
- Pareto efficiency and dynamic efficiency are other forms of efficiency.
- Markets fail for various reasons, leading to an inefficient allocation of resources.
- Externality is a common reason for market failure and results in negative and positive externalities for consumers and for firms.
- Cost–benefit analysis is a useful practical aid to decision making, especially in situations where it is necessary to consider the social costs and benefits.

Exam-style questions

1 a Using examples, explain what is meant by a negative externality. **[12]**

b Discuss the extent to which an indirect tax alone can rectify the problem of market failure due to negative externalities. **[13]**

2 a Using examples, explain why cost–benefit analysis is central to the decision making process in the allocation of public goods. **[12]**

b Discuss some of the limitations of cost–benefit analysis in the allocation of public goods. **[13]**

Chapter 7:
The price system and the microeconomy
A Level

Learning objectives

On completion of this chapter you should know:

- the law of diminishing marginal utility and its relationship to the derivation of an individual demand schedule
- the limitations of marginal utility theory and why consumers are not always rational
- how indifference curves can be used to represent what consumers want
- what a budget line is and how it can be used to show the income and substitution effects of a price change
- the short-run production function: fixed and variable factors of production; total product, average product and marginal product
- the law of diminishing returns; average cost, marginal cost
- the long-run production function and returns to scale
- how to explain the shape of the long-run average cost curve
- economies of scale, internal and external; diseconomies of scale
- how to define total, average and marginal revenue
- what is meant by normal and abnormal profit
- what is meant by market structure and how it can be explained
- the difference between perfect and imperfect competition
- the market structures of monopoly, monopolistic competition, oligopoly and natural monopoly
- what is meant by contestable markets and the implications of contestability in a market
- reasons for the growth and survival of small firms
- what is meant by profit maximisation; why there are other objectives of firms
- how firms make pricing decisions
- how it is possible to compare the performance of firms.

Introduction

This chapter builds upon and develops the content of Chapter 2 (AS Level). More specifically, it extends the description of how markets work to explain in more detail how consumers make choices at the margin The chapter also:

- explains how firms make decisions on how much they should produce at the margin
- analyses how firms behave in terms of setting prices and output in different market structures
- discusses the extent to which firms operate in an efficient way in these market structures.

Utility and marginal utility

Economists have long been interested in the way that consumers behave. Aspects of demand theory were introduced earlier in Chapter 2. For the demand curve, it was assumed that it could be derived from data collected for the demand schedule. Here we shall look behind the demand curve and explore why it really is the case that consumers buy more of a good when its price falls.

A relevant starting point is the notion of **utility**. This idea dates back to the nineteenth century and is a term used to record the level of happiness or satisfaction that someone receives from the consumption of a good. The concept assumes that this satisfaction can be measured, in the same way that the actual units consumed can be calculated. Two important measures are:

- **total utility** – the overall satisfaction that is derived from the consumption of all units of a good over a given time period
- **marginal utility** – the additional utility derived from the consumption of one more unit of a particular good. So, if someone gets ten units of satisfaction from consuming one bar of chocolate and 15 units after consuming two bars, then the marginal utility is five units.

KEY TERMS

Utility: the satisfaction received from consumption.

Total utility: the total satisfaction received from consumption.

Marginal utility: the utility derived from the consumption of one more unit of the good or service.

The marginal utility gained from the consumption of a product tends to fall as consumption increases. For example, if you buy an ice cream you will get a lot of satisfaction from consuming it, especially in hot weather. If you consume a second one, you will still get some satisfaction, but this is likely to be less than from the first ice cream. A third ice cream will yield even less satisfaction.

SELF-ASSESSMENT TASK 7.1

1 Table 7.1 below shows the total utility gained from the consumption of lemonade in a week.

Quantity consumed (bottles)	Total utility
0	0
1	20
2	35
3	45
4	53
5	58
6	54
7	48

Table 7.1

a Calculate the marginal utility as the quantity consumed increases.

b Sketch the total utility and marginal utility curves (put utility on the vertical axis, quantity consumed on the horizontal axis).

2 If the price of lemonade increases from $1 to $2 per bottle, how might it affect consumption? Explain your answer using the data above.

3 Comment on how confident you are on the answer you have provided to question 2.

This aspect of consumer behaviour is referred to as the law of **diminishing marginal utility**. As consumption increases, there may actually come a point where marginal utility is negative, indicating dissatisfaction or disutility.

KEY TERM

Diminishing marginal utility: the fall in marginal utility as consumption increases.

In considering the consumer's equilibrium, it is necessary to remember that it is assumed that consumers have limited incomes, behave in a rational manner and seek to maximise their total utility. A consumer is said to be in equilibrium, assuming a given level of income, when it is not possible to switch any expenditure from, say, product A to product B to increase total utility. This is referred to as the **equimarginal principle** and can be represented as:

$$\frac{MU_A}{P_A} = \frac{MU_B}{P_B} = \frac{MU_C}{P_C} \cdots = \frac{MU_N}{P_N}$$

where MU = marginal utility
P = the price
A, B, C and N = different products

So, if the marginal utility from consuming product A is ten units and the price is \$5, the consumer is in equilibrium when consuming 20 units of product B if its price is \$10 and so on.

KEY TERM

Equimarginal principle: consumers maximise their utility where their marginal valuation for each product consumed is the same.

It is possible to use marginal utility to derive an individual demand curve. The fundamental principle of demand is that an increase in the price of a good leads to a reduction in its demand. Using the above principle, this can now be proved. The value of the expression $\frac{MU_A}{P_A}$ will now fall as the price of A has increased. So, the marginal utility of A per dollar spent will now be less than on any other goods. The consumer will therefore increase total utility by spending less on good A and more on all other goods. This will in turn reduce the value of their marginal utility.

In other words, the consumer only maximises total utility by buying less of good A. The conclusion is that the demand curve for a good is downward sloping.

Are consumers rational?

The law of diminishing marginal utility assumes that consumers act and behave in a rational way in their purchasing decisions. This is a big assumption to make. Empirical evidence consistently shows that there are other factors apart from just utility that determine what we purchase. To understand the behavioural factors involved requires 'getting inside people's heads' to determine and then model such psychological influences.

A few examples will show why consumers often act in an irrational way.

- In the case of special offers such as 'buy one get one free'. Consumers may have no intention of buying the product until they enter the shop. Seeing the offer produces an impulsive cognitive response to buy.
- Where payment can be deferred. This allows consumers to purchase beyond their ability to pay outright at the time of sale – they may use a credit card to obtain what they want.
- Where a consumer is emotionally attached to a brand or where there is a prejudice against a brand, so influencing consumption.

This type of behaviour cannot be represented in a rational economic model. Interestingly, if consumers were rational, firms would have little need for marketing. Advertising that is designed to influence consumer choice would appear to be irrelevant. Behavioural economic models explore why consumers make irrational decisions, against what might have been predicted by conventional economic theory. It is therefore useful to bear these points in mind when evaluating the effectiveness of conventional economic models like that of utility.

Budget lines

As shown in Chapter 2, consumers are constrained in what they are able to buy due to their limited income and the prices of goods they wish to buy. These two important underpinning principles of consumer behaviour are brought together in the idea of a **budget line**. This shows numerically all the possible combinations of two products that a consumer can purchase with a given income and fixed prices.

KEY TERM

Budget line: the combinations of two products obtainable with given income and prices.

Quantity of A (US$20 each)	Quantity of B (US$10 each)
10	0
9	2
8	4
7	6
6	8
5	10
4	12
3	14
2	16
1	18
0	20

Table 7.2 Combinations of A and B with a budget of $200

Suppose someone has $200 to spend on two products, A and B. Assume the price of A is $20 and the price of B is $10. Table 7.2 shows the possible combinations that can be purchased. Each of the combinations would cost $200 in total. Figure 7.1a shows the budget line for this situation. Any point along this line will produce an outcome where consumption is maximised for this level of income.

If there is a change in the price of one good, with income remaining unchanged, then the budget line will pivot. For example, if the price of product B falls, then more of this product can be purchased at all levels of income. The budget line will shift outwards, from its pivot at point A. This is shown in Figure 7.1b. So, if the price of B falls by a third, then 30 of good B can now be purchased with an income of $200.

As the price of B has fallen relative to that of A, which is unchanged, consumers will substitute B for A. This is known as the **substitution effect** of a price change. It is always the case that the rational consumer will substitute towards the product which has become relatively cheaper. With the fall in the price of B, the consumer actually has more money to spend on other products, B included. Real income has therefore increased, which may mean that a consumer may now actually purchase more of product B. This is called the **income effect** of a price change.

KEY TERMS

Substitution effect: where following a price change, a consumer will substitute the cheaper product for the one that is now relatively more expensive.

Income effect: where following a price change, a consumer has higher real income and will purchase more of this product.

SELF-ASSESSMENT TASK 7.2

1 Re-draw Figure 7.1a to show how it would change:
   a if the price of B increased, leaving the price of A unchanged
   b if the price of A decreased, leaving the price of B unchanged.
2 In your own words, describe the substitution and income effects of:
   a an increase in the price of a normal good
   b a decrease in the price of an inferior good.

Indifference curves – representing what consumers want

The budget constraint referred to above showed what combination of goods a consumer could buy with given income and the prices of goods. This is only part of the

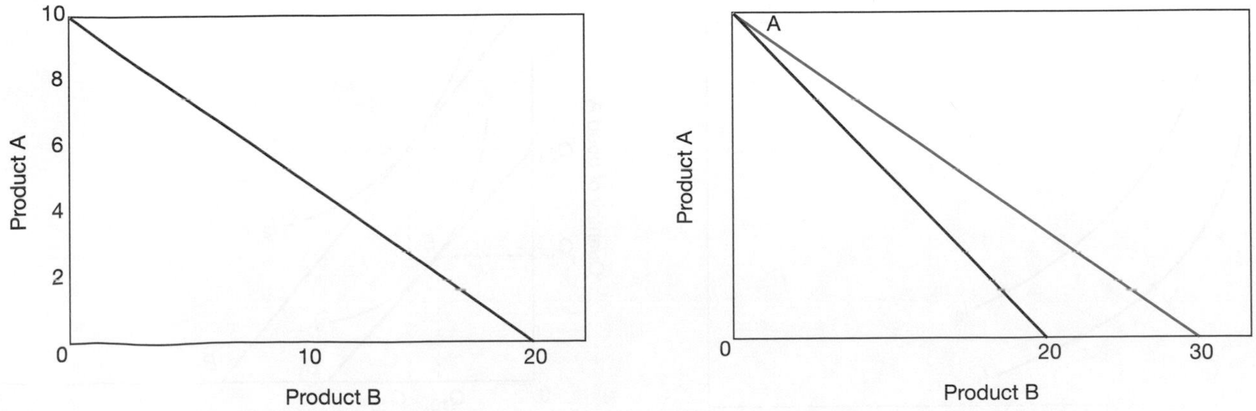

Figure 7.1 (a) Budget lines for an income of $200 (b) Budget lines – a fall in the price of B

reason why consumers buy particular goods – what is also relevant is consumer preference. Consumers will only buy a particular good if it is something that they actually want or prefer when having to choose between alternatives. Consumer preferences can be represented diagrammatically by what are known as **indifference curves**.

> **KEY TERM**
>
> **Indifference curve:** this shows the different combinations of two goods that give a consumer equal satisfaction.

As the name suggests, an indifference curve shows the different combinations of two goods that give the consumer equal satisfaction. Figure 7.2 shows two such indifference curves out of the many that can apply to a particular consumer. Considering indifference curve I_1, the consumer is indifferent with respect to combinations *X*, *Y* or *Z* since each are on the same indifference curve. If the consumer moves from point *Z* to *Y*, then the consumption of good B falls at the expense of an increase in consumption of good A. Point *Y* though still represents a situation where the consumer is still equally happy with the combination of goods that are being consumed.

The slope of the indifference curve is important – it represents the extent to which the consumer is willing to substitute one good for another. Looking at Figure 7.2, both the curves slope more steeply from left to right showing that when consuming large amounts of good A, the consumer is willing to give up rather more of this good when consumption of good B is small. The rate at which the consumer is willing to substitute one good for another in this way is known as the **marginal rate of substitution**.

> **KEY TERM**
>
> **Marginal rate of substitution:** the rate at which a consumer is willing to substitute one good for another.

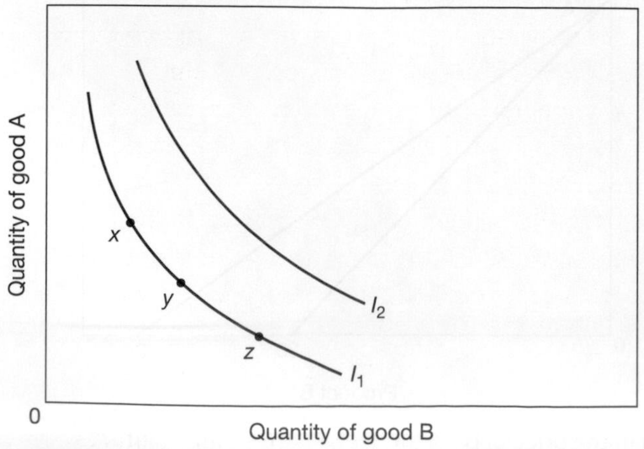

Figure 7.2 An indifference curve

Other points to note are:

- Higher indifference curves represent higher levels of consumption. Consumers therefore prefer to be on a higher rather than a lower indifference curve.
- All indifference curves are downward sloping to indicate that a fall in the quantity consumed of one good is accompanied by an increase in consumption of the other good.
- Indifference curves cannot cross.
- Indifference curves are concave or bowed inward to the origin.

> **KEY CONCEPT LINK**
>
> **Scarcity and choice:** A budget line represents the extent of a consumer's income; an indifference curve indicates the possible choices that are available. When combined, they show how the consumer can maximise satisfaction.

Effect of a change in income on consumer choice

The budget line constraint and the indifference curve can now be used together to show the effect of a change in income on the consumption of two goods. This is indicated in Figure 7.3. A consumer's choice is optimal at the point where the budget line touches or is at a tangent to the highest indifference curve. So, E_1 will give the consumer the maximum combined consumption of goods *A* and *B* given the budget constraint shown by the budget line B_1.

If income increases then this will allow the consumer to choose a better combination of goods *A* and *B*. This will usually be more of each good. So, if the budget constraint rises to B_2, then the consumer will increase consumption of good *A* and also of good *B*, albeit to a lesser extent. E_2 is the new optimal position, where more of both goods

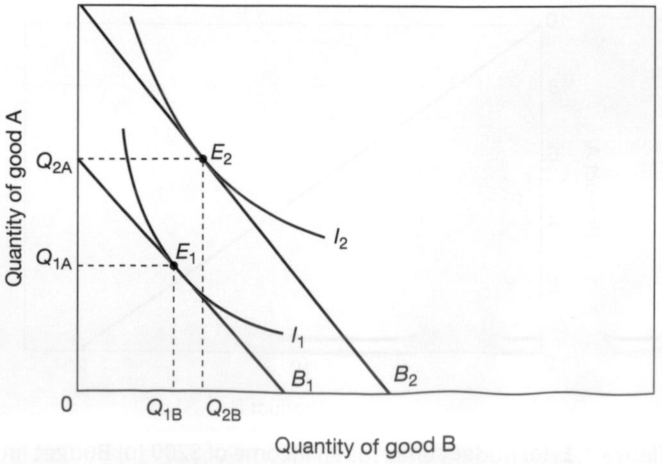

Figure 7.3 The effect of an increase in income

are being consumed. The change in position from E_1 to E_2 is what occurs when both goods are normal goods. If the increase in income or budget constraint results in less of one good being consumed then this is an inferior good.

When there is a fall in consumer income, the budget line shifts to the left in a parallel way. This indicates that both goods are normal and that less of each will be consumed.

Income and substitution effects of a price change using indifference curves

The income and substitution effects of a price change were briefly outlined earlier. These effects can now be interpreted using indifference curves. This is shown in Figure 7.4.

If the price of good A falls, then this means that the consumer has more spending power. This is represented by the new budget constraint B_2. The price of good B remains the same which is why B_2 pivots upwards to a new position. The extent of change that occurs consists of two stages. These are:

1. A movement along the initial indifference curve I_1 to point E_2. This is the substitution effect. It is so-called since the consumer buys less of good B as it is now relatively more expensive than good A.
2. A shift upwards to a higher indifference curve, moving from point E_2 to E_3. This is the income effect. As the consumer has more spending power, it is positive in the case of both goods, resulting in an increase in consumption of good B as well as good A.

In the case of good A, the income and substitution effects are both positive, resulting in a substantial increase in consumption. For good B, the substitution effect is negative but the fall in consumption is to some extent offset by the positive income effect. So here, the income

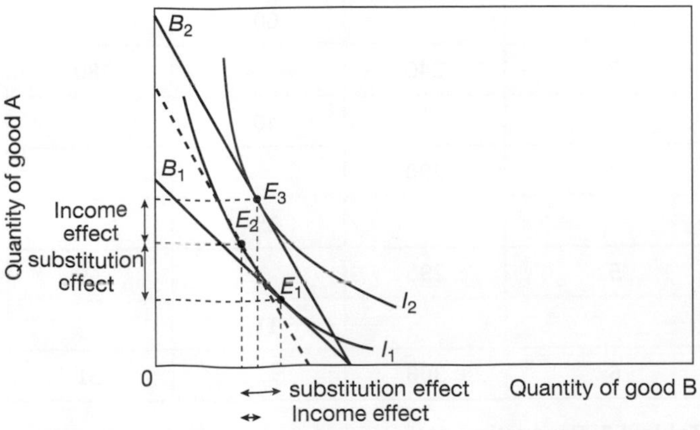

Figure 7.4 The income and substitution effects of a price change

and substitution effects are pulling in opposite directions. In Figure 7.4 there is a fall in consumption of good B as the substitution effect is stronger than the income effect.

In the case of inferior goods, as we saw in Chapter 2, when incomes rise above a certain point consumers tend to substitute more expensive and better quality alternatives. Here, the income effect is negative. Whether this leads to a fall in consumption will depend on the relative strength of the substitution effect. If this is greater than the income effect, then more of the inferior good will be consumed.

KEY CONCEPT LINK

Scarcity and choice, the margin and change: Using indifference curves and budget lines, the income and substitution effects of a price change are very relevant examples of how decision making by individuals is based on choices at the margin.

TOP TIP

Budget lines and indifference curves assume we are dealing with rational consumers; the reality is that this is not necessarily true for many consumers.

Types of cost, revenue and profit, short-run and long-run production

Introduction to production

In Chapter 1 four factors of production were identified. These were land, labour, capital and enterprise. In all cases, the demand for these factors of production comes from a producer who wishes to use them to make various goods or products. The producer is normally a business whose demand for factors of production is derived from the needs of its operations. Let us take the case of a clothing manufacturer to elaborate this important point.

As a consequence of globalisation, many items of clothing are now produced in the developing economies of South East Asia, North Africa and Central Europe. Designer labels, such as Nike, Calvin Klein, Ralph Lauren, Lacoste and Dolce & Gabbana are no longer produced in the home country of their corporate producer. Producers need all the factors of production in order to make goods for sale in markets that are mainly in developed economies. Their task is to combine the factors of production in an effective way to be efficient, competitive and profitable in the world market. The most important decision they have to make concerns the relative mixture of labour and capital. Therefore the task for the firm is to find the least cost or most efficient combination of labour and capital for the production of a given quantity of output.

Clothing is a typical example of a business where labour and capital are in direct competition with each other. If labour costs are relatively cheap, as in developing and emerging economies, then the production process is likely to take place using much more labour than capital. In most developed economies, however, the reverse is true. High-tech machines can often be used to replace labour, largely because it is more cost effective to do so. So, in this case, the same amount of output is produced using more capital and far less labour than if it were taking place in a developing economy.

Firms therefore have to choose between alternative production methods. Returning to the case of the clothing manufacturer, Figure 7.5 shows three different methods of production, each of which combines different levels of labour and capital to make items of clothing. Line A shows a method whereby labour and capital are used in equal proportions; line B shows a production method that uses twice as much capital as labour and line C shows the output resulting from twice as much labour as capital being used. On these lines, points *X*, *Y* and *Z* show the respective amounts of labour and capital that are needed to produce 100 units of clothing. If we join these points, then it gives us what is known as an **isoquant,** a curve that joins points that give us a particular level of output. This isoquant can of course be extended for other combinations of labour and capital not shown on Figure 7.5.

KEY TERM

Isoquant: a curve showing a particular level of output.

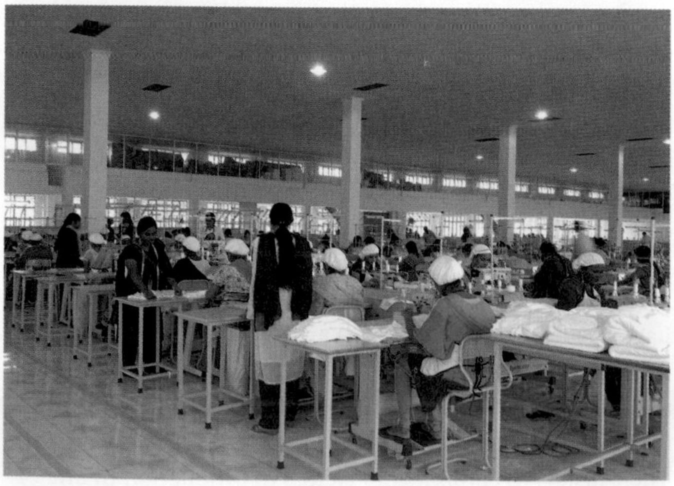

A clothing factory in India

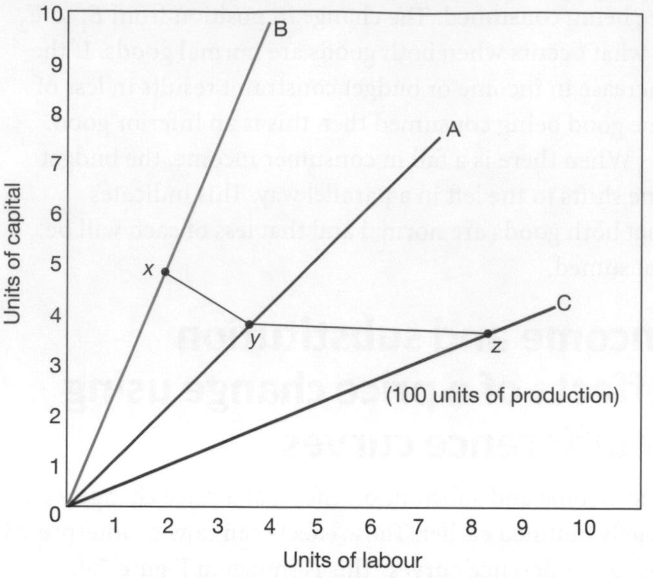

Figure 7.5 Alternative production methods

The short-run production function

To simplify our analysis, let us assume that the size of a clothing factory is given and that the only way in which the units of clothing produced can be varied is through varying the input of labour. This time period is referred to as the short run. In terms of factors of production, labour is the usual variable factor of production; all others – that is, capital, enterprise and land – are fixed factors of production. Table 7.3 shows how the quantity of clothing

Number of workers	Total product	Marginal product	Average product
0	0		0
		100	
1	100		100
		80	
2	180		90
		60	
3	240		80
		40	
4	280		70
		15	
5	295		59
		11	
6	306		51

Table 7.3 Production data

produced depends on the number of workers employed. For example, if there are no workers in the factory, there is no output or **total product**; with one worker, total product is 100 units. When there are two workers, the total product is 180 units and so on.

> **KEY TERM**
>
> **Total product:** total output.

Figure 7.6 is a graph of the first two columns of data in Table 7.3. It shows the relationship between the quantity of factor inputs (labour/workers) and the total product or output of clothing. This graph is called the **production function**. The third column of Table 7.3 shows the **marginal product**, the increase in total product that occurs from an additional unit of input (labour in this case). The data in this column show that, when the number of workers goes from one to two, output increases by 80 units; when it goes from two to three workers, the marginal product is 60 units. As the number of workers increases, the marginal product declines. This concept is known as a diminishing return and is often referred to as the law of **diminishing returns**. This well-known principle is clearly evidenced in many organisations. Adding more workers can be a short-term way of increasing what is being produced but there comes a point where the marginal return falls and might even become negative.

> **KEY TERMS**
>
> **Production function:** this shows the maximum possible output from a given set of factor inputs.
>
> **Marginal product:** the change in output arising from the use of one more unit of a factor of production.
>
> **Diminishing returns:** where the output from an additional unit of input leads to a fall in the marginal product.

The final column of Table 7.3 shows another important variable, average product. This is calculated by dividing the total product by the number of workers employed. It is a simple measure of labour productivity, i.e., how much output is produced by each worker.

> **KEY CONCEPT LINK**
>
> **The margin and change:** The law of diminishing returns is a very relevant illustration of firms making choices at the margin.

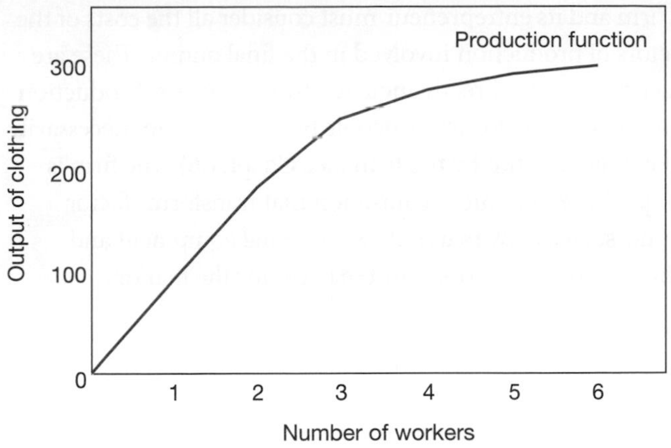

Figure 7.6 A production function

> **SELF-ASSESSMENT TASK 7.3**
>
> **a** Using data from Table 7.3, draw a graph with lines to show:
> - the marginal product of labour
> - the average product of labour.
>
> **b** What do you notice about the shape of the two and what does this indicate?
>
> **c** What production implications do these concepts have for a clothing firm planning how much to produce?

The firm's costs of production

Although we have already referred to the **firm**, we have not as yet defined it. The term 'a firm' is used by economists to describe a unit of decision making which has particular objectives such as **profit maximisation**, the avoidance of risk-taking and achieving its own long-term growth. At its lowest level the firm may be a sole trader with a small factory, a hawker's food stall or a local shop. The term is also used for national or multinational corporations with many plants and business establishments such as Nestlé, Sony, Tata and Toyota. In economic theory, all firms are headed by an entrepreneur (see Chapter 1).

> **KEY TERMS**
>
> **Firm:** any business that hires factors of production in order to produce goods and services.
>
> **Profit maximisation:** the assumed objective of a firm where the difference between total revenue and total cost is at a maximum.

A firm and its entrepreneur must consider all the costs of the factors of production involved in the final output. These are the private costs directly incurred by the owners. Production may create costs for other people but these are not necessarily taken into account by the firm (see Chapter 6). The firm is simply the economic organisation that transforms factor inputs such as raw materials with capital equipment and labour to produce goods and services for the market.

Short-run costs

These consist of:

- **Fixed costs:** These are the costs that are completely independent of output. Total fixed cost data when drawn on a graph would appear as a horizontal straight line. At zero output, any costs that a firm has must be fixed. Some firms operate in a situation where the fixed cost represents a large proportion of the total. In this case it would be wise to produce a large output in order to reduce unit costs and so make the firm more efficient.
- **Variable costs:** These include all the costs that are directly related to the level of output, the usual ones being labour and raw material or component costs. In other words, variable costs are incurred directly in the production process.

KEY TERMS

Fixed costs: those costs that are independent of output in the short run.

Variable costs: those that vary directly with output; all costs are variable in the long run.

Important definitions are:

$$\text{Total cost (TC)} = \text{total fixed cost (TFC)} + \text{total variable cost (TVC)}$$

These costs are shown on Figure 7.7.

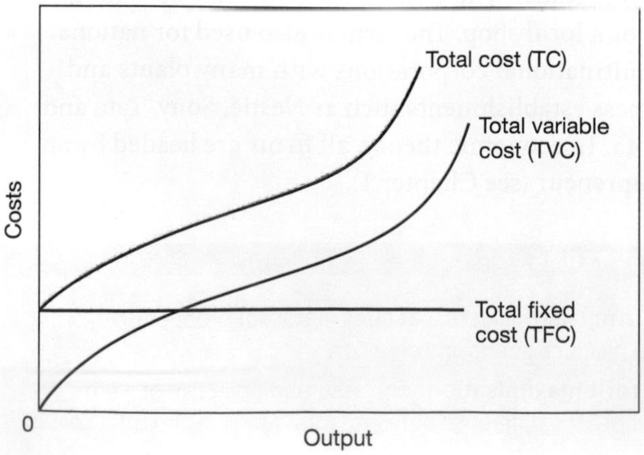

Figure 7.7 Total cost curves

Further cost measures can now be derived. They are:

$$\text{Average fixed cost (AFC)} = \frac{\text{total fixed cost}}{\text{output}}$$

$$\text{Average variable cost (AVC)} = \frac{\text{total variable cost}}{\text{output}}$$

$$\text{Average total cost (ATC)} = \frac{\text{total cost}}{\text{output}}$$

Marginal cost is the addition to the total cost when making one extra unit and is therefore a variable cost. These cost measures are shown in Figure 7.8.

The most important cost curve for the firm will be the ATC, showing the cost per unit of any chosen output. For most firms the decision to increase output will raise the total cost; that is, the marginal cost will be positive as extra inputs are used. Firms will only be keen to do this when the expected sales revenue will outweigh the extra cost. Rising marginal cost is also a reflection of the law of diminishing returns (see above). As more of the variable factors are added to the fixed ones, the contribution of each extra worker to the total output will begin to fall. These diminishing marginal returns cause the marginal and average variable cost to rise, as shown in Figure 7.8.

The shape of the short-run ATC is the result of the interaction between the average fixed cost and the average variable cost: AFC + AVC = ATC. As the firm's output rises, the average fixed cost will fall because the total fixed cost is being spread over an increasing number of units. However, at the same time, average variable cost will be rising because of diminishing returns to the variable factor. Eventually this will outweigh the effect of falling AFC, causing ATC to rise.

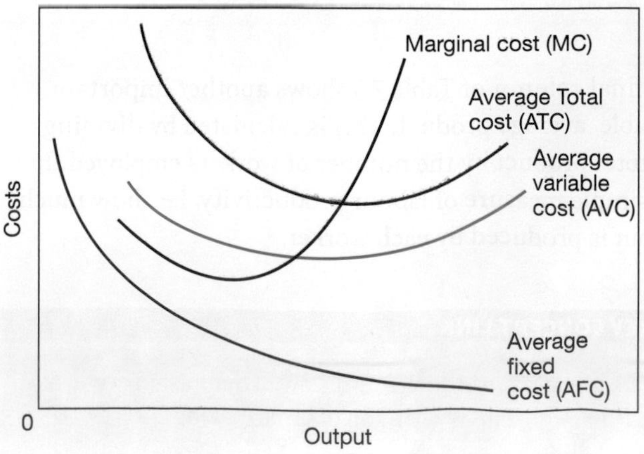

Figure 7.8 Average and marginal cost curves

This gives the classic 'U' shape to the ATC curve. On a graph of cost data, the MC will always cross AVC and ATC at their lowest points. In this situation, the most efficient output for the firm will be where the unit cost is lowest. This is known as the optimum output. It is where the firm is productively efficient in the short run; the most efficient output is not necessarily the most profitable since profit maximisation may only be possible in the long run. For a firm wishing to maximise its profits, its chosen output will depend on the relationship between its revenue and its costs.

TOP TIP

Decision making by firms is very dependent upon marginal cost. The significance of this will become clear in the rest of this chapter.

From short-run to long-run

As stated above, the short run is a period of time in Economics when at least one of the factors of production is fixed. The factor that tends to be easiest to change is labour as we have already seen. The factor that takes longest to change is capital. Students often ask the question, 'How long is the short run?' This is not an easy question to answer, as it tends to differ for different industries. In the clothing industry it is likely to be no more than a few weeks: the time that is taken to install new machines and to get these operational to produce clothing. In other industries, it will be much longer. A country building a new hydroelectric power station will, for example, take much longer to plan, install and make such a new facility operational. Ten years may well be a realistic estimate in this case. This time is still referred to as the short run since capital is fixed over this time. So, the short run is *not* defined in terms of a specific period of time; it refers to the time when not all factors of production are variable.

All factors of production are variable in the long run. This gives the firm much greater scope to vary the respective mix of its factor inputs so that it is producing at the most efficient level. So if capital becomes relatively cheaper than labour or if a new production process is invented and this increases productivity then firms can reorganise the way in which they produce. Firms must therefore know the cost of the factors of production they use and see this in relation to the additional product that accrues. Knowing costs is quite easy in the case of labour and some other basic inputs; it is more difficult to estimate for other factors of production. The best combination of factors can be arrived at as their price varies. Firms should aim to be in a position where:

$$\frac{\text{marginal product factor A}}{\text{price of factor A}} = \frac{\text{marginal product factor B}}{\text{price of factor B}} = \frac{\text{marginal product factor C}}{\text{price of factor C}}$$

and so on for all factors of production they use. For them to be able to do this all factors of production must be variable.

If we go back to the principles introduced in Figure 7.6, it is possible to derive the long-run production function for a firm by initially constructing an isoquant map. This shows the different combinations of labour and capital that can be used to produce various level of output. This is shown in Figure 7.9.

Let us again assume that this is for a clothing manufacturer. Figure 7.9a consists of a collection of isoquants for output levels of 100, 200, 300, 400 and 500 units of production. From this it is possible to read off the respective combinations of labour and capital that

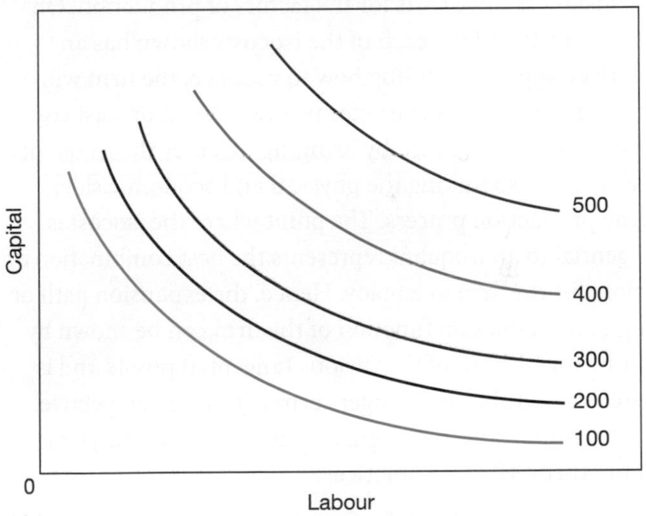

(a) Isoquant map

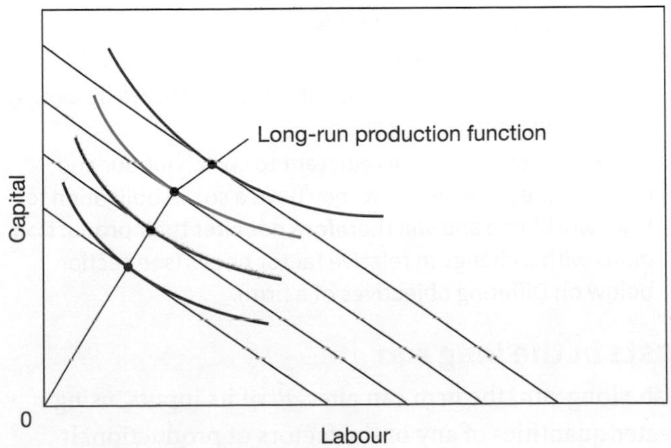

(b) Long-run production function

Figure 7.9 Isoquants and isocosts

could produce these output levels. (Remember that this is only looking at output from a physical standpoint.)

If you look at the diagram carefully you will see that as production increases from 100 to 200, relatively less capital and labour is required per unit of output. This is referred to as **increasing returns to scale**. As production expands further, increasing amounts of capital and labour are needed to produce 100 more units and so move up to the next isoquant. In contrast, this indicates **decreasing returns to scale**.

KEY TERMS

Increasing returns to scale: where output increases at a proportionately faster rate than the increase in factor inputs.

Decreasing returns to scale: where factor inputs increase at a proportionately faster rate than the increase in output.

In the long run, both labour and capital can be varied and, as stated above, the actual mix will depend upon their prices. Figure 7.9b shows what are known as isocosts: lines of constant relative costs for the factors of production. On this figure, therefore, each of the isocosts shown has an identical slope. In deciding how to produce, the firm will be looking for the most economically efficient or least cost process. This is obtained by bringing together the isoquants and isocosts, so linking the physical and economic sides of the production process. The point where the isocost is tangential to an isoquant represents the best combination of factors for the firm to employ. Hence, the expansion path or long-run production function of the firm can be shown by joining together all of the various tangential points and is therefore useful from a longer-term planning perspective.

It is important to recognise that the above analysis is highly theoretical. In practice:

- It is often very difficult for firms to determine their isoquants – they often do not have the data or the experience to be able to do this.
- It is also assumed that in the long run it is quite possible to switch factors of production. This may not always be as easy as the theory might indicate.
- Some employers may be reluctant to switch labour and capital – they may feel that they have a social obligation to their workforce and will therefore not alter their production plans with a change in relative factor prices (see section below on Differing objectives of a firm).

Costs in the long run

In the long run, the firm can alter *all* of its inputs, using greater quantities of any of the factors of production. It is now operating on a larger scale. So all of the factors of production are variable in the long run. In the very long run, technological change can alter the way the entire production process is organised, including the nature of the products themselves. In a society with rapid technological progress this will shrink the time period between the short run and the long run. In turn this will shift the firm's product curves up and its cost curves down since firms are more efficient as a consequence of new technologies. There are now examples in consumer electronics where whole processes and products have become obsolete in a matter of months let alone years as a result of more powerful microchips increasing the volume and speed of the flow of information. One has only to see how mobile phones have changed and will continue to change in the future. Another example is in air transport where the new generation of supersized jets have greatly improved fuel efficiency and reduced average costs per passenger.

It is possible that a firm can find a way of lowering its cost structure over time. One way might be by increasing the amount of capital used relative to labour in the production process, with a consequent increase in factor productivity. Car manufacturing and assembly plants are a very good example of this.

The long-run average cost (*LRAC*) curve shows the least costly combination of producing any particular quantity. Moving from its short-run equilibrium shown in Figure 7.10a, part b of this figure shows a firm experiencing falling *LRAC*s over time. This would enable it to lower the price without sacrificing profit. Products such as laptops, digital cameras, iPhones and games players are examples where prices have fallen through competition and changing technology.

The shape of the *LRAC* is derived from a series of short-run situations. As output increases so too does the scale of the firm's operations. The *LRAC* curve is a curve that just touches or is tangential to each of these short-run cost curves. It is therefore the lowest possible average cost for each level of output where the factors of production are all variable. It should be pointed out, however, that the firm is not necessarily producing at the minimum point on each of its *SRAC* curves.

Figure 7.11 shows the *LRAC* curve. This represents the firm's planning or envelope curve as it is sometimes known. It is a flatter U-shape than the *SRAC* curves and can be explained by **economies of scale** and **diseconomies of scale**.

KEY TERMS

Economies of scale: the benefits gained from falling long-run average costs as the scale of output increases.

Diseconomies of scale: where long-run average costs increase as the scale of output increases.

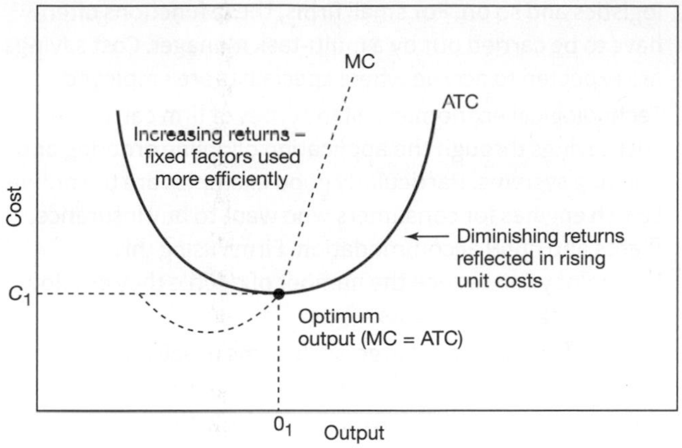

(a) Costs in the short run

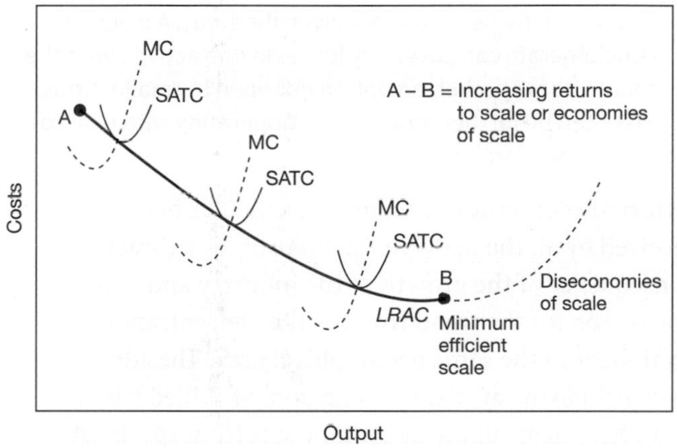

(b) Costs in the long run

Figure 7.10 A firm's costs in the short run and in the long run

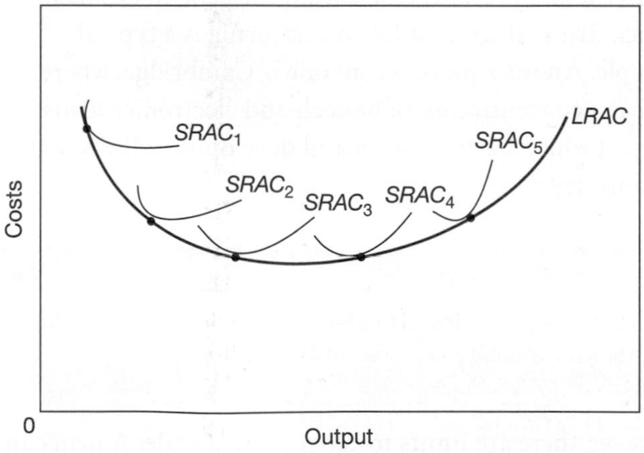

Figure 7.11 LRAC envelope curve

Economies of scale

Economies of scale occur when average costs decrease as the firm increases its output by increasing its size or scale of operations. They can therefore only accrue to a firm in the long run. Internal economies of scale are the benefits that accrue to a firm as a result of its decision to produce on a larger scale. They occur because the firm's output is rising proportionally faster than the inputs, hence the firm is getting increasing returns to scale. If the increase in output is proportional to the increase in inputs, the firm will get constant returns to scale and the *LRAC* will be horizontal. If the output is less than proportional, the firm will see diminishing returns to scale or diseconomies of scale. These are represented on Figures 7.10 and 7.11 by points on the LRAC curve beyond the minimum point.

The principal advantage for a firm benefiting from economies of scale is a reduction in the cost per unit produced, i.e., a fall in the ATC. The possible benefits

SELF-ASSESSMENT TASK 7.4

1 The following items are a selection of business costs:

- the rent of a factory
- taxes paid on turnover
- pay of production workers
- electricity charges
- interest on outstanding loans
- management salaries
- transport costs
- depreciation on fixed capital.

Indicate whether each one is likely to be fixed or variable in the short run.

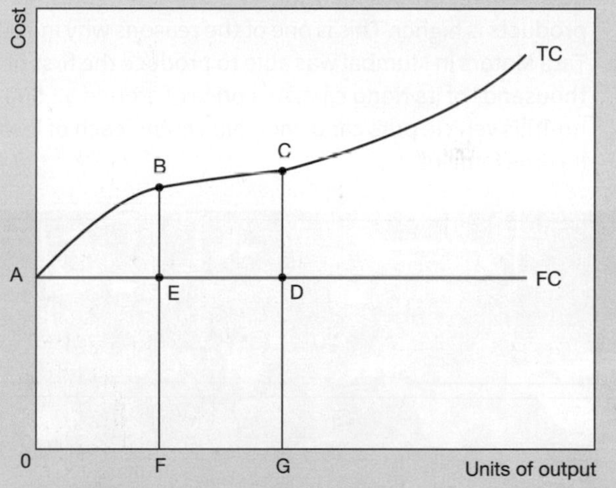

Figure 7.12

2 Study Figure 7.12. What is the:

a ATC at output G?
b AVC at output F?
c AFC at output G?
d TC at output F?

or economies depend on the nature of the economic activity. Some of the following may apply in a particular firm or industry:

- Technical economies: This refers to the advantages gained directly in the production process. Some production techniques only become viable beyond a certain level of output. A good example is in the case of container vessels, which over the years have continued to grow in size, resulting in a lower average cost per container carried. Making full use of capacity is also important on a production line. Car production is the result of various assembly lines. The number of finished vehicles per hour is limited by the pace of the slowest sub-process. Firms producing on a large scale can increase the number of slow-moving lines to keep pace with the fastest, so that no resources are standing idle and the flow of finished products is higher. This is one of the reasons why in 2009 Tata Motors in Mumbai was able to produce the first of thousands of its Nano cars. At a price of around $2,500, this no-frills vehicle puts car ownership within reach of lower-income families.

Car production in India – an example of technical economies of scale

- Purchasing economies: As firms increase in scale, they increase their purchasing power with suppliers. Through bulk buying, they are able to purchase inputs more cheaply, so reducing average costs. One of the best examples of this is the US retail giant Walmart, which uses its purchasing power to stock goods in its stores at rock bottom prices. All major retailers behave in this way.
- Marketing economies: Large-scale firms are able to promote their products on television and in newspapers at lower rates because they are able to purchase large amounts of air time and space. They are also likely to be able to make savings in their costs of distribution because of the large volumes of products being shipped.
- Managerial economies: In large-scale firms these come about as a result of specialisation. Experts can be hired to manage operations, finance, human resources, sales, logistics and so on. For small firms, these functions often have to be carried out by a multi-task manager. Cost savings are expected to accrue where specialists are employed.
- Technological economies: Many types of firm can make cost savings through the application of online ordering and booking systems. Particularly good examples are the online search engines for consumers who want to buy insurance, flights and hotel accommodation. Firms using this technology can reduce the number of people they employ, so reducing average costs.
- Financial economies: Large-scale firms usually have better and cheaper access to borrowed funds than smaller firms. This is because the perceived risk to the lender is lower.
- Risk-bearing economies: These might explain why, as firms get larger, they become more risk averse by spreading their business activities in a more diversified way. A diversified conglomerate can cover any losses in one activity with the profits from another, an option not open to smaller firms. Risks can be further reduced by cooperating with rivals on large capital projects.

External economies of scale are particular benefits received by all the firms in the industry as a direct consequence of the growth of the industry and may be one reason for the trend towards the concentration of rival firms in the same geographical area. The advantages may include the availability of a pool of skilled labour or a convenient supply of components from specialist producers who have grown up to make the items for all the firms. They may all benefit from greater access to knowledge and research and the better transport infrastructure that will result from the general expansion of such firms. Silicon Valley in California is a typical example. Another more recent one is Cambridge, where there is a concentration of biotech and electronics firms, many of which have research and development links with the university.

156

KEY TERM

External economies of scale: cost savings accruing to all firms in an industry as the scale increases.

However, there are limits to economies of scale. A firm can expand its output too much with the result that unit costs start to rise; efficiency is therefore compromised. This may be the beginning of diseconomies of scale. The most likely source of these lies in the problems of coordinating large organisations and the effect size has on morale and motivation of the workforce.

In the same way as internal diseconomies of scale are possible, the excessive concentration of economic activities in a narrow geographical location can also have disadvantages. External diseconomies may exhibit themselves in the form of:

- traffic congestion which increases distribution costs
- land shortages and therefore rising fixed costs
- shortages of skilled labour and therefore rising variable costs.

A firm that is producing at its optimum output in the short run and the lowest unit cost in the long run has maximised its efficiency. This is known as the **minimum efficient scale** since it is the lowest level of output where average costs are minimised. In industries where the minimum efficient scale is low there will be a large number of firms. Where it is high, competition will tend to be between a few large players.

KEY TERM

Minimum efficient scale: lowest level of output at which costs are minimised.

SELF-ASSESSMENT TASK 7.5

Read the feature below and then answer the questions that follow.

Transport firms gain economies of scale

Despite recession and uncertainty in the global economy and overcapacity in the industry, the world's largest sea container shipping companies are ordering new vessels in order to benefit from economies of scale. Maersk Line, the largest, took delivery in 2012 of five huge new Type-E vessels, each capable of carrying 18,270 TEUs (twenty-foot equivalent units). Another 16 vessels of the same size are currently under construction in South Korean shipyards and will be delivered to Maersk by the end of 2014.

In order to accommodate this increased capacity, Maersk, like its main rivals, is scrapping smaller vessels as these are more expensive to operate and maintain. The Asia-EU and Asia-USA markets are highly price competitive so these newer vessels will help the company to consolidate its position as the world's number one.

A second example is in air transport. The Airbus A380 is a double deck, wide body jet manufactured by the Anglo-French Airbus Corporation. It is the world's largest passenger aircraft with a maximum capacity of 853 passengers in a single class configuration or 525 passengers in the more conventional three class configuration. The aircraft's four engines are quieter and more fuel efficient compared to the aircraft it is replacing, notably the ageing Boeing 747s. There is a clear opportunity to benefit from economies of scale, particularly on busy routes where this aircraft could replace two smaller ones.

a Using the information provided, explain the likely types of economies of scale that might be gained by:
- Maersk Line
- airlines using A380s.

b How might these firms and their customers benefit from economies of scale?

c What diseconomies might arise as container vessels and aircraft increase in size?

Maersk Line container vessel

A380 aircraft

KEY CONCEPT LINK

Equilibrium and efficiency: The two examples in Self-assessment task 7.5 provide clear evidence as to how these transport markets have become more efficient over time. As a consequence, the price of air travel and the cost of moving containers from Asia to Europe is not only competitive but is likely to be falling in real terms.

The firm's revenue

In the theory of the firm, there are only two possible revenue relationships. In a competitive market, each firm has to accept the ruling market price. Its demand curve is horizontal, meaning that all it sells is at this one price. A firm in any other type of market will face a downward-sloping demand curve for its product. If the firm chooses to increase its output, the extra sales will depress the price. To look at it another way, the sales will only increase if the price is reduced from its present level. An increase in price would lead to a fall in the volume of sales. This is consistent with the basic principles of how markets operate as discussed in Chapter 2. The following definitions are used by economists when looking at a firm's revenue:

Total revenue (TR) = price × quantity
Average revenue (AR) = total revenue ÷ output.

The firm's demand curve therefore is the average revenue line.

Marginal revenue (MR) is the addition to the total revenue resulting from the sale of one additional unit. Because the firm can only sell more by reducing the price, it follows that the value for MR will always be lower than AR.

Profits

Very simply, **profit** is what is left over when total costs are deducted from total revenue. The economist's view is rather wider than the view of an accountant since the latter's approach does not fully recognise the full private costs of economic activity. As well as money paid out to factors of production, there must be an allowance for anything owned by the entrepreneur and used in the production process, such as any loans that may have been made to the business. This factor cost must be estimated and included with other costs. As we saw in Chapter 1, the idea of opportunity cost is relevant. The entrepreneur may have capital that could have been used elsewhere at no risk and this would have earned an income. So, this cost needs to be taken into account.

KEY TERM

Profit: the difference between total revenue and total costs.

An entrepreneur, therefore, will expect a minimum level of profit to reflect what could have been earned elsewhere with the resources at his or her disposal. In Economics this is known as **normal profit**. It is the entrepreneur's reward as a cost of production because without it, nothing would be produced by the firm. It is therefore the minimum return that a firm must receive to remain in business. So:

Profit = total revenue – total costs, including normal profit

KEY TERM

Normal profit: a cost of production that is just sufficient for a firm to keep operating in a particular industry.

Anything above normal profit is called **abnormal profit** or supernormal profit. The prospect of making abnormal profit motivates an entrepreneur to take risks. It can, though, act as a signal for other firms to move into a market, lured by the prospects of making abnormal profit for themselves.

KEY TERM

Abnormal profit: that which is earned above normal profit.

SELF-ASSESSMENT TASK 7.6

A small family-run engineering company has a productive capacity of 9,000 units per year. Market research suggests that the market will take up all of this output at a price of $8 per unit. The firm's cost structure is as follows:

- direct labour costs $1.50 per unit
- raw materials costs $0.50 per unit
- other variable costs $1.00 per unit, including normal profit
- the total fixed costs are $27,000 a year.

1 Calculate:
   a AFC
   b AVC
   c ATC
   d AR.
2 If the factory produced its capacity output, what would the firm's abnormal profit be?
3 Suppose that consumer tastes change away from the product and the firm has to reduce the price to $6 in order to get rid of unsold stock. What situation is the firm now in?

Firms and industries

We can now extend the earlier definition of a firm. 'Firm' is a generic term to denote a business organisation that buys or hires factors of production in order to produce goods and services that can be sold at a profit. From an organisational standpoint, firms are of many types including:

- sole traders or one-person businesses
- partnerships
- cooperatives
- private or public limited companies
- state-owned firms
- multinational or transnational firms.

Firms can range from small simple organisations to ones that are almost too complex to control and where there is some conflict of interests between the members. The characteristics and behaviour of the firm depend on the type of economic activity and the nature of competition. The factor mix in firms varies enormously, with most firms in the service sector being highly labour intensive. This contrasts with some types of manufacturing industry that are capital intensive. The decisions that firms take will vary according to the cost and availability of factors of production and be a function of the different economic systems in which they operate. In the former command economies of Central and Eastern Europe, for example, there was more emphasis on employing labour, as unemployment was virtually unknown. This has not been the case in market and mixed economies. There has been a trend in the rich Western economies of the EU to make large parts of manufacturing more capital intensive to the point where some major activities, such as car manufacturing and food processing, can largely be done by robots and computer-controlled machinery. Another trend has been increased concentration of ownership in the hands of large multinational conglomerates. At the same time, as we shall see later, there remain opportunities for new small firms to make an impact. In some developed economies like the UK, **small and medium enterprises (SMEs)** are an important engine of growth for the economy.

KEY TERM

Small and medium enterprises (SMEs): firms with fewer than 250 employees; small firms have fewer than 50 employees.

The Industry

In a competitive market structure, the **industry** is simply the sum of all the firms making the same product. This is the total market supply. In other markets, the industry is taken to be the total number of firms producing within the same product group, i.e., things that are close substitutes for each other. It is sometimes difficult to draw the line between different industries; for example, are motor cars and motorcycles in the same product group? In reality many multi-product firms operate in more than one industry at the same time. A **multinational corporation (MNC)** can be in several industries across the global economy. A particularly good example is the Indian-owned Tata Group, which has global interests in steel, vehicle production, upmarket hotels, tea production, telecommunications and electronics. Another is Nestlé, which produces a wide range of food and confectionery products worldwide.

KEY TERMS

Industry: all firms making the same product or in the same line of business.

Multinational corporations (MNCs): firms that operate in different countries.

The industry is therefore a collection of business organisations that supply similar products to the market. When a firm's market share is discussed it tends to be in terms of the sales of the firm as a percentage of the total sales of all firms in the industry. The terms 'industry' and 'market' are interchangeable in this context.

Tata Group companies

Market structures

The term **market structure** describes the way in which goods and services are supplied by firms in a particular market or industry. More specifically, it relates to how a market is organised in terms of the number of firms and the **barriers to entry** for new firms wishing to join the market.

KEY TERMS

Market structure: the way in which a market is organised in terms of the number of firms and the barriers to the entry of new firms.

Barriers to entry: any restrictions that prevent new firms from entering an industry.

Over the years, economists have developed models of market structures. These are an idealistic representation of a market; their value is that any real market can be compared or benchmarked against the models and conclusions drawn with respect to their efficiency.

Figure 7.13 shows the four models of market structure that are widely applied in Economics. It indicates the two limiting cases of **perfect competition** and **monopoly**. They are at opposite ends of the spectrum of competition. In between are **monopolistic competition** and **oligopoly**, both of which are evidenced in most economies. Apart from perfect competition, all other market structures on this figure are referred to as being in **imperfect competition**.

KEY TERMS

Perfect competition: an ideal market structure that has many buyers and sellers, identical or homogeneous products, no barriers to entry.

Monopoly: a pure monopoly is just one firm in an industry with very high barriers to entry.

Monopolistic competition: a market structure where there are many firms, differentiated products and few barriers to entry.

Oligopoly: a market structure with few firms and high barriers to entry.

Imperfect competition: any market structure except for perfect competition.

The following stages can help to identify a market structure within this spectrum of competition:

- Counting the number of firms. The larger the total, the closer to perfect competition.
- A better guide is to use a concentration ratio to see the combined market share of the biggest three, four or five firms in the industry as a percentage of the industry total. This is calculated by adding the percentage market shares in terms of volume or sales revenue for the largest three, four or five firms. The bigger the percentage, the closer the industry will be to the oligopoly and monopoly models.
- By considering how easy or difficult it is for new firms to set up and how easy it is for firms to exit the industry. Barriers are indicative of market structures on the less competitive side of the spectrum.
- By considering the importance of economies of scale to firms. The more important they are, the closer the industry will be to an oligopoly.

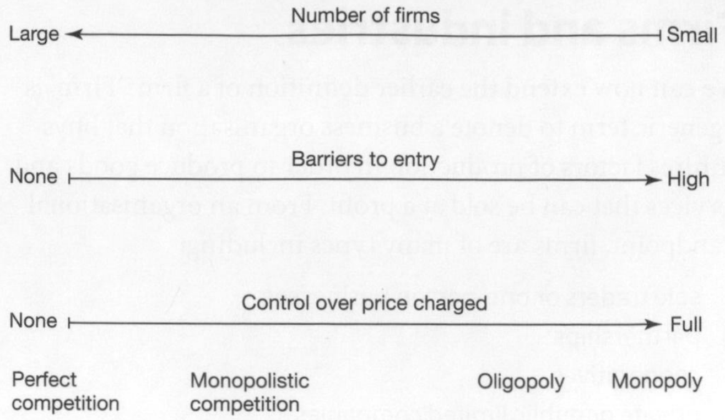

Figure 7.13 The spectrum of competition

Figure 7.14 shows a competition road map. This shows the characteristics and some aspects of the behaviour of firms for each of the main models. In terms of a journey, it indicates how markets move from being fully competitive and allowing new entrants to join to being heavily protected from competition. The obvious judgement might be 'competition good', 'no competition bad'. This is often true but, as we shall show, the opportunity to compete is invariably crucial in determining efficiency in a market.

Perfect competition

Perfect competition is a theoretical extreme. The main point of studying this model is that it acts as a benchmark for real-world competition. The performance of actual firms can be judged against this most efficient model. (Some of the characteristics are shared by the next most competitive model, which somewhat confusingly is known as monopolistic competition.)

Perfect competition has the following characteristics:

- There is a large number of buyers and sellers who have perfect knowledge of market conditions and the price that is charged.
- No individual firm has any influence on the market price. Firms are described as being price takers. The ruling price is determined by the forces of market demand and the output of all the firms.
- The products are homogeneous or identical. This means that they are all of the same quality and are identical in the eyes of the consumer.

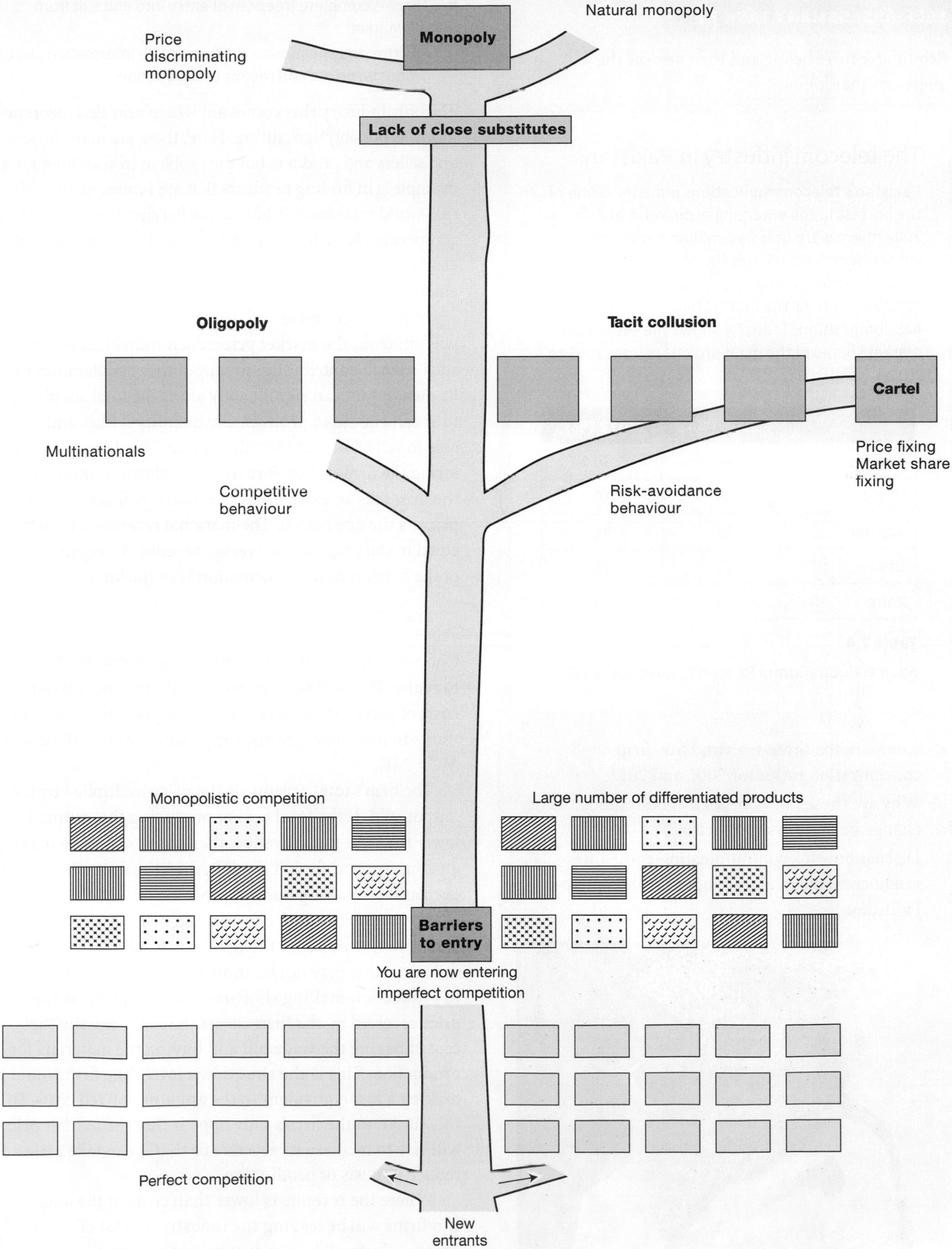

Figure 7.14 A competition road map

SELF-ASSESSMENT TASK 7.7

Read the feature below and then answer the questions that follow.

The telecom industry in Pakistan

Pakistan's telecommunications industry is one of the hottest in the emerging economies of Asia. In 2002, there were only two million mobile phone subscribers; by 2005, this figure had grown to around 40 million and by mid-2012, it had soared to 125 million. As the market has grown, so too has competition. Table 7.4 shows the estimated market shares of the main providers from 2005 to 2012.

	2005 (%)	2012 (%)
Mobilink	49	30
Warid	14	10
Telenor	11	25
Ufone	21	15
Zong	1	14

Table 7.4

Source: BuddeComm Research, Australia, 2013

a Compare the three-firm and five-firm concentration ratios for 2005 and 2012.

b Why are these not necessarily good indicators of change in the market structure?

c Discuss how telecommunication companies might compete in a growing market like that of Pakistan.

- There is complete freedom of entry into and exit from the market.
- All firms and consumers have complete information about products, prices and means of production.

The only industry that comes anywhere near this theoretical model is possibly agriculture. Here, there are many buyers and sellers and products but the problem in searching for an example is in finding products that are homogeneous. Most real-world markets also have some barriers to entry. Perfect competition has a lot of appeal as a yardstick because, if it were to operate, there would be consumer sovereignty and efficient production with no possibility of exploitation.

In perfect competition, the firm cannot do anything that will influence the market price. Each individual firm makes such a small contribution to output that no alteration in its own output can significantly affect the total supply. The firm can choose to produce any quantity it likes and will be able to sell all of it at the ruling price. The demand curve facing the firm is therefore perfectly elastic at this price. If the firm sells an extra unit of output, it will get the same price as the one before. The marginal revenue is therefore equal to the price or the average revenue. In Figure 7.15, all of the firm's revenue information is in the line:

$$D = AR = MR$$

Choosing the output is the only decision that the firm has to make. This will be done by considering the relevant costs of production. Given the assumption that the firm wants to maximise profits, the chosen output will be where MC = MR.

The firm's total revenue is the price multiplied by the output sold. If the total cost of producing this output is lower than the total revenue, then the firm will be making an abnormal profit. If TC = TR, then the firm would break even and be making normal profit.

It is possible that the costs could be higher than the revenue, in which case the firm may be about to exit the industry. This may not be immediate: a firm can continue in production making short-run losses, as long as the price received by the firm covers the AVC, usually the cost of paying the wage bill and buying the materials for production. This is the shut-down price. The firm would be making a loss equivalent to the amount of fixed costs. In this situation the firm's only hope is that the market price will rise to increase its revenue or that it can take action to reduce its costs of production.

Where the revenue is lower than costs in the long run firms will be leaving the industry. If a lot of them do, the effect will be a reduction in the overall market supply, which will raise the market price, giving the rest

SELF-ASSESSMENT TASK 7.8

Read the feature below and then answer the questions that follow.

Public transport in Hong Kong

Hong Kong is a very densely populated city of over seven million people. It is also relatively affluent by Asian standards yet has a very low level of car ownership at around 70 per thousand population. An efficient public transport system is absolutely critical in allowing this busy city to function.

Hong Kong has a diverse public transport system consisting of modern surface rail (KCR) to the New Territories as well as to Guanghou in mainland China. It has an extensive mass transit system (MTR), franchised bus services, tram services, various ferry services, minibuses and public taxis. All are privately owned. Unusually, no subsidies are paid for their operation by the Hong Kong government.

In 2007, the KCR and MTR companies were amalgamated to form a new integrated company, the MTR Corporation. This move was designed to cut out wasteful competition and duplication while providing scope for economies of scale. It was also seen as a way of generating new investment in the rail system, not least because of the extensive property portfolio owned by the MTR Corporation.

Franchised bus services are operated by five large companies. Each has its own geographical group of services. Fares, frequency levels, types of vehicle, routes and even bus stops are all part of the franchise arrangement with the government. There are a few pinch points and stretches of route where they compete with each other.

The famous Star Ferry, with cross-harbour services, and the Hong Kong Tramways Company on Hong Kong Island are long-established operators that charge very low fares and have a unique brand and a loyal customer base. They are the only providers of their modes of transport although buses and taxis as well as private cars compete with them. Victoria Harbour has three privately operated road tunnels, the oldest and most congested of which is the Cross Harbour Tunnel. The tolls charged are competitive.

Hong Kong has 4,400 minibuses, known locally as public light buses. The 2,800 green-topped ones can carry 16 seated passengers on fixed routes. The remaining red ones are more flexible and not as strictly regulated. The fares charged are competitive and can be determined by the driver. Many are owned by the driver or by small companies.

Finally, Hong Kong has 15,000 red urban Toyota taxis. Fares are strictly regulated by meter and vehicle numbers fixed by the government. Most are privately owned or leased from small local companies by their drivers.

1 Use the evidence above to provide examples of monopoly, natural monopoly, oligopoly and monopolistic competition. Justify your answers.
2 Explain what additional information you might need to be more certain of these market structures.
3 Discuss the extent to which similar market structures can be found in the public transport system in your own country.

an opportunity to continue producing and at least make normal profit. In the long run, firms will only supply the market if they can cover all of their costs and make a normal profit. The minimum supply for the firm will be the optimum output where average costs are lowest.

In perfect competition, firms will only make different amounts of profit from each other if they have different cost structures. Their behaviour is strictly limited and the only way to boost profit would be to increase productivity and lower average total cost.

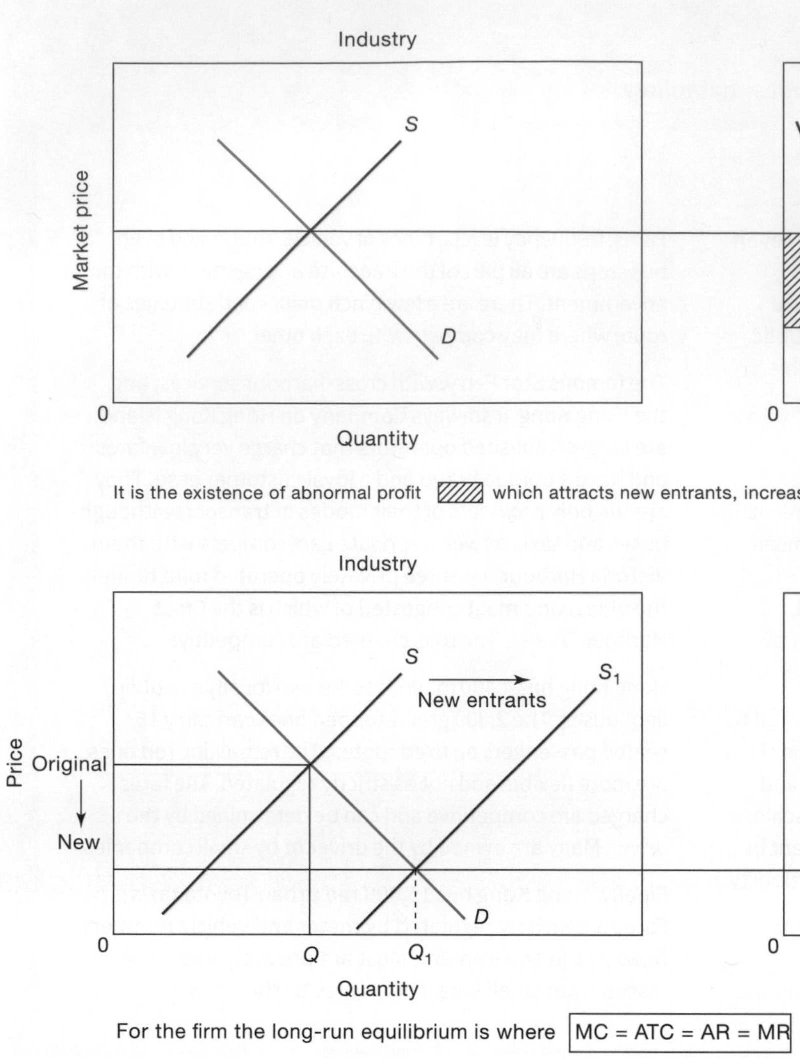

Figure 7.15 The perfect competition model

Abnormal profit will only be a feature of perfect competition in the short run. This is because its existence will act as an incentive for the entry of new firms. The absence of barriers to entry means that the total supply in the market will rise. The effect of this on the existing firms is that the market price will fall and the abnormal profit will diminish. When the abnormal profit goes, the entry of new firms dries up, and the existing ones will simply be covering costs. It is the competitive force of large numbers of new entrants that destroys abnormal profit.

The long-run equilibrium is therefore where the only firms left are the most efficient ones, making a normal profit. In this situation, there is no action that the firm can take to prosper at the expense of rivals. It has no market power. Firms' behaviour is easy to understand. The appeal of this model is that abnormal profit is competed away and the only firms that participate in the market in the long run are productively and allocatively efficient. It is this efficient economic performance which occurs in perfect competition that can be used to criticise real-world market structures.

KEY CONCEPT LINK

The market and change: The idealistic model of perfect competition is the most efficient in the long run. All other market structures are inefficient to varying degrees.

TOP TIP

Perfect competition is sometimes called total competition.

SELF-ASSESSMENT TASK 7.9

Study the diagrams in Figure 7.16 and then answer the questions that follow.

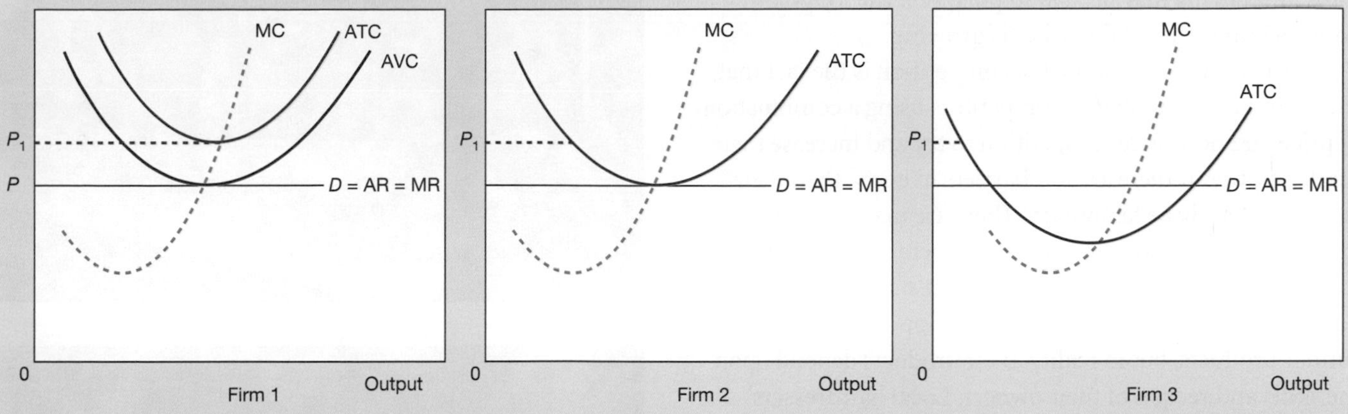

Figure 7.16 Perfect competition – three different cost situations

1. Describe each firm's position with respect to profit.
2. If market demand increased and price rose to P_1, how would it affect each firm?
3. According to the theory of perfect competition, what will then happen?
4. What output does a firm in perfect competition choose?
5. How can an individual firm increase its profits?

Monopolistic competition

This is the market structure closest to the model of perfect competition because of the large number of competing suppliers.

Monopolistic competition has the following characteristics:

- There is a large number of buyers and sellers.
- There are few barriers to entry into the market and it is easy for firms to recoup their capital expenditure on exit from the market.
- Consumers face a wide choice of differentiated products. Each firm has a slight degree of monopoly power in that it controls its own brand through quality and physical differences.
- Firms have some influence on the market price and are therefore price makers.

Each firm is competing with a large number of similar producers. In this situation the demand curve facing the individual firm will be downward-sloping but relatively price elastic because of the presence of substitutes. It is an option for firms to reduce their price in order to increase total revenue. As in perfect competition, the firms can make abnormal profit in the short run but the key restraint on their power is the free entry of rivals. In the long run, profit-maximising firms will only be able to achieve normal profit covering all the production costs and the opportunity cost of capital.

The clue to the behaviour of firms in this market structure lies in the concept of product differentiation. The development of a strong brand image must be seen as an act of investment on the part of the individual firm. This highlights the important role that advertising and promotions play in this market structure. Successful advertising will not only shift the firm's demand curve to the right at the expense of rivals but will also reduce the price elasticity of demand if the consumers feel there are no close substitutes. This is what is meant by brand loyalty – people will not easily shift back to rival products. There are problems associated with advertising because it is a competitive tool taken up by all firms. One could argue that the advantage will be temporary and that advertising will simply add to the firm's costs and bring little benefit to its demand curve. If advertising is not effective for all firms, those who are successful might take advantage of their greater market share and brand loyalty to charge a higher price. These firms would increase their sales revenue and by doing so move to the portion of the demand curve where price elasticity of demand has a value less than 1, i.e., inelastic.

It is easy to see how each firm can try to strengthen its market power in the short run. The constraint on firms is that there is freedom of entry into the market, which will threaten the existence of abnormal profit in the long run. By a combination of marketing and product innovation, individual firms may be able to postpone the long-run equilibrium if the total market is growing.

At the heart of this model of competition is the fact that there are a large number of competitors using a combination of price and non-price competition to try and increase their market power. If there are few barriers to entry, then their success will only be temporary. There are many typical examples of this market structure in operation. Take-away food outlets and local privately owned restaurants are particularly good examples. They may appear to be selling similar products, but in reality, their products depend upon the skills and recipes of their owners. Local hairdressers' shops, market stalls, driving schools and travel agents also exhibit the characteristics of this market structure.

Figure 7.17 shows the equilibrium price and output in monopolistic competition. In the short run, the profit-maximising firm will be seen to make abnormal profits. In time these will be competed away by the entry of new firms, which will shift the firm's original demand curve to the left. This process will continue until all firms in the industry are making normal profit. A key point though is that in both the short and the long run the firm is inefficient. This because it operates on but above the minimum point of its average total cost curve resulting in a situation of excess capacity. Additionally, the firm is not allocatively efficient as $P > \text{MC}$.

TOP TIP

Monopolistic competition is not the same market structure as monopoly; firms in monopolistic competition do though have a type of monopoly over the differentiated products they sell.

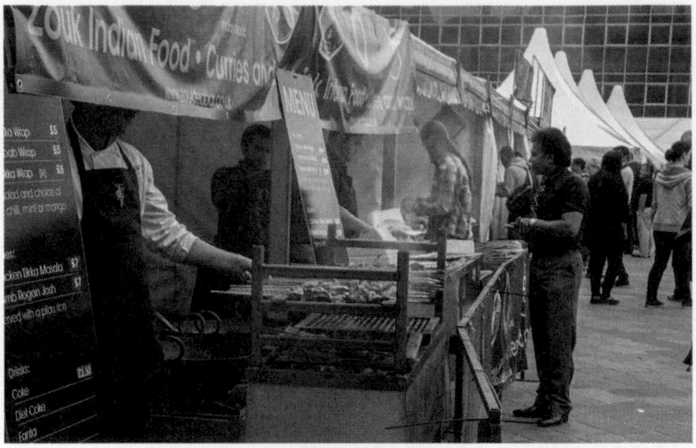

Take-away food outlets in Islamabad (top) and Bradford (below)

Barriers to entry

The existence of substantial barriers to entry into an industry differentiates oligopoly and monopoly from monopolistic competition and perfect competition.

Barriers to entry are a range of obstacles that deter or prevent *new* firms from entering a market to compete with existing firms. They give firms a degree of market power in that decisions can be made by existing firms without

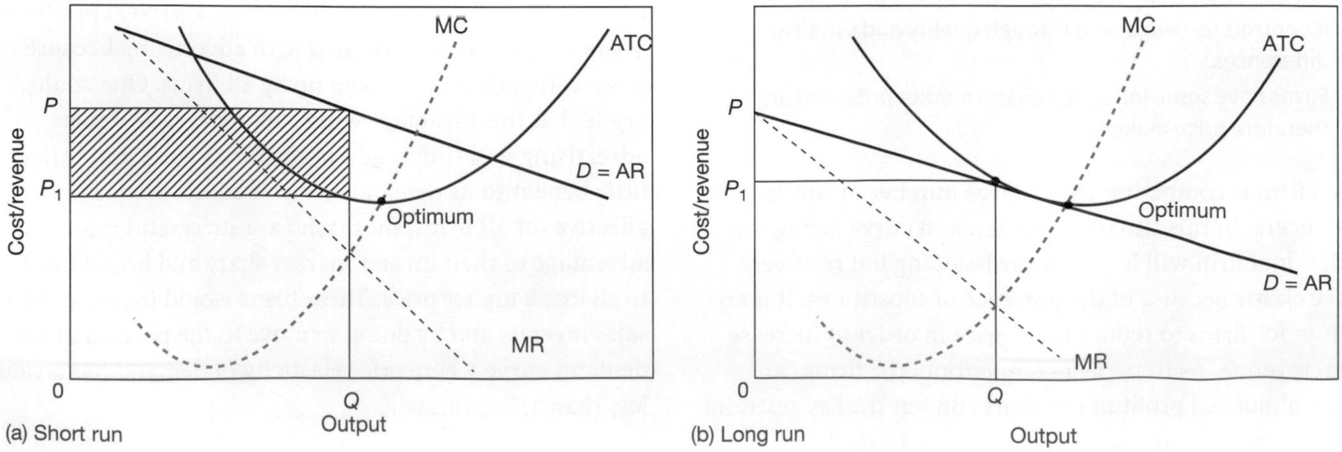

Figure 7.17 Monopolistic competition in the short and the long run

SELF-ASSESSMENT TASK 7.10

Read the feature below and then answer the questions that follow.

Bradford, Curry Capital of Britain, 2013

Bradford in West Yorkshire has once again been voted Britain's Curry Capital. In a hard-fought competition, this city of half a million people beat its long-term rival Glasgow, with Wolverhampton in third place.

Bradford has an eclectic mixture of hundreds of Asian eateries. These range from some top end fine dining restaurants to a multitude of local cafés and take-aways. Virtually all are small businesses, operated and managed by their Pakistani, Indian and Bangladeshi owners.

To the outsider, a curry might be just a curry. In Bradford, this is most certainly not the case. Each establishment tends to have its own take on rogan josh, biryani, vindaloo and that British staple, chicken tikka masala, a very mild curry dish. Variations in the product are usually indicative of the region where the owners or their families lived before coming to Bradford.

The business is competitive, although prices tend not to vary within particular market segments. Quality is essential for owners to remain in business. Most outlets do not openly advertise but rely heavily on word of mouth and strong repeat business to earn a living.

1 What evidence is there to suggest that the market is monopolistically competitive?

2 What additional evidence might you need to be more certain?

3 Why is the market for curry establishments in Bradford not perfectly competitive?

the risk of their market share or price being challenged from outside. The construction and maintenance of these barriers can become part of the firm's behaviour. Below are some of the main barriers:

- In some countries, it may be impossible for new firms to enter an industry because the economic activity is state-owned or the good is produced under licence from the government. This is a legal monopoly usually created to achieve social and political objectives. The economic justification might lie in the concept of a **natural monopoly**, where it is more efficient to have a single producer than to have competing firms, for example in the case of railways. Alternatively, in countries where the former state-owned resources have been privatised and the market has been deregulated, the economic justification is that the injection of competition will bring additional economic and social benefits through a more efficient allocation of resources.
- The high fixed cost or setup cost in activities such as electricity generation, aircraft and car production and pharmaceuticals may deter potential entrants. The barrier here is access to capital. Only very large firms will be able to fund the necessary investment. Research and development costs will represent a high proportion of total costs and it will require high sales over a long period of time before the activity becomes profitable.
- If a firm is shutting down and some costs such as research and development costs cannot be recovered. The resources are specialised and are not easily transferrable to other uses. They are regarded as sunk costs and act as a **barrier to exit** from the industry because the capital investment will be lost. It is therefore the risk of entering and the high cost of failure that deters potential entrants and so acts as a barrier to entry.
- Advertising and brand names with a high degree of consumer loyalty may prove a difficult obstacle to overcome. This explains why firms regard their expenditure on advertising and promotion as a type of investment. Existing firms can make entry more difficult through brand proliferation, giving consumers an apparent abundance of choice and closing market niches. Successful advertising can not only shift a firm's demand curve to the right but it can also reduce its price elasticity of demand.

KEY TERM

Natural monopoly: where a single supplier has substantial cost advantages such that competing producers would raise costs and where duplication will produce an inefficient use of resources.

KEY TERM

Barrier to exit: any restriction that prevents a firm leaving a market.

This gives the firm greater market power because consumers do not see the rival firm's product as a close substitute on account of extensive persuasive advertising.

- Economies of scale can be a barrier because the existing large producers are able to produce at a lower average cost than those just starting up. They also give large firms an opportunity to cut their price in order to eliminate any high-cost producers. This is the concept of predatory pricing, which can be used to eliminate any new firms that do enter the industry.
- The production process or the products of a firm may be protected by a legal monopoly in the form of a patent, whereby competitors cannot copy without the permission of the owner. The idea is to guarantee a reward to entrepreneurs with original ideas for a reasonable period of time. The barrier here is access to either technology or information.
- Some existing firms may have monopoly access to raw materials, components or retail outlets, which will make it difficult for new entrants to make an impact. Vertically integrated manufacturing businesses, where a firm is a specialist in different stages of production, will be protected by the fact that their rivals' costs will be higher.
- In activities such as consumer electronics, the pace of product innovation is so rapid that the existing firms will be working on the next generation of products while launching the current range. Unless the new entrants have original ideas or can exploit a new market segment, they are destined to fail.
- It may be possible for existing firms to hide the existence of abnormal profit by what is called **limit pricing**. This involves deliberately setting a low price and temporarily abandoning profit maximisation as their objective to deter new entrants. It may be in the interest of all the firms to do this and if they agree, it becomes a form of collusion.
- Collaboration between existing producers to develop new products may act as a barrier in that the resources necessary to compete are beyond the means of single new producers.
- Market conditions, such as a fall in demand resulting from recession, can leave producers with surplus productive capacity and this will deter entry.

KEY TERM

Limit pricing: where firms deliberately lower prices and abandon a policy of profit maximisation to stop new firms entering a market.

Where the barriers are strong, the market is likely to be dominated by a few large producers. New firms will only enter if they think that the economic returns will be greater than the cost of breaking down the barriers to entry.

The concept of barriers to entry is central to understanding where the models of oligopoly and monopoly fit within the spectrum of competition.

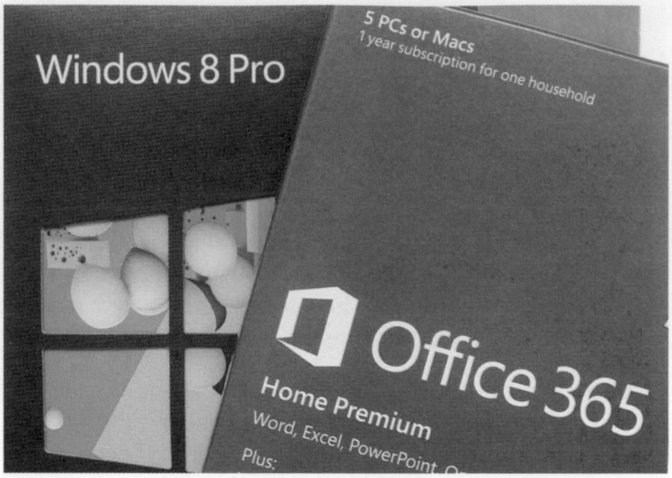

Microsoft Windows and Office software: a patented product

Oligopoly

Oligopoly is defined as a market situation where the total output is concentrated in the hands of a few firms. It is possibly the most realistic model of market structure but, ironically, the theory does not provide the definite predictions regarding the price and output of the firm that exist in every other model. An effective oligopoly can exist in an apparently competitive industry even when a handful of firms dominate the market.

An oligopoly has the following characteristics:

- The market is dominated by a few firms.
- Their decisions are interdependent. Firms must decide their market strategy to compete with close rivals, but they must also try to anticipate their rivals' reactions and think what the next step should be in the light of this response.
- There are high or substantial barriers to entry.
- The products may be differentiated or undifferentiated.
- The uncertainty and risks associated with price competition may lead to price rigidity.

There are many examples of oligopolistic markets. The telecommunications industry in Pakistan is like this (see Self-assessment task 7.7). The retail grocery supermarket business in the UK is a particularly good example; Tesco, Asda, Sainsbury's and Morrison's have more than 70% of the market. Another very relevant example is the growing car manufacturing and assembly industry in China (See Figure 7.18).

The difficulty in studying oligopoly is that behaviour can follow two very different routes. There is evidence of aggressive competition in some industries, while in others there is a suggestion of cooperation and even collusion.

Oligopolists are price makers but one of the dangers of using this weapon is that the firm can get drawn into a price

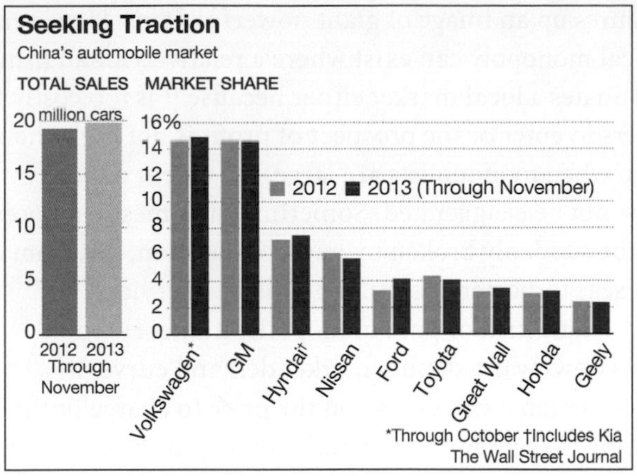

Figure 7.18 China's automobile market
Sources: the companies; China Association of Automobile Manufacturers

war. An oligopolist would only start a price war if its costs of production were significantly lower than those of its rivals. A price war may be the natural outcome of events, such as overcapacity in the industry or the entry of new firms. It could also be a defensive tactic where an oligopoly is losing market share to its rivals. A very good example of this is in the supermarket business in the UK where the market leaders, Tesco especially, are being increasingly challenged by non-UK discounters such as Aldi and Lidl. Where the firms are highly diversified, a firm may be prepared to sacrifice profits by cutting the price, in an attempt to increase or even retain market share. Profits from some of its activities may be used to cover short-term losses elsewhere in the business.

Although they each have market power in the form of influence over the prices they charge, the uncertainty surrounding the outcome of competitive tactics means that firms may prefer non-price competition. The observation is that prices tend to be similar between oligopolists and are stable over time.

The firm will therefore be better off concentrating on non-price competition to increase revenue. This may include the following:

- advertising and promotions
- product innovation – the attempt to make the products more appealing to consumers
- brand proliferation – where the firm produces lots of brands to saturate the market and to leave no gaps for rivals
- market segmentation – producers may decide that there are markets where the consumers have different characteristics and needs, and these market niches will be catered for through product innovation
- process innovation – usually seen as a way of reducing average costs, allowing the firm to cut the price without sacrificing profits.

KEY TERM

Horizontal integration: where a firm grows through a merger or acquisition of another firm in the same sector of an industry.

One way for a firm to grow rapidly would be to take over one of its rivals. This so-called **horizontal integration** may in fact be the cheapest way of getting growth in sales if the competing oligopolists are of a similar size. If a takeover or merger is likely to be resisted, a firm wanting to get rapid growth may prefer to look for more profits by producing in different countries and eventually become a multinational corporation.

The difficulty of choosing competitive strategies and of predicting the response of rivals may change the objectives of the firm. Profit-maximising strategies may be replaced by 'satisficing' (see below). The firm's management becomes more cautious, preferring to make just enough profit to keep the shareholders happy. The focus shifts towards maintaining market share.

Cooperation and collusion between oligopolists

There are situations where big firms find that it is in their interest to cooperate with rivals. One of the best examples is where research and development costs are a high proportion of the total costs and where the pace of technological change is very rapid. It is in the interests of all the firms to pool their knowledge and agree on technical standards, perhaps taking part in joint ventures.

Collusion is altogether different. It is an anti-competitive action by producers. Informal or tacit collusion, however, is not illegal and usually takes the form of **price leadership**, where firms automatically follow the lead of one of the group. The objective is to maximise the profits of the whole group by acting as a single monopolist. The price leader is invariably the dominant firm and has sufficient market power to determine a price change that other firms follow. On the other hand, a **cartel** is a formal price or output agreement between firms in an industry to restrict competition. This is illegal. Figure 7.19 below shows what happens when firms join a cartel and agree prices. By doing this, they are operating as a monopoly and maximising their profits.

KEY TERMS

Price leadership: a situation in a market whereby a particular firm has the power to change prices, the result of which is that competitors follow this lead.

Cartel: a formal agreement between firms to limit competition by limiting output or fixing prices.

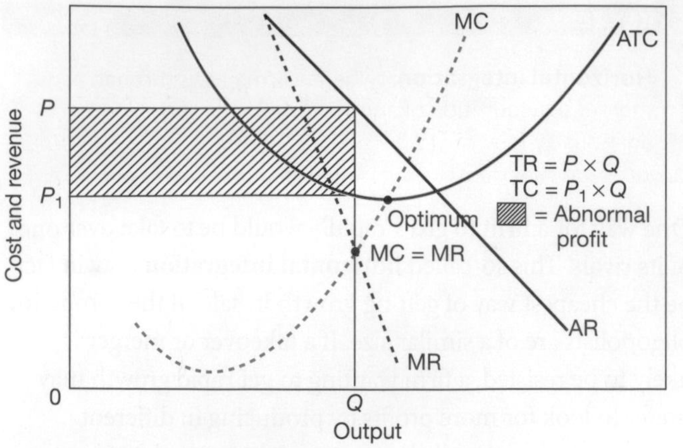

Figure 7.19 The equilibrium of a pure monopoly

Collusion is more likely to be tacit where the behaviour of each firm is the result of an unwritten rather than formal agreement. As noted above, one of the simplest forms is a follow-the-leader agreement, where each firm will only adjust its price following a move by the dominant firm. There are other price leadership models, such as using a typical firm as the yardstick for price. This will only change if a rise in costs affects the profit margin. The principle is the same: each firm will act in the same way in the interests of the group as a whole.

In practice, it is difficult to identify either tacit or formal agreements. This is because price similarities can be the result of either aggressive pricing in a competitive oligopoly or the outcome of a collusive agreement. This makes investigations into anti-competitive behaviour by organisations such as the UK's new (2014) Competition and Markets Authority difficult and invariably inconclusive.

Monopoly

A monopoly is where a single firm controls the entire output of the industry. This is called a pure monopoly and is at the opposite end of the spectrum to perfect competition. In practice, this strict definition is relaxed in so far as a monopoly can occur when a firm has a dominant position in terms of its market share. In the UK, for example, a legal monopoly is when a firm has more than 25% of the total market; if this share exceeds 40% then the monopoly is said to be 'dominant'.

In theory, a monopoly has the following characteristics:

- a single seller
- no close substitutes
- high barriers to entry
- the monopolist is a price maker.

A monopoly is protected from competition by the barriers to entry explained earlier. The word 'monopoly' conjures up an image of giant powerful firms. However, a local monopoly can exist where a relatively small firm dominates a local market either because it is too costly for others to enter or the prospect of profit is not high enough. Even when monopolists are large, the extent of power must not be exaggerated. Sometimes a domestic monopoly can be suddenly broken by new competition, say, from an overseas importer of similar goods and services.

A single firm or pure monopolist in theory would face a downward-sloping market demand curve. In this situation it can decide on the price to charge or the quantity to supply, but not both. There may be situations where the monopolist is unable to make abnormal profits despite having market power. One such example would be where the fixed costs are so high that the necessary price would be outside the range that the consumers could afford. This could occur, for example, in the case of a new groundbreaking pharmaceutical product. It may be that all the monopolist can hope for is that the revenue covers the production costs.

Figure 7.19 shows the equilibrium output of a pure monopolist. A profit-maximising monopolist would choose the output where MC = MR. This output will be somewhere over the price range where demand is price elastic and will be sold at the price consumers will pay. If the total revenue is higher than the production costs, it will make abnormal profit. This will be a permanent feature. In monopoly, there is no distinction between the short run and the long run because of the barriers that prevent the entry of competitors. There is no economic incentive for the monopolist to move away from the profit-maximising output *Q*.

The monopolist's profits could be increased in certain circumstances by a practice known as price discrimination. This occurs where the monopolist chooses to split up the output and sell it at different prices to different customers. This practice will be analysed in more detail towards the end of this chapter.

> **TOP TIP**
> The pure monopoly model assumes that the firm controls the whole market; in practice, a monopoly may have as little as 25% market share.

Natural monopoly

A natural monopoly is a market situation where a monopolist has overwhelming cost advantage. In theory this can come about where a monopoly has sole ownership of a resource or where past ownership of capital resources means that it is difficult and extremely expensive for competitors to duplicate these installations. It would also be extremely wasteful to do so.

The natural monopoly case is one that has consistently been put forward in support of public ownership of services such as water, gas and electricity. It is also applicable to railways and canals. In all of these cases, fixed costs are a very high percentage of total costs. As output increases, average fixed costs will decline offering the prospect of substantial benefits to be gained from economies of scale. With a canal, for example, long-run average costs per vessel using the canal will fall since the total costs are spread over an increased number of vessels. The same argument applies in the case of rail track.

Figure 7.20 is the usual representation of a natural monopoly. It shows a falling long-run average cost curve, indicative of continuing economies of scale. A monopoly firm would set price at P_1, provide Q_1 output and earn abnormal profits. If it behaved like a competitive firm, the equilibrium position would be where price equals long-run marginal cost – price would be lower at P_2, the quantity provided higher at Q_2. This is a loss-making position. The problem is that this will only happen if the government is prepared to subsidise the monopoly on the grounds that what it is providing is an essential public service. The alternative is for the service to be provided by the public sector.

The natural monopoly case is particularly strong in the case of railways, canals, piped water supplies and electricity. There is little economic logic in having rival companies competing with each other especially as, with rail, government subsidies are required to keep the system functioning at a social optimum level.

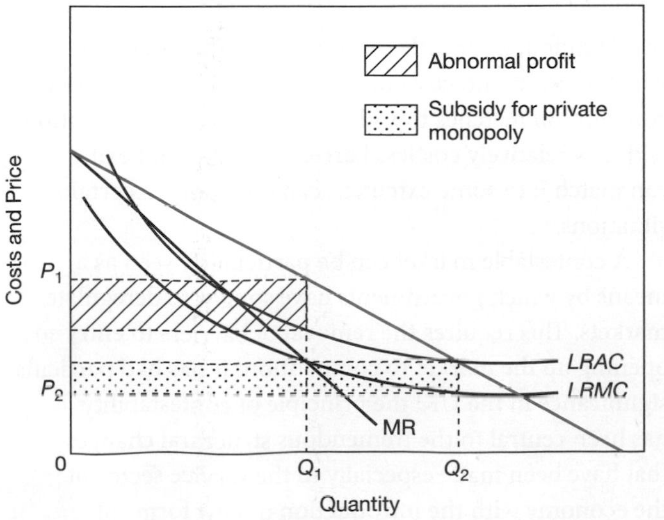

Figure 7.20 Natural monopoly

Comparing monopoly with perfect competition

Figure 7.21 shows the equilibrium price and output of a monopolist charging a single price in a market free of government intervention and what would occur in a perfectly competitive industry.

The classic case against a monopoly is that its conduct and performance is undesirable when compared with that of firms in more competitive markets. The following observations can be made comparing the two equilibrium positions:

- The price in monopoly is higher than it is in perfect competition.
- The monopoly output is lower.
- The monopolist is making short- and long-run abnormal profits.
- The firm in perfect competition is productively efficient, producing the optimum output.
- It is also allocatively efficient, producing where price = MC.
- The monopolist captures consumer surplus and turns it into abnormal profit.
- The monopolist is productively inefficient, producing less than the optimum output in the search for extra profit.
- The price charged is well above marginal cost and so is not allocatively efficient.
- If a perfectly competitive industry was turned into a monopoly, there would be a welfare loss of area *x* in addition to greater allocative inefficiency.

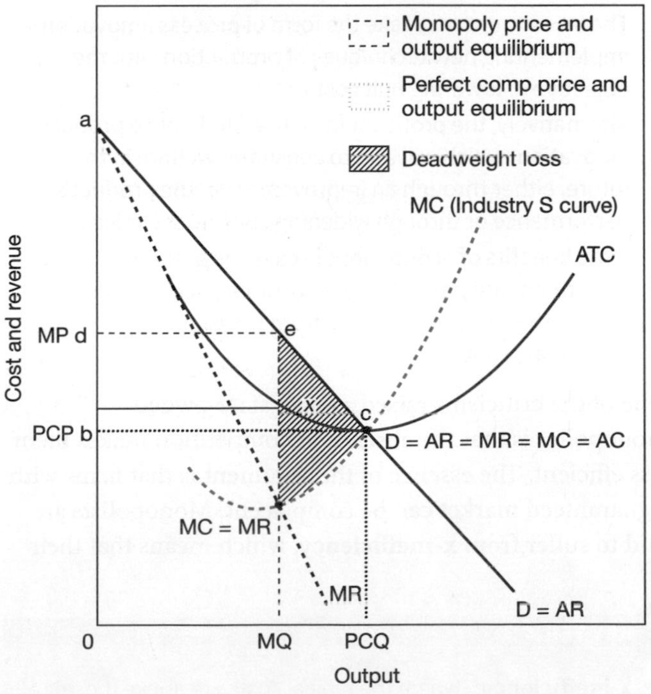

Figure 7.21 A comparison of a perfectly competitive industry with a profit maximising monopolist

The criticisms of real-world monopolies based on a comparison with perfect competition may not be valid for two reasons. First, perfect competition is a theoretical ideal. To have more applicability, monopoly must be compared with the more relevant models of monopolistic competition and oligopoly. These are also characterised by productive and allocative inefficiency. They may also involve a waste of resources in competitive advertising. Secondly, Figure 7.21 is drawn on the assumption that the costs in monopoly will be the same as in perfect competition. This ignores the possibility that the monopolist can achieve internal economies of scale that would reduce unit costs. It is possible that a monopolist could charge a lower price than would occur in perfect competition, making consumers better off, even though the monopolist is making abnormal profits.

There are, however, positives that can be said of monopolies in the following circumstances:

- A monopolist cannot always make abnormal profit – it depends how high its costs are. There may be situations where the fixed costs are so high relative to the total cost that the market price only just covers the average costs. In this case the monopolist would only make normal profit.
- The concept of abnormal profit must be considered carefully. One of the criticisms of a competitive market is the uncertainty of profits in the long run. A monopolist however can plan future investment and finance it through what are guaranteed profits. This may offer customers better products and the workforce greater security.
- The investment may take the form of process innovation, implementing new techniques of production with the objective of lowering unit costs.
- Alternatively, the profit could be used to finance product innovation, which will add to consumer welfare in the future, either through an improvement in the product's performance or through widening consumer choice.
- If the benefits of economies of scale and greater investment are passed on to consumers, it could be argued that they have gained from the existence of abnormal profit.

One of the criticisms raised against state-owned monopolies is that the absence of competition makes them less efficient. The essence of the argument is that firms with a guaranteed market can be complacent. Monopolists are said to suffer from **x-inefficiency**, which means that their cost levels are higher than they would be in competitive firms because they do not have the incentive for process innovation. They become less dynamic, doing things in a particular way simply through tradition. In addition, some of their investment may take the form of erecting barriers to maintain the level of abnormal profit by excluding potential rivals. This will add to costs in the short run. It may be true but there is the possibility that these inefficiencies are outweighed by economies of scale that lower average costs.

KEY TERM

X-inefficiency: where the typical costs are above those experienced in a more competitive market.

It is clear that monopolies can operate in ways that lead to inefficiency or consumer exploitation. However, one can make a positive case for monopoly. This explains why the investigation of monopoly practices is difficult and each case must be judged on its own merits. It is dangerous to assume that monopoly is always harmful; the performance of a monopolist may be little different from that of firms in oligopoly.

Contestable markets

So far, in dealing with market structures, the four models shown in Figure 7.13 have been analysed. A **contestable market** is not listed here. This is because although contestability increasingly features in many markets throughout the world, it is not really a market structure as such. It is best seen as a set of conditions that can apply in any market structure.

KEY TERM

Contestable market: any market structure where there is a threat that potential entrants are free and able to enter this market.

By definition, a *perfectly* contestable market is one in which there are no costs of entry and exit. So, only perfect competition matches this ideal; monopolistic competition, with few relatively costless barriers to entry and exit, can match it to some extent, as can oligopoly in certain situations.

A contestable market can be particularly seen as a means by which governments have sought to deregulate markets. This requires the removal of barriers to entry so opening up the market to competition. It has had particular significance in the UK; the principle of contestability has been central to the tremendous structural changes that have been made especially to the service sector of the economy with the introduction of new forms of competition into formerly protected markets.

The important features of a contestable market are as follows:

- Free entry, which implies that new and existing providers will have the same cost structure as in a perfectly competitive market.
- The number and size of firms are irrelevant. If a contestable market has only a few large firms, any cost differences should be a reflection of a decision by a particular firm to charge a given price.
- Only normal profits can be earned in the long run. If firms are making abnormal profits, then this is the signal for others to enter the market. This could be on a 'hit and run' basis – a firm sees an opportunity, enters the market, collects the gains and leaves at no cost.
- The threat of potential entrants into the market is overriding. Oligopolists and even a monopolist are obliged to offer consumers the benefits that they would receive in a more competitive market structure. Otherwise, new firms will enter from the pool of potential entrants.
- All firms are subject to the same regulations and government control irrespective of size.
- Mechanisms must be in place to prevent the use of unfair pricing designed by established firms to stop new firms from entering the market.
- Cross-subsidisation is eliminated since firms are unable to make normal profits if they sell any of their services below cost.

The application of contestability to the airline market is particularly interesting since, prior to deregulation, routes were strictly regulated by governments through the International Air Transport Association (IATA) and there was little competition. The 'open skies' policy of a deregulated market has led to lower fares and a greater choice of routes for passengers. This has particularly been the case in the US domestic market and in Europe, where new low-cost airlines such as easyJet and Ryanair have entered the market and challenged the established national carriers. More recently, deregulation has had a huge impact on the provision of air services in southern and South East Asia.

Other examples of contestable markets include:

- local bus services and rail services in the UK through deregulation and privatisation
- the provision of public services such as electricity, gas and water supplies
- telecommunications, particularly through the choice of network suppliers
- personal and corporate banking and finance through deregulation.

The extent to which markets are contestable varies from one country to another. In theory and in practice, any market, even a monopoly, can be contestable. This state of affairs will come about if there is a pool of potential entrants waiting to enter a market if they see existing firms making abnormal profits. The cost of entry and exit is the main factor that determines whether a market really is contestable. Deregulation, the removal of barriers to entry, is the main way in which markets can be opened up to competition. In many cases, deregulation has been implemented alongside a policy of privatisation. This twofold policy is one that has been implemented by many governments worldwide, often in markets where previously the state or public sector has been the only provider of a service.

SELF-ASSESSMENT TASK 7.11

For your own economy, analyse the extent to which the four typical examples given above are contestable markets.

KEY CONCEPT LINK

Equilibrium and efficiency: The underpinning rationale for contestability in markets is that of efficiency. By opening up markets to competition, and having a situation where market entry is easy for new entrants, this puts continual pressure on incumbent firms to be more efficient. Any hint of abnormal profits being made should be a signal for the entry of new firms.

Growth and survival of firms

Small vs. large firms

At least 90% of business units in the UK are small firms employing fewer than ten people. This is typical of most economies, although in developing economies the percentage will be even higher. These small firms are to be particularly found in the service sector, in retail, food production, automotive, personal and business services. A recent trend in many developed economies is for small knowledge- and research-orientated firms to provide services for much larger manufacturing companies often in developing economies. The reasons why so many small firms exist in a world where the economic power lies with large MNCs are as follows:

- There are economic activities where the size of the market is too small to support large firms.
- The business may involve specialist skills possessed by very few people.
- Where the product is a service – e.g., solicitors, accountants, hairdressers, dentists and small shops – the firm will be small in order to offer the customers personal attention for which they will pay a higher price.

SELF-ASSESSMENT TASK 7.12

Read the feature below and then answer the questions that follow.

Airline alliances

The international airline business is a particularly good example of an oligopoly. It has moved from an industry where, 20 years ago, individual carriers competed with each other on particular routes to one where groups of airlines compete with each other on a network basis. These groups are known as alliances. Three alliances cover most of the world's airlines. Their market shares of the global scheduled air market are indicated in Table 7.5 along with their full members in 2012.

Continental Airlines is the latest big addition to the Star Alliance. A long drawn-out merger with United Airlines eventually went ahead in 2010. It has not been without its problems. The way the new battleground is shaping up, since the US and the EU entered into an 'open skies' agreement in 2009, is that Star Alliance members compete with SkyTeam and both compete with Oneworld. But is this really in the best interests of the airlines and their passengers?

Oneworld: 23%	British Airways, American Airlines, Cathay Pacific, Qantas, JAL Japan Airlines, Finnair, Iberia plus six others
SkyTeam: 21%	Air France, KLM, Aeroflot, China Airlines, Delta Airlines, Alitalia, Czech Airlines plus 12 others
Star Alliance: 29%	Lufthansa, Swiss, Singapore Airlines, Air Canada, United, US Airways, Air New Zealand, Thai, TAP plus 19 others

Table 7.5

1 Explain the possible benefits to an airline of becoming a member of an alliance.

2 Explain the possible benefits to passengers of airline alliances.

3 The US Department of Justice remains concerned about the anti-competitive behaviour of airline alliances. Comment on this concern.

- Small firms may simply be the big firms of tomorrow. Although the number of small firms is high, only a very small percentage of them ever grow to become big businesses.
- There are particular obstacles to the growth of small firms. Probably the largest of these is access to borrowed capital because of the perceived risk on the part of banks.
- The entrepreneur may not want the firm to get bigger because extra profit is not the only objective and growth might involve a loss of control over the running of the business.
- Recession and rising unemployment can trigger an increase in the number of business start-ups as former employees try to become self-employed.
- Small businesses may receive financial help under government enterprise schemes because of their employment and growth potential.
- The increased access to technology through the Internet and mobile phones has reduced the optimum size of business unit and made small businesses more efficient and therefore competitive with larger ones.

The growth of firms

Although the number of large firms is small, it is true that they dominate both national and international trade. Business growth is strongly linked with the pursuit of profit but the motives behind a firm's growth may include the following:

- The desire to achieve a reduction in ATC over time through the benefits of economies of scale. This allows firms to compete more effectively with rivals because they can afford to cut prices without sacrificing profits.
- To achieve a bigger market share, which would boost sales revenue and therefore profits. This is sometimes referred to as the monopoly motive, but it could be a defensive strategy to maintain market share in anticipation of action by rivals. In the global economy there is a strong argument that only big firms can compete in markets where multinationals are present.
- To diversify the product range. A multi-product firm has the advantage of being able to spread business risks. If one branch of its activity is stagnating or going into decline, there will still be the revenue from others to keep the firm afloat. Firms often see new business opportunities in related areas.

SELF-ASSESSMENT TASK 7.13

Read the feature below and then answer the questions that follow.

Small firms in Pakistan's pharmaceutical industry

On the surface, the pharmaceutical industry is not one that immediately comes to mind when researching small firms. Yet in 2011, there were around 600 pharmaceutical companies in Pakistan, almost 400 of which were manufacturers. Multinational corporations (MNCs) such as GlaxoSmithKline and locally owned Getz Pharma have a large share of the market but the growth of small firms has severely damaged their market share. Less than half of total production is now in the hands of MNCs compared to more than 70% five years ago.

The changes to the pharmaceutical industry are best seen in a national context. Pakistan is a poor economy with an increasing population that requires more and more resources to be put into its health care system. The economy has had its fair share of woes in recent years: slow growth, high inflation and the ongoing devaluation of the rupee against other major currencies. As a consequence, the Ministry of Health is only prepared to pay low prices for the drugs it needs. This clearly helps small firms.

National firms have seen the country's economic position as an opportunity to produce generic drugs, products that have to be prescribed by medical professionals. The patents for these are invariably held by MNCs; when these expire then it is a signal for small producers to enter the market.

Source: Adapted from M. Aamir and K. Zaman, *International Journal of Business and Information Technology*, June 2011.

1 Elaborate the reasons given for the growth of small firms in the Pakistan pharmaceutical industry.

2 What obstacles might small pharmaceutical firms face when trying to grow?

This is at the heart of successful entrepreneurship. Sometimes they can use the same production facilities so keeping the costs down. These benefits are called **economies of scope**.

- To capture the resources of another business. Sometimes, firms may realise that resources are being underutilised in another firm and that the real value of the firm is currently above its accounting valuation. The resulting takeovers and mergers can lead to the firm being brought back into profit or being broken up. This is because the sum of the parts sold separately is greater than the current valuation of the whole enterprise. It is sometimes called 'asset stripping' and the cash may be ploughed back into improving the core business.

KEY TERM

Economies of scope: reduction in ATC made possible by a firm increasing the different goods it produces.

How do firms grow?

Firms can grow in two main ways. These are through:

- Internal growth: A firm decides to retain some of the profit rather than pay it out to the owners. It is ploughed back in the form of new investment in order to increase the productive capacity. This is most likely to occur in capital-intensive activities where the market is expanding. The timing will be influenced by the stage of the business cycle, most investment occurring when the national economy is approaching a boom period.
- External growth: The business expands by joining with others via takeovers or mergers. The objective in a takeover bid is to buy sufficient shares from the owners of the firm to get 51% of the total and therefore have control of the business. A merger often has the same result, a new larger legal entity, but the name implies less of a struggle and that both parties have agreed to the action. Mergers may be more numerous when there is a downturn in the economy or where there is a shrinking market and firms are left with excess productive capacity.

In practice, both types of growth can be going on at the same time. External growth may be a quicker and cheaper route for firms than internal growth, especially when there are high fixed costs. For example, it may be cheaper for one oil company to buy the assets of another than to expand existing operations, unless there are large recoverable reserves.

A further and common way in which firms grow is through **diversification**. This is where a firm, small or large, produces or sells a range of different products. The reasons behind this tend to be to spread risk or more aggressively, to exploit an opportunity in the market. Diversification is particularly in evidence in so-called conglomerates such as Unilever, Nestlé,

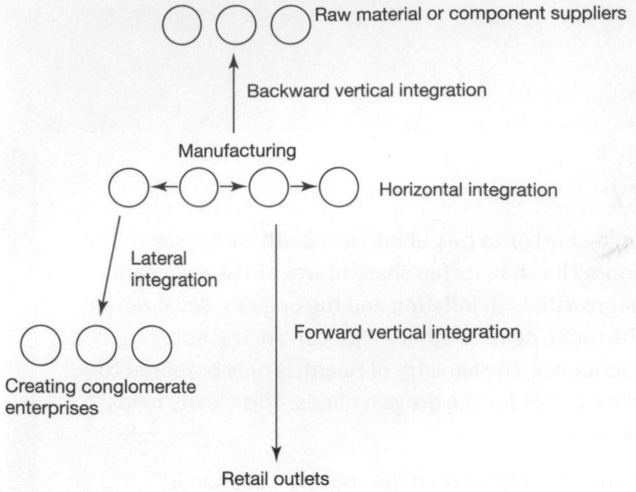

Figure 7.22 The routes to integration

> **KEY TERM**
>
> **Diversification:** where a firm grows through the production or sale of a wide range of different products.

Bosch and Tata Group. The latter which is Indian owned has extensive business interests in steel production, vehicle manufacturing, tea growing and packing and luxury hotels.

Integration

In general terms, integration refers to the ways in which the individual parts of, say, a business have come together. This could be through:

- a merger whereby two firms agree to join up with each other
- acquisition or purchase whereby one firm takes over control of another.

The various forms of integration are shown in Figure 7.22.

Horizontal integration is a process or strategy used by firms to strengthen their position in an industry. It involves the merger or acquisition of a business that is in the same sector of an industry. Typical examples are United Airlines' merger with Continental (see Self-assessment task 7.12), Kraft Foods taking over Cadbury in the UK and Mittel Steel's purchase of Arcelor, in Spain, France and Luxembourg. In such cases, the outcome is one of consolidation; an oligopoly or even a monopoly is likely. The prime motive for this growth is to reap the benefits of economies of scale. Research and development costs can be pooled, production plants can be rationalised, marketing costs reduced and so on. Horizontal integration can also lead to access to new markets, increased market power and, by reducing competition, the opportunity to make abnormal profits. The danger is that this sort of growth may sometimes be blocked by governments who are concerned about possible monopoly abuse.

> **KEY TERM**
>
> **Horizontal integration:** where a firm merges or acquires another in the same line of business.

Vertical integration is different. This is where a firm grows by moving into a forward or backward stage of its production process or supply chain, such as a manufacturer moving into retail (forward) or taking control over some of its supplies (backward). Typical examples are in the oil industry where BP, Shell and ExxonMobil are involved in exploration, fuel production, refining, transport and forecourt sales. Nestlé and other food producers are increasingly involved in the production of coffee beans, cocoa and milk as well as in their manufacture and distribution to retailers and other consumers. Vertical integration has various benefits including improved security and quality of supplies and reduced supply chain costs. There are, however, disadvantages, in particular potentially higher costs if the newly acquired businesses are not effectively integrated. This can also be a major problem with any merged operation.

> **KEY TERM**
>
> **Vertical integration:** where a firm grows by producing backwards or forwards in its supply chain.

Self-assessment task 7.14 contains two contrasting experiences of mergers prompted by the perceived benefits of horizontal integration. This task should be considered alongside the results for tasks 7.12 and 7.13.

Cartels

As referred to earlier when considering oligopoly, a cartel is a formal agreement between member firms in an industry to limit competition. The agreement may involve fixing the quantity to be produced by each member or fixing the price for which the product is sold. Other restrictions may also be applied. A cartel maximises profits in the same way as a monopolist (see Figure 7.19).

The Organisation of Petroleum Exporting Countries (OPEC) is the best known, long-standing example of a cartel. It currently has 12 members and membership is

SELF-ASSESSMENT TASK 7.14

Read the two features below and then answer the questions that follow.

Pharmaceutical industry mergers beat recession

Ten years ago the global pharmaceutical industry experienced a spate of mergers. That was when Glaxo and Astra Zeneca were created and Pfizer became the world's number one after taking over Warner-Lambert and, in 2003, Schering-Plough.

In early 2009 three new multi-billion dollar deals were announced. These were:

- Roche buying Genentech ($47 billion)
- Merck's takeover of Schering-Plough ($41 billion)
- Pfizer's purchase of Wyeth ($68 billion).

Each of the newly merged giants has their specialisms. Roche is big in cancer-treating drugs, Merck in cholesterol-reducing drugs, while the largest of all, Pfizer, is big in vaccines, anti-depressants, oral contraceptives and impotence aiding products.

The global industry is not short of cash. The reasons for the latest mergers stem mainly from fierce ongoing competition from generic drug manufacturers. These companies can make cheaper copies of drugs once patents have expired. Many such products are made in

the emerging economies of southern Asia. The knock-on effects are that big conglomerates are cutting back on new product development. Instead they are concentrating resources on new products such as the Tamiflu vaccine, which is difficult to copy. They are also buying new products from small businesses and then using their power to produce these for the global market.

Source: Adapted from A. Townend, *Daily Telegraph*, 16 March 2009.

Airline mergers – one too many?

Recession has hit the global airline business hard. Many of the world's flag-flying national carriers have found it necessary to embark on a series of mergers, largely to cut costs and so reduce their eye-watering trading deficits. Significant mergers have been:

- British Airways and Iberia
- Lufthansa and Swiss
- Delta and Northwest Airlines
- United and Continental Airlines
- Southwest Airlines and AirTran Airways

But is there a block on yet another US merger, that of American Airlines with US Airways? The Justice Department claims that the proposed merger 'threatens substantial harm to consumers'.

A law professor at the University of Iowa has argued that the relevant question is not so much why the Justice Department has moved to block this latest merger but why it approved that between United and Continental. If this new merger goes ahead, the US would have just three main airlines.

Earlier airline mergers in the USA, it is claimed, have resulted in reduced capacity and higher prices. These are not the benefits that were promised. For example, after the United-Continental merger, the combined airline had a 79% share of services between Chicago and Houston. Three months after the merger, fares were 57% higher than three years earlier. This compares with an increase of only 16% for the same period over the rest of United's network.

Source: Adapted from *The New York Times*, 16 August 2013.

1 What are typical reasons for business mergers?

2 To what extent do these reasons apply to mergers in the global pharmaceutical industry and in the airline industry?

3 What benefits might consumers get from larger companies in the two industries?

open to any countries that are substantial net exporters of crude petroleum. As a cartel, OPEC is widely criticised. Members produce about one-third of the world's oil yet own around 80% of known crude oil reserves as well as half of the reserves of natural gas. It clearly has much power in the market to determine not only current but, significantly, future prices. With projected growth in global demand, it is easy to see why there are calls for OPEC to increase production, otherwise stocks in consumer countries will be depleted to a dangerously low level.

The only thing that will weaken OPEC's economic power is if new suppliers outside of the cartel appear or consumers take action that will reduce consumption. Technology may provide alternatives to oil in the future. The cartel will weaken if there is disagreement over the target price or the production quotas allocated to each member country.

OPEC denies that it is acting as a single monopoly, cutting output in order to charge high prices to consumers and points out that Western governments make more money from the tax on oil than the producing countries receive in revenues from selling the oil.

At the retailing end of the industry, the supply is in the hands of an oligopoly of oil companies who deny that they are charging too much, insisting that their profit margin is low because of fierce competition. Total profits are only high because of the large turnover.

Some analysts predict that there will be further horizontal integration between oil companies that are already vertically integrated. The oil industry will continue to be dominated by a few big players mainly because of the high fixed cost and risks associated with exploration and drilling. If their controversial attempts to find oil in areas like the Arctic and Antarctic are successful, then OPEC's power could diminish.

The long-term survival of a cartel depends upon the high barriers to entry. However, there are threats to a cartel, such as:

- The possibility of a price war, whereby one firm breaks rank to capture a bigger market share.
- If some members have higher costs than others, resulting in fewer profits due to the agreed fixed price.
- If there is no dominant member that has the power to control others.
- Legal obstacles such as in the EU and USA where cartels are illegal since they restrict competition and do not act in the best interests of consumers.

Differing objectives of a firm

Profit maximisation

We saw earlier how the profit earned by a firm is referred to as normal profit and abnormal profit. The standard assumption made by economists, as made clear in our analysis of market structures, is that firms will seek to maximise their profits, i.e., maximise the difference between the total revenue and total cost (including normal profit). A firm making the minimum level of normal profit is said to be producing at the break-even output. No abnormal profit is being made. Most firms, though, will want to make abnormal profit as a reward for taking risks.

If the firm produces up to the point where the cost of making the last unit is just covered by the revenue from selling it, then the profit margin will have fallen to zero and total profits will be at their greatest. In Figure 7.23, a firm producing an output to the left of *Q* is sacrificing potential profit. It can raise total profit by increasing its output, because each further unit sold adds more to revenue than it does to costs. A firm producing to the right of *Q* is making a loss on each successive unit, which will lower the total

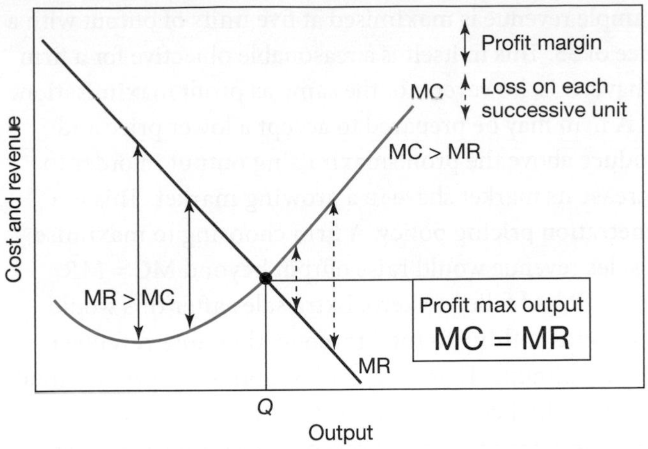

Figure 7.23 The profit maximisation rule

SELF-ASSESSMENT TASK 7.15

Self-assessment task 3.1 considered the case for introducing maximum price for essential commodities in Kenya. This has occurred because the government has been unable to enforce its competition law forbidding the operation of cartels. There is a generally held view that large suppliers have been colluding and charging exorbitant prices for their commodities to exploit consumers and so earn massive profits. It is firmly believed that the formation of these cartels is a major contributing reason for high consumer prices.

1 Using a diagram, explain how a cartel is able to charge high prices.
2 Comment on why the Kenyan government has been unable to enforce its competition law forbidding the operation of cartels.
3 Discuss the extent to which the benefits of cartels like those in Kenya might offset the exorbitant prices charged.

profit. It would be better off cutting output back to *Q* where MC = MR and the area of abnormal profit will be maximised.

There may be several reasons why firms do not operate at the profit maximisation output:

- In practice, it is difficult to identify this output. The firm may simply work out the average total cost and then add on a standard profit margin in order to determine the selling price. This cost-plus pricing technique may not result in maximum profit.
- Short-term profit maximisation may not be in the long-term interest of the company since:
  - firms with large market shares may wish to avoid the attention of government watchdog bodies, such as the Competition and Markets Authority in the UK and the US Justice Department
  - large abnormal profit may attract new entrants into the industry
  - high profits may damage the relationship between the firm and its stakeholders, such as its consumers and the company workforce as they may see senior managers and shareholders earning large returns
  - profit maximisation may not appeal to the management, who may have different objectives – high profits might trigger action by the firm's rivals and it could become a target for a takeover bid.

Other objectives of firms

Dissatisfaction with the traditional assumption of profit maximisation has led to a number alternative objectives being put forward to explain how firms behave. These are invariably based on empirical investigation and are referred to as managerial or behavioural objectives of firms.

Sales revenue maximisation

Figure 7.24, which is derived from the accompanying data, shows that when the price changes from \$9 to \$8, the marginal revenue is 7. The addition to total revenue is gradually falling as the price falls until when five units are sold MR = 0. At this point total revenue or sales is maximised.

In the above example, the firm would be facing a straight-line demand curve. Even so, the consumers' reaction to a price change varies at different prices due to the way in which the price elasticity of demand (PED) varies along the demand curve.

As the price falls in steps from \$10, sales increase more than proportionally, giving PED a value greater than 1, until the output of 5 when total revenue is unchanged. This gives a PED value of 1. Beyond this output PED has a value less than 1 and the result is that further price cuts will reduce total revenue.

A relationship between price elasticity and marginal revenue can also be seen. In the elastic part of the demand curve where PED > 1, the marginal revenue is positive and total revenue will be increasing as output increases. When the PED = 1, MR will be zero and total revenue will be maximised. When PED < 1, MR will be negative, reducing the total revenue.

The most important thing about the concept of price elasticity from the firm's point of view is that it determines what happens to total revenue when the price is altered. It would make sense for any firm operating in the elastic part of the demand curve to reduce price and boost total revenue. Conversely, in the inelastic part, the firm should raise its price if it wants to see higher revenue. In this

Revenue data

Price (*P*)	Units sold (*Q*)	*TR* (*P* × *Q*)	*MR*
10	0	0	
			9
9	1	9	
			7
8	2	16	
			5
7	3	21	
			3
6	4	24	
			1
5	5	25	
			−1
4	6	24	
			−3
3	7	21	
			−5
2	8	16	
			−7
1	9	9	

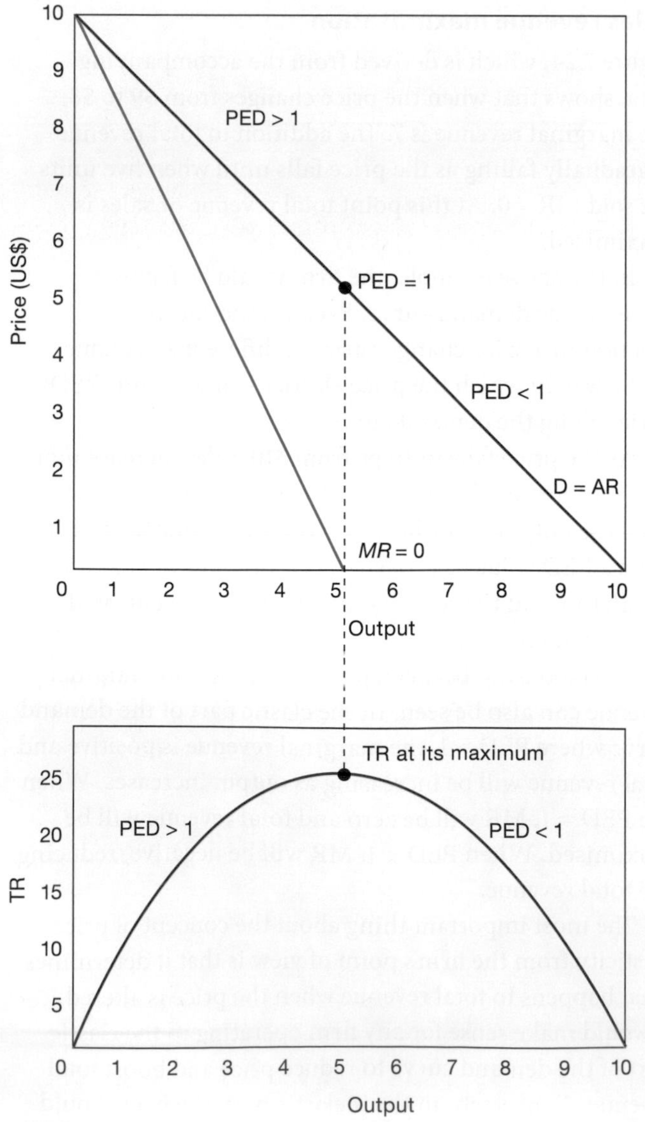

Figure 7.24 The relationship between average revenue, marginal revenue and total revenue

example revenue is maximised at five units of output with a price of $5. This in itself is a reasonable objective for a firm to have; it is, however, not the same as profit maximisation.

A firm may be prepared to accept a lower price and produce above the profit-maximising output in order to increase its market share in a growing market. This is a penetration pricing policy. A firm choosing to maximise its sales revenue would raise output beyond MC = MR until MR had fallen to zero. Extra sales after this would contribute nothing to total revenue, therefore revenue is at its maximum. There may still be abnormal profit if total revenue is higher than total cost but this is not always the case. The reason why **sales revenue maximisation** might be chosen in a large firm is that management salaries might be linked to the value of sales. Shareholders might be more interested in profit. The solution to this conflict of interests is to offer management some shares as a bonus or to link their salaries to profits.

KEY TERM

Sales revenue maximisation: a firm's objective to maximise turnover.

Sales maximisation

This option maximises the *volume* of sales rather than the sales revenue. In **sales maximisation** the firm would increase output up to the break-even output where the total revenue just covered the total cost. A higher output than this implies loss-making behaviour. The only situation where this would be possible is where the firm could use the profit from some other activities to cover these losses. This is referred to as cross-subsidisation. It could be that a state-owned firm, such as one running local bus services, uses the profits from city services to retain lower density routes that are loss-making. In this case there are social objectives lying behind price and output decisions. The company might be instructed to keep prices down, to cover their ATC, or to make sufficient profit to be self-financing when it comes to new investment.

KEY TERM

Sales maximisation: a firm's objective to maximise the volume of sales.

A firm in the private sector would not go beyond the break-even output in order to expand sales unless it is part of a diversified grouping where cross-subsidisation is being practised. If it did, then it would be making fewer profits.

However, deliberately cutting the price to reduce profit might be a strategy to deter new entrants into the market. This was referred to earlier as predatory pricing. If new entrants still appear, a price war may be a tactic to squeeze them out.

Satisficing

Satisficing occurs when a firm seeks to make a reasonable level of profits, sufficient to satisfy the shareholders but also to keep the other stake-holding groups happy, such as the workforce and, of course, consumers. The firm is seen as a coalition of interest groups, each with its own objectives, which may change over time. Workers will expect pay rises and improvements in working conditions which may raise costs. Consumers may expect to see prices falling, particularly if there are rival producers. This is a long way from the simple profit-maximising theory as firms may choose to sacrifice some potential short-term profits to satisfy these expectations.

KEY TERM

Satisficing: a firm's objective to make a reasonable level of profit.

Where the firm's shareholders are divorced from control of the firm, there may be a conflict of interests. The management's motives may be concerned with growth rather than profit. They may place a lot of importance on comfortable working conditions, job security, status and fringe benefits, such as company cars, private health care and pension rights. Time and money spent on these issues can raise costs. If the firm has close rivals, it may make management more cautious because the risk of failure will threaten their job security and career advancement prospects.

Satisficing can also be a feature of firms that have enjoyed a high market share over a long period of time. Complacency can lead to firms losing focus on their cost structure or failing to devote resources to either product or process innovation. Either situation can lead to a loss of profits. It could in the extreme lead to a firm having to exit the market. An example might be a firm that produces blank VHS tapes and nothing else and which finds its core product now obsolete.

Loss minimisation

In some situations firms may have a short-term objective of minimising losses. This is most likely to be where a firm is facing serious unexpected external threats such as the loss of its best customer or a downturn in the economy due to some external shock. Survival in such circumstances becomes a priority in order to allow the firm to develop a revised strategy to stay in business.

There is, however, a limit to the time and to the scale of losses that can be tolerated. If a firm is not covering its variable costs, then closure would seem to be the only sensible outcome. If variable costs (but not total costs) are being recouped, then it is possible for the firm to continue in business a little longer so that it can try to map out a retrieval strategy. In the UK, for example, retailers of fashion clothes, electrical goods, books and music products have been badly affected by the growth of Internet sales. Not all have been able to implement a successful retrieval strategy.

Ethical objectives

In some respects satisficing can be viewed as an ethical objective for a firm to pursue as the pursuit of maximum profit is not always in the best interests of society. Much wider is the notion of corporate social responsibility and why many firms now incorporate aspects in their mission statements.

An important consideration here is the growing number of cases where unscrupulous firms appear to put self-interest before the wider interest of others. Typical examples are:

- the growing instances of serious damage to the natural environment caused by firms, resulting in pollution, the loss of renewable resources and damage to the natural habitat
- the exploitation of child and adult labour, particularly in the production of clothing in developing economies
- exposing workers to serious health risks in the production of toys and consumer goods
- paying poor farmers in developing economies low prices for their produce.

It is within this context that a growing number of firms have stepped back from the endless pursuit of profit and sought to have a more responsible attitude to how what they are selling is sourced and produced.

One of the earliest and best examples in the UK of an ethically focused firm is The Body Shop, which has sought to bring sustainable products to its customers worldwide. It has also been at the forefront of supporting many environmental projects, animal welfare initiatives and educational programmes in developing economies. Other examples are banana exporters and coffee, tea and cocoa manufacturers who only source from fair trade farmers and suppliers. In this way, producers receive a guaranteed price for what they produce, so avoiding the vagaries of the market.

It can be argued that ethical objectives eat into profits. This is so. The danger all firms face is that consumers could react very unfavourably to purchasing products that come from unethical sources of supply. Given this risk, the cost of promoting corporate social responsibility is often a small price to pay.

The principal agent problem

In setting the various objectives of firms it is assumed that those who set these objectives have the authority and ability to do so. For example, in order to pursue an objective of profit maximisation, managers must be able to determine the price and output. The problem is that, in large firms especially, there is a divorce between management and ownership; shareholders and other owners are invariably not in a 'hands on' position in the firm to really know whether the decisions being taken are the right ones in relation to stated objectives.

This issue is known as the principal agent problem. The 'principal' is the owner who hires an 'agent' to run a business in return for a salary and the usual fringe benefits and bonuses that go with it. There is a case of information failure since the principal is unable to ensure that the appointed agent is taking the necessary decisions to run the firm in the best interests of owners and shareholders. This could mean, for example, that the agent is following an objective of satisficing when the principal believes he or she is implementing a policy of profit maximisation. The risk is that the agent has his or her own agenda, essentially ignoring the wishes and best interests of the principal. The principal's intended objective for the firm is therefore not being implemented and it inevitably leads to friction between the two parties. There have, for example, been a number of disputes in the designer fashion business where the head of design's ideas for the business have not coincided with those of the company's board and shareholders. These usually surface when a firm is losing market share or is receiving critical reviews in the media.

Pricing strategy and the prisoners' dilemma

Suppose two prisoners A and B are waiting in their cells at night. Tomorrow morning they have to give their respective pleas of 'Guilty' or 'Not guilty'. Both had been arrested for the same crime. The judge and jury knew that one of them was guilty but were unsure whether both were. If both prisoners were to plead guilty, then both would be assumed to be guilty and given a four-year sentence. If one were to plead guilty and the other not guilty, the one pleading guilty would receive a sentence of eight years in prison; the other would be assumed not guilty and therefore released. However, if both pleaded not guilty, then both would be assumed to have committed the crime and would receive six years in prison. The dilemma for both is how they should plead, guilty or not guilty?'

A pay-off matrix can be drawn up to show these options:

		B	
		Confess	Deny
A	Confess	4/4	0/8
	Deny	8/0	6/6

The obvious conclusion is that turning the other prisoner in is the best response. By remaining silent, a prisoner runs the risk of being hit with a long sentence, eight years, while the other prisoner walks away. By speaking up and saying the other is guilty, a prisoner hopes that the second prisoner remains silent, in which case he goes free. On the other hand, if both prisoners speak, they both get some jail time; the risk of remaining silent is seen as greater than the risk of speaking out.

So what has this to do with Economics and the theory of the firm? It can be used to show some of the strategies involved when firms are deciding their pricing strategies. **Game theory** suggests that firms are unlikely to trust each other, even in a cartel. This is especially the case if a decision has been taken to increase prices. Not all members can be trusted to keep in line. Some, for example, may keep prices the same in order to gain market share from their rivals even if this is only for a short time. This point will be elaborated below when looking in more detail at the behaviour of oligopolists.

> **KEY TERM**
>
> **Game theory:** where competing firms exhibit interdependent behaviour whereby the actions of one will impact on all other firms.

Behaviour of oligopolistic firms

The difficulty in studying oligopoly is that the behaviour of firms can follow two different routes – in some industries there may be cut-throat competition between aggressive firms, while in others, there may well be cooperation or tacit evidence of collusion. Consequently, just how one firm actually reacts will depend on how it expects competitors to react. All of this means that it is difficult

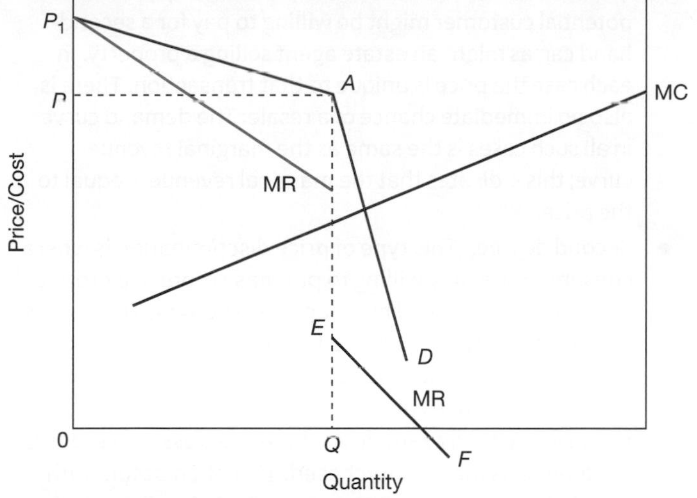

Figure 7.25 The kinked demand curve

to put forward one completely acceptable theory of oligopolistic behaviour. Nevertheless, there are two main theories that attempt to explain how oligopolists behave. These are the theory of the **kinked demand curve** and game theory as referred to above.

KEY TERM

Kinked demand curve: a means of analysing the behaviour of firms in oligopoly where there is no collusion.

Oligopolists are price makers. They have the power to set their own prices but what they are unable to gauge is the reaction of their competitors. This uncertainty means that firms may prefer non-price competition in the form of branding, customer service, location, range of products and so on. The underpinning explanation for this is the kinked demand curve (see Figure 7.25). This can be used to explain why prices in oligopolistic markets are often rigid in so far as they are stable for relatively long periods of time.

In Figure 7.25, it is assumed that a firm is producing at price *P* and output Q. If the firm increases its price above *P*, other firms in the market will not follow. This is because these firms will be able to sell more themselves, attracting customers from the firm that increased its price. So, the firm's demand curve is *AD* and its marginal revenue curve is MR. This demand curve is relatively elastic to an increase in price. If the firm lowers its price, it assumes that other firms in the market will follow this lead so as not to lose market share. This starts a price war, the result of which is likely to be that all firms lose out. The demand curve below A is inelastic and indicated by *AD*. The marginal revenue curve is EF.

B's Price \ A's Price	£1	90p
£1	£2m each	£1m B £2.2m A
90p	£2.2m B £1m A	£1.5m each

The cells show each firm's expected profits

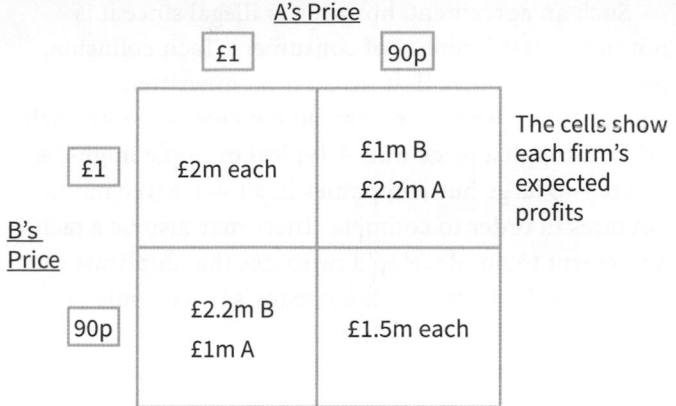

Table 7.6 An oligopoly game matrix

So, overall the oligopolist's demand curve appears to be P_1AD. Price will be rigid at *P* since there is no incentive for a firm to increase or decrease the price it charges. If it did, either way, it would lose out.

The kinked demand curve is in some respects a useful way to explain the behaviour of oligopolists. Empirical evidence unfortunately does not always support what this model tells us. For example, prices in an oligopolistic market may be no more rigid than in other markets. Also, the reason for price rigidity may have more to do with commercial practices than the firm's awareness of the kinked demand curve.

It is for this reason that, in recent years, game theory has increasingly been applied in order to understand the behaviour of oligopolists. The 'game' is that firms have to make decisions about the price they charge and their level of output. Decisions are taken based on assumptions about the responses of rival firms; these decisions have particular implications for the profits earned.

Table 7.6 shows the game matrix facing two firms, A and B, that have large market shares in an oligopolistic market. Suppose at present there is no price competition and that each firm sells its product for £1. In order to increase market share, both firms are considering reducing their prices by 10% to 90p.

At £1, each firm is making an annual profit of £2 million. If B decided to reduce its price to 90p, its profits would increase to £2.2 million. This is not good news for A, which has left its price at £1 and seen profits fall to £1 million. Alternatively, A could cut its price to 90p, with B leaving its price at £1. A's profits would increase to £2.2 million, with B's falling to £1 million. In this situation both firms know what each other is considering – if prices are cut to 90p then both firms experience a fall in profits to £1.5 million. Both firms lose out so the obvious option is for them to collude to retain their prices at £1 in order to gain higher profits.

Such an agreement, however, is illegal since it is not in the best interests of consumers. Tacit collusion, however, is not illegal. It involves an unwritten agreement between two firms to not compete with each other through a price war. A typical example might be where two large bus companies in a town agree not to cut fares in order to compete. There may also be a tacit agreement to not develop new routes that duplicate each other's services since each company's costs would rise and profits reduce accordingly.

The behaviour of oligopolists continues to give concern to regulatory bodies such as the UK's Competition and Markets Authority. A particular cause for concern is the anti-competitive behaviour of firms which collude. This is illegal but very difficult to prove. It is, though, indicative of mutual interdependence as in the earlier analysis of cartels. Collusion in some markets is likely to be tacit whereby rival firms have an unwritten agreement not to compete directly with each other or to engage in a price cutting campaign. Here, the oligopolists would seem to be satisfied with the profit levels they are achieving.

Pricing policy

Aspects of pricing policy were referred to earlier in our discussion of oligopoly and monopoly. In this section, price discrimination, limit pricing and price leadership will be considered. Each of these are examples of where firms charge prices that are not what might be expected in the conventional theory of the firm.

Price discrimination

Price discrimination was briefly mentioned in the context of a monopolist. It can, however, be used by any firm to increase its profits by reducing consumer surplus and converting this into producer surplus. The only exception is in perfect competition. To price discriminate, the firm must have some control over price; in other words, its demand curve must be downward-sloping.

There are three recognised types of price discrimination. They are:

- First degree: This is a situation where the firm sells each unit of a product to a different consumer, charging each the price (ideally the maximum) that they are willing to pay. In practice this is difficult. Most examples are in the service sector. A private doctor may charge each patient what he feels that person can afford to pay. If he is feeling kind, then richer patients might be charged more than those on low incomes. A car dealer is likely to weigh up just what a potential customer might be willing to pay for a second-hand car, as might an estate agent selling a property. In each case the price is unique to that transaction. There is also no immediate chance of a resale. The demand curve in all such cases is the same as the marginal revenue curve; this indicates that the marginal revenue is equal to the price.
- Second degree: This type of price discrimination is where consumers are only willing to purchase more of a product if price falls as more and more units are bought. This means that a higher price is charged for the first unit followed by a lower price as successive units are purchased. A type of discounting takes place as the quantity purchased increases. A good example is where progressive discounts are offered as more is purchased. This often occurs with certain food items, car tyres or season tickets to watch a Premier League football team in the UK. The consumer benefits as does the firm whose output, total revenue and profits can be expected to increase.
- Third degree: This is the most common form of price discrimination. It requires firms to actively discriminate between consumers and is based on the presumption that groups of consumers have a different price elasticity of demand for the product. So, where consumers have a low inelastic demand, this demand is not price sensitive. They need the product and can be expected to pay a higher price for it than consumers whose demand is more price elastic. A good example is with air fares – flights booked earlier have a lower price than those booked closer to departure. Rail travel in many countries is priced on a peak and off-peak basis, whereby commuters travelling in the peak time slots pay higher fares than off-peak leisure travellers, for whom price is more important. Another interesting case is where students may be given a discount at a food stall or the cinema. The overall outcome here is not entirely predictable. The firm's revenue and profits should increase, otherwise there is no point in discriminating. The problem is that some consumer groups benefit yet others do not because of the higher prices they have to pay.

It may be possible for a monopolist to use price discrimination to produce at a profit when competitive firms or a monopoly charging a single price could not cover costs. Figure 7.26 shows that at the single price profit maximisation output, the total revenue would be $3 \times 40 = 120$ and the total cost would be $3 \times 45 = 135$, giving a loss of 15. If the output was sold separately for what consumers would pay for each individual unit, the revenue would be $60 + 50 + 40 = 150$, giving an abnormal profit of 15. The monopolist has effectively tapped into the consumer surplus and turned it into producer surplus or profit. If triangle A in the diagram

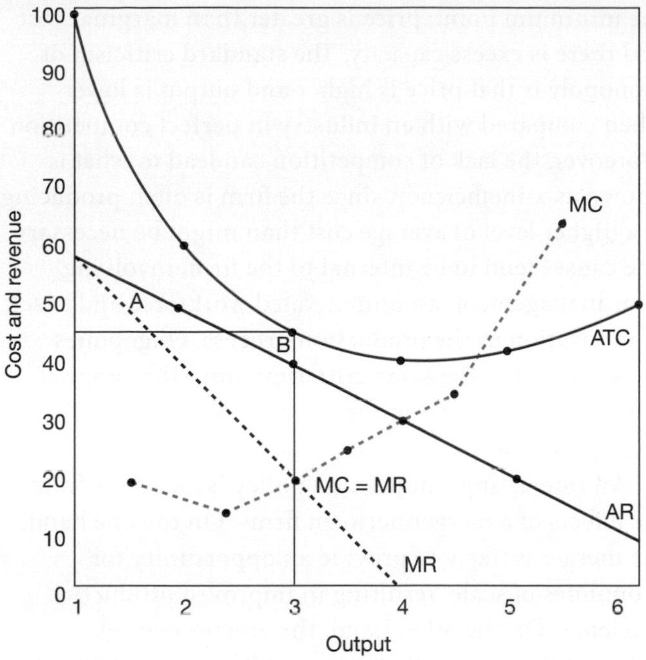

Figure 7.26 A price discriminating monopolist

is the same size as triangle B, which is the shortfall in cost, the firm will break even, but if it is larger then it makes abnormal profit. As long as the consumers are prepared to pay the higher price, there is no consumer exploitation. The competitive market price would generate losses and therefore there would be zero output in the long run.

If a firm wishes to split the market up into different segments and charge different prices, it must have a mechanism for keeping the markets separate. It must also avoid the possibility of consumers buying at a cheap price and then selling on the product at a higher price. Crucially, price discrimination will only work where consumers have a different willingness to purchase or have different price elasticities of demand for the product.

Price discrimination has certain advantages and disadvantages for firms and consumers. It results in an improvement in allocative efficiency but this is often achieved by converting consumer surplus into profit. From an equity standpoint this is a disadvantage to consumers.

KEY CONCEPT LINK

Regulation and equity: Price discrimination tends to favour producers over consumers; some form of regulation may be required to ensure that consumers are not exploited.

SELF-ASSESSMENT TASK 7.16

a Taking each type of price discrimination in turn, give examples of each from your own country.

b Explain who you believe is benefiting from price discrimination.

Limit pricing

Limit pricing is a pricing policy that is used by monopolies as well as oligopolies. As referred to earlier, it involves firms setting a lower short-run price to deter new firms from entering a contestable market. These firms might have been attracted by the abnormal profits that were being earned. At this new price, the incumbent firm no longer maximises profits but this is only to be expected for a short period of time. The lower price effectively acts as a barrier to entry. To work, a monopolist or oligopolist needs to increase output or the services provided to such a level that a new firm is not in a position to make a profit. An example might be in an unregulated taxi market where a firm might reduce rates and at the same time increase the number of its vehicles so making it impossible for a new entrant to make an impact; the likelihood is that these tactics will deter the new operator from trying to enter that particular market.

TOP TIP

Limit pricing has a different objective to predatory pricing. Limit pricing seeks to keep new firms out of a market whilst predatory pricing seeks to remove existing firms from the market.

Price leadership

Price leadership is a common feature of oligopolistic markets. All firms in the market accept the price that is set by the leading firm, which is often the one with the largest market share or the brand leader. They then alter their own prices in line with those of the leader. It is seen as a way of avoiding price competition yet maximising total profits for all firms while allowing various forms of non-price competition to prevail. A good example in many countries is petroleum retailing where the market leader is a well-known MNC. Other examples are in the markets for certain types of retail goods or branded fast food.

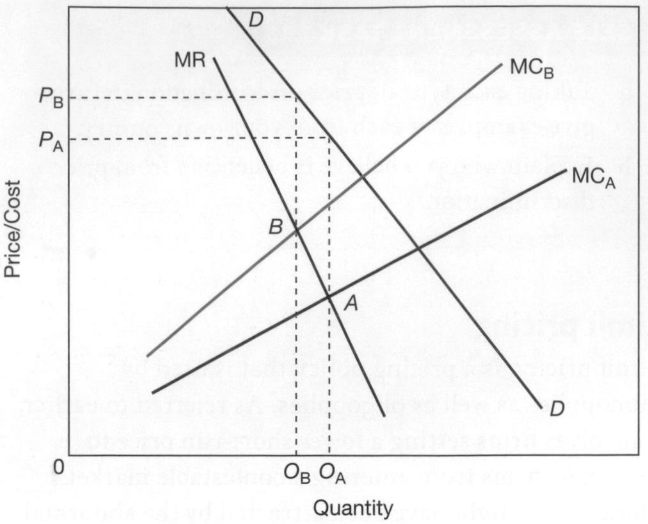

Figure 7.27 Price leadership under oligopoly

When the leading firm announces a price increase, all others quickly follow, sometimes in just a matter of hours. It is the same when a price fall is announced; smaller rivals are forced to follow the fall in price to retain market share. The downside, however, is that since their costs are higher, matching a price decrease could result in sustained losses and their eventual exit from the market.

Figure 7.27 shows a simple representation of price leadership. It assumes there are two firms in the market, *A* and *B*. DD is their demand curve. Firm *A* is the lower cost producer and price leader. It maximises its profits at point *A* where MC=MR. Its output O_A is sold at price P_A. Firm *B*'s ideal price is at P_B but if it fixes price here, it will not be able to compete with A's lower price. It is therefore compelled to lower its price to P_A with lower profits due to its higher costs of production.

Comparisons of performance of firms: some conclusions

Much of this chapter has been concerned with how firms operate in terms of:

- their production, costs and revenue
- their behaviour in different market structures
- their objectives and how they price their products in the market.

In terms of efficiency, perfect competition is the only market structure where firms are productively and allocatively efficient in the long run. It is for this reason that this model acts as a benchmark for assessing the efficiency of other market structures. In monopolistic competition, the average cost of production is not at the minimum point; price is greater than marginal cost and there is excess capacity. The standard criticism of monopoly is that price is higher and output is lower when compared with an industry in perfect competition. Moreover, the lack of competition can lead to what is known as x-inefficiency, since the firm is often producing at a higher level of average cost than might be necessary. The causes tend to be internal to the firm, involving poor management, an unmotivated workforce and a lack of innovation in the production process. Oligopolies are subjected to the same criticisms since they apply practices that give them the opportunity to gain monopoly power.

An interesting competition policy issue arises from the effects of a merger between firms. On the one hand, the merger is likely to provide an opportunity for economies of scale, resulting in improved productive efficiency. On the other hand, the greater market power of the merged firm may result in increased prices, so widening the difference between price and marginal costs. The firm is now even less allocatively efficient.

Differences in barriers to entry have a bearing on the level of profits in imperfectly competitive markets. They also may prevent a market from becoming contestable or, depending on their strength, allow a market to actually remain contestable. In monopolistic competition, there is relatively free entry and exit. This is very similar to perfect competition where there are no barriers to entry or exit. With oligopoly and monopoly, in contrast, barriers to entry determine market power; there are also sunk costs of exit.

In perfect competition firms are price takers. Any firm that moves away from a policy of charging more or less than the prevailing market price will have to leave the industry in the long run. In monopolistic competition and oligopoly, firms are price makers, although there may be some price competition. Consequently, non-price competition, where firms compete in terms of product promotion through branding, packaging or advertising, is particularly relevant in monopolistic competition and oligopoly. A monopolist, however, has complete control over the prices that are charged.

Other aspects of pricing were discussed in the cases of oligopoly and monopoly. Price leadership was stated as being prevalent in oligopoly. Here, a market leader may be the price leader. This firm sets prices and others follow. The rigidity of prices in this market was shown by the kinked demand curve, a clear recognition of the mutual interdependence of firms.

So, in imperfect competition, firms compete with others through a mixture of price and non-price competition. It is only when there are very close substitutes that their conduct becomes less predictable. In this way, firms are interdependent. The extent to which they feel they can take risks with regard to their rivals' responses can lead to a change in a firm's pattern of behaviour. The outcome is often one of collusion.

The models of market structure make an assumption that, whatever the market structure, each firm will seek to maximise its profits all of the time. In reality this is clearly not the case. There is a particularly strong argument for relaxing this assumption when investigating how oligopolists operate. Alternative motives therefore often make it difficult to predict the conduct of firms in respect of price and output.

SUMMARY

In this chapter it has been shown that:

- The principle of diminishing marginal utility can be used to explain the shape and derivation of the demand curve.
- A consumer will choose a combination of goods where the value of the marginal utility divided by the price of the good is equal for all goods.
- A price change for a good can be divided into a substitution effect and an income effect.
- In the short run, at least one factor of production is fixed; all factors are variable in the long run.
- The short-run production function shows how the quantity produced varies with changes to the input of a variable factor of production, normally labour.
- The demand for all factors of production is a derived demand.
- Economists split a firm's costs of production into fixed and variable costs; marginal and average costs are particularly useful in explaining how costs vary with a firm's output.
- In the long run, as output expands, the benefits from falling average costs are known as economies of scale; these benefits can accrue both within and from outside of a particular firm.
- The structure of markets can be explained by various characteristics including the strength of barriers to entry, the number and size of firms, the nature of the product and the availability of information.
- Economists recognise various models of market structure, namely perfect competition, monopoly, monopolistic competition and oligopoly; these models are useful for making comparisons with real markets.
- Many real-world markets are increasingly contestable in their structure.
- Firms compete in various ways depending upon the market structure in which they operate.
- Although economic power rests with large firms, small firms are more typical and are able to survive for many reasons.
- Firms can grow through integration, diversification and mergers; they also form cartels.
- The normal objective of a firm is profit maximisation; other objectives may also be relevant in some types of market structure, especially in oligopoly.
- Price discrimination, limit pricing and price leadership are all forms of pricing policy practised by oligopolies.
- The main models of market structure themselves can be compared in terms of their relative output, profits and efficiency.

Exam-style questions

1

'Stores Wars' hits the UK supermarket business

The supermarket business in the UK is dominated by the so-called 'Big Four'. Their market shares in March 2014 are shown below:

Tesco	28%
Asda	19%
Sainsburys	18%
Morrisons	11%

Other established supermarkets, notably the Co-operative and Waitrose, are way behind with market shares of 5–6%.

Over the year to March 2014, Tesco and Morrisons have lost out whilst the other two have hung on to retain or marginally increase their market share.

UK supermarkets are in a fiercely competitive business. Since 2008, consumer spending on food has been cut mainly as a result of recession. At the same time, established supermarkets have faced a new challenge from German-owned discounters Aldi and Lidl. When they first entered the market a few years ago, they had a 'no-frills' image and often sold products that were unknown to UK consumers. That has now changed. Both have expanded their market shares in the last year, notably Aldi which has now around 4% of the market. They have also begun to stock new products that have appeal to a wider spectrum of customers.

The response of the Big Four has been to embark on a vicious no holds barred price war.

Recently:

- Asda announced at the end of 2013 that it would spend £1bn cutting prices over the next five years.
- Tesco then announced a £200m cut in its prices of core products, including fresh vegetables, and a scheme to reduce the price of petrol to its loyal customers.
- Morrisons then followed a year of heavy losses by announcing that it was cutting its prices by £1bn over three years.
- Sainsburys has remained committed to its 'Brand Match' policy of refunding to its customers any difference in its prices on selected items compared to competitors.

Tesco has until now been the price leader. Its profit margin is greater than its rivals although this has been shrinking. Whether it will be forced into taking further action on prices is by no means clear. It could well be that the price-cutting campaigns that have been launched are a battle that none of the Big Four can win. Only time will tell.

a What evidence is there to indicate that the UK supermarket business is an oligopoly? What further evidence might you need to be more certain that this is the case? **[4]**

b Comment on the suggestion that Tesco's position as price leader is being undermined. **[4]**

c Other than price cutting, analyse the ways in which the Big Four might restrict the growth of new entrants such as Aldi and Lidl. **[6]**

d Discuss the extent to which the stores wars described above is in the best interests of the UK consumers. **[6]**

2 **a** Analyse the factors that might lead to contestability in a market. **[12]**

b Discuss the extent to which a rise in contestability in a market is beneficial for consumers as well as firms. **[13]**

3 **a** Analyse the likely benefits that a car manufacturing firm might gain through expanding its scale of operations. **[12]**

b Discuss whether gaining these benefits will mean that the firm is maximising its profits. **[13]**

Chapter 8: Government microeconomic intervention

A Level

Learning objectives

On completion of this chapter you should know:

- why an efficient allocation of resources is desirable
- what is meant by deadweight loss
- how fiscal policies can be used to correct market failure where there are production and consumption externalities
- how a range of other policies can also be used to correct market failure
- what is meant by equity and how governments can use various policies to redistribute income and wealth
- how labour markets operate and why government intervention is invariably necessary
- how to evaluate the effectiveness of government microeconomic intervention.

Introduction

An introduction to market failure and government intervention was provided in Chapters 1, 3 and 6. This chapter builds upon this introduction by considering policies that might be used by governments to achieve a more efficient allocation of resources.

As economies grow and develop, then it becomes increasingly difficult for the unfettered or free market mechanism to work to achieve the best allocation of resources. This does not mean that the market mechanism is not important. It is, but if markets are to achieve what is their purpose, then they must be supported by government policies to correct their failings.

A common form of government intervention is through various types of indirect taxation and subsidy, the basis of which was explained in Chapter 3. In this chapter, we shall see how indirect taxes and subsidies are widely used to correct market failure and to provide a more efficient allocation of resources. We shall also look at a range of other policies that are available for governments to use to achieve the same objectives.

Deadweight loss

As seen in Chapter 6, government intervention in markets is justified where allocative efficiency is not being achieved. Going back to the simple analysis of markets in Chapter 2, the demand curve represents the benefits that consumers derive from consuming a good as measured by the prices they are willing to pay. For this reason, the demand curve is also known as the marginal private benefit (MPB) curve. The supply curve shows the firm's costs of production; these are marginal costs, hence the supply curve is also known as the marginal private cost (MPC) curve. If there are no externalities present, then the best outcome is at price P_e and output Q_e shown in Figure 8.1. Any variation from this optimum will be a situation of market failure or allocative inefficiency.

Market failure can also be understood through an economic concept known as **deadweight loss.** This term refers to the loss of economic welfare due to the fact that potentially desirable production and consumption does not take place. There is not as much producer and consumer surplus as there would be if all such desirable trade took place. This loss of surplus is called 'deadweight loss.'

KEY TERM

Deadweight loss: the welfare loss when due to market failure desirable consumption and production does not take place.

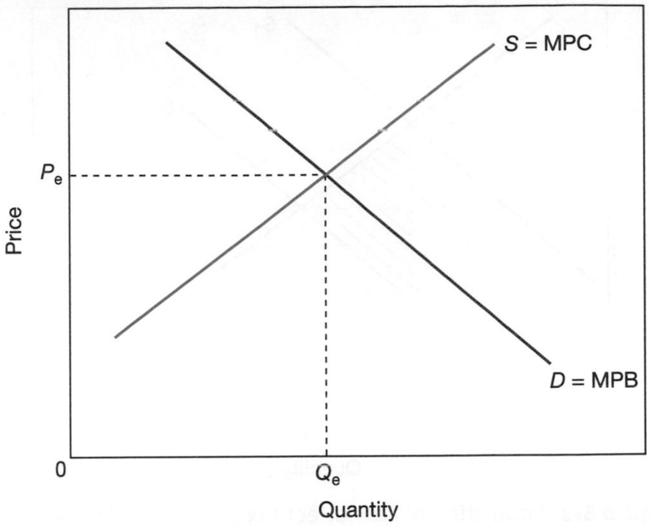

Figure 8.1 Allocative efficiency

Deadweight loss can be seen to occur in a monopolistic market when comparing that market with a competitive market. This is due to the market power of the monopolist and is shown in Figure 8.2. The competitive outcome is given in this diagram by price P_1 and output Q_1. This represents the optimum production and consumption position. Just the right amount of resources is being used to provide this product. This is in contrast to the outcome under monopoly given by price P_2 and quantity Q_2. Here, there is underproduction and underconsumption. Too few resources are used in the production of this good because the price is too high. A measure of the resulting loss of economic welfare is given by the shaded triangle in the diagram. This indicates the loss of net consumer and producer surplus due to the monopoly. It is the deadweight loss due to the monopoly. For consumers, the reduction in consumer surplus amounts to a reduction in real income.

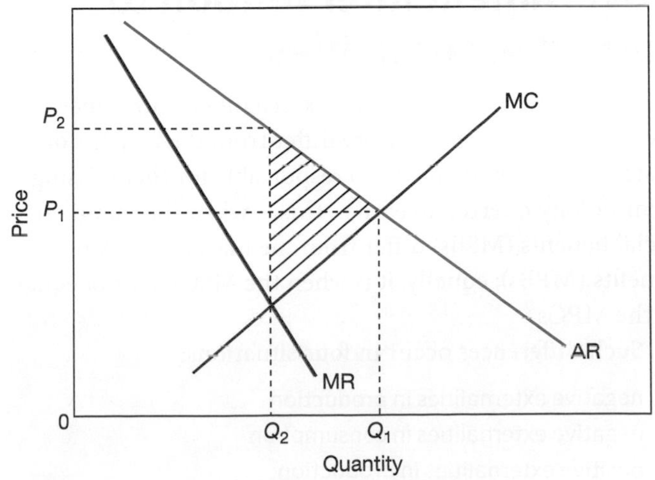

Figure 8.2 Deadweight loss under monopoly

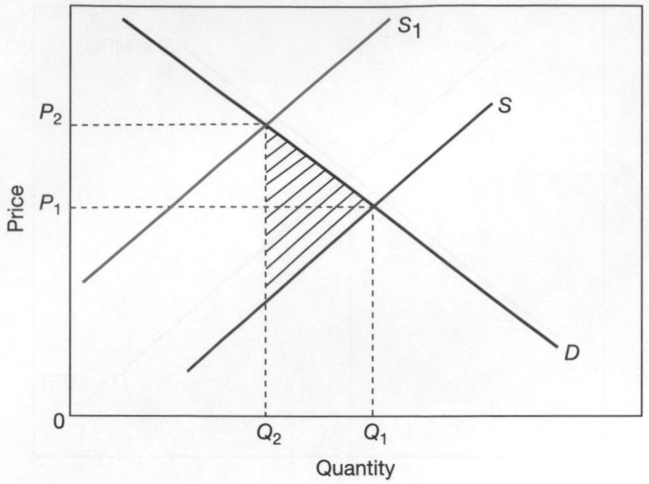

Figure 8.3 Imposition of an indirect tax

Deadweight loss can also be seen to operate when a government imposes an indirect tax on a product. This is shown in Figure 8.3.

The price and quantity of the product are given by the intersection of supply and demand before the tax is imposed. This gives a price of P_1 and a quantity of Q_1. The imposition of the tax is the equivalent of an increase in the costs of production and thus it shifts the supply curve to the left (S to S_1). This leads to a higher price, P_2, and a lower quantity, Q_2. This means a deadweight loss for the same reason as in a monopoly. Desirable production and consumption are discouraged because of the higher price. The resulting overall loss of economic welfare is shown by the shaded triangle. It gives a measure of the amount of deadweight loss due to the imposition of the tax. From a wider perspective, excessive taxes can undermine competitiveness in a market.

Government intervention to correct externalities

As referred to in Chapter 6, an externality occurs when the benefits or costs to society differ from the benefits or costs to the individual who is responsible for them. Using terminology referred to earlier, this is when the marginal social benefits (MSBs) differ from the marginal private benefits (MPBs); equally, it is when the MSCs are not equal to the MPCs.

Such differences occur in four situations:

1. negative externalities in production
2. negative externalities in consumption
3. positive externalities in production
4. positive externalities in consumption.

Intervention to correct externalities takes many forms including:

- use of indirect taxes
- various types of regulation
- property rights
- provision of information
- pollution permits
- subsidies.

Recent interest has also focused on behavioural insights and the so-called 'nudge' theory.

Let us now consider how these interventions might be applied in each of the four situations where externalities occur.

Negative production externalities

This is a particularly common form of market failure. A typical example is the case of a firm that pollutes the environment as a result of its production processes. An indirect tax (ideally a green tax) would normally be imposed on the individual or firm that causes the negative externality. This is consistent with the so-called 'polluter pays' principle.

In Figure 8.4, where there is no government intervention, the equilibrium occurs at point E, where supply, S_1, which is given by marginal private cost (MPC), equals demand, D, given by marginal private benefit (MPB). However, if external costs are taken into account, then the supply curve becomes S_2 or marginal social cost (MSC). The vertical distance between these two supply curves is marginal external cost (MEC). The socially optimal level of output is now equal to Q_2, where S_2 cuts the demand curve. At this socially optimal level of output, the marginal external cost is equal to the vertical distance AB.

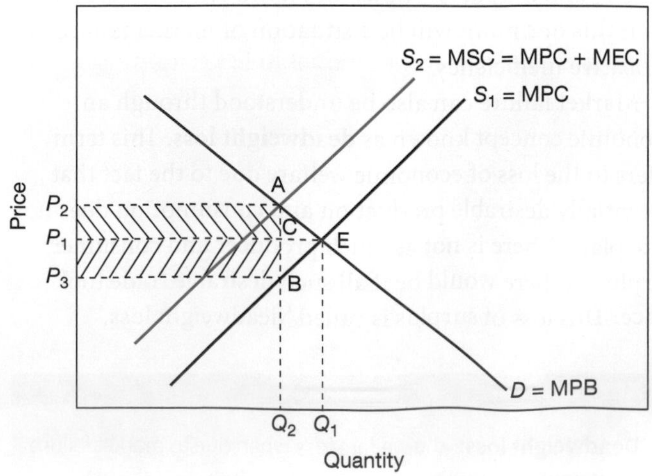

Figure 8.4 External costs and use of indirect taxation

The government intervenes in this market and imposes an indirect tax, which is *ideally* equal to the marginal external cost. This tax is added to the cost of producing the product; the supply curve S_2 is now equal to the MPC plus this tax. From Figure 8.4, you can see that the price at which the product is sold has increased from P_1 to P_2. This is less than the tax applied by the government. At first sight this may appear a little strange, but the producer has accepted a cut in the price received from P_1 to P_3. The producer has borne the burden of part of the tax. The total tax paid is equal to the area P_2ABP_3, of which the consumer's share of the burden is P_2ACP_1 and the producer's share is P_1CBP_3. The effect of the negative externality is now internalised within the market. This is an ideal situation; in practice, the big problem is being able to know or estimate the exact value of the tax that is to be imposed.

Second, governments frequently use **regulations** to overcome market failures caused by production externalities. Let us consider the case of a mining company that pollutes the surrounding countryside. The government might intervene by setting standards that restrict the amount of pollution that can be legally dumped. The government would then need to regulate and inspect the company to make sure that these restrictions are enforced. It can do this in several ways, such as by imposing large fines on any company that contravenes the law. Exhaust fumes from cars pollute the atmosphere and, to reduce this problem, the government can set legal limits on the amount of carbon particles that are emitted from a car's exhaust pipe.

A third form of intervention is through **pollution permits**. Unlike indirect taxation and regulations, pollution permits are a free market solution as they can be bought and sold. They are issued by governments or, as with the Emissions Trading Scheme (ETS), the European Union. Polluting firms (and also airlines) are given a certain number of 'permits to pollute' over a given time period. If a firm emits a lower level of pollution, it can sell its spare permits in the market to firms needing to buy more permits since they have used up those allocated to them. As well as the EU, similar permit schemes are in place in Australia, China and Singapore; the USA has recently introduced a 'cap and trade' system for reducing carbon emissions.

KEY TERMS

Regulations: a wide range of legal and other requirements that come from governments and other organisations.

Pollution permits: a form of licence given by governments that allows a firm to pollute up to a certain level.

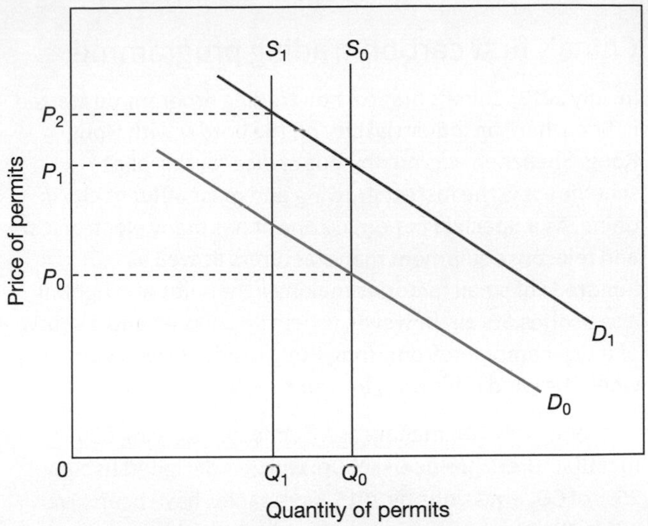

Figure 8.5 Market for pollution permits

Figure 8.5 shows how the system operates. When introduced, the supply of pollution permits is S_0 with a demand of D_0. The market price is therefore P_0. Assume over time that demand increases (more pollutants are being emitted); with supply fixed at S_0, the price rises to P_1, giving every incentive to polluting firms to be more environmentally efficient. A more ambitious approach, as being applied in the US's Green Budget, is to reduce the number of permits available over time. Hence, the supply curve shifts left to S_1, with the price of permits rising to P_2. This puts even more financial pressure on firms to invest in cleaner technologies, so cutting greenhouse gas emissions.

The use of pollution permits has many attractions but they are not without their critics. The EU's ETS, introduced in 2005, has suffered from an oversupply of permits mainly as a consequence of how global recession has hit industrial production. The price of permits peaked at €30 in 2008; in 2013 the price was around €5. Such low prices are unlikely to provide the incentive many firms need to reduce their greenhouse gas emissions. One likely solution, as indicated in Figure 8.5, is to cut back on the supply of permits (see the box 'China's first carbon trading programme').

A fourth way to correct this type of negative externality is by means of **property rights**. As the name indicates, individuals, firms, governments and others have the right to own resources such as housing, factories, mines, farms, rivers and so on. This is a central feature of a capitalist economy. This right gives the owner the legal right to use

KEY TERM

Property rights: where owners have a right to decide how their assets may be used.

China's first carbon trading programme

In July 2013, China's first carbon trading programme started in Shenzhen, an industrial city on the border with Hong Kong. Shenzhen was an obvious choice for this pilot scheme – it is the fastest growing and most affluent city in China. As a Special Economic Zone, it has many electronics and telecom equipment manufacturers as well as hundreds of small factories making light bulbs and lighting accessories. Its air, however, is heavily polluted and a source of much complaint from Hong Kong residents who suffer when the wind is blowing foul air their way.

A carbon emission management scheme involving 635 manufacturers has been set up, which is designed to cut 25% of CO_2 emissions by 2015. Companies have been given 100 million tons of free carbon credits over the next three years. Those who exceed their quota will be fined at the rate of three times the average market price per ton. At the launch of the scheme, two large manufacturers each bought 10,000 tons of credits as a form of investment. If a company fails to cut back on its emissions at the agreed rate and its value added output does not increase as quickly as estimated, the municipal government will take back a proportion of the carbon credits that have been allocated.

Shenzhen has learned a lot from the ETS's experience. In particular, the adoption of an adjustable credit allocation should keep the price of credits at a reasonable level. Typically this is 30 yuan per ton. With limited allowances, companies are under pressure to cut their emissions. Many are also expected to take advice from consultants who can advise on the application of greener technologies.

Shenzhen's factories emitting pollution

The Shenzhen programme is clear evidence that China is now serious about saving energy and reducing emissions. Extending this scheme as is planned will involve a major overhaul of the administrative and regulatory systems. If Shenzhen is successful, then this will go part of the way to reducing China's image as a heavy polluter.

Source: Adapted from *China Daily*, 29 July 2013.

the property as set down and to enforce property rights accordingly. If these rights are assigned, then bargaining may be undertaken to achieve an optimum level of pollution.

Two possibilities can occur. They are:

1. If a polluting firm has property rights, then those who are affected by its activities could pay the polluter to reduce the scale of activity and hence the pollution. In principle the polluter would require payment equal to the loss of profit. An example of this might be a situation where a long-established but polluting firm is asked to relocate as its emissions are affecting an increased number of people who live in the vicinity. The firm has property rights, so why should it move? And if it does move, it should not have to pay the cost of a move as it could stay where it has always been. The government could threaten to use new regulations, so bargaining is likely to take place until a solution is reached.
2. If those affected by negative externalities are assigned property rights, then a polluting firm may be sued by the owners and obliged to compensate them in some way. In this situation there is likely to be a difference in the bargaining power of the two parties. An individual with property rights is likely to experience all sorts of problems if taking on a large powerful multinational corporation (MNC). The chance of success will be greater if others with property rights join the action against the polluting firm. Again, much will depend on the bargaining that is carried out before a settlement is reached.

KEY CONCEPT LINK

Regulation and equity: Negative production externalities are a common form of market failure. The challenge for governments is to use various forms of regulation and control without unduly restricting firms in their operations.

Negative consumption externalities

These externalities are the spillover costs caused by consumers. A good example is the case of urban road traffic congestion. Where roads are congested, there is overconsumption and excessive exhaust emissions are poured out into the atmosphere, causing problems of poor

SELF-ASSESSMENT TASK 8.1

Read the feature below and then answer the questions that follow.

City counts cost of chemical spill

Business owners with empty dining rooms and quiet shops in Charleston, West Virginia's capital in the US, are now counting the cost of a massive chemical spill.

As much as 19,000 litres of industrial chemical leaked into the Elk River from a tank belonging to Freedom Industries, a company that produces specialised chemicals for the mining, steel and cement industries. As a consequence, more than 300,000 residents in Charleston were without safe drinking water. They faced not being able to shower, let alone drink any tap water for several days.

Most visitors have left the city; locals are staying at home or driving out of the area to get hot food. The spill is catastrophic for the environment and also for local businesses. Restaurants have had to close as they cannot prepare food or wash dishes, and employees are unable to clean their hands. Hotels are empty and retail stores have long sold out of bottled water and fizzy drinks. The city's airport has had to close.

People have been admitted to hospital with symptoms such as nausea, vomiting, dizziness, diarrhoea and reddened skin, while 73 people have had to have emergency treatment.

Source: Adapted from *South China Morning Post*, 13 January 2014.

1. Identify examples of
   - private costs
   - external costs

   that have resulted from the chemical spillage.
2. Explain the problems of putting monetary values on these costs.
3. How might the costs of the externalities be internalised on Freedom Industries?
4. Discuss what measures might be put in place to ensure that such a spillage does not occur in the future.

air quality. These negatively impact on third parties such as residents and pedestrians. For road users, the speed of traffic falls below the optimum, causing delays to all road users (see Self-assessment task 8.2). Another example is the case of passive smoking and its effects on non-smokers; there is also the problem of aircraft noise, which can seriously affect the lifestyles of people who live close to a major airport, many of whom may never travel by air.

Figure 8.6 shows these situations. Because of the external costs, MSB is below MPB. The market equilibrium, however, is at P_1 and Q_1 where MPB = MPC. The social optimum is below this at Q_0, where MSB and MPC intersect. Market failure can be corrected by imposing an indirect tax on those who have caused the negative consumption externality. The supply curve shifts to the left; if the tax is the same as the external cost, then the quantity traded will fall to Q_0. Allocative efficiency will now be achieved.

Legislation is also widely used in these situations. There are strict laws in place that prohibit smoking in public buildings, close to schools, in restaurants, shopping malls, railway stations and so on. There are regulations in place in many countries that put noise and time restrictions on when aircraft can take off and land. The noise from vehicles is also subject to strict regulations in most developed economies.

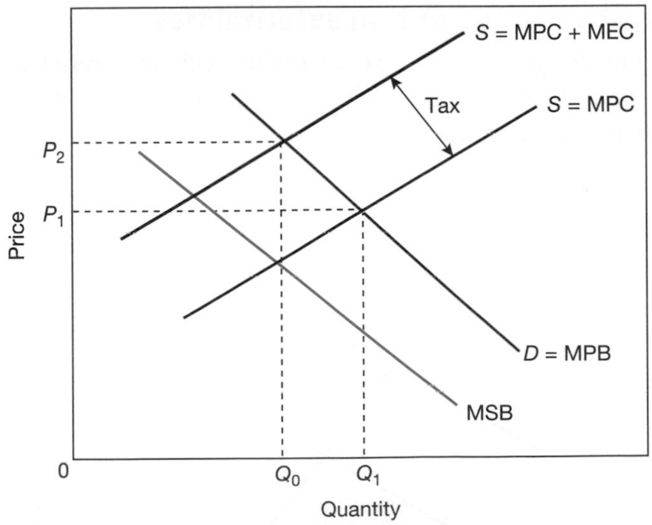

Figure 8.6 Negative consumption externalities

The provision of information is also appropriate in this case of market failure. Warnings and photographs are now placed on packets of tobacco products to deter smoking; information is provided on the packaging of many processed food products to indicate their sugar and salt content as well as their nutritional qualities. Bottled water usually contains details of the composition of the contents. Another example is for air travel, where it is possible for passengers to know the carbon footprint they are causing and how this might in some way be offset.

Positive production externalities

These occur when there are positive spillover benefits created by producers. A particularly good example is in the case of inoculations; vaccines that have been developed to combat serious medical conditions like polio, cholera and smallpox benefit not only those receiving them but also the community as a whole. The same is true in other fields of research and technological development. Initially the inventor but subsequently many others are able to benefit from the private costs that have been spent by a firm.

Figure 8.7 shows how a subsidy to the firm generating these benefits would correct market failure. Here, MSC is below MPC. The market equilibrium is at P_1 Q_1; the market under allocates resources at this point. It is implied that the government should provide a subsidy to the firm equal to the external benefit. As a result, there will be an increase in the quantity produced to Q_2 and a lower price at P_2. Allocative efficiency is now being achieved.

Positive consumption externalities

In this situation, the positive externality occurs as a result of decisions taken that impact favourably on consumers. The provision of secondary education is a good example. Being

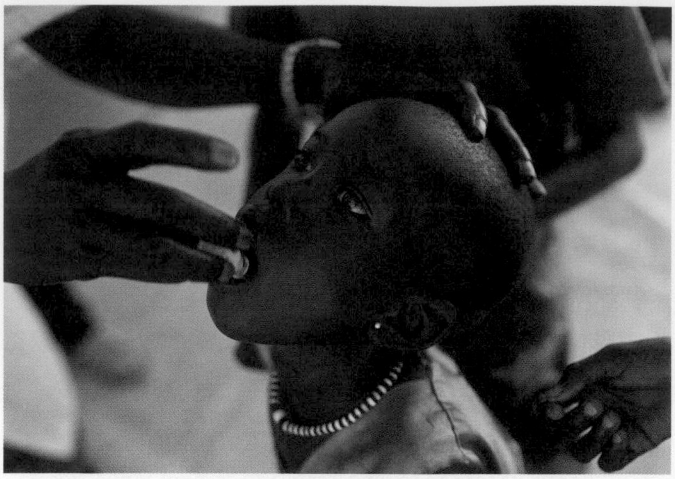

A child in Africa receiving a cholera inoculation

educated not only benefits the individual; it produces other spillover benefits for the economy in the form of a better educated workforce that is likely to be more productive and able to provide an important source of future economic growth. Another example is where local rail and bus services are subsidised. The subsidy benefits all travellers but provides most benefit to low wage earners who are able to access a wider geographical range of job opportunities.

The effect of a subsidy in this case is shown in Figure 8.8. The equilibrium without government intervention is at point F where MPC = MPB or $D_1 = S_1$. The marginal external benefit (MEB) is added to the MPB curve to give the MSB, the marginal social benefit. The MSB represents society's demand curve for the product.

If the government subsidises production of this product, then the supply curve shifts to the right from S_1, which equals MPC, to S_2, which equals MPC plus the subsidy. The marginal cost of supplying the good is reduced by the amount of subsidy and the vertical distance GH is equal to the value of the subsidy.

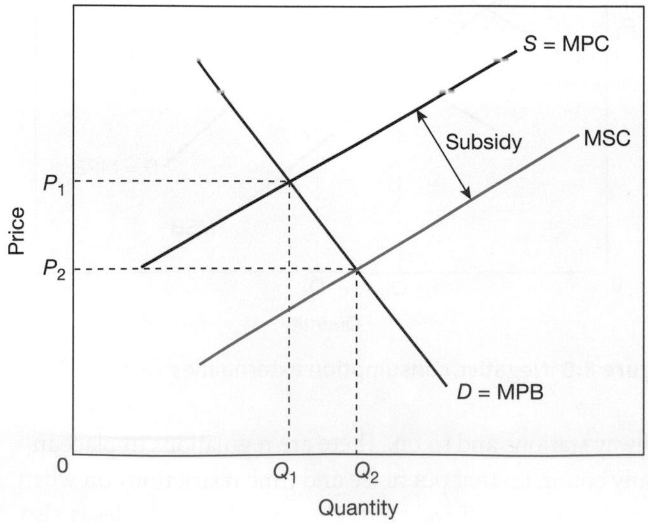

Figure 8.7 Positive production externalities

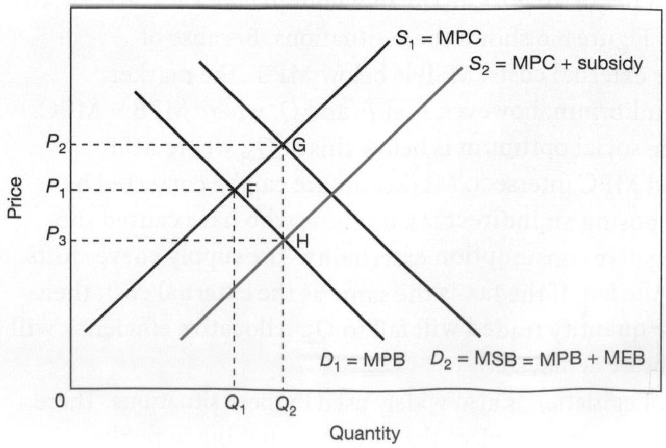

Figure 8.8 External benefits and use of a subsidy

SELF-ASSESSMENT TASK 8.2

Read the feature below and then answer the questions that follow.

A tale of two cities: Delhi and Singapore

Contrary to what many may believe, the worst traffic congestion is to be found in emerging economies that are experiencing a boom in car ownership. India's capital, Delhi, is no exception.

Recent reports suggest that very shortly peak traffic speeds will be little more than 5 km per hour. Delhi's congestion problems are the worst in the whole of India and four times worse than Mumbai. The problem is on the demand side; Delhi has more than six million vehicles, with 1,200 new ones being added each day. At the same time, the supply of road space lags behind. This can only have negative results: commuter stress, loss of valuable working time, excessive exhaust fumes polluting the air and wastage of fuel. The only way out in the eyes of the current administration is to pump money into the public transport system. By 2020, if Delhi is to not be facing gridlock, public transport needs to be carrying 80% of all trips made in the city as against 40% at present. A big ask!

At the same time there is now a remarkable consensus among economists that road pricing is the only way in which congestion problems can be resolved. It is seen as a sensible way of dealing with the problem of a scarce resource, road space, which is inefficiently used and, as a consequence, generates substantial costs to the community. Road pricing, whereby there is a direct charge to use congested roads, is a fair and logical outcome to what is a classic example of market failure.

For many years the Singapore government has imposed high customs duties on imported cars and set stiff registration fees and high annual road taxes. In addition it requires anybody buying a new car to get a permit, currently priced at between S$27,000 and S$49,000, well above the average annual income per head. If this were not enough, for the past 30 years, to enter a restricted

city zone, drivers must pay a $2 flat rate charge in the morning peak period, falling to $1.30 at off-peak times. When the peak charge was extended to the rush hour in 1989, it further reduced traffic.

From spring 1998, a new automatic 'pay-as-you-go' system replaced the above rather crude system. Using the latest microchip technology, charging is automatic (smart cards can be pre-loaded up to S$150) and is based on the actual contribution to congestion made by individual car users. The system is now well established. To the economist it is in many respects a 'dream ticket' – it matches in full the well-known 'polluter pays' principle so strenuously advocated in textbooks yet so very rarely applied in practice.

But will it work in Delhi? This is highly problematic, not least because, unlike Singapore, Delhi does not currently have a world-class public transport system to provide a realistic alternative for urban travellers. There are many other issues as well.

Source: Adapted from *India Today*, 23 July 2012.

1 a Explain why traffic congestion is a classic example of market failure.

  b How in theory should a government deal with the problem of traffic congestion?

2 Suppose you have been invited to make a presentation to politicians and planners on how the experience of Singapore in dealing with its congestion problems might assist your country in reducing its urban transport problems. Briefly draft this presentation under the following headings:

- the main benefits of road pricing in Singapore
- the data you would need to be able to measure these benefits
- why the experience of Singapore may not be entirely relevant for your own country.

Thus the equilibrium after the subsidy is at point H, which is where D_1 crosses S_2 and the optimal amount of goods Q_2 is sold by the market at the lower price of P_3. This is clearly more beneficial for consumers.

In the case of education, legislation is used in some countries to make state-funded education compulsory up to a certain age. Sadly, this is often not the case in many poorer countries. Information is also provided by governments to persuade consumers to buy more goods that produce positive externalities. In most developed economies, people are urged to eat more fruit and vegetables to reduce the possible risk of health problems such as diabetes and obesity.

KEY CONCEPT LINK

Regulation and equity: So far in this chapter it has been shown that effective government intervention can produce not only a more efficient allocation of resources but can, by correcting market failure, also result in greater social equality and equity.

TOP TIP

It is sometimes difficult to distinguish between a production and consumption externality as an action may involve both.

Behavioural insights and 'nudge' theory

Reference has been made earlier to behavioural approaches to decision making. By way of correcting market failure, there is growing interest in how 'nudge' theory might lead to a more efficient allocation of resources.

The basis of nudge theory lies in the provision of information. Thaler and Sunstein used the concept to explain what they called 'choice architecture'. They argued that by presenting choices in a better way, people make wiser decisions. This avoids the need for more formal government intervention since, when applied, individuals retain their freedom to choose. It is in some respects a form of paternalism whereby governments or individuals interfere with the affairs of people against their will yet with their best interests in mind.

Nudge theory therefore is a way of achieving beneficial economic and social outcomes without the need for regulations. In the case of market failure, it can be applied through letters, emails or personal communications.

A typical example is in the case of a free inoculation (merit good) that is available to all people over 60 years old. These people can be targeted by a simple letter that makes them fully aware of the benefits of having the inoculation and how they can get one. In this way, they are 'nudged'; without such a nudge, take up would likely be less and, over time, involve greater costs to the health service.

A second example might be in the case of a city that is seeking to reduce the number of cars on its roads (negative externality). There could be a media campaign that focuses on the benefits of cycling or of using other more environmentally acceptable forms of transport like buses. This campaign could nudge motorists into using another form of urban transport.

The key question is 'Does nudge work?' The answer is that it does but to only a limited extent and that it is best used and most effective when used alongside other policies that are already dealing with market failure.

Price and output decisions under nationalisation and privatisation

Privatisation is a process whereby there is a change in ownership of an activity from the public or state sector to the private sector. In the UK, for example, important former nationalised industries such as coal, gas, water, electricity, telephones, railways and bus services were privatised in a very short period of time from the mid-1980s to the mid-1990s. Privatisation has also been prevalent in other developed economies, emerging economies like China and the new EU members from Central and Eastern Europe, and in many developing economies.

KEY TERM

Privatisation: where there is a change in ownership from the public to the private sector.

There are many reasons for privatisation, some political as well as economic. From a microeconomic perspective, the most significant is the belief that breaking up a state monopoly will produce greater efficiency. In other words, it is believed that the private sector will be able to achieve a better allocation of resources than a nationalised industry. In part this comes about because the managers of private companies are accountable to their shareholders; in contrast, the general public has only limited property rights over a nationalised company.

X-inefficiency is also relevant. As we saw in Chapter 6, this is a situation where, in this case, a nationalised company is likely to become increasingly inefficient over time.

Average costs and hence consumer prices will be higher than if the company was in private ownership. This situation relates to the property rights issue referred to earlier whereby there is little or no pressure on managers to be more efficient. Consequently, productive efficiency declines. A further related argument is that in a private business, managers have the freedom to manage; they can raise funds for investment and are not restricted by how the government says that they should manage. Efficiency, therefore, is a key issue.

There are, however, valid arguments for the nationalisation of certain activities, again from an efficiency standpoint. One of the best reasons is the natural monopoly argument put forward in Chapter 7, where it was suggested that it does not make sense for there to be more than one provider of, say, a railway line or a canal. With privatisation and competition it can be argued that duplication will ensue, leading to inefficiency, higher prices and less output. A second reason is that privatisation can often lead to a private monopoly replacing a state-owned monopoly. This will produce few, if any, benefits for consumers – the monopolist will be able to exert power in the market to raise prices and restrict output.

Another argument is that, following privatisation, it is invariably necessary for some degree of regulation and control to be put in place to protect consumers from the market power of large private companies. Without such controls in place, prices would rise faster than under state ownership and the consumer would lose out. These are all valid reasons for retaining state ownership of an industry. Whether an industry is privatised or remains in state control is often a political decision and not one solely based on economics.

KEY CONCEPT LINK

Regulation and equity: Privatisation allows firms a greater freedom to operate in the market; government regulation is invariably necessary to ensure that consumers are not exploited and that social equity is not compromised.

Equity and policies towards income and wealth redistribution

Introduction: equity versus efficiency

Efficiency is a term that we have used widely so far in many of our discussions of microeconomics and refers to how limited resources can be used in the best possible way. **Equity** is different in so far as it refers to a distribution that is fair or just. This distribution could be of income, poverty, government benefits, wealth and so on. A fair distribution of income, for example, is not the same as an equal distribution of income.

KEY TERM

Equity: where the distribution of, say, income or wealth is fair.

Equity has two sides to it. These are:

1 horizontal equity, whereby consumers and others with the same circumstances should pay the same level of taxation
2 vertical equity, whereby taxes should be fairly apportioned between the rich and the poor in society.

The various types of market failure discussed in Chapters 3 and 6 have resulted in efficiency and equity being major objectives of microeconomic policy. But herein lies a problem – policies that are used to promote efficiency may have the effect of increasing inequality. For example, when a consumer good is scarce, its price rises; those most able to pay will continue to consume but the increased price will hurt those on lower incomes much more. Also, those who work hard and take risks are likely to be better off than others. As a consequence, governments invariably find it necessary to have a trade-off between equity and efficiency. Creating a more equal distribution on income may require incentives to be made to improve efficiency. These incentives are designed to prompt people to take risks and so improve the standard of living for all concerned.

TOP TIP

Equity is not the same as equality. Governments seek to reduce inequality in the distribution of income in various ways but have had only limited success. At the same time they have to ensure that the distribution is equitable through its policies being fair to all of the population.

Income and wealth

It is important to distinguish between income and **wealth**. Income, as we saw in Chapter 1, is the reward for the services of a factor of production. For labour, it is paid in wages and salaries or rent, interest and profits in the cases

KEY TERM

Wealth: an accumulated stock of assets.

of the other factors of production. Wealth is the term used for the accumulation of a *stock* of assets such as property, shares, bonds or bank accounts. These assets are there to provide an income stream for the future.

Measuring inequality

A **Lorenz curve** is a simple, well-used way of representing inequality in an economy. Figure 8.9 is a typical example. If there was a completely equitable distribution of income, then this would be represented by the 45° line on this diagram. The extent of inequality is shown by area A. As inequality rises, this area increases, moving towards the bottom right of the diagram. When area A shrinks, the distribution of income among the population becomes more equal.

The **Gini coefficient** is a numerical measure of the extent of inequality. On Figure 8.9 it is calculated as (area A) ÷ (area A + area B). If the income distribution is equal, this coefficient will have a value of 0. At the other extreme, if all income accrues to just one person, then the Gini coefficient is 1. Both extremes do not occur in reality – the norm is for coefficients to be somewhere between these two values. A Gini coefficient of 0.3 therefore indicates a more equal distribution of income than say a coefficient of 0.5. The smaller coefficient would be indicated by a slimmer segment on the Lorenz curve. Table 8.1 contains some typical examples.

KEY TERMS

Lorenz curve: a graphical representation of inequality.

Gini coefficient: a numerical measure of inequality.

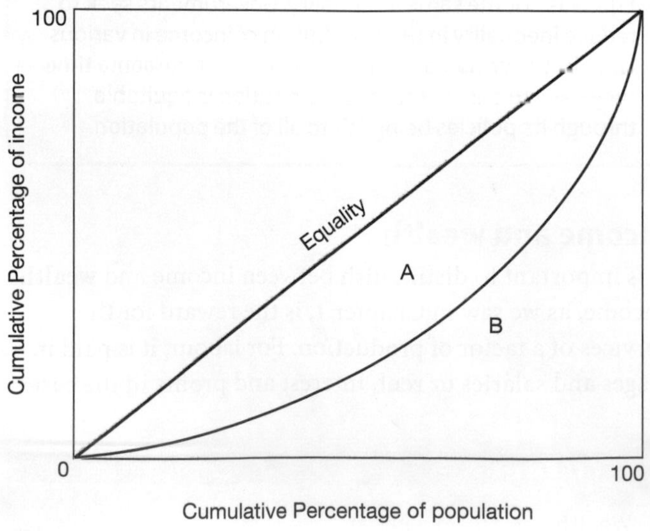

Figure 8.9 The Lorenz curve

Seychelles	0.66	PR China	0.42
South Africa	0.63	USA	0.40
Central African Republic	0.56	UK	0.36
Zimbabwe	0.50	India	0.33
Nigeria	0.48	Pakistan	0.30
Sierra Leone	0.43	Denmark	0.25

Table 8.1 Selected Gini coefficients (various dates)

Source: World Bank, 2013

SELF-ASSESSMENT TASK 8.3

Table 8.2 shows the extent of income inequality in Pakistan and in its Punjab region in 2011.

	Pakistan	Punjab
% Population	**% Income**	**% Income**
9	2.6	4.3
18	7.1	9.5
36	19.5	17.7
45	27.1	24.6
73	54.8	56.5
91	77.4	85.5

Table 8.2

1 Use the above data to sketch the two Lorenz curves.

2 Comment on any differences you observe.

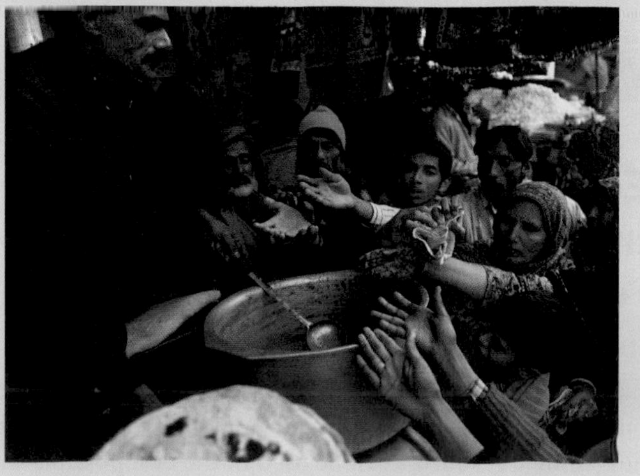

Government policies to redistribute income and wealth

There are three main types of policies that are available to reduce inequality in the distribution of income and wealth. These are:

1 providing benefits
2 through the tax system
3 through other policies.

Providing benefits

A simple way to redistribute income is to pay benefits out of government spending to those on low incomes. Money raised through the tax system is then paid to low income persons and families in order to increase their disposable income. There are two types of such benefits:

1 **Means-tested benefits:** These benefits are only paid to those on low incomes. They are targeted directly at those who are seen to be most in need. An example would be income support or unemployment benefit. What is available varies between countries. In general more is likely to be provided in developed economies, since they have a more robust tax base to draw upon. However, such benefits are not always claimed by those for whom they are designed. They can also create a disincentive to work. This is the so-called **poverty trap** and is where a person or family is financially worse off working rather than living off the range of benefits available. Such a situation can occur where there is a low income tax threshold and generous means-tested benefits up to a certain level of income.
2 **Universal benefits:** These are paid out to everyone in certain categories, often age related, regardless of their income or wealth. Examples include universal state pensions and child benefit. Such benefits overcome the two problems associated with means-tested benefits. However, they imply paying out money to many who do not need it and therefore tend to be expensive to operate.

KEY TERMS

Means-tested benefits: benefits that are paid only to those whose incomes fall below a certain level.

Poverty trap: where an individual or a family are better off on means-tested benefits rather than working.

Universal benefits: benefits that are available to all irrespective of income or wealth.

Through the tax system

The tax system can be used in order to reduce inequalities in income and wealth. This is specifically through the use of **progressive taxation**. Progressive income taxes lead to those earning higher incomes being taxed a higher percentage of their income than those on lower incomes. In some economies the top rate of income tax might be as high as 80% compared to other rates of 40% and 20%. Thus income differentials are reduced. Most income tax systems are like this example and are therefore progressive in nature. The average rate of tax rises as people earn higher incomes. The main problem, however, is that for some people, the result is a disincentive to work and possibly even to live in a high taxation regime.

Indirect taxes such as a general sales tax on products tend to be **regressive**. They have to be paid for by all who consume and so have no potential for redistributing income. Rich and poor people pay the taxes at the same rate.

KEY TERMS

Progressive tax: one where the rate rises more than proportionately to the rise in income.

Regressive tax: one where the ratio of taxation to income falls as income increases.

Taxes can also be imposed to reduce wealth inequalities. One example is inheritance tax. Individuals who inherit more than a certain amount of wealth have to pay some of the value of that wealth in tax to the government. Another similar example is that of capital gains tax, whereby a tax is payable on the financial gain a person may have made in the time that an asset such as property or a financial portfolio has been owned. The overall impact of such measures remains modest.

Other policies

A further way of reducing inequalities in society is for the government to provide certain important services free of charge to the user. Such services are financed through the tax system. If such services are used equally by all citizens, then those on lowest incomes gain most as a percentage of their income. Inequality is thus lowered.

The two most significant examples of such free provision in many economies are health care and junior and secondary education. These markets are characterised by various market failures. However, these failures do not, according to standard economic theory, justify free provision to the consumer. The justification must be on the grounds of equity. The view is that everyone should have access to a certain level of health care and education regardless of income and wealth. Thus, these services are provided universally free: they are the material equivalent of monetary universal benefits.

It can also be argued that price stability can assist in the redistribution of income. In such circumstances, the price level rises slowly and there is a steady rate of inflation. As shown in Chapter 10, this provides relatively stable conditions for the macroeconomy. The income stream from taxation is secure, there is less pressure on government spending and likely to be more resources available to reduce income tax thresholds or the basic income tax rate. In a modest way, income inequalities may be reduced.

As referred to earlier, means-tested benefits can result in people on low incomes being trapped with little chance of becoming better off. Universal benefits overcome this problem but are invariably far too expensive to apply. One possible way around this problem is **negative income tax**. Under such a system, there would be a flat rate of taxation (say 25%) and

SELF-ASSESSMENT TASK 8.4

Read the feature below and then answer the questions that follow.

Income disparity: the very uneven rise in Pakistani incomes

The distribution of income in Pakistan continues to be an important economic and political issue. Since 2000, per capita income has increased rapidly but there is a very disturbing fact – household income for the growing urban middle class has continued to rise, yet the rural poor have seen their real incomes fall. This is often the case in emerging economies like that of Pakistan.

The widening disparity in incomes has got worse since 2000. It has persisted when the economy was expanding rapidly, when it has been slowing down and when it has been almost stagnant. This is difficult to explain. Moreover, the implications for the poorest people are worrying economists and the government; for the poorest people the period of growth this century has meant nothing. Yet the rest of the country's population has got richer, some stupendously so.

There have been wide geographical variations in income growth since 2002. The fastest growth has been in the Punjab and urban Khyber-Pakhtunkhwa regions where the incomes of the top 20% have risen in real terms by an average of 3.8% per annum. In contrast, the worst off have been in rural Sindh where the real incomes of the bottom 20% have fallen by 4.4% per annum. Interestingly, the very poor in Balochistan experienced real income growth of 4% a year, albeit from a very low base.

Over the past decade, the well-being of the overwhelming majority of Pakistan's population has depended on how well the national economy has been performing. This majority is not the middle class, nor are they in the poorest class. These are the ones whose votes will count at the next election.

Source: Adapted from F. Tirmizi, *Express Tribune*, 30 July 2012.

1 Explain **one** likely consequence of the widening gap in the incomes of the urban and rural populations.

2 Comment upon how the Pakistani government and businesses might be able to improve the well-being of the rural population.

every person or family would receive a fixed annual benefit of, say, $4,000. If the tax paid on earnings is less than this annual benefit then the person receives the difference from the government; in other words, a negative income tax. Where the difference is positive, in the case of higher earners, then this is the amount of direct tax that has to be paid.

A final issue to consider is that of **intergenerational equity**. This relates back to sustainability and the need for the present generation to take responsibility for the well-being of future generations. Wealth can be passed down from one generation to the next. Although taxes on wealth can marginally reduce inequality, it is important that current government policies work in such a way as to not compromise the opportunities for there to be a more equitable future distribution. This represents a substantial challenge for policy-makers.

KEY TERMS

Negative income tax: a unified tax and benefits system where people are taxed or receive benefits according to a single set of rules.

Intergenerational equity: the responsibility that government has to provide for a more equitable future distribution of income and wealth.

SELF-ASSESSMENT TASK 8.5

Go back and study the information in Table 8.1 and then answer the questions that follow.

1 Using a Lorenz curve, briefly describe the difference in the distribution of income between
   - the Central African Republic and Sierra Leone
   - India and Pakistan.
2 For your own country, discuss the ways in which your government is seeking to reduce income inequalities.

Labour market forces and government intervention

When you leave school or college (hopefully with a CIE A Level in Economics), the wage or salary you get paid will be determined largely by what type of job you take. If you get a post as a clerk, you are likely to get more pay than if you are a street cleaner. Equally, if you go on to become a teacher, you will get paid more than a clerk. In turn, the manager of a multinational company will probably get paid more than a teacher. So why is it that some workers get paid more than others? Why is it that some people with exceptional talent – for example Lionel Messi, Roger Federer, Maria Sharapova, Madonna or Amitabh Bachchan – are so highly paid? The answer to these questions, like many such questions in Economics, is that it all depends on supply and demand. To understand why some people get paid more than others, economists have looked at the labour market and have sought to put forward various principles based on the characteristics of this market.

Lionel Messi

Amitabh Bachchan

Demand for and supply of labour

Demand for labour

Many of the principles introduced in Chapter 2 can be applied to the labour market. However, there is one fundamentally different point: the demand for labour is a **derived demand**. By this, we mean that the firm's demand for labour is due to its decision to produce certain goods or services. Labour is therefore demanded not for its own sake but because it is essential for the production of goods or services. If we go back to our earlier examples, clerks are employed because they are necessary for a firm to carry out its business. The streets need cleaning, therefore street cleaners are employed. Children need education so teachers are required. This may seem obvious but it does underpin the whole basis of labour economics. A small number of film stars, rock idols and sports personalities have exceptional talents – the demand for their services is very high indeed and they can command a high fee for their services.

KEY TERM

Derived demand: where the demand for a good or service depends upon the use that can be made from it.

The analysis that follows is based upon two important assumptions:

1 The firm wishing to hire labour is operating in a competitive market. There are many buyers and sellers of labour, and no single firm or worker can affect the wage that is paid.
2 The firm is a profit maximiser. Its demand for labour and supply of labour are based on it maximising the difference between total revenue and total costs.

TOP TIP

The demand for labour is unusual since it is derived from the benefits that accrue to those who hire labour. This makes the demand for labour different from most other things that are demanded.

The marginal revenue product of labour

The profit-maximising firm is concerned with how much the output it produces is worth to the business. We must therefore take into account the cost of employing labour – the wage rate. Let us assume that this is $600 per month and, using earlier data from Table 7.3, let us assume that a unit of clothing sells for $10.

When the firm hires the first worker, this worker generates $1,000 of revenue for the firm; this in turn represents $400 of profit. The amount of revenue generated by an additional worker is referred to as the **marginal revenue product** of labour. Adding a further worker generates another $800 and $200 profit. There comes a point when, after the third worker has been employed, a further worker adds more to costs than to revenue (it still costs $600 to employ the worker but only $400 worth of clothing is produced). So, above this level of employment, the value of the marginal product that is being produced is less than the wage. This clearly makes no sense to the firm. It can therefore be deduced that the firm should hire workers up to the point where the value of the marginal product of labour equals the wage that is being paid. The demand curve for labour can therefore be represented by the value of the marginal product curve. This is shown in Figure 8.10. So, in general terms:

- a firm should continue to hire labour as long as the additional worker adds more to revenue than he or she adds to the firm's costs
- the market wage is determined by the marginal revenue product of labour
- the marginal revenue product curve is therefore the firm's demand curve for labour
- if the wage rate rises or falls, then fewer or more workers will be employed.

It follows from this analysis that the wages paid to workers are a direct reflection of their marginal revenue product. So, a street cleaner has a lower marginal

KEY TERM

Marginal revenue product: the addition to total revenue as a result of employing one more worker.

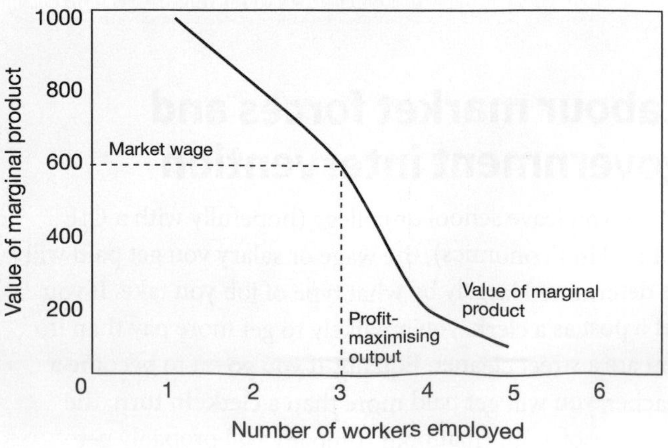

Figure 8.10 The value of the marginal product of labour

revenue product than a clerk, who in turn has a lower marginal revenue product than a teacher, and so on. It also follows that it is actually possible to measure marginal revenue productivity. This is a very big assumption to make. In a manufacturing firm it may be possible to do this, but in many occupations this is not possible. How, for example, can we measure the marginal revenue product of a teacher? The answer is 'with great difficulty'. We therefore need to look at the other side of the labour market, that involving the supply of labour, to give a proper explanation of how wages are actually determined.

KEY CONCEPT LINK

Scarcity and choice, the margin and change: When firms are deciding how much labour they need, the decision is based on choice at the margin. Any change in the wage rate or in the marginal revenue product of labour will lead to a change in the firm's demand for labour.

Supply of labour

The supply of labour is the total number of hours that labour is able and willing to work at a particular wage rate. The general principles of supply introduced in Chapter 2 apply here. However, it is important to remember that in this case we are talking about people and their willingness to participate (or otherwise) in the labour market depending upon the rate or price that they are offered for their services. It is useful to consider labour supply at three levels: that of the individual worker, that of a firm or industry and that of the economy as a whole. Different factors affect supply depending upon which of these levels we are dealing with. Let us look briefly at each in turn.

The individual's supply of labour

As with any supply, price (or wage in this case) has an important bearing on the decision of any individual worker to enter the labour market. If the wage is too low, someone may determine that it is not worth the effort of going to work and will decide to stay at home. Not many people are in this position – most of us need to work to live. Economic theory assumes that there is a positive relationship between labour supply and the wage rate. So, as the wage rate increases, more people are willing to offer their services to employers. This is represented by the individual's labour supply curve, which mainly slopes upwards (see Figure 8.11).

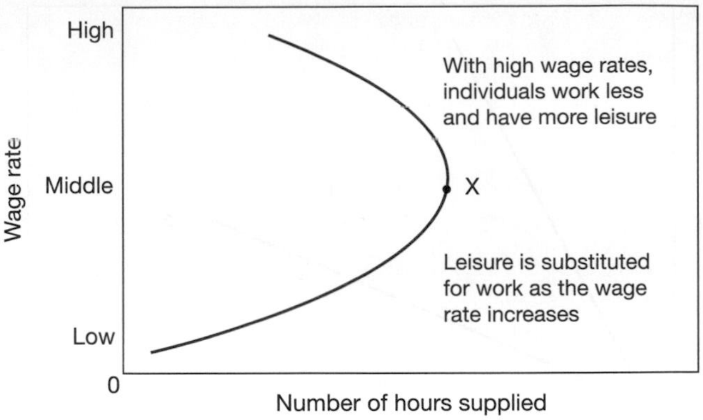

Figure 8.11 An individual's labour supply curve

Beyond a certain point, individuals will take the view that they prefer leisure to work. This point is indicated by the backward-sloping curve from point X. Before this point, an individual worker is more willing to supply his or her labour as the wage rate increases. It must be stressed that this point depends on the individual's attitude to work and leisure – point X on any individual's supply curve will vary.

A further factor that can affect an individual's supply of labour is the income tax rate. In all countries this tends to be progressive, as we noted earlier. Low-wage workers pay little or no tax. As wages rise, more of the increase is paid in tax to the government. In the UK, for example, the standard rate of income tax in 2014 was 20%, with a maximum rate of 45% for the highest income earners. In other developed countries this higher rate is often above 50%. The downside could be that a high tax rate stifles the incentive to work. Governments must therefore be very careful to not do this as it will adversely affect economic prospects if key workers are not encouraged to work because of the high tax rates.

Labour supply to a firm or industry

This supply curve consists of the sum of the individual supply curves of all workers employed in a firm or industry. It is usually upward sloping throughout (see Figure 8.12). As with an individual worker, the number of workers wanting to supply their labour increases with the wage rate that is offered. The slope of this supply curve is measured by the elasticity of supply of labour, the extent to which labour supply responds to a change in the wage rate. Figure 8.12 shows two different supply curves, one inelastic (L_1) and the other elastic with respect to the wages being paid.

There are various reasons for this difference. An obvious one is the skills required to carry out a particular occupation. In general, the more skills required, the more

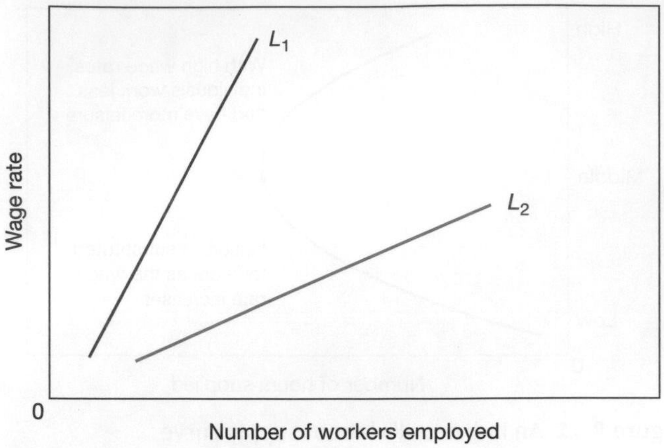

Figure 8.12 The supply curve of labour to a firm or industry

inelastic will be the supply of labour. This also applies to the amount of education and training that is required to carry out a particular job. Anyone who teaches has to spend at least four years after college acquiring the necessary qualifications. Supply to such an occupation will be more inelastic than to, say, road sweeping, where no skills and little or no education and training are needed.

The supply curve L_2 in Figure 8.12 is therefore likely to be that for an industry where wages are low and where there is a plentiful supply of labour with no particular skills or training.

In a competitive labour market, the wage rates offered in all other industries or occupations will be important in determining the supply of labour to a particular industry. In developing economies, an obvious example could be the difference in wages in agriculture compared with wages in expanding manufacturing or food-processing industries, which usually pay more to their workers.

The long-run supply of labour

This is of particular significance for the economy as a whole. There are important contrasts here between developed and developing economies, involving wider economic factors including the following:

- The size of the population: In some developed economies, the total population is relatively stable; in others it is increasing at a modest rate mainly due to increasing immigration. In contrast, the population of Italy is actually declining quite markedly. With life expectancy increasing, there are relatively fewer people of working age. In contrast, in most developing economies there is an increase in the overall supply of labour from within mainly due to higher birth rates and improved medical care for young children. Consequently, increasing numbers of young people join the labour market. This means the long-run supply curve for labour shifts to the right, indicating that more workers are willing to supply their labour at a given wage rate.
- The labour participation rate: This term is used to determine the proportion of the population of working age actually in employment. In many developed economies, workers often choose to leave the labour market, by taking 'early retirement', before the normal age for retirement, so reducing the labour participation rate. At the lower end of the age range, with more students electing for higher education, the labour participation rate is also falling slightly. The combined effect has been for a slight reduction in the labour participation rate, so shifting the long-run labour supply curve to the left.
- The tax and benefits levels: As we saw earlier in Figure 8.11, there comes a point where the work–leisure trade-off affects an individual's labour supply. This also affects the supply of labour for the economy as a whole, particularly in developed economies. Governments therefore have to be very careful in their taxation and social security policies to ensure that the long-run supply of labour is not adversely affected through a reduction in the willingness of people to work. In the UK, the top rate of income tax was reduced from 50% to 45% in 2013 – 20 years ago it was much more progressive, with marginal tax rates as high as 80% of the increase in income for the highest-paid. In such circumstances, there is clearly a huge disincentive for someone to stay in the labour market. The level of unemployment and social security payments can also affect the long-run supply of labour in a similar way as we saw earlier. Through their supply side policies, therefore, governments seek to provide incentives for certain types of labour to remain active in the labour market (see Chapter 5).
- Immigration and emigration: These affect the long-run supply of labour in an economy. Where there are labour shortages, as was the case in the UK during the late 1950s and early 1960s, migrants moved from Commonwealth countries such as Barbados, Jamaica, Bangladesh, India and Pakistan, often to work in relatively low-pay industries and the public services. This increased the supply of labour. Emigration from these countries in turn relieved pressures in their labour markets. In the past, the UK has faced labour shortages in nursing, teaching and 'high-tech' industries as well as in other skilled manual occupations. Since 2004, the geographical enlargement of the EU has seen a huge influx of well over one million migrant workers from the new member states in Central and Eastern Europe.

The above factors determine the long-run supply of labour. Shifts to the left and to the right in the long-run supply of labour are shown in Figure 8.13.

In the long run, the supply of labour to a particular firm, as distinct from the economy, is influenced by the net advantages of a job. These include pecuniary advantages and non-pecuniary advantages.

Polish migrant workers arriving at Victoria Coach Station

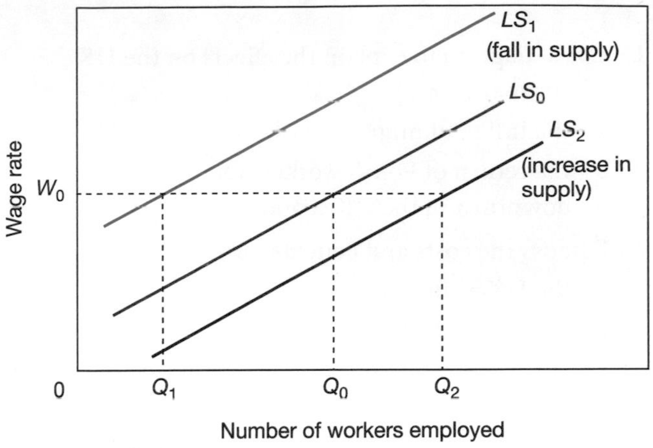

Figure 8.13 Shifts in the long-run supply of labour

A pecuniary advantage includes things such as the weekly wage or monthly salary, any bonus payments, the opportunity to work paid overtime and pension prospects. Non-pecuniary advantages are numerous and cover an almost endless list of factors that have to be taken into account by a person considering whether to remain in a job, change jobs or even to change occupations. These include the hours of work, job security, holiday entitlement, promotion prospects, location of the workplace and whether the job is pleasant or satisfying. For many workers, these non-pecuniary advantages rather than pecuniary advantages often have a major bearing on their choice of occupation.

SELF-ASSESSMENT TASK 8.6

Read the feature below and then answer the questions that follow.

Polish migrant workers leave Britain in droves

When Poland and seven other Central and Eastern European (CEE) countries joined the EU in May 2004, the UK experienced one of the largest single waves of immigration the country had ever seen. This was mainly because the UK, unlike other member states, gave free access to the citizens of six of these eight countries. (Free access for migrants from Bulgaria and Romania followed in 2014.)

By 2008, there were well over one million new CEE migrant workers registered for work or who were self-employed in the UK. Around 700,000 were from Poland, the largest of the new member states. Their motives for coming to the UK were economic and included high unemployment in Poland, low wages at less than one quarter of the UK average, and an opportunity to send money back home to their struggling families.

Around 80% of the Polish migrants were younger than 34 years old. Many went to London and to the East Anglia region where there was a desperate shortage of agricultural labour. Unlike former Commonwealth migrants, Polish workers went to almost every corner of the country in search of work. They continue to play an important part in the manufacturing, construction, hotel and catering industries as well as in agriculture. Polish-owned businesses, restaurants and shops have also become a common sight.

As recession has hit Britain, Polish workers are leaving the country and going home in droves. Some of those leaving have become unemployed; others have become disillusioned by the high cost of living in the UK and the effects of the depreciation of the Polish zloty. They have also been attracted by the better state of the Polish economy and the consequent opportunity to work for a more realistic wage in their home country.

Source: Adapted from C. Blume, *VOA News*, 31 March 2009.

1 Use a diagram to explain the effects on the UK labour market of:
   a the influx of migrant workers
   b the return of Polish workers following the downturn in the UK economy.
2 Discuss the costs and benefits for
   a the UK economy
   b the Polish economy
   of labour migration on the scale reported above.

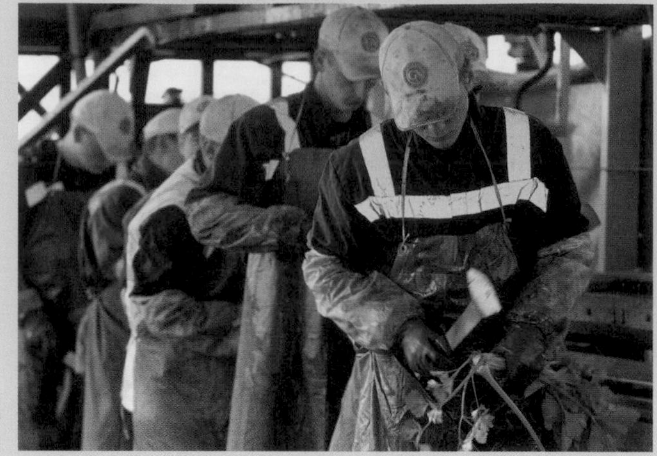

Polish agricultural labourers in East Anglia

Wage determination in perfect markets

So far, we have established two important features of the workings of labour markets. These are:

1 the wage paid to labour equals the value of the marginal product of labour
2 the willingness of labour to supply their services to the labour market is dependent upon the wage rate that is being offered.

In some respects, it might seem surprising that the wage can do both of these things at the same time. However, it is all tied up with how wages are actually determined in a competitive labour market.

The price of labour, the wage, is no different from any other price in so far as it depends on demand and supply. Figure 8.14 shows how the wage and quantity of labour adjust to balance demand and supply. As the demand curve reflects the value of the marginal product of labour, in equilibrium workers receive the value of their contribution to the production of goods and services. Each firm therefore purchases labour until the value of the marginal product equals the wage. Therefore, the wage paid in the market must equal the value of the marginal product of labour once it has brought demand and supply into equilibrium. The market therefore clears at the equilibrium wage.

The labour market, however, is dynamic, like any market – any change in the demand or the supply of labour will change the equilibrium wage. The value of the marginal product of labour will also change by the same amount as, by definition, it must always equal the wage rate.

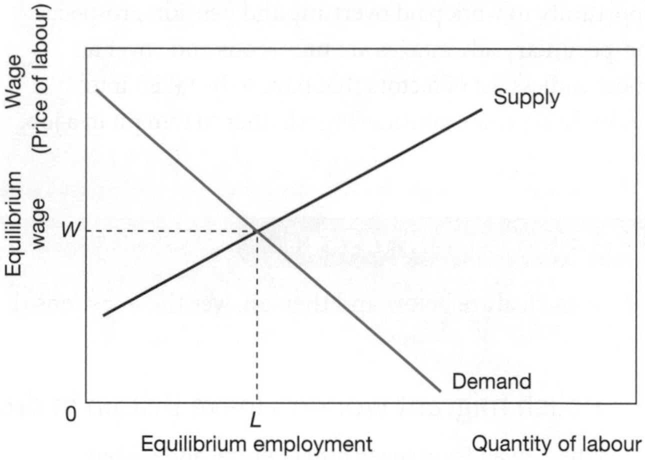

Figure 8.14 Equilibrium in the labour market

Let us now analyse how a change in the demand for labour and a change in the supply of labour affect the market equilibrium.

If we go back to the earlier example of clothing, we can see that an increase in the income of consumers in developed economies will shift the demand curve for clothing to the right, indicating that more will be demanded at any price. In turn, this affects the demand for labour producing the clothing – this is shown in Figure 8.15 by a shift to the right. The outcome is that the equilibrium wage rises from W_1 to W_2, and employment increases from L_1 to L_2. The change in the wage rate therefore reflects a change in the value of the marginal physical product of labour.

A change in the labour supply will also affect the market equilibrium. Suppose that there is an increase in the number of migrant workers and that this increases

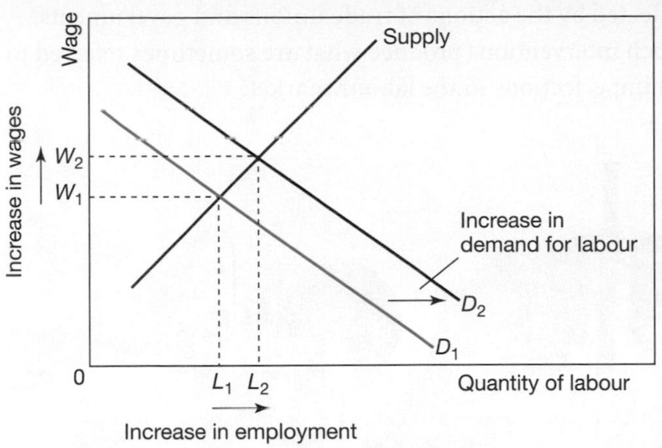

Figure 8.15 Effects of an increase in demand for labour

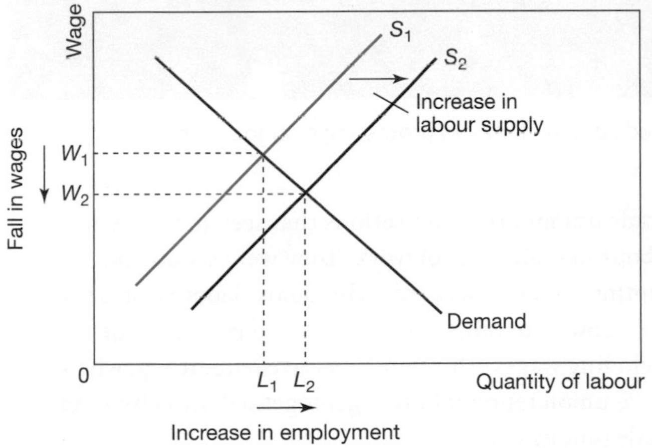

Figure 8.16 Effects of an increase in the supply of labour

the number of workers who are able to produce clothing. When this happens, the labour supply curve shifts to the right. This surplus labour has a downward effect on wages, making it more profitable for firms producing clothing to hire more labour. As the number of workers increases, so their marginal physical product falls, as does the value of their marginal revenue product. The outcome in this case is that wages are reduced for all workers, although the level of employment rises. This is shown in Figure 8.16.

Transfer earnings and economic rent in the labour market

In our introduction to the labour market we posed the question:

> Why is it that some people with exceptional talent – for example, Lionel Messi, Roger Federer, Maria Sharapova, Madonna or Amitabh Bachchan – are so highly paid?

The answer to this question can in part be given in the same way as to that as to why a teacher is paid more than a street cleaner – supply and demand. In order to answer why these differences in earnings occur, economists find it useful to split earnings into two elements:

1 **Transfer earnings:** This is the minimum payment necessary to keep labour in its present use.
2 **Economic rent:** Any payment to labour which is over and above transfer earnings.

KEY TERMS

Transfer earnings: the amount that is earned by a factor of production in its best alternative use.

Economic rent: a payment made to a factor of production above that which is necessary to keep it in its current use.

Both are shown in Figure 8.17a. Transfer earnings are indicated by the area under the labour supply curve. As we have seen, this is upward sloping. Although the equilibrium wage is *W*, at wage rates below this there are workers who are willing to offer their services to employers. In fact, at any wage rate from zero upwards, workers will join the labour market, until at wage *W*, *L* (labour supply) is available. In all cases up to *W*, the wage that a worker receives is their best alternative. For those workers willing to work for less than *W*, then any wages they get over and above what they will accept is their economic rent. This is shown by the triangular area in Figure 8.17a.

It follows, therefore, that different workers receive different amounts of transfer earnings and economic rent even in the same job. Take a bus driver as an example. Some people are very willing to drive buses for a low wage. These have low transfer earnings and some economic rent. Others, however, will be attracted just by the equilibrium wage paid to bus drivers. In such cases they have little or no economic rent, the wage almost entirely consisting of transfer payments.

The case of superstars can be explained using Figure 8.17b. Such people have a scarce and, in some respects, unique talent. Their labour supply curve is completely inelastic and their earnings consist entirely of economic rent. In contrast, workers who have a completely elastic supply, such as many unskilled workers and others in menial jobs, have no economic rent at all as their earnings consist entirely of transfer earnings. Employers can hire an infinite supply of labour at the market wage, *W*. This situation is shown in Figure 8.17c.

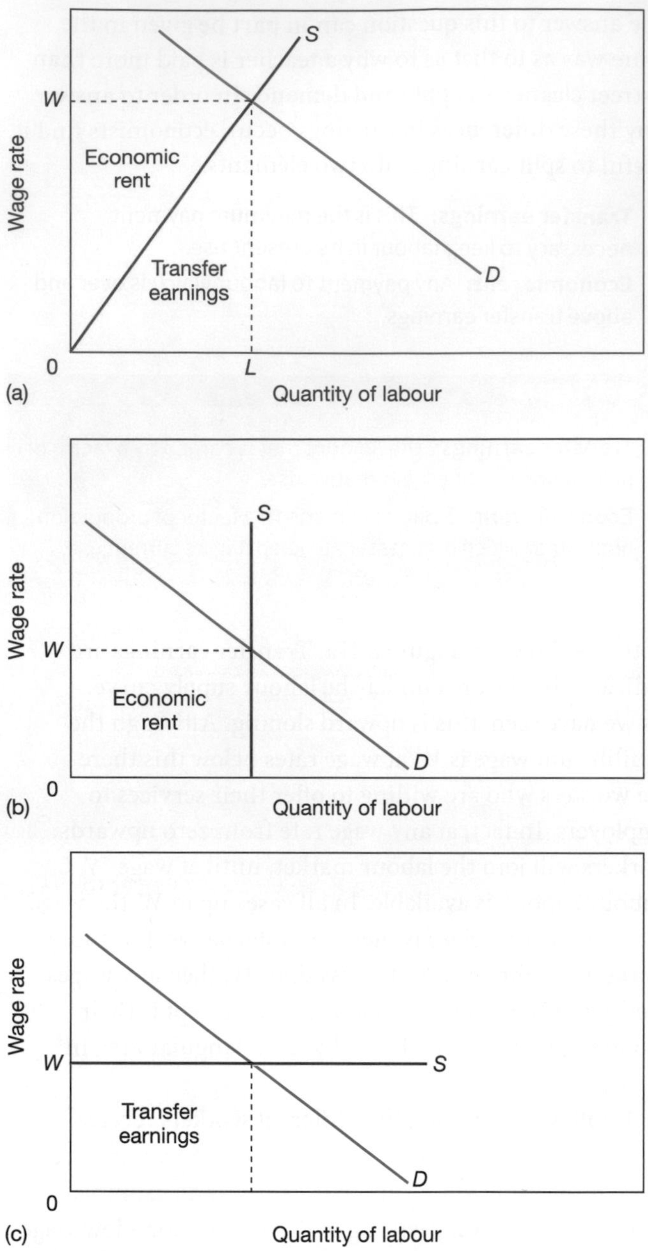

Figure 8.17 Transfer earnings and economic rent in the labour market

Wage determination in imperfect markets

The role of trade unions and government in wage determination

So far in our analysis of how wages are determined we have assumed that the respective forces of demand and supply operate freely with no intervention. In many respects this is an unrealistic assumption as in many labour markets, the demand and supply of labour are affected by the actions of trade unions and governments. Such interventions produce what are sometimes referred to as imperfections in the labour market.

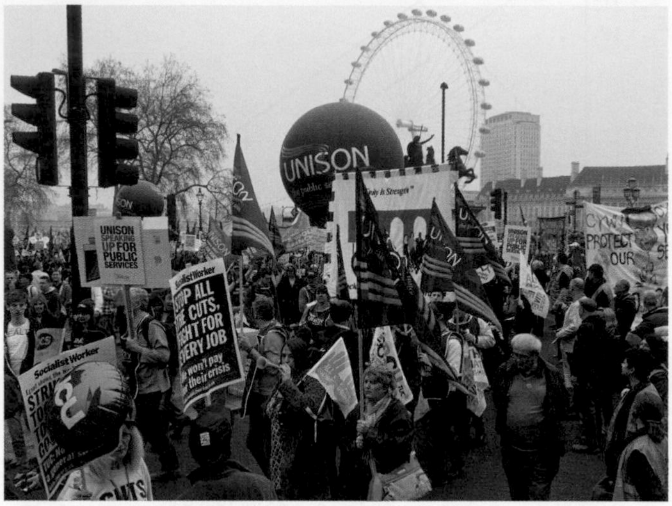

Trade union members protesting over job cuts

Trade unions are organisations that seek to represent labour in their place of work. They were set up and continue to exist because individuals (labour) have very little power to influence conditions of employment, including wages. Through collective bargaining, where trade union representatives get together with employers, trade unions aim to:

- increase the wages of their members
- improve working conditions
- maintain pay differentials between skilled and unskilled workers
- fight job losses
- provide a safe working environment
- secure additional working benefits
- prevent unfair dismissals.

Traditionally, in the UK, trade unions have been strong in the public sector and manufacturing and less important in the service sector. They are, however, particularly strong in the transport industry. As the structure of the UK economy has changed, so total membership has fallen to around 6.5 million workers in 2012, less than one in four of the working population. Consequently, the power of the trade union movement is not as strong as it was when membership was at a peak of 11 million in 1979.

Economic analysis suggests that, in a competitive labour market, a powerful trade union is able to secure wages for its members above the equilibrium wage rate explained earlier in Figure 8.14. The basis for this claim is shown in Figure 8.18. At the equilibrium wage, the quantity of labour employed is *L*. If a strong trade union can force up wages to say W_u, which is above the equilibrium, the number of workers who are offered jobs by employers falls to L_u. At this wage the number of people who would like to work is higher. This is shown by L_c. Consequently, there is a shortfall between those who want to work and those who can actually work, due to the influence of the trade union. This is shown in Figure 8.18 as the difference between L_c and L_u.

In practice, it is really quite difficult to prove whether or not this theory actually applies in labour markets. A much-quoted example is that of actors and actresses in the UK and USA, where there are very strong unions that restrict the numbers able to work in films, television and theatres. The wages of their members are supposedly supported in this way. Other examples are likely to be in labour markets where a trade union has a monopoly over workers with a particular type of skill. Increasingly such practices have been made illegal, so restricting their powers to act in this way.

Trade unions that try to behave in this way are playing a dangerous game with employers. The fear is that because of high labour costs and restrictive practices, employers will go out of business or transfer production to countries where wage levels are lower. This threat has been particularly severe for UK car manufacturers – production has been switched to other EU countries, such as Spain, the Czech Republic, Poland and Slovakia, where labour costs can be as little as one-fifth of those in the UK. Consequently, trade unions have very little real influence over the wages paid to their members in these circumstances.

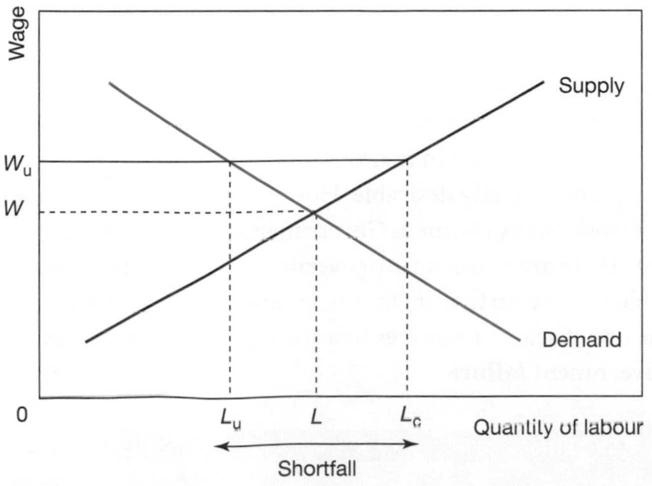

Figure 8.18 The effect of a strong trade union in a competitive labour market

The labour market has seen explicit government intervention through the introduction of national minimum wages. In the UK, after considerable deliberation, the government's Low Pay Commission recommended a national minimum wage from early 1999 for all workers above the age of 21. The main aim of a minimum wage such as this is to reduce poverty and the exploitation of workers who have little or no bargaining power with their employers. In the UK, many women employed in shops, small businesses and low-skill jobs, such as home working and cleaning, were being paid very low wages and, in the eyes of the government, were being exploited. The introduction of the minimum wage was of particular significance for them.

Whether there should be a minimum wage is controversial. Additionally, it was argued that the amount of state benefits being paid to low-income families would be reduced with the introduction of a minimum wage. There might also be a small increase in tax revenue. Opponents were not convinced by these arguments, believing that jobs would be lost and that other low-paid workers would seek an increase to maintain their differential with the lowest paid. Cost-push inflation could well result, so affecting the economy as a whole.

The economics of a minimum wage are shown in Figure 8.19. The effect on an industry is particularly dependent upon the elasticities of demand and supply for labour in that industry. Figure 8.19a shows the effects where there is an inelastic demand for labour. The loss of jobs here is much less than shown in Figure 8.19b where the demand for labour is more wage elastic. In both cases there is an excess supply of labour at the higher minimum wage. This excess is more pronounced in Figure 8.19b, where both the demand for and supply of labour are relatively elastic. It can also be seen that the higher the minimum wage is set above the competitive equilibrium ($2.50 in the case of Figure 8.19), the greater will be the excess supply of labour willing to work at the national minimum wage.

A problem with the minimum wage in the UK is that it applies across the entire country. It does not take into account variations in the cost of living. In London, for example, the cost of accommodation, food and other living costs are much higher than elsewhere. Consequently, it is very difficult to survive on the minimum wage alone unless long hours are worked. Recently, a 'living wage' has been promoted. It is calculated on the basic cost of living but unlike the minimum wage, employers choose to pay this on a voluntary basis. In London in 2014, this was £8.80 per hour compared with £7.65 elsewhere. The minimum wage was less, at £6.31 per hour.

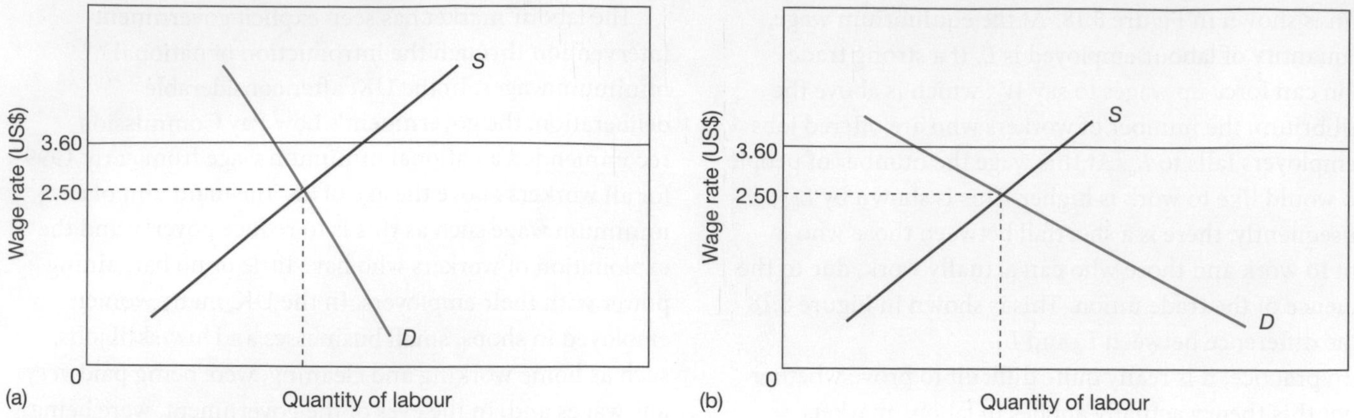

Figure 8.19 The effects of the introduction of a minimum wage

Evidence suggests that employees are more motivated and that there is less absenteeism where a living wage is being paid. Staff retention also improved. The living wage, however, is not the answer to poverty – it is just part of a package of measures including a range of benefits designed to improve the standing of those who are most vulnerable.

Monopsony in the labour market

A **monopsony** occurs when there is a single or dominant buyer, in this case of labour. The monopoly buyer is able to determine the price that is paid for the services of the workers that are employed. Unlike other labour market examples we have looked at, in this situation we are now dealing with an imperfect rather than competitive market.

KEY TERM

Monopsony: where there is a single buyer in a market.

Figure 8.20 shows how the monopsonist can affect the market equilibrium. The monopsonist will hire workers by equating the marginal cost paid to employ a worker with the marginal revenue product gained from this employment. This is the profit-maximising position. The wage that the monopsonist pays to hire labour is W_m. This is actually below the wage that should be paid if they were paying the full value of their marginal revenue product, that is W_{mrp}. The level of employment is L_m.

In this situation the power of the employer in the labour market is of overriding importance and the employer can set a low wage because of this buying power. Monopsonists often exist in local labour market situations, for example where there is just one major employer in a town or where workers may be employed in an extractive industry located well away from where they normally live. In this way the

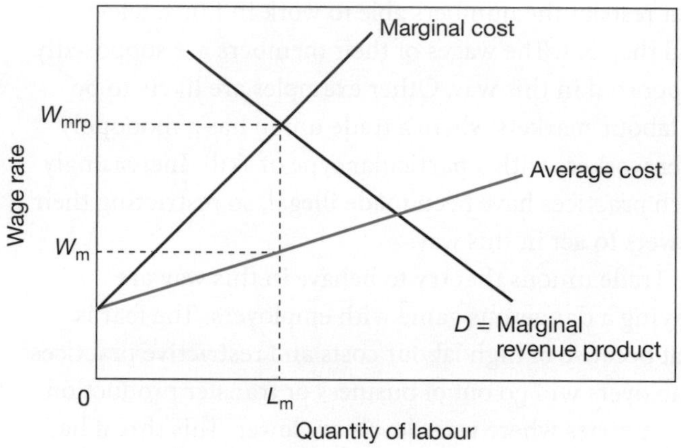

Figure 8.20 A monopsony buyer of labour

employer dominates the labour market, setting down wages and all other conditions of employment.

Government failure in microeconomic intervention

The effectiveness of government policy

In principle, government policies to reduce market failures make economic sense. They increase the level of economic efficiency in markets and thus must be judged to be economically desirable. However, in practice, all may not work out as planned. Governments may themselves fail. There are reasons why government intervention may in fact create further inefficiencies and so not improve the use of scarce resources in a society. This is known as **government failure**.

KEY TERM

Government failure: where government intervention to correct market failure causes further inefficiencies.

There are three main reasons why government failure may occur. These are as a result of:

1 imperfect information
2 undesirable incentives
3 policy conflict.

Problems of imperfect information

Once the government starts to intervene in the running of markets, it needs information. The correct policies can only be introduced if governments have the correct information. The problem is that governments may have inaccurate information. In this case, they may introduce policies that lead to greater economic inefficiency. Some examples of this problem could be the following:

- There is a lack of information about the true value of a negative externality. It is often very difficult to give an accurate figure for the value of a negative externality such as pollution. It is difficult both to put an accurate figure to all of the external costs imposed and to trace the source of the pollution itself. The problem with this is that it then becomes very difficult to impose the correct value of a tax that attempts to reduce production to an efficient level. The wrong level of tax will lead to the wrong level of production.
- There is a lack of information about the level of consumer demand for a product. If the government is providing a product free of charge to the consumer, then some estimation of the level of consumer demand is required. This could be the case with a public good. However, the government must try to provide the right amount of such goods. If it does not estimate the level of demand accurately, then the wrong amount will be produced and thus there is inefficiency.

Problems of undesirable incentives

A further problem arises with government intervention in the economy due to the creation of undesirable incentives. These can create inefficiencies. Some examples of the ways in which this can happen are as follows:

- The imposition of taxes can distort incentives. As we have seen, the most obvious example of this is the possible impact of an income tax upon the incentive to work. High marginal rates of taxation can create disincentives for people to work harder and gain more income. If this happens, then scarce resources are not being used to their best effect and there is inefficiency. A similar point can be recalled from the earlier discussion of the deadweight loss of a tax. The disincentive to consume and produce created by the tax led to the wrong amount of a product being produced.
- Politicians may be motivated by political power rather than economic imperatives. Politicians are often seen as being motivated principally by the desire to remain in government. If this is so, then economic policies may be designed by governments to try to retain power rather than to try to ensure maximum efficiency in the economy. For example, road pricing is a very unpopular tax in the eyes of car users despite its tremendous potential to reduce congestion and hence correct market failure. It is likely to be avoided due to a government's fears that its introduction could lead to a loss of votes.
- Those running public services may have inappropriate incentives. Once products are provided by the government, then the profit motive of the private sector is largely removed. The question then remains as to what may motivate those in charge of providing public services. There is no entirely clear answer to this question. At its worst, it could become a total lack of incentive to produce the product well or attempts to defraud the system.

Problems of policy conflict

Government intervention in the running of the economy is often justified by the need to reduce inequality. However, it is possible that government intervention might sometimes increase existing inequality. This is simply understood by recognising that the imposition of any tax will have a distributional effect. Thus, a tax on energy use that aims to reduce harmful emissions of greenhouse gases will have different effects on different groups of people. If the tax is on the use of domestic fuel, then older members of society may bear the greatest effect as they use proportionately more domestic fuel for heating than others in society. This could be seen as unfair and increasing inequality in society.

It is also possible to see how government failure can occur in the case of subsidies on the costs of fossil fuels. These encourage production and their use in coal-fired power stations, both of which contribute increased environmental pollution. The subsidies might enhance competitiveness of manufacturing industries

Spicejet, a low-cost airline in India

and keep workers in jobs but they are completely inconsistent with the need for more sustainable development policies.

A final example, again including sustainability, is in the case of air transport. In the US, EU and increasingly in Asia, markets have been deregulated. The effects have been for new firms to enter the market, for reduced fares and for more people to travel. Obviously there are many benefits, but there is the clear conflict involved with respect to diminishing global fuel resources and the now proven negative effect of increased air transport use as a serious contributor to global warming and climate change.

Are agricultural subsidies causing more harm than good?

In 2001 at the Doha Round of talks, representatives from many developing countries were like-minded to heavily criticise the huge agricultural subsidies being paid by the US and the EU to their farmers. They argued very strongly that high subsidies force prices down, reduce farm incomes and maintain poverty in developing economies.

What a difference 12 years makes! The BRIC countries especially have increased their own agricultural subsidies the fastest of all. China, for example, spent more than $160 billion in 2012. This was much, much higher than the $19 billion spent by the US and the $67 billion spent by the EU. Brazil's subsidies to its farmers have increased rapidly since 2007 to $10 billion; India has spent more than the US in its price support policy for domestically produced wheat and rice.

So, where is the government failure? The point is that if these subsidy policies are done well, they can support innovation, feed the hungry, produce surpluses for export and pull millions out of poverty while helping to build a stronger middle class. Once this has been evidenced then the subsidies should be removed; they should not be seen as long-term support for inefficient farmers, in which case, innovation will be stifled, production remain uncompetitive and farmers will be even more dependent on the government. As a result, many will end up doing less for more. A clear case of government failure.

Source: Adapted from J. Clay, *The Guardian*, 8 August 2013.

SELF-ASSESSMENT TASK 8.7

Explain why each of the following is an example of government failure:

- **a** An underestimation of the full benefit to society of public transport that means only a small subsidy is being provided by the government.
- **b** The building of a new road that has unclear benefits in an area where the government fears that it could lose votes at the next election.
- **c** A high tax on health care, which forms a significant part of many poorer people's budgets.
- **d** A high level of unemployment benefit that means that people can sometimes earn more by not having paid employment.

SUMMARY

In this chapter it has been shown that:

- Governments apply a range of policies to correct market failure including indirect taxation, subsidies, permits, licences, regulations and the recognition of property rights.
- Governments seek to develop policies that will improve the distribution of income and wealth through benefits, progressive taxation and a range of other measures.
- The demand for labour is a derived demand; the firm's demand curve can be determined from the value of the marginal revenue product of labour.
- The supply of labour to a firm depends on the wage rate.
- The wage rate in a market is determined by the supply of labour and demand for labour.
- Transfer earnings and economic rent can be used to explain why some workers end up being paid more than others.
- Labour markets can be influenced by the actions of trade unions and the government.
- Government failure can occur as a result of intervention in markets.

Exam-style questions

1 As economies grow and develop, the market has less of a role and government a greater role in securing an efficient allocation of resources. Discuss the extent to which you agree with this view. **[25]**

2 In 2013 the Intergovernmental Panel on Climate Change published clear evidence that the growth in air transport was one of the main contributors to climate change.

a Using a diagram, explain the market failure associated with the increased use of air transport. **[12]**

b Discuss the extent to which an indirect tax on air passengers might reduce the demand for air transport. **[13]**

3 The differences in wage rates paid in different occupations are caused entirely by the differences in the elasticity of supply of labour. The way, therefore, to overcome the differences in wage rates is to increase the training available to workers. Discuss whether economic analysis supports this argument. **[25]**

Source: Cambridge International AS and A Level Economics 9708 Paper 41 Q4 October/November 2012.

Chapter 9: The macroeconomy
A Level

Learning objectives

On completion of this chapter you should know:

- what is meant by economic growth, economic development and sustainability
- the distinction between actual and potential growth in output
- the factors contributing to economic growth
- the costs and benefits of growth, including using and conserving resources
- how national income statistics are used as measures of economic growth and living standards
- the meaning of the national debt
- the distinction between gross domestic product (GDP), gross national product (GNP) and gross national income (GNI)
- what is meant by the national debt (government or public sector debt)
- other indicators of living standards and economic development; monetary, non-monetary, Human Development Index (HDI), Measure of Economic Welfare (MEW), Multidimensional Poverty Index (MPI) and the Kuznets curve
- the characteristics of developed, developing and emerging (BRICs) economies; by population growth and structure, employment composition, external trade and urbanisation in developing economies
- how economic growth rates and living standards are compared over time and between countries
- what influences the size and components of the labour force
- what is meant by labour productivity
- the distinction between full employment and the natural rate of unemployment
- the causes and consequences of unemployment
- how to distinguish between the types of unemployment
- what is meant by the unemployment rate and the pattern and trends in (un)employment

- why there are difficulties involved in measuring unemployment
- the policies to correct unemployment
- the distinction between a closed and an open economy
- the circular flow of income between households, firms, government and the international economy; the multiplier, average and marginal propensities to save and consume
- what is meant by aggregate expenditure, its components and determinants
- how inflationary and deflationary gaps can be analysed
- what is meant by the full employment level of income and equilibrium level of income
- the difference between autonomous and induced investment
- what is meant by the accelerator
- the Quantity Theory of Money
- the distinction between broad and narrow money supply
- what are the sources of money supply in an open economy (commercial banks and credit creation, role of central bank, deficit financing, quantitative easing, total currency flow)
- the difference between Keynesian and monetarist theoretical approaches to how the macroeconomy functions
- what the liquidity preference theory involves
- what are the types of aid
- the nature of dependency
- the role of trade and investment, multinationals and foreign direct investment (FDI)
- the impact of external debt
- the role of the International Monetary Fund (IMF) and World Bank
- the impact of corruption and legal framework in an economy.

The macroeconomy

The output of an economy changes over time and such changes can have an impact on the development of the country and the living standards of its inhabitants. Another key measure of living standards is the Human Development Index (HDI), which is discussed below. The issue of what influences living standards and the quality of people's lives is currently receiving considerable attention from economists.

Developed, emerging and developing economies have a number of differences including differences in GDP (income) per head. Economic growth can increase GDP per head and is, in turn, influenced by changes in the quantity and quality of the labour force. Unemployment is likely to reduce a country's economic prospects.

Whether an economy achieves full employment will be influenced by the level of aggregate expenditure. A rise in investment would increase aggregate expenditure. Firms may finance such spending on capital goods by borrowing from banks.

Banks are one source of an increase in the money supply in an economy. Changes in the money supply can alter interest rates. There are differences between the Keynesian and monetarist views of how changes in the money supply affect an economy. These are discussed in this chapter.

An economy's economic performance is also influenced by international trade and the role of international organisations such as the International Monetary Fund (IMF) and the World Bank, which are described below.

In this chapter the key concepts of progress and development figure prominently. The concepts of scarcity and choice, efficiency and equity and the margin and change also appear.

Economic growth, economic development and sustainability

Economic growth

Economic growth is an increase in an economy's output and the economic growth rate is the annual percentage change in output. For people to enjoy more goods and services, output has to increase by more than any growth in population. In such a case, GDP per head (per capita) would increase. For many years it was assumed that poverty would be eradicated if countries managed to sustain economic growth. As a result, economic growth was seen as synonymous with economic development. If economies grew they would also experience development. It was assumed that increased availability of goods and services in an economy would lead to a 'trickle down' effect that would have an impact upon all, including the poor members of society, in terms of jobs and other economic benefits. In reality, however, economic growth does not result in a rise in the living standards and quality of life of everyone in an economy. It is also possible for a high proportion of people to achieve an improvement in their living standards and quality of life even if economic growth does not occur if there is, for instance, a more even distribution of income or a reduction in pollution. As a result, a wider perception of **economic development** is now accepted that is related to, but distinct from, economic growth. In other words, economic development is the process of improving people's economic well-being and quality of life.

KEY TERMS

Economic growth: in the short run an increase in a country's output and in the long run an increase in a country's productive potential.

Economic development: an increase in welfare and the quality of life.

KEY CONCEPT LINK

Progress and development: Economic growth is perhaps the key measure of progress in an economy. This can be assessed by examining economic data. To assess whether an economy is developing is a more normative judgement.

Economic development

In its World Development Report of 1991 the World Bank offered the following view of development:

> The challenge of development . . . is to improve the quality of life. Especially in the world's poor countries, a better quality of life generally calls for higher incomes – but it involves much more. It encompasses as ends in themselves better education, higher standards of health and nutrition, less poverty, a cleaner environment, more equality of opportunity, greater individual freedom and a rich cultural life.

This statement remains true. Although it acknowledges that economic growth is important, it makes clear that higher income in itself is not sufficient to ensure that there is a rise in the quality of life for the citizens of a country. This is a much broader view of development than one confined purely to increases in GDP. It is one that provides a different focus for those responsible for development policy planning, and moves away from measures designed purely to increase and maintain an economic growth target. Todaro states that development must be seen as a multidimensional process.

> Development . . . must represent the whole gamut of change by which an entire social system, tuned to the diverse basic needs and desires of individuals and social groups within that system, moves away from a condition of life widely perceived as unsatisfactory toward a situation or condition of life regarded as materially and spiritually better.
>
> (M.P. Todaro, *Economic Development*, 1995)

Sustainability

Very rapid economic growth may be achieved but this may be at the expense of the living standards and quality of life of future generations if it results from the reckless use of resources. Both developed and developing countries are now becoming more concerned to achieve **sustainable development**. This occurs when output increases in a way that does not compromise the needs of future generations. Materials such as aluminium, paper and glass can be recycled. More use could be made of renewable resources in preference to non-renewable resources, and improvements in technology may both increase output and reduce pollution. Cutting back on CO_2 emissions, reducing landfill and dumping less waste into rivers and the sea are all central to realising improved sustainability.

KEY TERM

Sustainable development: development that ensures that the needs of the present generation can be met without compromising the well-being of future generations.

Pursuing sustainable development ensures that economic growth improves living standards and the quality of life not only in the present but also for the future. To achieve this requires a deliberate and concerted effort to balance economic, social and environment objectives. More specifically:

- Economic objectives require a better use of resources. To be sustainable, growth should ensure that sufficient resources are available to invest in human capital as well as physical capital. Education and training programmes are central to this requirement.
- Social objectives focus on the distribution of the benefits of growth. Food, housing, health care and secondary education are essential if people's lives are to be productive. A sustainable approach involves an education system that gives girls the same opportunities as boys, is serious about reducing fertility rates, controlling the spread of HIV/AIDS and providing for the elderly.
- Environmental objectives require the responsible use of natural resources. This means that mineral extraction and forest depletion especially should be done in such a way that the benefits are not just short-term. Many people in developing countries lack clean water and proper sanitation, a reason why charities such as UNICEF invest heavily in these areas.

Actual and potential economic growth

Actual economic growth occurs when output increases. It can be achieved as the result of greater utilisation of existing resources or as the result of the utilisation of more resources. Figure 9.1 uses a production possibility curve (PPC) diagram

KEY TERM

Actual economic growth: an increase in real GDP.

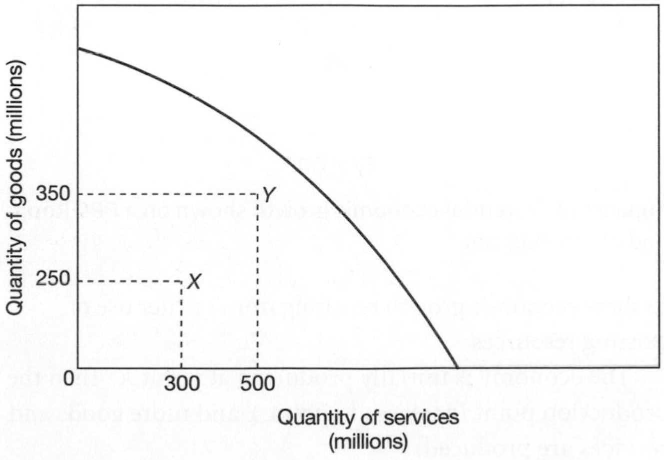

Figure 9.1 Actual economic growth shown on a production possibility curve

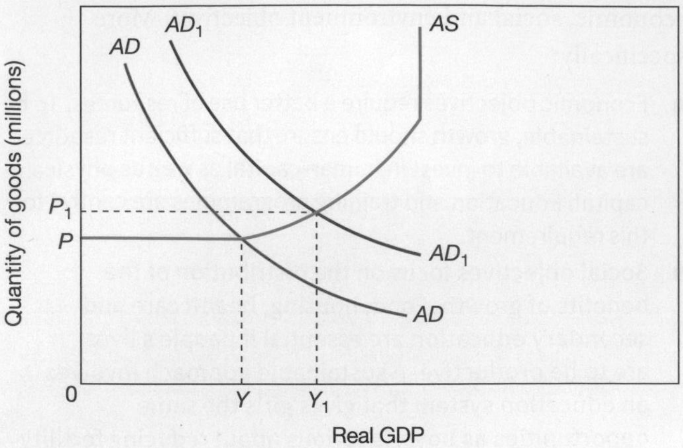

Figure 9.2 Actual economic growth shown on an *AD/AS* diagram

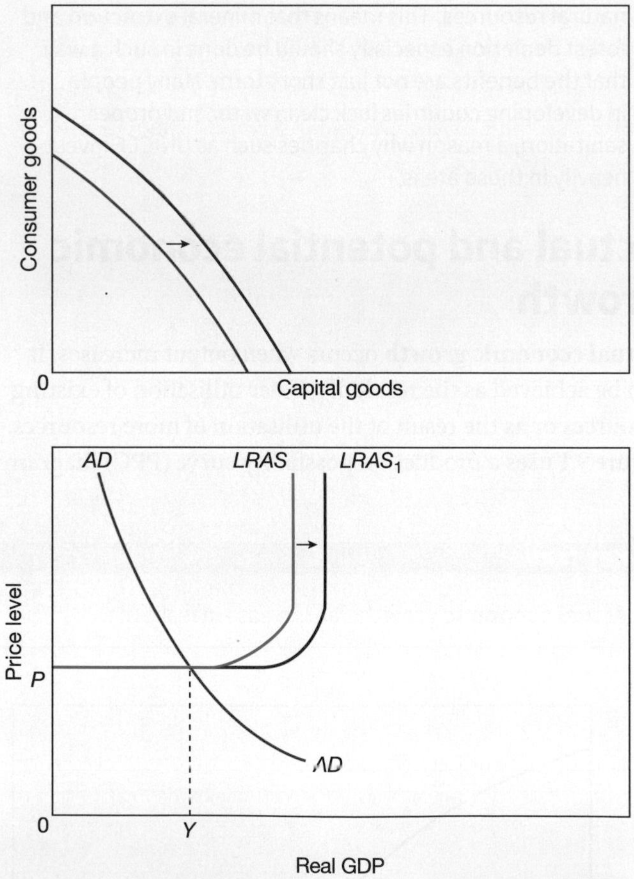

Figure 9.3 Potential economic growth shown on a PPC (top) and *AD/AS* diagram

to show economic growth resulting from greater use of existing resources.

The economy is initially producing at point *X*. Then the production point increases to point *Y* and more goods and services are produced.

Actual economic growth can also be shown using an *AD/AS* diagram. Figure 9.2 shows an increase in aggregate demand in an economy with spare capacity. The increase in

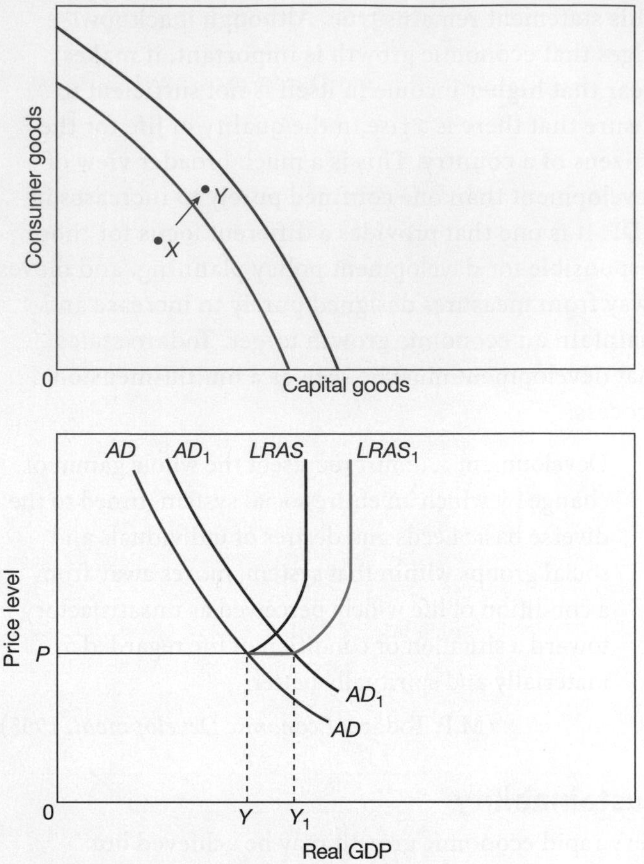

Figure 9.4 Actual and potential economic growth

aggregate demand brings into use previously unemployed resources and output (measured by real GDP) increases from *Y* to Y_1.

For an economy to continue to grow, it is necessary for **potential economic growth** to occur. Figure 9.3 shows potential economic growth using both a production possibility curve and an *AD/AS* diagram. Both diagrams illustrate an increase in the maximum output the economy is capable of producing.

For potential economic growth to lead to higher output, the rise in productive potential must be utilised. Figure 9.4 again uses two diagrams, this time to show both actual and potential economic growth.

TOP TIP

In distinguishing between actual and potential economic growth it is useful to draw diagrams.

KEY TERM

Potential economic growth: an increase in the productive capacity of the economy.

SELF-ASSESSMENT TASK 9.1

Read the feature below and then answer the questions that follow.

Slowdown in Latin America's economies

The economies of Latin America grew by an annual average of 4.5% between 2004 and 2012. In 2013 the growth rate fell to 2.6%. Of course, the economic growth rate varied between the economies of the different countries. Brazil's growth rate was 2.3%, while Peru's was 5%. Unemployment also varied between the economies with, for instance, Brazil's unemployment rate being 5% and Peru's being 6.5%.

Potential economic growth also experienced a decline. Two of the key influences on the growth in potential output are increased investment and increased productivity. Investment in the region did increase in 2013. On average, investment accounted for 25% of GDP but it was only 18% in Brazil. Productivity also increased but only by a small percentage. Indeed, productivity actually fell in Mexico. There were thought to be four major reasons for the low average growth in productivity in Latin America. These were relatively poor education performance, a lack of innovation, poor transport infrastructure and a lack of competition, particularly in services.

1 What was happening to output in Latin America in 2013?
2 Explain whether Brazil's or Peru's actual output was closer to its potential output.
3 Analyse how productivity influences economic growth.
4 Explain why productivity growth was low in Latin America in 2013.

Output gaps and the trade cycle

The difference between actual and potential output is known as the **output gap**. Figure 9.2 shows a **negative output gap**. In this situation, there is a lack of aggregate demand and there is unemployment of resources.

KEY TERMS

Output gap: a gap between actual and potential output.

Negative output gap: a situation where actual output is below potential output.

It is also possible that an economy may experience a **positive output gap**. This occurs when an economy is producing more than its maximum potential as shown in Figure 9.5. Output may be beyond maximum potential for a while because, in response to high aggregate demand, machinery may be worked flat out and workers may be persuaded to work long hours of overtime. However, this cannot be sustained since a time will come when machines have to be serviced or repaired and when workers will want to reduce the number of hours of overtime they work.

Output gaps arise during the course of a trade cycle. A **trade cycle**, which can also be called an economic or business cycle, involves fluctuations in economic activity.

KEY TERMS

Positive output gap: a situation where actual output is above potential output.

Trade cycle: fluctuations in economic activity over a period of years.

Actual output varies around the trend growth in productive potential. Figure 9.6 illustrates a trade cycle with *ab* showing a negative output gap and *cd* a positive output gap.

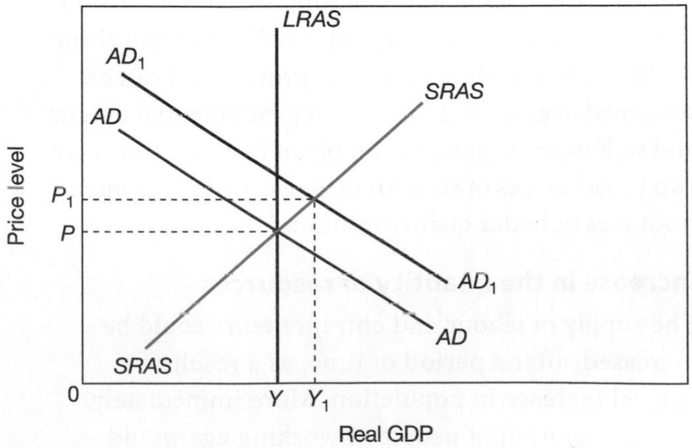

Figure 9.5 A positive output gap

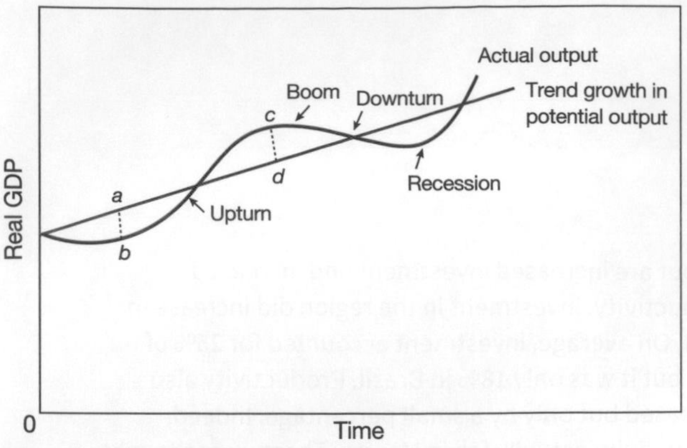

Figure 9.6 The trade cycle

TOP TIP

In analysing changes in economic activity, it is often useful to mention output gaps.

KEY CONCEPT LINK

Equilibrium and efficiency: Closing output gaps increases the efficiency with which resources are being used. This will lead to progress either in the form of higher output if a negative output gap is closed or a reduction in inflationary pressure and a more sustainable output in the case of a positive output gap.

The factors contributing to economic growth

As noted above, in the short run if there is spare capacity, output can be increased as a result of an increase in aggregate demand. For instance, greater consumer confidence may lead to higher consumer expenditure and so an increase in aggregate demand. Similarly, expansionary fiscal policy measures may result in more factors of production being employed and output rising.

In order to achieve economic growth that can be sustained over time, it is necessary for potential output and so long-run aggregate supply to increase. There are two broad causes of such an increase, which are more resources or better quality resources.

Increase in the quantity of resources

The supply of labour and entrepreneurs could be increased, after a period of time, as a result of a natural increase in population. More immediately, net immigration of people of working age would be likely to lead to a greater availability of workers and entrepreneurs. The number of workers and entrepreneurs may also be increased as a result of government policy measures. For example, a rise in the retirement age would increase the supply of labour and deregulation and privatisation may promote entrepreneurship.

The supply of capital goods will be increased if there is net investment with firms buying more capital goods than are needed to replace those capital goods that are taken out of use.

The quality of land may be increased by discoveries, for instance, of new oil fields and gold mines.

Increase in the quality of resources

Improvements in the quality of resources will increase the productivity of the factor inputs. The quality of labour and entrepreneurship can be improved through education and training and better health care. The quality of capital goods is improved as technology advances. The application of fertilisers and irrigation and drainage schemes may improve the quality of land.

Economic growth in some developing countries

The main obstacle to increases in the quantity and quality of resources in some developing countries is the opportunity cost of devoting resources away from their current use. For example, devoting more resources to education may mean that fewer resources can be devoted, for instance, to health care. Producing more capital goods may mean sacrificing consumer goods in the short run, which would lead to a decrease in living standards. Research and development that can result in advances in technology also use resources that have alternative uses.

Some emerging economies have, nevertheless, achieved high economic growth rates in recent years. China has witnessed particularly rapid economic growth. Indeed, after two decades of rapid economic growth China has become the second largest economy in the world and it is predicted it will soon overtake the USA for the top spot. China's increase in output has been driven by increases in investment and exports. The high rates of saving in China have freed up some resources for investment and the relatively low value of the Chinese currency, the renminbi, has contributed to the rise in demand for Chinese exports. India's economic growth rate has been boosted by an increase in the size of the labour force and advances in information technology.

KEY CONCEPTS LINK

Scarcity and choice: The choice between producing extra capital goods and fewer consumer goods or producing the same quantity of both types of goods arises because of scarcity.

TOP TIP

Remember the performance of an economy and which economies are considered to be developed, developing and emerging will alter in the future.

The costs and benefits of economic growth

Costs

As indicated above, if an economy is operating at full capacity, there will be an opportunity cost involved in achieving economic growth. To produce more capital goods, in order to increase the country's productive capacity some resources will have to be moved from producing consumer goods to producing capital goods. So the current consumption of goods and services will have to be reduced. However, this will only be a short-run cost since, in the long run, increased investment will increase the output of both capital goods and consumer goods and services.

There are some other potential costs that may exist in both the short run and the long run. These include increased stress and anxiety. A growing economy is a dynamic economy that undergoes structural changes. Workers may have to learn new skills and may have to change their occupation and/or where they live. Some workers may find such changes difficult to cope with. Economic growth may also be accompanied by increased working hours and pressure to come up with new ideas and improvements. There is a marked difference in the number of hours people work in different countries. In 2013, for instance, the average annual hours worked per person in South Korea was 2,193 whereas it was only 1,408 in Germany.

In addition, economic growth may be accompanied by the depletion of natural resources and damage to the environment. Higher output may, for example, involve firms using more oil, depleting fish stocks, building on greenfield sites and creating more pollution.

Benefits

The main benefit of economic growth is the increase in goods and services that become available for the country's citizens to enjoy. This raises their material living standards. Economic growth makes it easier to help the poor. Higher incomes and more spending increase tax revenue and some of this extra revenue may be given to the poor in the form of higher benefits, better housing, better education and better health care. Without any increase in output and income, a government may have to raise the tax rates on higher income groups, and so reduce their living standards, in order to help the poor.

Economic growth may also be accompanied by a rise in employment. A rise in real GDP caused by higher aggregate demand is likely to create extra jobs. An increase in aggregate supply may make a country's products more internationally competitive and so may generate more jobs.

A stable rate of economic growth tends to increase business and consumer confidence. This encourages investment. Indeed, economic growth can create economic growth. In addition, economic growth may increase a country's international prestige and power. For example, China's rapid economic growth since the early 1990s has increased its status as an economic and political power.

Some economists in rich countries debate whether the benefits of economic growth outweigh the costs. For those in poor countries, however, economic growth is seen as essential to bring people out of poverty.

KEY CONCEPT LINK

Progress and development: Comparing the benefits and costs of economic growth brings out the difference between progress and development. An economy that is growing will be progressing in terms of higher output but it may not be developing if the quality of people's lives is declining.

Using and conserving resources

Using natural resources now can increase economic growth, at least in the short run. For example, cutting down trees in a rainforest, hunting animals in a wildlife reserve or increasing the amount of gas extracted from gas fields can increase output and create jobs. It can also increase exports and so improve the current account position on the country's balance of payments. In addition, the higher output can increase tax revenue that can be used, for instance, to improve the country's infrastructure and education, which can further generate economic growth.

There are, nevertheless, some arguments for conserving resources. For example, maintaining rainforests and wildlife in a reserve may encourage tourists to visit the country. Maintaining rainforests may also help the environment by absorbing carbon dioxide. Conserving resources also enables future generations to benefit from them and may mean that they can be sold at higher prices in the future.

There are a number of factors that may influence the decision as to whether to use or conserve resources.

SELF-ASSESSMENT TASK 9.2

Read the feature below and answer the following questions.

The world's most polluted city

In 2014 the levels of air pollution in Delhi overtook those in Beijing, making India's capital the most polluted city in the world. The population of Delhi, which was 22 million in 2014, is continuing to grow and this is increasing car ownership. Exhaust fumes from cars was the largest single contributor to the increase in pollution in the city in 2014. The higher pollution level was also contributed to by rises in industrial emissions, dust from construction sites and smoke from burning rubbish.

1 Explain why economic growth tends to increase car ownership.

2 Discuss whether economic growth always causes increased pollution.

One is consideration of whether demand for the products created by the resources is likely to increase or decrease in the future. If it is thought that demand will fall in the future, there is an argument for using the resources now. If the resources are non-renewable, it would be important that any revenue earned from using them now should be invested into developing other industries.

It may be advisable to conserve a resource if the country does not currently have a comparative advantage in producing the related product but may have in the future. For example, a country may have significant gold deposits but they may currently be too expensive to extract. If a country has serious debt problems, it may feel forced into using its resource now.

It is interesting to note that the Ecuadorean government between 2007 and 2013 sought, unsuccessfully, to get individuals, firms and governments throughout the world to pay it to leave oil underground in its Yasuni National Park, which is part of the Amazonian rainforest. Oil drilling will create income and employment but will reduce tourism and may generate a range of external costs.

KEY CONCEPT LINK

Scarcity and choice: In assessing whether to conserve or use resources, scarcity and choice are clearly important concepts. The reason why a choice has to be made is because resources are limited.

TOP TIP

Remember that what may have been renewable resources, such as fish stocks, may become non-renewable resources if they are overexploited.

National income statistics

A government measures a country's total output to assess the performance of the country. An economy is usually considered to be doing well if its output is growing at a sustained and sustainable rate. Economic growth has the potential to increase people's living standards. If an economy is growing at a slower rate than it is considered capable of, a government is likely to introduce policy measures to stimulate the economy.

National income statistics are used to compare countries' economic performance and to give a perspective to key economic indicators. For instance, in 2013 the output of Turkey increased to US$811.2 billion from US$780 billion the previous year and the output of Russia increased from US$2.52 trillion to US2.55 trillion.

KEY TERM

National income: the total income for an economy.

However, given the relative size of the outputs of the two countries, the Russian economy grew by only 1.2% whereas Turkey's grew by 4%.

Gross domestic product, gross national product and gross national income

The most widely used measure of national income is known as gross domestic product (GDP). Gross means total, domestic refers to the home economy and product means output. So, for example, Pakistan's GDP is a measure of the total output by the factors of production based in Pakistan. GDP is calculated by adding up consumers' spending, government spending on goods and services, total investment, changes in stocks and the difference between exports and imports.

From GDP, a number of other measures of national income can be found. GDP plus net property income from abroad gives **gross national income (GNI)**. This used to be referred to as gross national product (GNP). Net property income from abroad is the income that the country's residents earn on their physical assets (such as factories and leisure parks) owned abroad and foreign financial assets (such as shares and bank loans) minus the returns on assets held in the country but owned by foreigners. So GNI gives a measure of the income of a country's residents.

KEY TERM

Gross national income (GNI): the total output produced by a country's citizens wherever they produce it.

The ways of measuring GDP

There are three ways of calculating GDP. These are the output, income and expenditure methods. They should give the same total because they all measure the flow of income produced in an economy. So the value of output is equal to the incomes that it generates, meaning wages, rent, profit and interest. If it is assumed that all incomes are spent, expenditure will, by definition, equal income.

The output measure

The output method measures the value of output produced by industries such as manufacturing, construction, distributive, hotel and catering and agricultural industries or sectors.

In using this measure it is important to avoid counting the same output twice. For example, if the value of cars sold by manufacturers is added to the value of output of the tyre firms, double counting will occur. Value added is the difference between the sales revenue received and the cost of raw materials used. It is equal to the payments made to the factors of production in return for producing the good or service, so that if a TV manufacturing firm buys components costing $280,000 and uses them to make TVs that it sells for $350,000, it has added $70,000 to output. It is this $70,000 that will be included in the measure of output.

The income method

The value of an output produced is based on the costs involved in producing that output. These costs include wages, rent, interest and profits. All these payments represent income paid to factors of production. For instance, workers receive wages and entrepreneurs receive profits. In using this measure it is important to include only payments received in return for providing a good or service. So transfer payments, which are transfers of income from taxpayers to groups of individuals for welfare payments, are not included.

The expenditure method

What is produced in a year will either be sold or added to stocks. So, if additions to stocks are added to expenditure on goods and services, a measure is obtained that will equal output and income. In using this method it is necessary to add expenditure on exports and deduct expenditure on imports. This is because the sale of exports represents the country's output and creates income in the country, whereas expenditure on imports is spending on goods and services made in foreign countries and creates income for people in those countries. It is also necessary to deduct indirect taxes and add subsidies in order to get a value which corresponds to the income generated in the production of output.

SELF-ASSESSMENT TASK 9.3

Which of the following should be included in measuring GDP by the income method:

- government subsidies to farmers
- the pay of civil servants
- the pay of nurses
- supernormal profits
- state pensions?

TOP TIP

One way of remembering the three methods is to think about the circular flow (see later in this chapter).

Money and real GDP

Money (or nominal) GDP is GDP measured in terms of the prices operating in the year in which output is produced. It is sometimes referred to as GDP at current prices and is a measure that has not been adjusted for inflation.

Money GDP may give a misleading impression of how well a country is performing. This is because the value of money GDP may rise not because more goods and services are being produced but merely because prices have risen. For example if 100 billion products are produced at an average price of \$5, GDP will be \$500 billion. If in the next year the same output of 100 billion products is produced but the average price rise to \$6, money GDP will rise to \$600 billion. So to get a truer picture of what is happening to output, economists convert money into **real GDP**. They do this by measuring GDP at constant prices, meaning the prices operating in a selected year. By doing this they remove the distorting effect of inflation. For example, in 2016 a country's GDP is \$800 billion and the price index is 100. Then in 2017, money GDP is \$900 billion and the price index is 120.

$$\text{Real GDP} = \frac{\text{money GDP} \times \text{price index in base year}}{\text{price index in current year}}$$

$$\text{So } \$900 \text{ billion} \times \frac{100}{120} = \$750 \text{ billion}$$

The price index used to convert money into real GDP is called the GDP deflator, which measures the prices of products produced rather than consumed in a country. So it includes the prices of capital goods as well as consumer products and includes the price of exports but excludes the price of imports.

KEY TERMS

Money GDP: total output measured in current prices.

Real GDP: total output measured in constant prices.

TOP TIP

In analysing economic data, check carefully whether the data are in real or nominal terms.

SELF-ASSESSMENT TASK 9.4

In 2016 a country's GDP is \$1,000. In 2017 nominal GDP rises to \$1,092 and the price index increases by 4%. Calculate:

a real GDP

b the percentage increase in real GDP.

Comparison of economic growth performance over time and between countries

Changes in real GDP are used to calculate economic growth rates. For example, the real GDP of Indonesia grew from US\$846.8 billion in 2012 to US\$878 billion in 2013. This meant that the economic growth rate was 5.8%.

Table 9.1 compares the average annual growth rates for five Asian and five European economies, with the Asian economies experiencing more rapid economic growth. Indeed, Greece experienced negative economic growth meaning that its output declined.

In comparing economic growth rates over time and between countries, care has to be taken over a number of issues. One of these is that the official real GDP figures may understate the true change in output. This is because of the existence of, and changes in, what is called the shadow, hidden or underground economy. These terms refer to undeclared economic activity. There are two main reasons why people may not declare their earned income to the authorities. One is that they are seeking to evade paying tax. For example, a plumber may receive payment for undertaking jobs in his spare time and not declare the income he receives to the tax authorities. So some of the services he produces will not be included in GDP. Another reason for not declaring economic activity is that the activity is itself illegal, for example smuggling goods.

Asian country	Economic growth rate (%)	European country	Economic growth rate (%)
Malaysia	4.8	Germany	0.5
Pakistan	6.1	Greece	–3.6
Singapore	3.7	Norway	1.3
South Korea	2.7	Poland	1.5
Thailand	3.0	UK	1.8

Table 9.1 Economic growth rates for selected Asian and European countries, 2013

Some idea of the **shadow economy** can be found by measuring any gap between GDP as measured by the expenditure and income methods. This is because people will be spending income they have not declared!

KEY TERM

Shadow economy: the output of goods and services not included in official national income figures.

If the size of the shadow economy is relatively constant, the rate of economic growth may be calculated reasonably accurately. However, even a shadow economy can make international comparisons of economic growth rates difficult. This is because the size of the hidden economy varies between economies. It is influenced by the marginal rates of taxation, the penalties imposed for illegal activities and tax evasion, the risk of being caught and social attitudes towards, for example, different illegal activities.

Official GDP figures may also not provide an accurate measure of output and changes in output because of low levels of literacy, non-material goods and services and the difficulties of measuring government spending. In countries with low levels of literacy, it will be difficult for the government to gather information about all economic activity. Some people will be unable to fill out tax forms and others will fill them out inaccurately, so estimates will have to be made for some output. This is a particular problem in Pakistan, which had an adult literacy rate of just 58% in 2013 with females having a literacy rate of 45%.

Estimates also have to be made for non-marketed goods and services. The GDP figures only include marketed goods and services, that is goods and services that are bought and sold and so have a price attached to them. Goods and services that are produced and that are either not traded or are exchanged without money changing hands go unrecorded. For example, domestic services provided by homeowners, painting and repairs undertaken by home owners and voluntary work are not included in the official figures. The proportion of goods and services that people produce for themselves and the amount of voluntary work undertaken vary over time and between countries.

In comparing economic growth rates, it is also important to consider the nature of economic growth. A very high rate of economic growth may initially appear to be very impressive. However, it may not be possible to sustain this for any length of time if non-renewable resources are depleted and pollution is created that reduces the fertility of the land and the health of the labour force.

SELF-ASSESSMENT TASK 9.5

China's economic growth rate fell in 2013 to 7.5% from 7.8% in 2012. The economy's domestic demand would have supported a 9% growth rate, largely driven by investment. Weak exports due to the strength of the currency reduced the growth rate.

1. What is meant by a fall in a country's economic growth rate?
2. Explain how investment may promote economic growth.
3. Discuss whether a high exchange rate will reduce a country's economic growth rate.

Comparison of living standards over time

Real GDP per head figures have traditionally been used as one of the main indicators of living standards. If a country's real GDP per head is higher this year than last year, it is generally expected that the country's inhabitants will be enjoying higher living standards. This is often the case but may not always be so.

Real GDP per head is found by dividing total real GDP by the country's population to give an average figure. Real GDP is not evenly distributed so, while it is possible that real GDP per head may rise, not everyone will be better off. Indeed, some people may even experience a fall in their income.

The change in real GDP may not reflect the true change in the quantity of goods and services that households can enjoy if the level of undeclared economic activity changes over time.

To assess changes in living standards, changes in the type of products produced and the ways in which they are made must be considered. During a war, output may rise because more weapons are being produced but not many people will say that the quality of their lives is improving. The recruitment of more police to cope with more crime will increase real GDP but will be unlikely to cause people to feel better off.

More consumer goods and services, such as housing, food, clothing and transport, raise people's living standards. A shift of resources from consumer products to capital goods will enable more consumer products to be produced and enjoyed but only in the future. However, in the short run if the economy is operating at the frontier of its production possibility curve, such a move will cause people to enjoy fewer consumer products. Figure 9.7 shows a reduction in the output of consumer products in the short run but an increase in the long run.

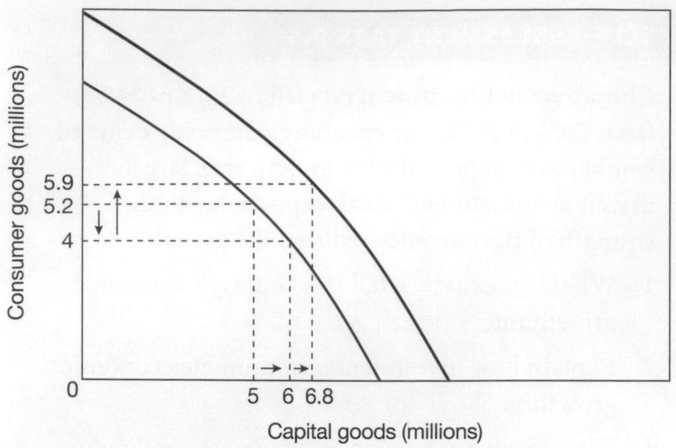

Figure 9.7 The effect of producing more capital goods in the short and long run

Even if people are able to enjoy more consumer goods and services, it does not necessarily mean that they will be happier. As access to more and higher-quality products rises, the desire for even more and better products may increase at even faster rate. For example, people who do not have a car are happy when they buy their first car but often, within a short space of time, they want a better model. This has particular implications for people in China and India where incomes and car ownership are increasing rapidly.

Real GDP measures the quantity of output produced but not the quality. Output could rise but if the quality of what is produced declines then the quality of people's lives is likely to fall. In practice, however, the quality of output tends to rise over time.

Working conditions also tend to improve over time and working hours usually fall. If real GDP per head stays constant from one year to the next but working conditions rise and/or working hours fall, people's living standards will rise.

Although workers tend to enjoy improved working conditions over time, the quality of the environment in some countries declines as a result of pollution and, for example, deforestation. A decline in environmental conditions will lower living standards but not necessarily real GDP. Indeed, if more resources have to be devoted to cleaning up the environment, real GDP will increase while living standards decline.

KEY CONCEPT LINK

Progress and development: Assessing changes in living standards over time and between countries involves distinguishing between economic growth and economic development. The concepts of progress and development are useful here.

Comparison of GDP per head between countries

The citizens of a country with a higher GDP per head are likely to enjoy higher living standards than people living in a country with a lower real GDP per head, but this is not necessarily the case.

To compare living standards between countries, it is necessary to convert the real GDP per capita into a common currency. To avoid the comparison

SELF-ASSESSMENT TASK 9.6

Read the feature below and then answer the questions that follow.

Not all benefitting from Asia's fast growth

Recently a number of Asian economies have experienced rapid economic growth and this has led to a fall in absolute poverty. The main beneficiaries, however, have been the rich. Income inequality has increased, particularly in China, India and Indonesia. In these three counties spending on education in 2013 was less than 4% of GDP, compared with an average of 5.2% in developed economies.

To ensure that economic growth provides the greatest benefits for the greatest number of people, some economists suggest that a fair and stable tax base has to be developed in a number of Asian economies, which would increase the ability of the governments to spread the benefits of economic growth.

1 Why may the rich benefit most from economic growth?

2 Explain how 'a fair and stable tax base' might result in more people benefiting from economic growth.

being distorted by exchange rate changes, economists usually adjust exchange rates to take into account their **purchasing power parities (PPPs)**. For example, suppose the exchange rate is 6 Malaysian ringgits equals US$1 and the USA has a real GDP per head of $50,000 while Malaysia has a real GDP of 12,000 ringgits. From this information, it might appear that, when Malaysia's real GDP is converted into dollars ($2,000) people in the USA are, on average, 25 times better off than people in Malaysia. However, if $1 can buy more goods and services in the USA than in Malaysia, then using the exchange rate to convert ringgits into dollars will exaggerate Malaysia's output. A basket of products may sell for $200 in the USA and for 2,400 ringgits in Malaysia. This would mean that in terms of ability to buy products (purchasing parities) 12 ringgits are worth $1. Using this as the basis for converting Malaysia's output into US dollars would show that people in the USA are 50 times better off than people in Malaysia.

KEY TERM

Purchasing power parity (PPP): a way of comparing international living standards by using an exchange rate based on the amount of each currency needed to purchase the same basket of goods and services.

Even if a country is found to have a higher real GDP per head than another country using purchasing power parities, it does not necessarily mean that its inhabitants will enjoy higher living standards. For example, Kuwait has one of the highest real GDP per head in the world but some immigrant workers in the country receive relatively low wages. Where income is very unevenly distributed, only a small number of households may benefit from a high average income.

When assessing living standards between countries, consideration must be given to factors that are not measured in real GDP per head, just as when making comparisons over time. For example, working hours, working conditions, fear of crime and freedom of thought may be taken into account.

National debt

National debt is often expressed as a percentage of GDP. Government or public sector debt is the total debt a central government or the whole public sector has built up over time. It is connected to budget deficits and budget surplus. If a government has a budget deficit in one year it will add to the country's national debt. In contrast, the extra revenue earned from a budget surplus can be used to pay off part of the national debt.

KEY TERM

National debt: the total amount of government debt.

The national debt tends to increase during economic downturns as this is when government expenditure tends to rise at a more rapid rate than tax revenue. There may also be a tendency for a government to spend more than its

SELF-ASSESSMENT TASK 9.7

The world's super-rich in 2013 were those with US$30 million or more in assets apart from their main homes. In that year there were 167,669 such people. In total they controlled more than US$20 trillion in assets, more than the combined GDPs of the US and Germany. London is home to more of the super-rich than any other city. New York is due to overtake London by 2023 but is then, in turn, expected to be overtaken by Asian cities. The number of super-rich is forecast to double in Africa and India and to increase by 80% in China by 2025. The super-rich buy homes throughout the world.

1 What may attract the super-rich to a particular city?
2 Explain one advantage and one disadvantage a city may experience as a result of attracting more of the super-rich.

SELF-ASSESSMENT TASK 9.8

Read the feature below and answer the questions that follow.

The Big Mac index

The Big Mac index, *The Economist*'s gauge of exchange rates, offers some food for thought. The index is based on the theory of purchasing power parity, which holds that currencies should in the long run adjust to rates that would make a basket of goods and services cost the same wherever they were bought. Our basket contains just one item, a Big Mac, since its ingredients are the same the world over, except in India, where the Maharaja Mac is made of chicken. Because buying a Big Mac in Norway, for instance, costs $7.80 at market exchange rates compared with $4.62 in America, our index suggests that the Norwegian krone is almost 70% overvalued.

Source: Adapted from *The Economist*, 25 January 2014.

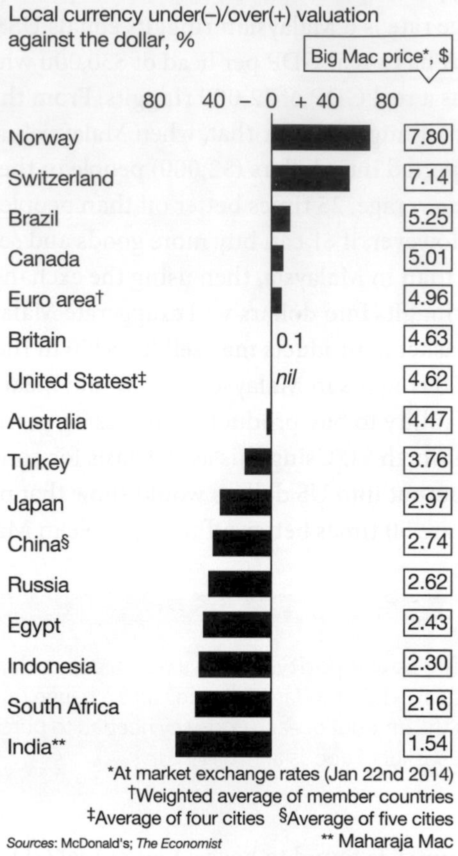

Figure 9.8 The Big Mac index

1 Explain what is meant by purchasing power parity.

2 Explain what effect using an undervalued exchange rate for Indonesia would have when comparing the GDP of Indonesia with that of the USA.

revenue even during economic booms (a structural deficit). In addition, military conflicts can result in significant increases to the national debt.

There are disadvantages in having a large and increasing national debt. There is the opportunity cost of interest payments on the national debt. The government revenue used to service the debt might have been used to finance, for instance, the building of new hospitals. A large national debt may make financial institutions, firms, individuals and governments reluctant to lend and may push up the rate of interest that has to be paid. National debt is not the same as external debt as some of the debt will be owed to citizens of the country. For example, some households may have purchased government saving certificates and some domestic banks may have bought government bonds. Payments to foreign lenders to the government, however, will involve an outflow of money from the country.

TOP TIP

Be careful to avoid confusing national debt with a budget deficit. The former is built up over time whereas the latter occurs over the course of one year.

Other indicators of living standards and economic development

In assessing living standards and economic development, economists use a wide range of indicators. Some of these are measured in monetary terms, for instance education spending as a percentage of GDP, while others are measured in non-monetary terms including, for example, infant mortality rates and the number of doctors per 1,000 of the population.

There are also a number of composite measures, which include a number of indicators of living standards and economic development with weightings to give a single, combined figure. One of these is **Measurable Economic Welfare (MEW).** This was developed in 1972 by two American economists, William Nordhaus and James Tobin. The measure seeks to give a fuller picture of living standards by adjusting GDP figures to take into account other factors that have an impact on living standards. Factors that improve living standards, including increased leisure time, are added to the GDP figure, while factors that reduce living standards are deducted. Of course, in practice, it is difficult and expensive to measure the value of non-marketed goods and services.

Perhaps the best-known measure of economic development is the United Nation's **Human Development Index (HDI)**. This takes into account GNI per head, education (as measured by mean years of schooling and expected years of schooling) and health care (as measured by life expectancy). These are included as it is thought that people's welfare is influenced not only by the goods and services available to them but also their ability to lead a long and healthy life and to acquire knowledge.

KEY TERMS

Measurable Economic Welfare (MEW): a composite measure of living standards that adjusts GDP for factors that reduce living standards and factors that improve living standards.

Human Development Index (HDI): a composite measure of living standards that includes GNI per head, education and life expectancy.

The HDI value for a country shows the distance a country has to cover to reach the maximum value of 1. Countries are divided into very high human development, high human development, medium human development and low human development. A country's ranking by HDI does not always match its ranking in terms of real GDP per head. Indeed, in some cases there are marked differences. For example, in 2012 Cuba's HDI ranking was significantly higher than its GNI per head ranking while Qatar's GNI per head ranking was significantly higher than its HDI ranking.

Table 9.2 shows details on the ten countries with the highest HDI rankings and the ten with the lowest HDI rankings in 2012.

A more recent composite measure is the **Multidimensional Poverty Index (MPI).** This was developed in 2010 by the Oxford Poverty and Human Development Initiative and the United Nations Development Programme. It measures indicators of living standards (cooking fuel,

KEY TERM

Multidimensional Poverty Index (MPI): a composite measure of deprivation in terms of the proportion of households that lack the requirements for a reasonable standard of living.

sanitation, safe drinking water, floor space and assets), education (years of schooling and school attendance) and health (child mortality and nourishment). The six indicators of living standards are given a total weighting of 33%, the two indicators of education a total weighting of 33% and similarly the two indicators of health have a weighting of 33%. A household is considered to be multidimensionally poor if they are deprived in at least 33% of the weighted indicators. This means a family would be regarded as poor if it has lost a child and has another child who is not attending school.

The Kuznets curve

This inverted U-shaped curve was first drawn by the American economist Simon Kuznets. The **Kuznets curve** suggests that as an economy develops, income becomes more unevenly distributed and then after a certain income level is reached, income becomes more evenly distributed as shown in Figure 9.9.

The thinking behind this initial rise in income inequality is that as an economy develops there will be a movement of labour from low-paid and low-skilled agricultural jobs to higher paid and more skilled manufacturing jobs.

This suggested trend, however, is not being followed in all developing economies. The curve also does not explain the rise in income inequality in some developed economies such as the UK.

KEY TERM

Kuznets curve: a curve that shows the relationship between economic growth and income inequality.

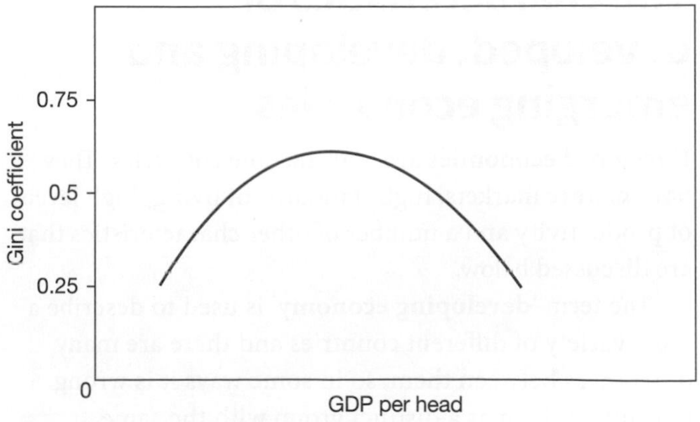

Figure 9.9 The Kuznets curve

Ranking	Very high human development Country	HDI value	Life expectancy at birth (years)	Mean years of schooling (years)	Expected years of schooling (years)	GNI per capita 2005 PPP (US$)
1	Norway	0.955	81.3	12.6	17.5	48,688
2	Australia	0.938	82.0	12.0	19.6	34,340
3	US	0.937	78.7	13.3	16.8	43,480
4	Netherlands	0.921	80.8	11.6	14.9	37,282
5	Germany	0.920	80.6	12.2	16.4	35,431
6	New Zealand	0.919	80.8	12.5	19.7	24,358
7	Ireland	0.916	80.7	11.6	18.3	28,671
7	Sweden	0.916	81.6	11.7	16.0	36,143
9	Switzerland	0.913	82.5	11.0	15.7	40,527
10	Japan	0.912	83.6	11.6	15.3	32,545
	Low human development Country					
176	Guinea-Bissau	0.364	48.6	2.3	9.5	1,042
177	Sierra Leone	0.359	48.1	3.3	7.3	881
178	Burundi	0.355	50.9	2.7	11.3	544
178	Guinea	0.355	54.5	1.6	8.8	941
180	Central African Republic	0.352	49.1	3.5	6.8	722
181	Eritrea	0.351	62.0	3.4	4.6	531
182	Mali	0.344	51.9	2.0	7.5	853
183	Burkina Faso	0.343	55.9	1.3	6.9	1,202
184	Chad	0.340	49.9	1.5	7.4	1,258
185	Mozambique	0.327	50.7	1.2	9.2	906

Table 9.2 The HDI rankings of 20 countries, 2012
Source: Human Development Report 2013, UNDP

The characteristics of developed, developing and emerging economies

Developed economies are high-income countries. They have mature markets, high standards of living, high levels of productivity and a number of other characteristics that are discussed below.

The term '**developing economy**' is used to describe a great variety of different countries and there are many differences between them, so in some ways it is wrong to think of them as a distinct group with the same characteristics. Very often the differences that exist between them are related to the geographical area in which the countries are located. This also means that developing countries located in the same region are usually affected by the same types of problems. The problems of developing countries in sub-Saharan

KEY TERMS

Developed economies: economies with high GDP per head.

Developing economy: an economy with a low GDP per head.

SELF-ASSESSMENT TASK 9.9

Study the information in Table 9.3 and then answer the questions that follow.

Region	HDI group	Life expectancy (years)	Mean years of schooling (years)	Expected years of schooling (years)	GNI per capita 2005 PPP (US$)
Arab states	0.652	71.0	6.0	10.6	8,317
East Asia and the Pacific	0.683	72.7	7.2	11.8	6,874
Europe and Central Asia	0.771	71.5	10.4	13.7	12,243
Latin America and the Caribbean	0.741	74.7	7.8	13.7	10,300
South Asia	0.558	66.2	4.7	10.2	3,343
Sub-Saharan Africa	0.475	54.9	4.7	9.3	2,010

Table 9.3 HDI by regions, 2012

Source: Human Development Report 2013, UNDP

1 Assess the extent to which the information suggests there is a positive correlation between education (as measured by mean years of schooling) and GNI per head.

2 Discuss whether the information shown suggests that the region of sub-Saharan Africa was the least developed in 2012.

SELF-ASSESSMENT TASK 9.10

Between 2006 and 2012 the number of people living in poverty in Rwanda, as measured by the Multidimensional Poverty Index (MPI) fell from 80% to 66%. This was largely due to improvements in access to water and sanitation. On the same measure, poverty in Nepal fell from 60% to 45%. This time it was largely the result of improved health.

Some critics of the MPI claim that not all relevant items are included while others think that the weightings are not appropriate. Defenders of the MPI argue that the MPI does include some of the most important indicators of poverty.

1 How is health poverty measured in the MPI?

2 Identify two indicators of poor living standards not referred to in the passage.

3 Explain why a lack of education is an important indicator of poverty.

Africa, may, for example, be quite distinct from those of developing countries in Asia.

A number of developing economies in Africa, Asia and Latin America do, however, suffer from **poverty cycles**, which are also sometimes referred to as **development traps**. Figure 9.10 shows two poverty cycles.

The term '**emerging economies**' describes those developing economies that have high rates of economic growth and are expected to give high rates of return on investment while carrying a greater risk than investment in developed economies.

KEY TERMS

Poverty cycles: the links between, for example, low income, low savings, low investment and low productivity.

Development traps: restrictions on the growth of developing economies that arise from low levels of savings and investment.

Emerging economies: economies with a rapid growth rate and that provide good investment opportunities.

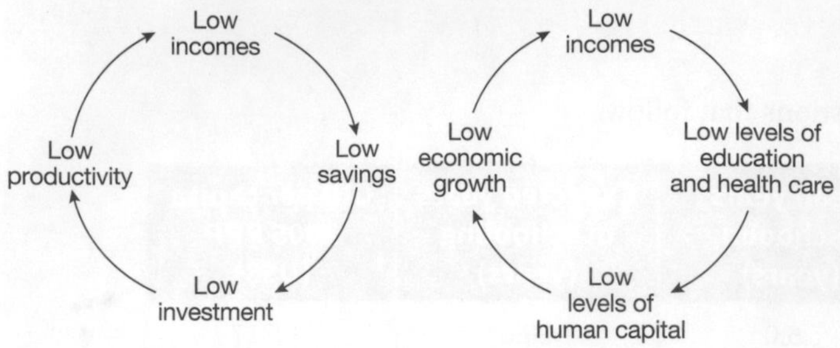

Figure 9.10 Poverty cycles

TOP TIP

Avoid thinking all developing economies are the same.

Classification according to levels of income

Economies are classified in a number of ways. The best known is according to the value of their GDP per head or GNI per head. This is used by the **World Bank**, which classifies every economy as low income, middle income (subdivided into lower and upper middle) or high income. Developing economies have low income or middle income. Emerging economies tend to have middle or high income and developed economies have high income.

KEY TERM

World Bank: an international organisation that lends money to developing economies for projects that will promote development.

Each year there are some changes. In the 2013 classification, Russia moved to high income and Chile, Lithuania and Uruguay also became high-income economies for the first time. Hungary slipped from high income to high middle income.

The thresholds between the categories are updated each year to account for the international rates of inflation. As a result the thresholds are constant in real terms over time.

Classifying economies according to income levels is relatively straightforward and can help to identify those economies in need of help and assistance from aid providers. It can, however, be misleading as some countries' economies may be growing while others may be contracting. It also does not capture all the influences on development.

Low income	US$1,035
Middle income	US$1,036 to US$4,085 (lower middle) US$4,086 to US$12,615 (upper middle)
High income	US$12,616

Table 9.4 Classification of economies, GNI per head, 2013

Classification according to levels of external indebtedness

Sometimes it is useful to classify developing economies according to the degree of their external indebtedness. These categories are: severely (or highly) indebted, moderately indebted and less indebted. The categorisation depends upon a number of measures of external indebtedness, the most important of which is the proportion of GNI that is devoted to servicing the debt. The fact that such a categorisation is used is a reflection of the extent to which external indebtedness is an obstacle to economic development.

As well as the ratio of debt service to GNI, economists measure the ratio of debt service to exports. If either the proportion of debt service exceeds 80% of GNI or the value of debt service to exports is 220% of exports, then the country is considered to be severely indebted. If either of the two rates exceeds 60% of the critical level, then the country is said to be moderately indebted. The presence of debt on such a scale diverts resources to debt repayment and away from spending on health and education, infrastructure and poverty relief.

Classification according to economic structure

Economic activity can be placed into the following sectors:

- **Primary sector:** This covers agriculture and the extractive industries such as oil extraction, gold mining and coal mining.
- **Secondary sector:** This includes all manufacturing industries and the construction industry.
- **Tertiary sector:** This covers all service industries. Some economists separate out from the tertiary sector the **quaternary sector**, to cover knowledge-based services such as education, financial planning, ICT, the media and research and development.

KEY TERMS

Primary sector: industries involved in farming and extracting natural resources.

Secondary sector: industries that manufacture products.

Tertiary sector: industries that produce services.

Quaternary sector: industries involved in providing knowledge-based services.

Developing economies typically have a high dependence on the primary sector. A high dependency on agricultural output makes developing economies vulnerable to the forces of nature. In those developing economies that are dependent upon agricultural output for subsistence, a drought can swiftly lead to famine. In those developing economies that are dependent upon agricultural products for their exports, a drought can wipe out their foreign currency earnings.

As an economy develops, the contribution to GDP of the primary sector tends to decline. The secondary sector becomes the major contributor and as the economy develops further, the tertiary sector usually makes the largest contribution to output. Resources also move into the secondary and tertiary sectors and away from the primary sector. A smaller proportion of the economy's labour force is employed in the primary sector but, given higher labour and capital productivity, the total value of the sector's output may increase.

Table 9.5 compares the economic structure of some developed, emerging and developing economies.

Classification by population growth and population structure

Developing economies tend to have high rates of population growth. This is due largely to natural increases in population size with the birth rate exceeding the death rate. There are a number of reasons why the birth rate tends to be high in developing economies. These include the need to have children to support parents in their old age, lack of availability of contraceptives, high infant mortality rates, the relatively low costs of raising children and a relatively low labour force participation.

Some economists suggest that the population theory of the Reverend Thomas Malthus, published in 1798, can be applied to the current population problems of the developing economies. The **Malthusian theory** has a pessimistic view of population growth.

KEY TERM

Malthusian theory: the view that population grows in geometric progression whereas the quantity of food grows in arithmetic progression.

	GDP contribution by sector of origin, 2013 (% estimates)		
Developed economies	**Agriculture**	**Industry**	**Services**
France	1.9	18.7	79.4
Germany	0.8	30.1	69.0
UK	0.7	20.5	78.9
USA	1.1	19.5	79.4
Emerging economies			
Brazil	5.5	26.4	68.1
India	16.9	17.0	66.1
Russia	4.2	37.5	58.3
South Africa	2.6	29.0	68.4
Developing economies			
Bangladesh	17.2	28.9	53.9
Central African Republic	56.6	14.5	28.9
Liberia	76.9	5.4	17.7
Sierra Leone	47.9	18.6	33.5

Table 9.5 The economic structure of selected economies

Source: *The World Factbook*, CIA, GDP composition/sector of origin (www.cia.gov/library/publications/the-world.../; www.cia.gov/library/publications/the-world=factbook/geos/)

The theory suggests that a country's population has a tendency to grow in geometric progression (i.e., 1, 2, 4, 8, 16, etc.) over time, while food supplies have a tendency to increase only in arithmetic progression (i.e., 1, 2, 3, 4, 5, etc.). He thought there was this tendency for population growth to outstrip food production because the quantity of land was in relatively fixed supply (the fixed factor) and, as increasing quantities of labour (the variable factor) were added in production, diminishing returns would set in. Malthus thought there were checks that kept population to a level sustainable by the available food supplies. He divided these checks into positive and preventative checks. Positive checks increase the death rate and include epidemics, diseases and war. Preventative checks reduce the birth rate and include delaying marriage and contraception.

The Malthusian theory has, however, been challenged on a number of grounds. The main weakness is that it fails to recognise the impact of changes in technology upon food production and distribution. Malthus could not have foreseen the huge changes that were to occur in agricultural production, such as mechanisation, the application of more effective fertilisers and insecticides and the introduction of new high-yield seeds and genetically modified crops. These changes mean that food supplies have increased to a level capable of supporting a much higher level of world population.

Nevertheless, malnourishment and famine remain problems in some developing economies. These problems arise from a range of factors, including uneven distribution of resources in the world, poor management of agricultural sectors, vulnerability to sudden supply shocks, such as floods and drought, and an inability to respond to these.

The higher birth rate of developing economies results in a relatively low average age of population. This creates a high proportion of dependent, non-productive members of the population. They are said to have very high **dependency ratios**. This means that a proportionally small working population has to produce enough goods and services to sustain not only themselves but also a large number of young people who are economically dependent upon them.

KEY TERM

Dependency ratio: the proportion of the economically inactive to the labour force.

Developed economies also face a range of population problems. The most common one is an ageing population. This arises from a decreasing birth rate and a decreasing death rate. Again dependency ratios are high, this time because there is a high proportion of old people who are reliant upon the productive proportion of the population for support. With people living longer, the cost of health care and pensions have been rising. To reduce the cost of pensions, a number of governments of developed countries have increased the retirement age.

In assessing the effects of differences in population size, economists make use of the concept of **optimum population**. The optimum population is said to exist when output per head is the greatest, given existing quantities of the other factors of production and the current state of technical knowledge. This is illustrated on Figure 9.11.

KEY TERM

Optimum population: the size of population that maximises GDP per head.

As the population grows it can make better use of the stock of the other factors of production such as land and capital. This is because increasing returns are enjoyed as the population grows. If population is below the optimum level, it can be described as underpopulated. When the population is beyond the optimum level and decreasing returns are being experienced, it is said to be overpopulated. In the real world, the situation is more dynamic and the state of technical knowledge is constantly improving. The quantity of the other factors also continuously changes so that the optimum population for a country is not a fixed entity. In addition, the criteria for assessing under- or overpopulation are purely economic and may be disputed by conservationists.

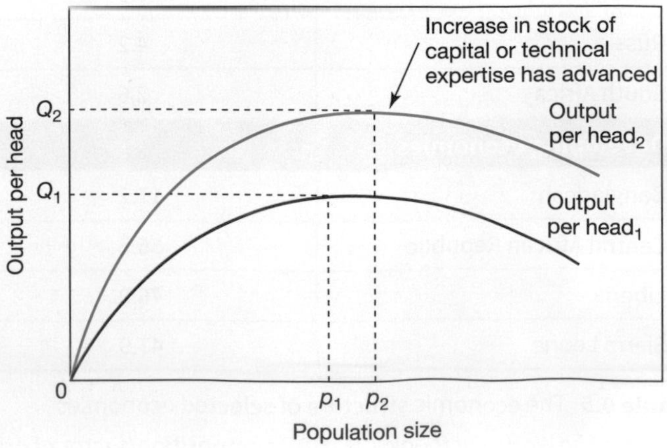

Figure 9.11 The optimum population

TOP TIP

Be careful not to confuse population growth and population size. Developing economies tend to have high population growth but not necessarily high population size. For instance, Zimbabwe has a population growth rate of 2.15% but a population of only 12.7 million whereas the US has a lower population growth of 0.85% but a higher population size of 320 million.

Classification according to income distribution

It is a characteristic of some developing countries that income is unevenly distributed. This is partly because income-generating assets, especially land, are owned by the few. As a result, there are great extremes of rich and poor. Income is particularly unevenly distributed in Latin America and in South Africa and Lesotho. Income is relatively evenly distributed in Scandinavian European economies.

The transition of Eastern European countries, including Poland and Russia, from centrally planned to market economies has increased inequality as a small number of people have benefited enormously from the new opportunities that have been forthcoming. Two exceptions are Slovenia and the Czech Republic, which have two of the least uneven distributions of national income in Europe.

SELF-ASSESSMENT TASK 9.11

Read the feature below and then answer the questions that follow.

China's one-child policy

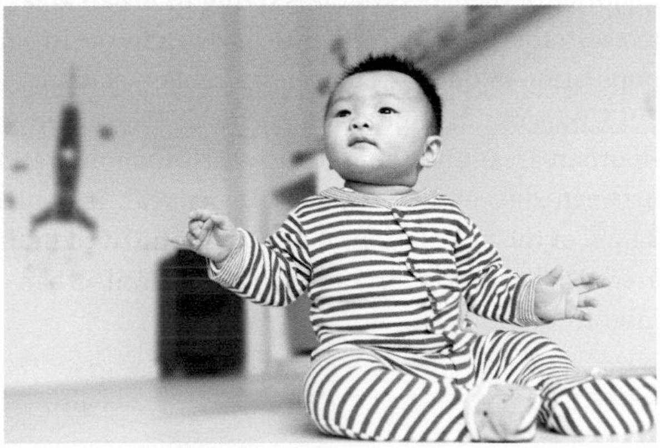

China has been relaxing its one-child policy. The policy came into force in the late 1970s and has been claimed to have prevented the births of 400 million extra people and saved China from food shortages. The number of exceptions to the policy has been increasing with, for instance, urban couples being allowed to have two children if both parents are only children and rural couples are permitted to have a second child if the first child is a girl.

One reason behind the relaxation is concern about China's ageing population. Longer life expectancy is increasing the proportion of elderly citizens and for the first time in decades the size of the country's working-age population is decreasing.

Some economists, however, have claimed that the relaxation of the policy will have little impact as rising incomes tend to reduce the birth rate anyway.

Table 9.6 compares population growth in China and India.

	Population size in billions	
Year	**China**	**India**
1970	0.8	0.5
1990	1.0	0.8
2010	1.3	1.1
2030*	1.5	1.3
2050*	1.4	1.5

Table 9.6 Population growth in China and India

*Predicted figures.

1 Explain what is meant by an 'ageing population'.

2 Explain two possible reasons for the differences in the trends of China's and India's population size shown in the table.

3 Why may increases in incomes reduce birth rates?

4 Discuss whether a larger population would always result in food shortages.

KEY CONCEPT LINK

Regulation and equity: The issue of income inequality raises questions of equity. Deciding whether income is too unevenly distributed is a normative issue that takes into account the concept of equity.

KEY TERM

Prebisch-Singer hypothesis: a theory that suggests that the terms of trade tend to move against developing economies so that developing economies have to export more to gain a given quantity of imports.

Classification according to external trade

In the case of a number of developing economies, primary products account for most of the export revenue earned. This makes them vulnerable in their trading relations because demand and especially supply can change significantly. For example, demand may decrease due to a health scare and supply may increase due to a good harvest. These changes mean that the market for primary products is subject to frequent and large fluctuations in price.

In addition, the demand for many primary products, especially food, is income inelastic. This means that as world income rises there is little impact upon the demand for primary products. In contrast, demand for manufactured goods is income elastic. This means that primary goods tend to become relatively cheaper than manufactured goods. As a result, over time there is a tendency for the terms of trade of primary goods to decline relative to manufactured goods. This tendency is known as the **Prebisch-Singer hypothesis**. Those developing economies that are dependent upon agricultural products may receive relatively low prices for their exports while having to pay relatively high prices for their imports.

Developed economies tend to export mainly manufactured goods and services. They also tend to export a wide range of products. Some developing economies, in contrast, rely heavily on exporting a narrow range of products. For example, in 2012 exports of coffee accounted for 60% of Ethiopia's export revenue.

Classification according to urbanisation

Developing economies tend to have a relatively high proportion of their populations living in rural areas but also rapid rates of rural-urban migration. This migration can put pressure on the infrastructure, housing and schools in urban areas.

Most developed economies already have the majority of their populations living in urban areas. As a result, there is relatively little growth in the urban population of developed economies. For example, in 2013, 83% of the population of the USA was living in urban areas and the rate of rural-urban migration between 2003 and 2013 was 1.3% per year. In contrast, 24.2% of the population of Burkina Faso lived in urban areas in the same year and the rate of rural-urban migration was 7.3%.

SELF-ASSESSMENT TASK 9.12

Read the feature below and then answer the questions that follow.

Population changes

In the recent past, Spain was Europe's largest recipient of immigrants. Its population grew from 40 million in 1999 to more than 47 million in 2010 largely as the result of immigration coming from, for example, Bolivia, Morocco and Romania. In 2010, however, the position changed. Migrants began to return home and more Spanish people emigrated. This reversal from net immigration to net emigration combined with one of the world's lowest birth rates is causing the population to decline for the first time since records began.

The decline in the size of Spain's population and the increase in the average age of the population are causing a number of problems. One is that they are reducing Spain's economic growth rate. With very little productivity growth, Spain's economic growth rate had been largely driven by increases in the size of the country's labour force. Another problem is that the ratio of workers to pensioners is declining. There is also the problem of Spain's national debt, which in 2014 amounted to 105% of GDP. In addition, with so many empty houses and flats, a smaller population depresses the housing market further.

Spain's population decline is in contrast with the relatively rapid rise in population in some African countries. While fertility rates* have fallen in most parts of Africa, they are still high at more than five in a number of countries including Nigeria, Uganda and the Democratic Republic of Congo. The increase in population is increasing urbanisation. For example, the population of Lagos in Nigeria is forecast to grow from 11 million in 2014 to more than 40 million in 2050. The number of children in Africa will also rise dramatically. In 2010 there were 411 million African children aged 14 or below. By 2050 it is predicted there will be 839 million.

*The fertility rate is the number of children a woman, on average, can expect to have in her lifetime.

1 What may cause a reversal from net immigration to net emigration?
2 What type of economic growth had Spain been experiencing in the recent past?
3 Why does a high national debt become more of a problem with a smaller population?
4 Explain two reasons why a country's fertility rate may be high.
5 Explain one advantage and one disadvantage of a high fertility rate.
6 Discuss whether rapid urbanisation is an advantage or a disadvantage.

	Average annual growth rate 2007–2012	% share of global output 2007	% share of global output 2012	% share of global exports of goods and services 2007	% share of global exports of goods and services 2012
BRIC countries					
Brazil	4.3	2.4	3.4	0.9	1.2
Russia	3.3	2.4	2.4	2.1	2.3
India	8.2	2.2	2.8	1.2	1.7
China	10.9	5.9	9.4	9.0	9.0
Developed economies					
Germany	1.2	6.1	5.3	8.8	8.4
Japan	0.2	8.0	7.8	4.7	4.6
UK	0.5	5.1	3.6	6.1	4.3
USA	0.8	25.2	23.1	11.5	11.3

Table 9.7 Selected economic data on BRIC and developed economies

Emerging economies

In 2014 emerging economies accounted for half of global GDP compared to less than a third in 1990. The most significant growth was in four of the largest emerging economies: Brazil, Russia, India and China. Jim O'Neill, an analyst working at the investment bank Goldman Sachs, labelled these four economies in 2001 as the BRICs. He identified these four economies as the ones with the greatest potential for economic growth and the ones providing the best opportunities for investment. Table 9.7 compares the growth rates and share of global output and exports of goods and services of the four BRIC economies and four developed economies.

The governments of the four countries now meet on a regular basis and they were joined in 2010 by the government of South Africa.

Influences on the size and composition of the labour force

The labour force in an economy is defined as the total number of workers who are available for work. It therefore refers to all males and females who can contribute to the production of goods and services. As well as those actually in employment, it also includes those who are unemployed and who are seeking employment. The size of a country's labour force depends upon a wide range of demographic, economic social and cultural factors, such as:

- the total size of the population of working age
- the number of people who remain in full-time education above the school leaving age
- the retirement age
- the proportion of women who join the labour force.

A country with a higher number of people of working age is likely to have a larger labour force than one with a smaller number of people in the age group. This, however, is not always the case. This is because the size of the labour force is also influenced by the labour force participation rate. This refers to the percentage of the total population of working age who are actually classified as being part of the labour force. For most economies the rate is usually between 50% and 70%. There are two main reasons why the labour force participation rate may be relatively low in a developed economy. These are a higher participation rate in higher education and a relatively large proportion opting for early retirement. In some developing economies, the difference is due to the contribution of women in the labour force being constrained by social and cultural factors.

Table 9.8 shows the total population size, the size of the working population age and the labour force of ten economies.

Labour productivity

Labour productivity refers to the quantity of goods and services that a worker is able to produce in a given period of time. It is usually measured in terms of output per worker hour.

An increase in labour productivity will increase an economy's productive potential. Labour productivity may increase as a result of improvements in education and training, greater experience, being able to work with more capital equipment and being able to work with technologically advanced equipment.

KEY TERM

Labour productivity: output per worker hour.

TOP TIP

Students sometimes confuse productivity and production. An economy's production may increase as a result of more people being employed, while productivity may fall. A rise in unemployment may reduce production while increasing productivity as it is likely that it will be the least efficient workers who will lose their jobs.

Country	Total population size (millions)	Size of working age population (millions)	Working age population as a % of total population	Size of the labour force (millions)	Labour force as a % of the working age population
Argentina	41	25	60.4	17	68.0
Bangladesh	165	104	78.6	79	76.0
Egypt	85	51	60.4	28	54.9
India	1,215	750	61.7	487	64.9
Italy	60	35	59.1	26	74.3
Nigeria	160	86	53.7	52	60.5
Pakistan	185	106	57.2	60	56.7
Russia	141	94	66.9	75	79.8
South Africa	51	32	62.4	19	59.4
USA	320	197	61.6	155	78.6

Table 9.8 Population and labour market data for ten economies

SELF-ASSESSMENT TASK 9.13

The UK's productivity gap with its main rivals increased in 2013. Output per worker hour in the UK was 21% lower than the average for the other six members of the G7 – the US, Germany, France, Italy, Japan and Canada. On an alternative measure, output per worker, the gap was even wider at 25%.

Low productivity can restrict economic growth and so limit economic growth. Productivity would be expected to grow over time because of new technology and better skills but the UK's productivity remained stagnant between 2011 and 2013.

1 Explain why output per worker hour is a better measure of productivity than output per worker.
2 Explain **two** reasons why a country's productivity may be lower than that of the other rival countries.

Unemployment

Definition

People are unemployed when they are able and willing to work but cannot find a job. The *level* of **unemployment** should be distinguished from the *rate* of unemployment. The level of unemployment refers to the total number of people who are unemployed whereas the rate of unemployment is the number of unemployed people as a percentage of the labour force. So in an economy with a labour force of 50 million people, 4.3 million of whom are unemployed, the rate of unemployment is 8.6%.

KEY TERM

Unemployment: the state of being willing and able to work but without a job.

KEY CONCEPT LINK

Equilibrium and efficiency: Unemployment is a clear example of inefficiency. An economy is not achieving productive efficiency as it is not making full use of its resources and not producing as much as possible.

Full employment and the natural rate of unemployment

Full employment is considered to be the highest level of employment possible. It is often considered to be achieved when the unemployment rate falls to 3%, although the rate may vary between countries. This may appear to be somewhat surprising as it might be expected that it would be 0% unemployed. However, in practice, at any particular time some people may be experiencing a period of unemployment as they move from one job to another job.

The **natural rate of unemployment** can also be referred to as the non-accelerating inflation rate of unemployment (Nairu). This is largely a monetarist concept. The natural rate of unemployment is the unemployment that exists when the aggregate demand for labour equals the aggregate supply of labour at the current wage rate and price level. The inflation rate is constant, with the actual inflation rate equalling the expected one at this rate of unemployment.

KEY TERMS

Full employment: the level of employment corresponding to where all who wish to work have found jobs, excluding frictional unemployment.

Natural rate of unemployment: the rate of unemployment that exists when the aggregate demand for labour equals the aggregate supply of labour at current wage rate and price level.

While monetarists argue that the natural rate of unemployment cannot be reduced, in the long run, by expansionary monetary or fiscal policy, it can change over time. The factors that determine the natural rate of unemployment are supply side factors. Over time the natural rate of unemployment may fall as a result of:

- an increase in the mobility of labour
- an improvement in the education and training levels of workers
- a reduction in trade union restrictive practices
- a reduction in state unemployment benefits
- a cut in income tax.

TOP TIP

Be careful to avoid confusing the economically inactive and the unemployed. The economically inactive are not part of the labour force whereas the unemployed are.

The causes of unemployment

Unemployment can be divided into three main types: frictional, structural and cyclical. Each of these types has different causes.

Frictional unemployment is unemployment that arises when workers are between jobs. One form of frictional unemployment is search unemployment. This arises when workers do not accept the first job or jobs on offer but spend some time looking for a better paid job. Casual and seasonal unemployment are two other forms of frictional unemployment. Casual unemployment refers to workers who are out of work between periods of employment including, for example, actors, supply teachers and construction workers. In the case of seasonal unemployment, demand for workers fluctuates according to the time of the year. During periods of the year, people working in, for example, the tourism, hospitality, building and farming industries may be out of work.

As its name suggests, **structural unemployment** arises due to changes in the structure of the economy. Over time the pattern of demand and supply will change. Some industries will be expanding and some will be contracting. If workers cannot move from one industry to another industry, due to a lack of geographical or occupational immobility, they may become structurally unemployed. Structural unemployment can take a number of forms. One is technological unemployment. In this case, people are out of work due to the introduction of labour-saving techniques.

KEY TERMS

Frictional unemployment: unemployment that is temporary and arises where people are in-between jobs.

Structural unemployment: unemployment caused as a result of the changing structure of economic activity.

When declining industries are concentrated in a particular area of the country, the resulting unemployment is sometimes referred to as regional unemployment.

Another form of structural unemployment is international unemployment. This is when workers lose their jobs because demand switches from domestic industries to more competitive foreign industries. For instance, the number of coal miners in the UK has fallen significantly over the past 40 years as the UK has lost its comparative advantage in coal mining.

Frictional and structural unemployment arise largely due to problems on the supply side of the economy. The third main type of unemployment, cyclical unemployment or demand-deficient unemployment, arises due to a lack of aggregate demand. **Cyclical unemployment** will affect the whole economy, with job losses occurring across a range of industries. Figure 9.12 shows the labour market initially in equilibrium at a

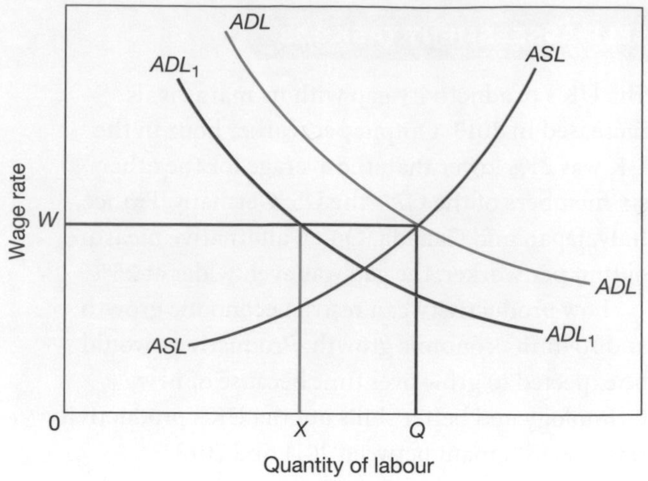

Figure 9.12 Cyclical unemployment

KEY TERM

Cyclical unemployment: unemployment that results from a lack of aggregate demand.

wage rate of *W*. Then as a result of a fall in aggregate demand, firms reduce the output and aggregate demand for labour shifts to ADL_1. If workers resist wage cuts, demand-deficient unemployment *XQ* will exist.

Even if wage rates fall, this type of unemployment may persist. This is because a cut in wages would reduce demand for goods and services as people would have less money to spend, which would cause firms to reduce both their output further and make more workers redundant.

TOP TIP

In explaining the different types of structural unemployment it is useful to give examples based on your own country.

The consequences of unemployment

Unemployment has consequences for the unemployed themselves, firms and the economy as a whole. Workers who lose their jobs are likely to experience a fall in income. They are likely to find it more difficult to get another job the longer they have been out of work. This is because they will miss out on training, will get out of touch with advances in technology and may lose confidence. They may also experience a decline in their physical and mental well-being. For a small number of people, there is a chance that a period of frictional or structural unemployment may give them the opportunity to search for a more rewarding job.

Firms wanting to expand may have a greater choice of potential workers. They may also benefit from workers not pressing for wage rises for fear of losing their jobs. They may, however, suffer from lower demand for their goods and services.

The economy will experience an opportunity cost. Output will be below its potential level. If the unemployed had been working, more goods and services would have been produced and living standards would have been higher. The tax revenue received by the government will be lower than with a higher level of employment. If state benefits are paid by the government, there will be an increase in government spending on the benefits which could have been put to other purposes.

SELF-ASSESSMENT TASK 9.14

In March 2014 more jobs were created in the US tertiary sector. These new jobs partly offset the number of jobs lost in construction as a result of the harsh winter weather. However, there was a rise in the unemployment rate from 6.6% to 6.7% and the number of people who had been out of work for more than a year increased to 38% of the total unemployed. Some economists blame long-term unemployment on globalisation for shifting low-skilled jobs overseas or on advances in technology replacing them. Other economists suggest that it is unemployment itself that is causing the problem. The latter economists argue that when people are out of work for a long time they become 'scarred' and find it difficult to be rehired and tend to lose the work habit.

1 Explain what type of unemployment some US construction workers suffered in March 2014.

2 Explain what type of unemployment would be caused by globalisation 'shifting low-skill jobs overseas and advances in technology replacing workers'.

The pattern and trends in (un)employment

Over time the pattern of employment and unemployment tends to change. As an economy develops, comparative advantage changes as workers become more skilled. The proportion of the labour force employed in the primary sector tends to decline. At first the proportion employed

SELF-ASSESSMENT TASK 9.15

In 2013 the number of female workers in the UK passed 14 million despite a rise in overall unemployment. Of this number, 57% were in full-time employment with 43% in part-time employment. There were thought to be a number of reasons for this, including a rise in the female retirement age, an increase in the tertiary sector, more grandparents looking after the grandchildren during the day and cuts in benefits.

1 Explain how a rise in employment may occur at the same time as a rise in unemployment.

2 Which of the reasons given for the rise in female employment would have increased the size of the UK's labour force?

in the secondary sector tends to increase. Then the proportion employed in the tertiary sector rises.

There may also be shorter trends in employment and unemployment, with industries within sectors declining and expanding. For example, while the number of workers employed in agriculture may be declining the number of workers employed in oil mining may be increasing with the discovery of new oil fields.

Difficulties of measuring unemployment

Most governments use two main measures of unemployment. One measure is the number of people in receipt of unemployment-related benefits – this is called the **claimant count** measure. It has the advantage that it is relatively cheap and quick to calculate as it is based on information that the government collects as it pays out benefits. However, the figure obtained may not be entirely accurate. It may over- or understate the true figure as it may include some people who are not really unemployed and may omit some people who are genuinely unemployed. Some of those receiving unemployment benefits may not be actively seeking employment (voluntary unemployment) and some may be working and so claiming benefit illegally. On the other hand, there may be a number of groups who are actively seeking employment but who do not appear in the official figures. These groups may include those above retirement age, those on government training schemes and those who choose not to claim benefits. As this measure is based on those

KEY TERM

Claimant count: a measure of unemployment based on those claiming unemployment benefits.

receiving benefits, it changes every time there is a change in the rules on who qualifies for unemployment benefit.

The more widely used measure involves a **labour force survey** using the International Labour Organization definition of unemployment. This includes as unemployed all people of working age who, in a specified period, are without work, but who are available for work in the next two weeks and who are seeking paid employment. This measure picks up some of the groups not included in the claimant count. It also has the advantage that it is based on internationally agreed concepts and definitions, so makes international comparisons easier. More information is found on, for example, the qualifications job seekers have. However, the data are more expensive and time-consuming to collect than the claimant count measure. Also, as the data are based on a sample survey, they are subject to sampling error and to a multitude of practical problems of data collection.

KEY TERM

Labour force survey: a measure of unemployment based on a survey that identifies people who are actively seeking a job.

Policies to correct unemployment

To reduce cyclical unemployment, a government will use **reflationary fiscal or monetary policy measures** to increase aggregate demand. Among the reflationary fiscal policy measures it may use are:

- a reduction in indirect or direct taxation to increase consumer expenditure
- a cut in corporate taxes to stimulate investment
- an increase in government spending.

The possible monetary measures include:

- reducing the rate of interest to increase consumer expenditure and investment
- increasing the money supply to, again, increase consumer expenditure and investment
- lowering the exchange rate, either through a formal devaluation or through intervention in the foreign exchange market in the case of a managed float, to increase net exports.

The extent to which reflationary fiscal or monetary policy measures increase aggregate demand will depend on a number of factors. These include the size of the

KEY TERM

Reflationary fiscal or monetary policy measures: policy measures designed to increase aggregate demand.

multiplier (see below) and the response from consumers and firms. The larger the size of the multiplier and the more confident consumers and firms are, the greater the final rise in aggregate demand is likely to be.

KEY TERM

Multiplier: a numerical estimate of a change in spending in relation to the final change in spending.

It is also important, but not easy, to get the size of the changes right. For example, if a government underestimates the size of the multiplier, it may, for instance, cut income tax rates by too much. Figure 9.13 shows aggregate demand increasing and eliminating a negative output gap but at the cost of increasing the price level.

To reduce frictional and structural unemployment, a government is likely to introduce supply side policy measures. It may reduce unemployment benefit and income tax rates to increase the reward from working and so encourage people to spend less time between jobs. Improved education and training may increase workers' occupational mobility and so reduce structural unemployment. Trade union reform may stop trade unions pushing up the wage rates of their members above the equilibrium levels and taking industrial action. This may increase the efficiency of the country's labour and product markets.

TOP TIP

In evaluating what might be the appropriate policy measures to reduce unemployment it is important to consider the cause/s of unemployment and the possible adverse side effects of such measures.

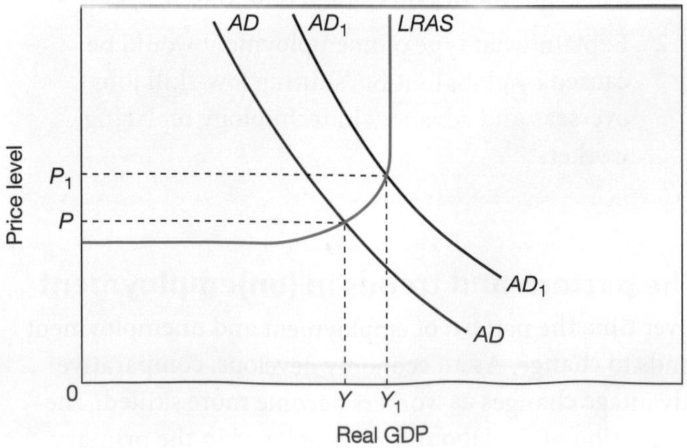

Figure 9.13 The effect of increasing aggregate demand

The circular flow of income

The distinction between an open and a closed economy

An **open economy** is an economy that engages in international trade. In contrast, a **closed economy** is one that does not export or import goods and services. Of course, no economy is a totally closed economy but such an economy can be used in a model of how an economy works.

KEY TERMS

Open economy: an economy that is involved in trade with other economies.

Closed economy: an economy that does not trade with other economies.

The circular flow in a closed economy and open economy

The **circular flow of income** shows how income and spending move around an economy. Figure 9.14 shows the process in a closed economy. The inner circle shows the real flow of products and factor services and the outer circle the money flow of spending and incomes.

KEY TERM

Circular flow of income: a simple model of the process by which income flows around the economy.

In practice, there are leakages out of the circular flow – some income is saved, some is taxed and some is spent on imports. Some expenditure is also additional to the spending that comes from the incomes generated by domestic output. These extra items of spending, known as injections, are investment, government spending and spending by foreigners on a country's exports. Figure 9.15 includes these leakages, also known as withdrawals, in a circular flow of income in an open economy.

KEY CONCEPT LINK

Equilibrium and equity: The circular flow of income shows how and why macroeconomic equilibrium can change.

The multiplier

This is also known as the national income multiplier or the Keynesian multiplier. It shows the relationship between an initial change in spending and the final rise in GDP. The multiplier effect occurs because a rise in expenditure will create incomes, some of which will, in turn, be spent and thereby will create incomes. For example, if people spend 80% of any extra income, an increase of government spending of $20 billion will cause a final rise in GDP of $100 billion. This is because the initial $20 billion spent will create higher incomes. People will spend $16 billion of these extra incomes, thereby generating a further rise of incomes. Of the $16 billion, $12.8 billion will be spent. This process will continue until incomes increase to $100 billion and the change in injections is matched by the change in withdrawals.

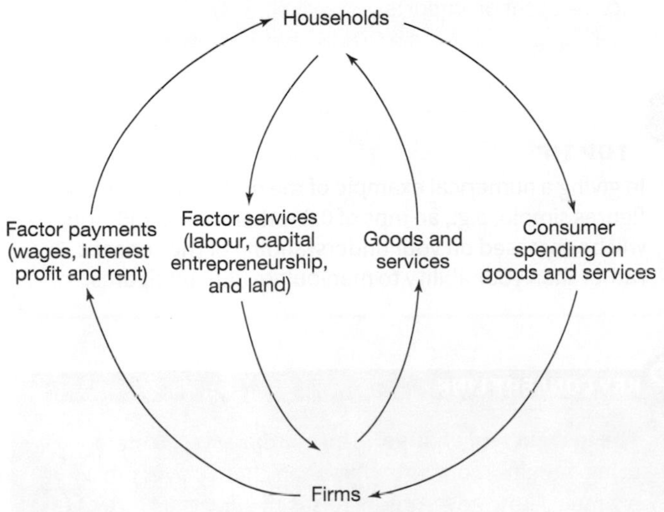

Figure 9.14 The circular flow of income in a closed economy

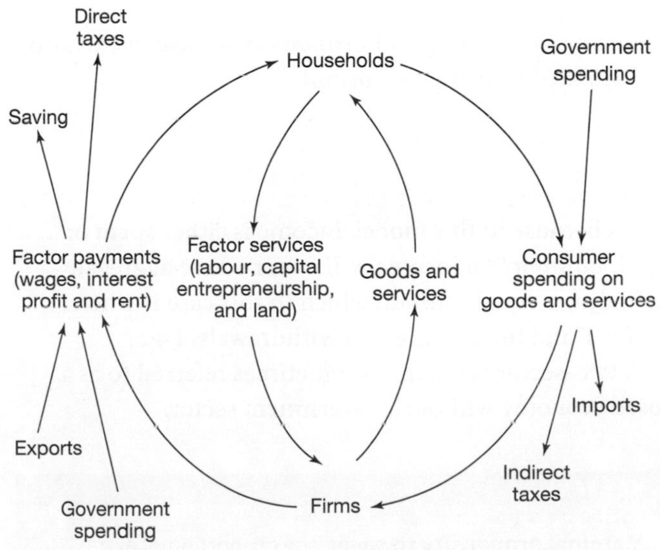

Figure 9.15 The circular flow of income in an open economy

In the example above, GDP rises until the \$20 billion of extra government spending is matched by withdrawals of \$20 billion. The value of the multiplier is calculated after the injection by using the formula:

$$\frac{\text{change in income}}{\text{change in injection}} = \frac{\Delta Y}{\Delta J}$$

In the example above the multiplier is $\frac{\$100\text{bn}}{\$20\text{bn}} = 5$

The multiplier can also be estimated in advance of the change by using the formula:

$$\frac{1}{\text{marginal propensity to withdraw}}$$

The multiplier and equilibrium income in two-, three- and four-sector economic models

As seen with the circular flow, economists often seek to explain their analysis first in a simplified model and then go on to include more variables. This is also the case with the multiplier where economists start with a simple model of the economy, which only includes two sectors and then move on to a model that includes three sectors and then finally one that includes all four sectors.

Two-sector economy

In a two-sector economy (households and firms) there is only one withdrawal (saving) (S) and one injection (investment). In such an economy, the multiplier can be found by using the formula:

$$\frac{1}{\text{mps}}$$

where mps is the **marginal propensity to save**. It can also be calculated by using the formula:

$$\frac{1}{1-\text{mps}}$$

This is because in this model, income is either spent or saved. Equilibrium income will occur where aggregate expenditure equals output, which in this case is where $C + I = Y$ and injections equal withdrawals, $I = S$.

A two-sector economy is sometimes referred to as a closed economy without a government sector.

> **KEY TERM**
>
> **Marginal propensity to save:** the proportion of extra income which is saved.

Three-sector economy

The additional sector in this model is the government. This gives an extra injection, G (government spending) and an extra withdrawal, T (taxation). The multiplier is now:

$$\frac{1}{\text{mps} + \text{mrt}}$$

where mrt is the **marginal rate of taxation** (the proportion of extra income which is taxed). Equilibrium income is achieved where aggregate expenditure equals output, $C + I + G = Y$ and injections equals withdrawals, $I + G = S + T$.

> **KEY TERM**
>
> **Marginal rate of taxation:** the proportion of extra income taken in tax.

Four-sector economy

This is the most realistic model as it includes all four possible sectors (households, firms, the government and the foreign trade sector) and is an open economy. Again, equilibrium income is where aggregate expenditure equals output, but this is now where $C + I + G + (X - M) = Y$, and injections equal withdrawals, which is now where $I + G + X = S + T + M$. The full multiplier is:

$$\frac{1}{\text{mps} + \text{mrt} + \text{mpm}}$$

where mpm is the **marginal propensity to import** (the proportion of extra income that is spent on imports).

> **KEY TERM**
>
> **Marginal propensity to import:** the proportion of extra income spent on imports.

> **TOP TIP**
>
> In giving a numerical example of the multiplier, keep the figures simple, e.g., an mps of 0.2 rather than 0.235. You will be assessed on your understanding of the concept rather than your ability to manipulate difficult figures.

> **KEY CONCEPT LINK**
>
> **The margin and change:** The multiplier is calculated using marginal concepts which can change over time. For example, if the government raises the marginal rate of tax, the size of the multiplier will fall.

SELF-ASSESSMENT TASK 9.16

In an economy, mps is 0.1, mrt is 0.1 and mpm is 0.2. GDP is $300 billion. The government raises its spending by $66 billion in a bid to close a deflationary gap of $20 billion. Calculate:

a the value of the multiplier

b the increase in GDP

c whether the injection of extra government spending is sufficient, too high or too low to close the deflationary gap.

Aggregate expenditure

Aggregate expenditure is the total amount that will be spent at different levels of GDP in a given time period. It is made up of consumption (*C*), investment (*I*), government spending (*G*) and net exports; that is, exports minus imports (*X* – *M*).

KEY TERM

Aggregate expenditure: the total amount spent in the economy at different levels of income.

While an aggregate demand curve plots total spending on the products the economy produces against different price levels, an aggregate expenditure curve plots total spending against different income levels.

Consumption

Consumption or consumer expenditure is spending by households on goods and services to satisfy current wants, for example, spending on food, clothes, travel and entertainment. The main influence on consumption is the level of disposable income. When income rises, total spending also usually rises with the rich spending more than the poor. However, while total spending rises with income, the proportion of **disposable income** that is spent tends to fall. Economists refer to this proportion as the **average propensity to consume** (apc):

$$\text{apc: } \frac{\text{consumption}}{\text{income}} = \frac{C}{Y}$$

When a person or country is poor, most if not all disposable income has to be spent to meet current needs. Indeed, consumption may exceed income with people or countries drawing on past savings or borrowing. This situation can be referred to as **dissaving**. However, when income rises, some of it can be saved. **Saving** is defined as disposable income minus consumption. The average propensity to save (aps) is the proportion of disposable income which is saved and is equal to 1 minus apc. As income rises, the actual amount saved and aps tend to increase. The rich usually have a lower apc and a higher aps than the poor.

The rich also have a lower **marginal propensity to consume** (mpc) and a higher marginal propensity to save (mps) than the poor. The mpc is the proportion of extra income which is spent:

$$\text{mpc: } \frac{\text{change in consumption}}{\text{change in income}} = \frac{\Delta C}{\Delta Y}$$

KEY TERMS

Consumption: spending by households on goods and services.

Disposable income: income minus direct taxes plus state benefits.

KEY TERMS

Average propensity to consume: the proportion of income that is consumed.

Dissaving: spending financed from past saving or from borrowing.

Saving: income minus consumption.

Marginal propensity to consume: the proportion of extra income that is spent.

1 – mpc gives mps which can also be calculated by:

$$\frac{\text{change in saving}}{\text{change in income}} = \frac{\Delta S}{\Delta Y}$$

The relationship between consumption and income and saving and income can also be investigated by using the consumption and saving functions. The **consumption function** indicates how much will be spent at different levels of income. It is given by the equation: $C = a + bY$,

KEY TERM

Consumption function: the relationship between income and consumption.

where C is consumption, a is autonomous consumption (that is the amount spent even when income is zero and which does not vary with income), b is the marginal propensity to consume and Y is disposable income. bY can also be defined as income-induced consumption because it is spending that is dependent on income. For example, if $C = \$100 + 0.8Y$ and income is \$1,000, the amount spent will be $\$100 + 0.8 \times £1{,}000 = \$900$.

The **saving function** is, in effect, the reverse of the consumption function and is given by the equation: $S = -a + sY$, where S is saving, s is the marginal propensity to save, Y is income and a is autonomous dissaving (i.e., how much of their savings people will draw on when their income is zero; this amount does not change as income changes). sY is induced saving; that is, saving that is determined by the level of income. The saving function can be used to work out how much and what proportion households will save at different income levels. For example, if $S = -\$200 + 0.2 \times \$4{,}000 = \$600$.

The **average propensity to save** will be \$600/\$40,000 = 0.15. This will also mean that apc = 1 − 0.15 = 0.85.

A number of other factors, apart from disposable income, influence consumption. These include the distribution of income, the rate of interest, the availability of credit, expectations and wealth. If income becomes more evenly distributed because of, for example, an increase in direct tax rates and state benefits, consumption is likely to rise. This is because the rich have a lower mpc than the poor. When rich people lose income they are unlikely to cut back on their spending significantly, while the poor who gain more income will spend most of the extra.

Households will also usually spend more when interest rates are low. This is because the return from saving will be reduced, buying goods on credit will be cheaper and households that have borrowed before to buy a house, for example, will have more money to spend. If it becomes easier to obtain loans it is likely that total spending will increase. However, people are unlikely to borrow and to increase their spending if they are pessimistic about the future. Indeed, expectations about future economic prospects are thought to be a significant influence on consumption. When people become more optimistic that their future jobs are secure and that their incomes will rise, they are likely to increase their spending. An increase in wealth, which may result, for example, from a rise in the value of houses or the price of shares, will also probably increase consumption.

KEY TERMS

Saving function: the relationship between income and saving.

Average propensity to save: the proportion of income that is saved.

TOP TIP

Be careful to avoid confusing the amount and the proportion of income people spend. Remember a rich person may spend much more in total than a poor person but this amount may be a smaller proportion of her/his income.

Investment

Investment is spending by firms on capital goods, such as factories, offices, machinery and delivery vehicles. The amount of investment undertaken is influenced by changes in consumer demand, the rate of interest, technology, the cost of capital goods, expectations and government policy.

If consumer demand rises, firms are likely to want to buy more capital equipment to expand their capacity. Similarly, a fall in the rate of interest is likely to stimulate a rise in investment. The cost of investment will fall. Firms that borrow to buy capital goods will find it cheaper and firms that use retained profits will find that the opportunity cost of investment will fall. Firms will also expect higher sales as lower interest rates will raise consumer demand.

Advances in technology will raise productivity of capital goods and so will probably stimulate more investment. Similarly, a fall in the price of capital equipment and/or cost of installation of capital goods is likely to raise investment.

As with consumption, expectations can play a key role in determining investment. When firms are optimistic that economic conditions are improving and demand for their products will rise, they will be encouraged to raise their investment. Governments can also seek to increase private sector investment by cutting corporation tax (the tax on company profits) and by providing investment subsidies.

Government spending

This covers spending on items such as medicines used in state hospitals, equipment used in state schools and government investment in new roads.

KEY TERM

Investment: spending by firms on capital goods.

The amount of **government spending** that is undertaken in any period is influenced by government policy, tax revenue and demographic changes. If a government wants to raise economic activity it may decide to raise its spending. Higher government tax revenue will enable a government to spend more, without resorting to borrowing. Pressure for a rise in government spending may come from an increase in the number of children (education) and/or an increase in the number of elderly people (health care).

KEY TERM

Government spending: the total of local and national government expenditure.

Net exports

The level of **net exports** is influenced by the country's GDP, other countries' GDPs, the relative price and quality competitiveness of the country's products and its exchange rate. When a country's GDP rises, demand for imports usually increases. Some products may also be diverted from the export market to the domestic market. When incomes rise abroad, demand for the country's exports is likely to increase. A rise in exports may also result from an improvement in the competitiveness of the country's products, due for example to a rise in productivity or improved marketing.

The level of the exchange rate can be a key influence on net exports. If the exchange rate falls in value, the country's exports will become cheaper and imports will become more expensive. If demand for exports and imports is elastic, export revenue will rise while import expenditure will fall, causing net exports to fall.

KEY TERM

Net exports: exports minus imports.

Income determination

Changes in income

The level of income in an economy is determined where aggregate expenditure is equal to output. If aggregate expenditure exceeds current output, firms will seek to produce more. They will employ more factors of production and GDP will rise. Whereas if aggregate expenditure is below current output, firms will reduce production. So output will change until it matches expenditure as shown in Figure 9.16.

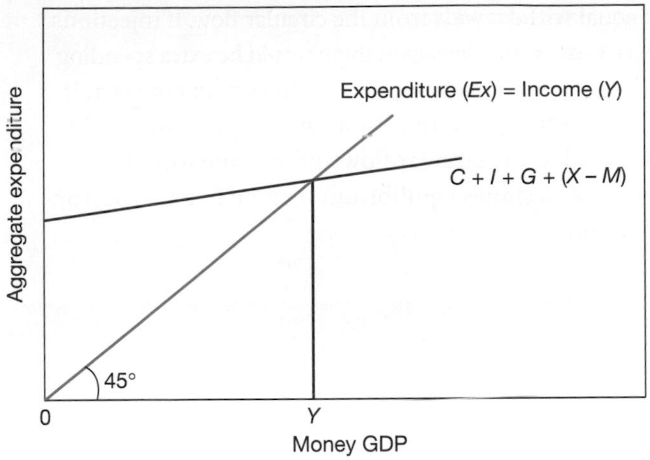

Figure 9.16 The Keynesian 45° diagram

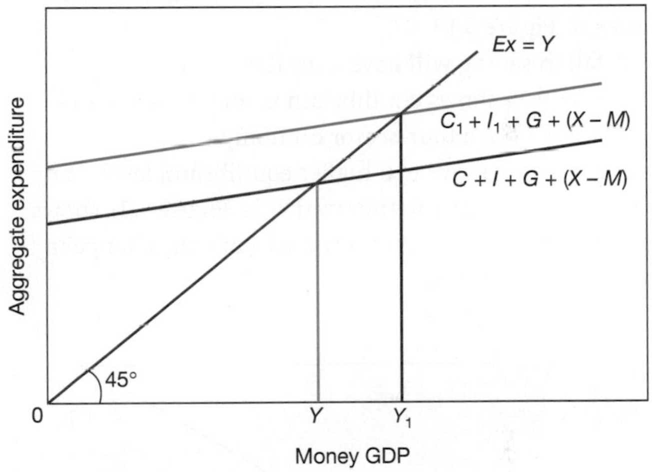

Figure 9.17 Impact of a rise in aggregate expenditure

The diagram is often referred to as the Keynesian 45° diagram. It measures money GDP on the horizontal axis and aggregate expenditure equals national income (GDP). Output is determined where the $C + I + G + (X - M)$ line cuts the 45 degree line.

If aggregate expenditure rises, perhaps because consumption and investment increase due to greater optimism, output will increase. Figure 9.17 shows GDP increasing from Y to Y_1.

TOP TIP

Remember that, while an aggregate demand curve shows total spending at different price levels, an aggregate expenditure curve shows total spending at different income levels.

Withdrawals and leakages

For income to be unchanged it is also necessary for **injections** of extra spending into the circular flow of income to equal **withdrawals** from the circular flow. If injections were greater than leakages, there would be extra spending in the economy, causing income to rise. In contrast, if withdrawals exceed injections, more spending would be added to the circular flow and income would fall. Figure 9.18 shows equilibrium income in a two-sector economy.

KEY TERMS

Injections: additions to the circular flow of income.

Withdrawals: leakages from the circular flow of income.

A rise in investment would cause a rise in GDP. This is shown in Figure 9.19.

A fall in saving will have a similar effect.

Figure 9.20 shows equilibrium income where $I + G + X = S + T + M$ in a four-sector economy.

Income will move to a higher equilibrium level if any injection rises or any withdrawal falls. Figure 9.21 shows what will happen if tax rates rise without any change in government spending.

A rise in saving will also cause GDP to fall. Indeed, a decision by households to save more can actually result in them saving less. This is because higher saving can reduce income and hence the ability of households to save. This is referred to as the **paradox of thrift**.

Inflationary and deflationary gaps

In the short run, and Keynesians argue also possibly in the long run, an economy may not achieve full employment. An **inflationary gap** will occur if aggregate expenditure exceeds the potential output of the economy. In such a situation, not all demand can be met, as there are not enough resources to do so. As a result the excess demand drives up the price level. Figure 9.22 shows that an economy is in equilibrium at a GDP of *Y*, which is above the level of output, *X*, that could be achieved with the full

KEY TERMS

Paradox of thrift: where the fact of people saving more results in a fall in saving due to lower spending and income.

Inflationary gap: the excess of aggregate expenditure over potential output (equivalent to a positive output gap).

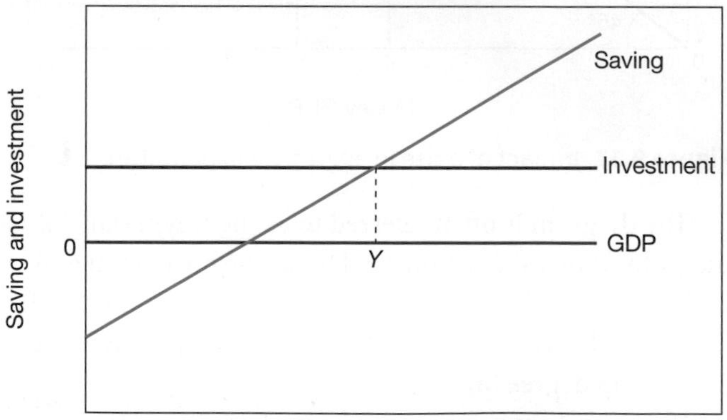

Figure 9.18 Equilibrium income in a two-sector economy

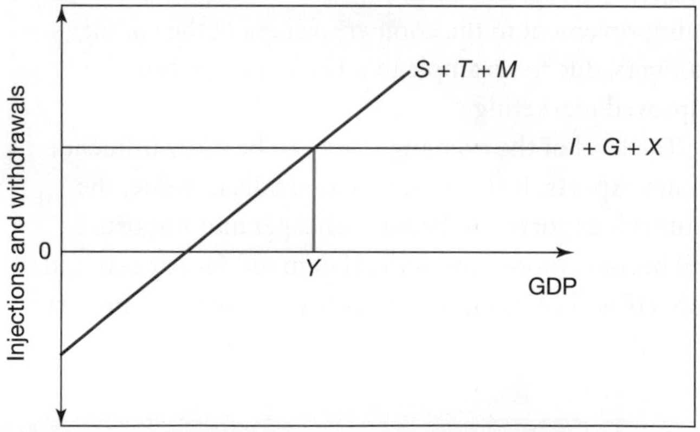

Figure 9.20 Equilibrium income in a four-sector economy

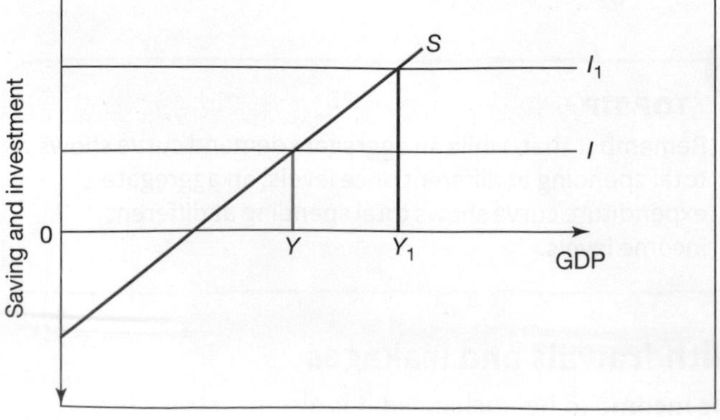

Figure 9.19 A rise in investment in a two-sector economy

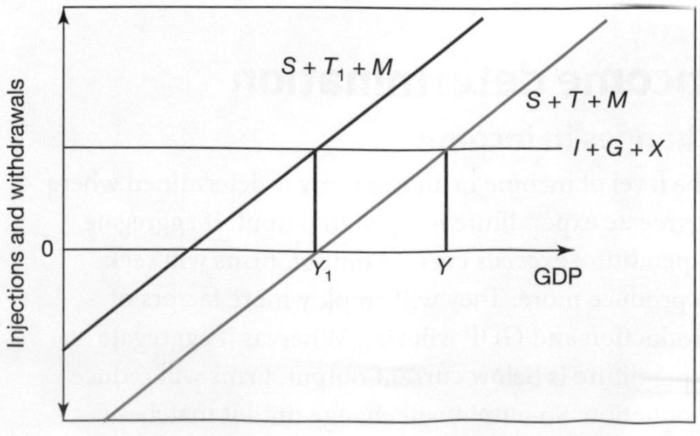

Figure 9.21 Impact of a rise in taxation on equilibrium income

employment of resources. The distance ab represents the inflationary gap.

A government may seek to reduce an inflationary gap by cutting its own spending and/or raising taxation in order to reduce aggregate expenditure. Figure 9.23 shows a reduction in government spending moving the economy back to the full employment level.

The equilibrium level of GDP may also be below the full employment level, In this case there is said to be a **deflationary gap**. Figure 9.24 shows that the lack of aggregate expenditure results in an equilibrium level of GDP of *Y*, below the full employment level of *X*. There is a deflationary gap of vw.

KEY TERM

Deflationary gap: a shortage of aggregate expenditure so that potential output is not reached (equivalent to a negative output gap).

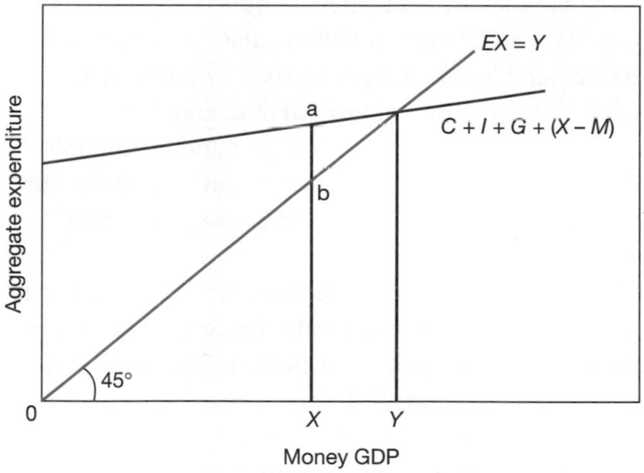

Figure 9.22 An inflationary gap

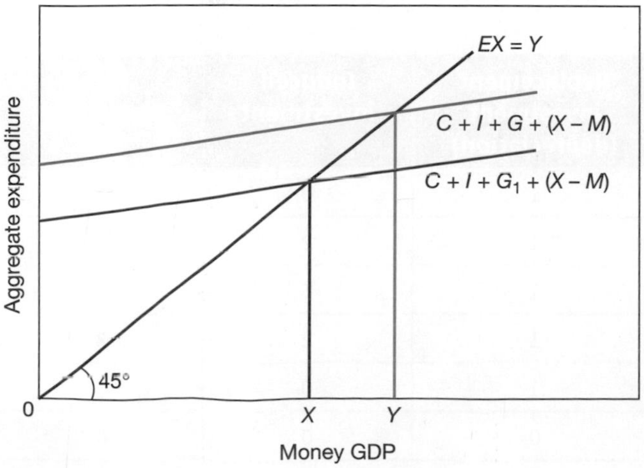

Figure 9.23 Impact of a cut in government spending

The Keynesian solution to a deflationary gap is increased government spending financed by borrowing. Figure 9.25 shows an increase in government spending eliminating a deflationary gap.

Autonomous and induced investment

Investment can rise or fall by significant amounts. Investment that is undertaken independently of changes in income is known as **autonomous investment**. For example, a firm may buy more capital goods because it is more optimistic about the future or because the rate of interest has fallen. In this case, the aggregate expenditure line will shift upwards as shown in Figure 9.26.

KEY TERM

Autonomous investment: investment that is made independent of income.

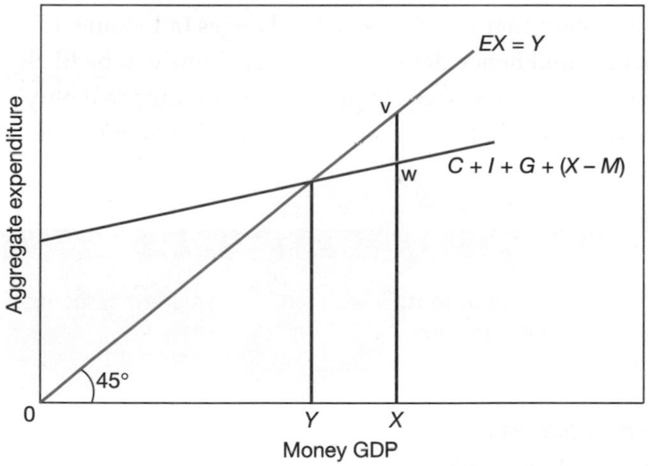

Figure 9.24 A deflationary gap

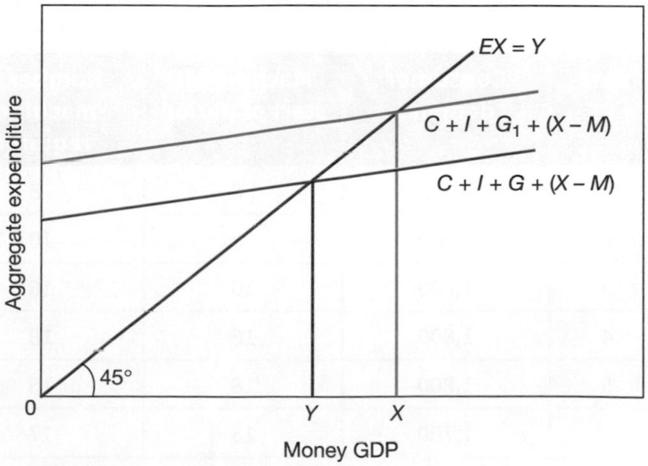

Figure 9.25 Impact of an increase in government spending

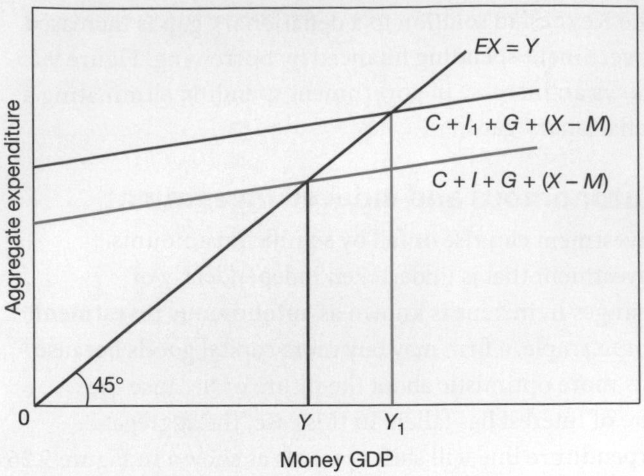

Figure 9.26 An increase in autonomous investment

As a result of an increase in investment from I to I_1, GDP rises by a multiple amount from Y to Y_1.

In contrast to autonomous investment, **induced investment** is illustrated by a movement along the expenditure line. This is because induced investment is investment that is influenced by changes in income. If income and hence demand increases, firms will be likely to buy more capital equipment. However, they will only continue to add to their capital stock if GDP continues to rise.

KEY TERM

Induced investment: investment that is made in response to changes in income.

The accelerator

The **accelerator theory** focuses on induced investment and emphasises the volatility of investment. It states that investment depends on the rate of changes in income (and hence consumer demand), and that a change in GDP will cause a greater proportionate change in investment. If a $1 million increase in GDP causes induced investment to rise by $3 million, the accelerator coefficient is said to be 3.

KEY TERMS

Accelerator theory: a model that suggests investment depends on the rate of change in income.

If GDP is rising, but at a constant rate, induced investment will not change. This is because firms can continue to buy the same number of machines each year to expand capacity. However, a change in the rate of growth of income can have a very significant influence on investment.

Table 9.9 provides an example. It is assumed that the firm starts the period with eight machines, that one machine wears out each year and that each machine can produce 100 units of output per year.

The table shows that when demand for consumer goods rises by 25% (from 800 to 1,000) in the second year, demand for capital goods rises by 200% (from 1 to 3). When the rate of growth of demand for consumer goods slows in year 4, demand for capital goods falls, investment falls to zero with the worn-out machine not being replaced, and hence production capacity is reduced.

However, an increase in demand for consumer goods does not always result in a greater percentage change in demand for capital goods. For instance, firms will not buy more capital goods if they have spare capacity or if they do not expect the rise in consumer demand to last. It may also not be possible for firms to buy many capital goods if the capital goods industries are working close to capacity. In addition, with advances in technology, the

Year	Consumer demand	Machines at start of period	Number of machines required	Replacement investment (depreciation)	Induced investment	Total investment
1	800	8	8	1	0	1
2	1,000	8	10	1	2	3
3	1,600	10	16	1	6	7
4	1,800	16	18	1	2	3
5	1,800	18	18	1	0	1
6	1,700	18	17	0	0	0

Table 9.9 Changes in investment

capital-output ratio may change with fewer machines being needed to produce a given output.

KEY TERM

Capital-output ratio: a measure of the amount of capital used to produce a given amount, or value, of output.

TOP TIP

It is often useful to bring out the link between the multiplier and the accelerator and how they tend to reinforce each other. If investment increases, real GDP is likely to increase by a multiple amount which in turn will increase investment.

The Quantity Theory of Money

Aggregate expenditure is influenced by the money supply and, in turn, can influence the money supply. One theory which seeks to explain how changes in the money supply can have an impact on the economy is the **Quantity Theory of Money**. This theory is based on what is called the **Fisher equation**, which is $MV = PT$. This is now more commonly written as $MV = PY$. M is the money supply, V is the velocity of circulation (i.e., the number of times money changes hands), P is the price level and T or Y is the transactions or output of the economy. Both sides of the equation have to equal each other since both sides represent total expenditure in the economy. To turn the equation into a theory, monetarists assume that V and Y are constant, not being affected by changes in the money supply, so that a change in the money supply causes an equal percentage change in the price level. For example, the money supply may initially be US$80 billion, the velocity of circulation 5, price level 100 and output is 4 billion. If V and Y are unchanged, an increase in the money supply by 50% to 120 would cause the price level to also rise by 50% to 150. The monetarist view is that inflation is a monetary phenomenon. Keynesians, however, argue that the equation cannot be turned into a theory since V and Y can change with a change in the money supply and so no predictions can be made about what effect a change in M will have on P.

KEY TERMS

Quantity Theory of Money: the theory that links inflation in an economy to changes in the money supply.

Fisher equation: the statement that $MV = PY$.

TOP TIP

In explaining the Quantity Theory of Money, it is always useful to give an example.

Broad and narrow money

The money supply is the total amount of money in an economy. It consists of currency in circulation plus relevant deposits. Governments measure the money supply to gain information about trends in aggregate demand, the state of financial markets and to help them in determining the direction of monetary policy.

In practice, measuring the money supply is not straightforward. This is because it is difficult to decide what to include in any measure of the money supply.

Economists define items as money if they fulfil the functions of money. However, the extent to which items carry out these functions varies and can change over time. As a result, governments use a variety of measures of the money supply, which are occasionally altered to reflect developments in the roles carried out by particular items.

There are two main measures of the money supply:

1 **Narrow money:** This is money that is used as a medium of exchange and consists of notes in circulation and cash held in banks and in balances held by commercial banks at the central bank. This is sometimes referred to as the monetary base.

2 **Broad money:** This consists of the items in narrow money plus a range of items that are concerned with money's functions as a store of value. An example is money in savings accounts.

KEY TERMS

Narrow money: money that can be spent directly.

Broad money: money used for spending and saving.

Sources of the money supply

There are five main causes of an increase in the money supply:

1 an increase in commercial bank lending
2 an increase in government spending financed by borrowing from commercial banks
3 an increase in government spending financed by borrowing from the central bank
4 the sale of government bonds to private sector financial institutions
5 more money entering than leaving the country.

Commercial banks

Commercial banks, also called high street banks and retail banks, make most of their profits by lending to customers, and when they lend they create money. This is because when a bank gives a loan (also called an advance by bankers), the borrower's account is credited with the amount borrowed. Banks are in a powerful position to create money because they can create more deposits than they have cash and other liquid assets (items that can be quickly converted into cash).

From experience, banks have found that only a small proportion of deposits are cashed. When people make payments, they tend to make use of credit cards, debit cards and electronic transfers. These means of payment involve a transfer of money using entries in the records that banks keep of their customers' deposits rather than by paying out cash. So, banks can create more deposits than they have liquid assets.

Nevertheless, they have to be careful when calculating what liquidity ratios (the proportion of liquid assets to total liabilities) to keep. The lower they keep the ratio, the more they can lend. However, they have to be able to meet their customers' demands for cash. If they miscalculate and keep too low a ratio, or if people suddenly start to cash more of their deposits, there is a risk of a run on the banking system. This was evidenced in 2008 when there were fears over the liquidity of some US and UK banks, the result being enforced government involvement. Indeed, banking is based on confidence. Customers have to believe there is enough cash and liquid assets to pay out all their deposits even though, in practice, this is not going to be the case.

The credit multiplier

By estimating what liquidity ratio to keep, a bank will be able to calculate its credit multiplier. This is also referred to as a bank or credit creation multiplier, and shows by how much additional liquid assets will enable banks to increase their liabilities. It is given by the formula:

$$\frac{\text{Value of new assets created}}{\text{Value of change in liquid assets}}$$

For example, if total deposits rise by $600 million as a result of a new cash deposit of $100 million, the credit multiplier is $600m/$100m = 6. It is also possible to calculate the **credit multiplier**, in advance, by using the formula:

$$\frac{100}{\text{liquidity ratio}}$$

KEY TERM

Credit multiplier: the process by which banks can make more loans than deposits available.

Liquidity ratio

If a bank keeps a **liquidity ratio** of 5%, the credit multiplier will be 100/5 = 20. Knowing this enables a bank to calculate how much it can lend. It first works out the possible increase in its total liabilities. This is found by multiplying the change in liquid assets by the credit multiplier. So, if the credit multiplier is 20 and liquid assets rise by $40 million, total deposits can rise by $40 million × 2 = $800 million.

To work out the change in loans (advances), the change in liquid assets is deducted from the change in liabilities. This is because the change in liabilities will include deposits given to those putting in the liquid assets. In the example, the change in loans can be $800 million – $40 million = $760 million.

In practice, however, a bank may not lend as much as the credit multiplier implies it can. This is because there may be a lack of households and firms wanting to borrow or a lack of credit-worthy borrowers. If banks persist in lending to borrowers with poor credit ratings, as was the case in the US sub-prime market, the risk of default is high and can have serious consequences on a bank's liquidity.

A bank is likely to change its liquidity ratio if people alter the proportion of their deposits they require in cash, if other banks alter their lending policies or if the country's central bank requires banks to keep a set liquidity ratio.

A central bank may seek to influence commercial banks' ability to lend. For example, it may engage in open market operations. These involve the central bank buying or selling **government securities** to change bank lending. If the central bank wants to reduce bank loans it will sell government securities. The purchasers will pay by drawing on their deposits in commercial banks and so cause the commercial banks' liquid assets to fall.

KEY TERMS

Liquidity ratio: the proportion of a bank's assets held in liquid form.

Government securities: bills and bonds issued by the government to raise money.

TOP TIP

In explaining the credit multiplier, it is useful to give a simple numerical example.

SELF-ASSESSMENT TASK 9.17

A bank keeps a liquidity ratio of 4%. It receives an additional cash deposit of $50,000. Calculate:

- **a** the credit multiplier
- **b** the potential increase in total liabilities (deposits)
- **c** the potential increase in bank lending.

Government spending financed by borrowing from commercial banks and the central bank

If the government spends more than it raises in taxation, it will have to borrow. If it borrows by selling government securities, including National Savings certificates, to the non-bank private sector (non-bank firms and the general public) it will be using existing money. The purchases will be likely to draw money out of their bank deposits. So the rise in liquid assets resulting from increased government spending will be matched by an equal fall in liquid assets as money is withdrawn.

However, if a budget deficit is financed by borrowing from commercial banks or the central bank, the money supply will increase. When a government borrows from the central bank it spends money drawn on the bank. This spending increases commercial banks' liquid assets, which will increase their ability to lend. Commercial banks will also be able to lend more if the government borrows from them by selling them short-term government securities. This is because these securities count as liquid assets and so can be used as the basis for loans.

Quantitative easing

When the rate of interest is very low, a central bank may decide to try to increase aggregate demand by engaging in **quantitative easing**. This involves a central bank buying government bonds from financial institutions, including commercial banks, in order to increase the money supply. With more liquid assets, it is hoped that the commercial banks will lend more which will increase investment and consumer expenditure and so aggregate demand and economic activity.

Quantitative easing was used in Japan in the 1990s and in the UK and USA following the global recession at the end of the first decade of the twenty-first century.

KEY TERM

Quantitative easing: a central bank buying government bonds from the private sector to increase the money supply.

Total currency flow

The **total currency flow** on the balance of payments refers to the total outflow or inflow of money resulting from international transactions as recorded in the current account, capital account and financial accounts. If a central bank maintains an exchange rate below the equilibrium level, there will be an inflow. This is because the central bank will sell the domestic currency, which will be bought by foreigners to pay for exports from the country. Exporters will deposit the money into the country's banks, which will lead to a multiple increase in the money supply.

KEY TERM

Total currency flow: the current plus capital plus financial balances of the balance of payments.

The monetary transmission mechanism

This is the process by which a change in monetary policy works through the economy via a change in aggregate demand to the price level and the real GDP. There are a number of links in this process. For example, an increase in the money supply may lower the interest rate which in turn may increase aggregate demand. Higher aggregate demand may increase output and/or the price level.

Keynesian and monetarist theoretical approaches

Keynesians are economists whose ideas are based on the work of the British economist John Maynard Keynes (1883–1946). They believe that if left to market forces there is no guarantee that the economy will achieve a full employment level of GDP. Indeed, they think that the level of GDP can deviate from the full employment level by a large amount and for long periods. In such cases they favour government intervention to influence the level of economic activity. They argue that if there is high unemployment, the government should use a deficit budget to increase aggregate demand. They believe that a government can assess the appropriate amount of extra spending to inject into the economy in such a situation. For most Keynesians, the avoidance of unemployment is a key priority.

KEY TERM

Keynesians: economists who think that government intervention is needed to achieve full employment.

John Maynard Keynes

Milton Friedman

In contrast, for **monetarists,** the control of inflation is seen as the top priority for a government. This group of economists, the best-known of whom was the American economist Milton Friedman (1912–2006), argue that inflation is the result of an excessive growth of the money supply, so they believe that the main role of a government is to control the money supply. They also maintain that attempts to reduce unemployment by increasing government spending will only succeed in raising inflation in the long run. They think that the economy is inherently stable unless disturbed by erratic changes in the growth of the money supply.

KEY TERM

Monetarists: economists who argue that control of the money supply is essential to avoid inflation.

The liquidity preference theory

Keynesians argue that the rate of interest is determined by the demand for and supply of money. They assume that the supply of money is determined by the monetary authorities and is fixed in the short run. The demand for money is explained by **liquidity preference**. There are three main motives for households and firms to hold part of their wealth in a money form.

The motive most people will be familiar with is the **transactions motive**. This is the desire to hold money to make everyday purchases and meet everyday payments. How much is held by a household or firm is influenced by the income received and the frequency of the income payments. Generally, the more income received and the more infrequently the payments are received, the higher the amount that will be held.

KEY TERMS

Liquidity preference: a Keynesian concept that explains why people demand money.

Transactions motive: the desire to hold money for the day-to-day buying of goods and services.

Firms and households usually hold rather more of their wealth in money form than they anticipate they will spend. This is so that they can meet unexpected expenses, and take advantage of unforeseen bargains. This is known as the **precautionary motive**. Money resources held for the transactions and precautionary motives are sometimes referred to as **active balances** as they are likely to be spent in the near future. They are relatively interest inelastic so that, for example, a rise in the rate of interest will not result in households and firms significantly cutting back on their holdings of money for transactions and precautionary reasons.

In contrast, the third motive for holding money balances, the **speculative motive**, is interest elastic. Households and firms will hold what are sometimes

KEY TERMS

Precautionary motive: a reason for holding money for unexpected or unforeseen events.

Active balances: the amount of money held by households or firms for possible future use.

Speculative motive: a reason for holding money with a view to make future gains from buying financial assets.

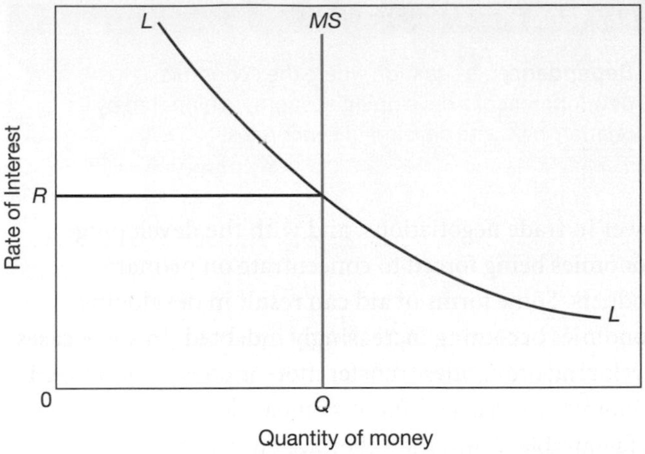

Figure 9.27 The liquidity preference theory of interest rate determination

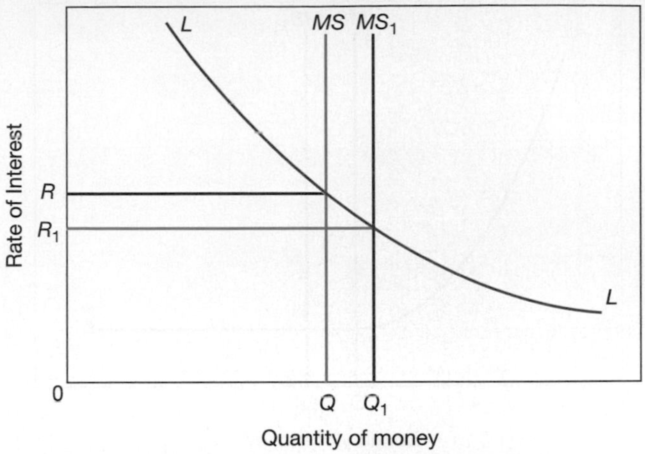

Figure 9.28 An increase in the money supply causing a fall in the rate of interest

called **idle balances** when they believe that the returns from holding financial assets are low. One financial asset that firms and households may decide to hold is government bonds. These are government securities that represent loans to the government. The price of government bonds and the rate of interest (in percentage terms) move in opposite directions. For example, a government bond with a face value of $500 may carry a fixed interest rate of 5% of its issue price. If the price of the bond rises to $1,000, the interest paid will now represent 2.5% of the price of the bond. Households and firms are likely to hold money when the price of bonds is high and expected to fall. This is because they will not be forgoing much interest and because they will be afraid of making a capital loss. The speculative demand for money will be low when the price of bonds is low and the rate of interest is high. Figure 9.27 shows the combined transactions, precautionary and speculative motives for holding money in the form of liquidity preference (or demand) for money. The rate of interest is at R, since this is where the liquidity preference curve intersects the supply of money curve.

An increase in the money supply will cause a fall in the rate of interest, as illustrated in Figure 9.28. The rate of interest falls because the rise in the money supply will result in some households and firms having higher money balances than they want to hold. As a result they use some to buy financial assets. A rise in demand for government bonds will cause the price of bonds to rise and so the rate of interest to fall.

KEY TERM

Idle balances: the amount of money held temporarily as the returns from holding financial assets are too low.

TOP TIP

It is interesting to note that, while the transactions and precautionary motives for holding money are interest inelastic, the demand for holding money for the speculative motive is interest elastic.

The liquidity trap

Although it is expected that an increase in the money supply will cause the rate of interest to fall, Keynes described a situation where it would not be possible to drive down the rate of interest by increasing the money supply. He described this situation as the **liquidity trap.** He thought it could occur when the rate of interest is very low and the price of bonds is very high. In this case, he thought that speculators would expect the price of bonds to fall in the future, so if the money supply was to be increased they would hold all the extra money. They would not buy bonds for fear of making a capital loss and because the return from holding such securities would be low. Figure 9.29 shows that at a rate of interest R, demand for money becomes perfectly elastic and the increase in the money supply has no effect on the rate of interest.

KEY TERM

Liquidity trap: a situation where interest rates cannot be reduced any more in order to stimulate an upturn in economy activity.

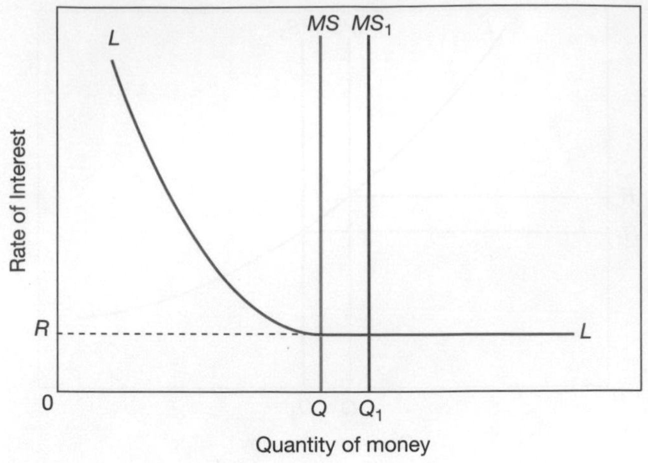

Figure 9.29 The liquidity trap

TOP TIP

The concept of the liquidity trap can be brought into an assessment of the effectiveness of monetary policy. This is because when the rate of interest is very low, it may no longer be worthwhile cutting it further and so this particular policy measure may not be an option.

Types of aid

Developing countries that need to borrow often find it relatively expensive to do so. A number have sought **foreign aid**. Such aid can take a number of methods. It may be as a grant, a loan at reduced interest rate, technical assistance or direct provision of goods and services.

KEY TERM

Foreign aid: assistance given to developing economies on favourable terms.

Aid can be tied or untied, bilateral or multilateral. Tied aid is aid that comes with conditions. For example, a grant may be given provided that it is spent on buying products from the donor country. Untied aid is aid given without conditions. Bilateral aid is aid given by one country to another country. In contrast, multilateral aid is aid given by countries to international organisations such as the World Bank or UN agency, which then distributes it to other countries.

Dependency

Some economists suggest that the problems of developing economies arise from their continued **dependence** on developed economies. International trade can be dominated by developed economies with terms of trade moving in their favour, as a result of them exercising more power in trade negotiations, and with the developing economies being forced to concentrate on primary products. Some forms of aid can result in developing economies becoming increasingly indebted. In some cases developing economies transfer more money to developed economies in terms of interest on past loans, even if given on favourable terms, than they are currently receiving in aid. Advice given and policies suggested or imposed on developing economies by international organisations, such as the **International Monetary Fund (IMF)** and the World Bank, are not always suitable given the conditions in the developing economies. For example, advising an economy to use capital intensive methods when it has a shortage of capital but an abundance of labour may not be the best advice. In addition, requiring a government to cut spending on primary education to cut a budget deficit may harm an economy's development and longer-term economic growth prospects.

KEY TERM

Dependence: a situation where the economic development of a developing economy is hindered by its relationships with developed economies.

KEY TERM

International Monetary Fund (IMF): an international organisation that promotes free trade and helps countries in balance of payments difficulties.

The role of trade, investment, multinationals and foreign direct investment

International trade

The governments of developing economies often argue for trade rather than aid. What they are actually arguing for is trade on fair terms. There are a number of reasons why international trade can act as an engine for growth. It can improve supply conditions and can reduce costs, which can lead to more efficient production as:

- economies of scale become possible because of the larger market
- the increased competition encourages domestic entrepreneurs to innovate and look for new techniques of production
- trade leads to a transfer of skills and technology from developed and developing economies
- specialisation and trade increases incomes and so provides the increased savings which can be used for investment.

International trade may also stimulate demand. The expansion of production to cater for the export market may increase employment. The result will be an expansion of spending power in the home market that will create demand for domestic output.

Although the beneficial effects of international trade upon the growth rate of developing economies have a strong theoretical basis, many economists have a far more pessimistic view. This is based upon the pattern of world trade that emerged as economies specialised. Developing economies have tended to specialise in primary products. Those developing economies that have specialised in agricultural products have been at a disadvantage in trading relations since the prices of agricultural products have declined relative to the prices of manufactured goods and services over time. This is for three main reasons:

1 The income elasticity of demand for primary products is low so that, as world incomes have risen, there has been little extra demand for agricultural products and demand has shifted to manufactured goods and services.
2 Producers of manufactured goods in developed economies have an element of monopoly power, which they have used to maintain high prices.
3 Subsidies provided to farmers in the USA and Europe put downward pressure on global agricultural prices. For instance, it is claimed that US subsidies given to its cotton farmers have deflated the global price and have given US cotton farmers an unfair competitive advantage.

As trading patterns have been seen by some governments as exploitative, a number of developing economies, such as Venezuela, have adopted import substitution policies and sought to diversify their economies. They have tried to prevent imports of manufactured goods from developed economies in order to develop their own manufacturing industries. Other developing economies, such as the Philippines, have gone for export-led growth. Generally, the secondary sector is becoming more important in developing economies and some are gaining comparative advantage in industries formerly dominated by developed economies.

Investment

Investment may not be easy for some developing economies to achieve because of the lack of savings and the lack of financial institutions to channel those savings that do exist from lenders to entrepreneurs wanting to establish new firms and to expand the output of existing firms. There may also be a shortage of entrepreneurs.

If, however, investment can be encouraged, a **virtuous cycle** may be created as shown in Figure 9.30.

One of the reasons China achieved rapid economic growth in the 1990s and first decade of the twenty-first century is, in part, because of high levels of investment.

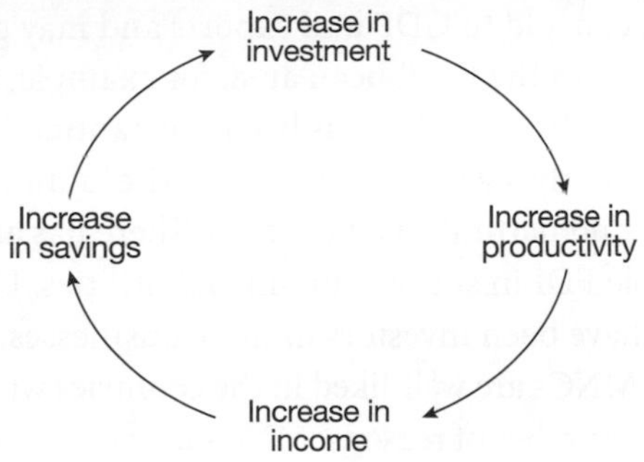

Figure 9.30 A virtuous cycle

> **KEY TERM**
>
> **Virtuous cycle:** the links between, for example, an increase in investment, increase in productivity, increase in income and increase in saving.

The country already had high levels of savings but over these two decades it also developed its range and sophistication of financial institutions.

Multinational corporations and foreign direct investment

One way that developing economies can achieve a rise in investment is to attract multinational companies. A multinational corporation (MNC) is defined as a firm that operates in more than one country. In other words, it is a business with a parent company based in one country but with production or service operations in at least one other country. The largest MNCs – such as the Coca-Cola Corporation, Ford, Hilton Hotels, Nestlé, McDonald's, Tata, Toyota and so on – are global operations, with manufacturing and retail outlets in many countries of the world. 259

Through their activities, MNCs provide **foreign direct investment (FDI)** to the economies in which they operate. This is investment that is necessary to produce a good or service in a foreign country. FDI, therefore, involves capital flows between countries. It should not be confused with portfolio investment, which is the purchase of shares by foreign investors in businesses that are located in another country.

> **KEY TERM**
>
> **Foreign direct investment (FDI):** the setting up of production units or the purchase of existing production units in other countries.

The activities of MNCs and the effects of FDI on the economies of the recipient countries have been the subject of much debate and discussion by economists and politicians. MNCs can bring in new technology, new ideas, can add to GDP and exports and may generate employment. In the Caribbean area, for example, the impact of FDI from MNCs has been substantial. It has been particularly significant in the bauxite, alumina, petroleum and natural gas industries. There has also been considerable FDI in sugar, tourism and utilities. US MNCs especially have been investors in these businesses.

Not all MNCs are well-liked in the countries where they invest, for a number of reasons. MNCs may not create higher employment and higher incomes if they replace domestic firms, they may deplete non-renewable resources and may create pollution. They may also send most of their profits back to their home countries and may employ foreign rather than home labour, especially in the top-paid jobs. Some of the products they sell may not improve people's living standards. For instance, faced with declining sales in their home markets, a number of European and US tobacco firms are now putting considerable time and effort into marketing their cigarettes in Asian and African economies. In addition, MNCs put pressure on governments to pursue policies that are beneficial to them but not the economies in which they are producing. Their mobility and considerable economic powers mean that they often negotiate favourable tax breaks and exemption from some environmental laws.

KEY CONCEPT LINK

Progress and development: In debating the effects of MNCs on developing economies, the concepts of progress and development are significant. The presence of an MNC in a developing economy may or may not increase its economic growth rate and its effects on living standards may or may not be beneficial.

TOP TIP

Remember that while an MNC may pay lower wages in a host country than it pays in its country of origin, it may still benefit workers in the host country if it pays more than paid by domestic employers to similar workers.

The impact of external debt

External debt can be a major obstacle to future economic development. As mentioned earlier, repaying the debt can divert funds away from improving the welfare of the population and increasing the economy's growth potential.

A high level of external debt can make it difficult and expensive for a developing economy to attract more funds for development.

Some governments reduce their ability to borrow more in the future by defaulting on past loans. These governments may consider that, for instance, avoiding cutting spending on education and health care may be more important than meeting their obligations to repay loans.

SELF-ASSESSMENT TASK 9.18

Read the feature below and then answer the questions that follow.

China's expansion into other economies

Although China's outward FDI is growing fast, it is still less than inward FDI. China's FDI first grew largely because of its search for energy, minerals and land in African economies. It is now moving into richer markets in a bid to get more recognition for its products and to take advantage of advanced technology.

Its investment in the Caribbean is relatively low but may increase in the future, partly because its location makes it an appropriate base to export to the USA and Canada. The region does, however, have relatively high wages and modest resources.

1 Analyse what effect an excess of inward FDI over outward FDI will have on a country's balance of payments.

2 Discuss whether China is likely to invest more in the Caribbean in the future.

The role of the International Monetary Fund and the World Bank

The International Monetary Fund

The International Monetary Fund (IMF) was set up in 1945 after the Bretton Woods Conference, to help promote the health of the world economy after World War II. With headquarters in Washington, DC, it currently has 188 members. Non-members include Cuba and North Korea.

The purposes and responsibilities of the IMF include:

- to promote international monetary cooperation
- to facilitate the expansion and balanced growth of international trade
- to provide exchange rate stability
- to assist in setting up a multinational system of payments
- to make resources available to members experiencing balance of payments difficulties, on condition that adequate safeguards are provided.

These activities have been central to the development of global trade since a stable system of international payments and exchange rates is necessary for trade to take place between two countries. In carrying out its responsibilities, the IMF has three main functions that are known as surveillance, technical assistance and lending. The first two are in line with its mission of promoting global growth and economic stability by encouraging countries to adopt sound economic policies. The third function is used where member countries experience difficulties in financing their balance of payments.

The World Bank

Like the IMF, the World Bank was established at the Bretton Woods Conference. Its function is to provide financial support for internal investment payments such as building new roads, improving infrastructure and constructing new health facilities.

It is best described as the World Bank Group through the activities of its five constituent agencies. These are:

- International Bank for Reconstruction and Development (IBRD)
- International Finance Corporation (IFC)
- International Development Association (IDA)
- Multilateral Investment Guarantee Agency (MIGA)
- International Centre for Settlement of Investment Disputes (ICSID).

The IBRD and IDA provide low- or no-interest loans and grants to countries that do not have favourable access to international credit markets. Therefore, the focus of activities is very much on developing economies. Grants are only provided to the world's poorest economies. Loans cover areas such as:

- health and education – in order to enhance human development in a country for improving sanitation and combating AIDS
- agriculture and rural development – for irrigation programmes and water supply projects
- environmental protection – for reducing pollution and for ensuring that there is compliance and pollution regulation
- infrastructure – roads, railways, electricity
- governance – for anti-corruption reasons.

Loans tend to be linked to conditions that involve wider-reaching changes being made to the economic policies of the recipient economies. But the IMF and World Bank have been criticised for imposing the so-called 'Washington Consensus' on developing economies. The Washington Consensus was devised by a US economist, who proposed ten economic policy prescriptions. These policy prescriptions, which include privatisation, deregulation and trade liberalisation, are based on increasing the role of market forces. Such an approach may increase efficiency, which would increase productive potential. It may, however, increase income inequality and may not work if the problem that is holding back development is not too much government intervention but market failure such as a lack of financial markets.

The headquarters of the IMF

SELF-ASSESSMENT TASK 9.19

Between 2011 and 2014 the Bolivian economy grew at its fastest rate for 30 years. This coincided with a marked reduction in its poverty rate and a change in its budget position from a deficit to a balance. The Bolivian government was praised by both the IMF and the World Bank for its sound fiscal policy.

1 Analyse why rapid economic growth may be associated with:
   - a fall in poverty
   - a change in the budget position from a deficit to a balance.

2 Explain what type of fiscal policy the IMF and World Bank may describe as 'sound'.

The impact of corruption and legal framework in an economy

An inadequately developed legal framework can encourage corruption. If firms and governments are corrupt, funds that could have been used for development may be diverted to the owners of the firms and to government officials. For example, a lack of property rights may result in firms polluting local rivers without any penalties. Corrupt government officials may steal money given as aid or raised in tax revenue. They may also be bribed to give contracts to certain firms.

SUMMARY

In this chapter it has been shown that:

- Economic development involves more than economic growth.
- Actual growth involves a movement within a PPC towards the curve, whereas potential growth is shown by a shift of the PPC to the right.
- Economic growth is caused by increases in the quantity and quality of resources.
- Economic growth may increase material living standards but may also create pollution and deplete resources.
- GDP is the income of a country, whereas GNI is the income of a country's population wherever they earn it.
- There are a number of measures of living standards including GNI per head, the HDI and MPI.
- The size of a country's labour force is influenced by the number of people of working age, the school leaving age, the retirement age and the proportion of women who work.
- Full employment may be achieved by increases in aggregate demand, while supply side policy measures may reduce the natural rate of unemployment.
- The main types of unemployment are frictional, structural and cyclical.
- Unemployment results in lost output, lost tax revenue and increased government spending on unemployment benefits.
- Patterns of (un)employment change as countries develop, and as demand and technology change.
- There are two main measures of unemployment: the claimant count and the labour force survey. Both measures have their shortcomings.
- Reflationary fiscal and monetary policy measures and supply side policy measures are used to try to reduce unemployment.
- A closed economy is one that does not engage in international trade, whereas an open economy is one with an international trade sector.
- Initial changes in aggregate demand result in greater final changes in aggregate demand because of the multiplier effect.
- Aggregate expenditure consists of consumption, investment, government expenditure and net exports.
- An increase in aggregate expenditure will increase money GDP.
- An inflationary gap will occur if aggregate expenditure exceeds the full employment level of output.
- An increase in investment may be caused by changes in income or by changes in other influences such as changes in technology and changes in business optimism.
- The accelerator theory states that the level of investment depends on the rate of change in GDP.
- The Quantity Theory of Money states that changes in the price level are directly related to changes in the money supply.
- The narrow money supply is used largely to make payments whereas the broad money supply is money used both to make payments and to save.
- Commercial banks create money by lending to their customers.
- Keynesians favour government intervention to achieve full employment, while monetarists argue that control of the money supply is necessary to avoid inflation.
- The liquidity preference theory states that there are three motives for demand in money which are the transactions, precautionary and speculative motives.
- Aid may be given from one country to another country or through an international organisation.
- The development of a developing economy may be hindered by its relationship with developed economies.
- Trade and investment may promote development if trade is on fair terms and if investment, including FDI, raises GDP and employment and does not generate pollution and deplete resources.
- The IMF and World Bank are international organisations that help economies with balance of payments difficulties that are in need of loans and grants.
- Corruption and a lack of a developed legal framework can hinder development.

Exam-style questions

1 a Why may a country experience a rise in unemployment? [12]

b Discuss whether an increase in unemployment is always harmful. [13]

2 A country experiences an increase in its GDP. Discuss whether this means that its citizens will enjoy an increase in their standard of living. [25]

3 **High taxes do not help in a recession**

In 2009, there was an economic recession in many countries. One aspect of the recession was that unemployment rose. Governments paid large subsidies to a number of industries to try to stop the rise in unemployment. This increased the government's debt and affected its other expenditue.

In an attempt to recover part of the extra expenditure, some governments increased income tax rates on people who had high salaries.

However, critics of this policy argue that higher tax rates do not work. They say that the proportion of revenue received from top taxpayers falls and does not rise as taxes increase and the higher taxes cause damaging effects on the economy. It is better, they say, to decrease taxes. The decrease in taxes brings the government more revenue, not less revenue. Their opinion is supported by evidence from the past, as is seen in the effect on tax receipts of changing tax rates in the US as shown in Figure 9.31.

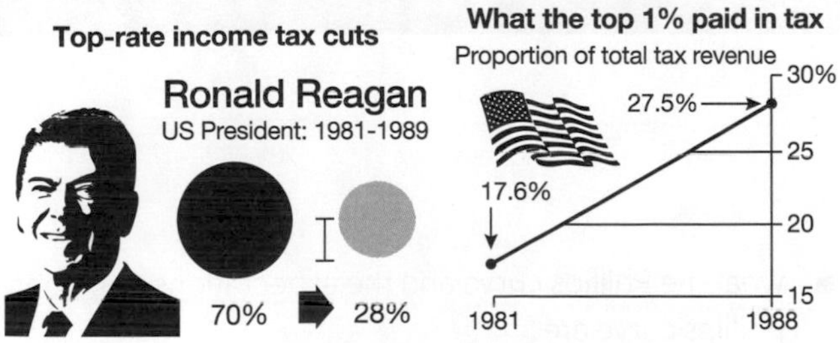

Figure 9.31 Cutting taxes raises revenue

Source: The Times, 7 May 2009 p.28.

It is suggested that this opposite policy of reducing tax rates is better. Lower tax rates actually boost both the economy and tax revenues. For example, Russia, Latvia and Estonia reduced their highest tax rate and replaced a complicated system of taxes with a single income tax rate of 10%. They enjoyed a huge economic boost as a result.

Another aspect of the recession was that businesses found it difficult to borrow money from the commercial banks. In order to try and make borrowing easier and help businesses, some central banks lowered their interest rates. The central banks also bought government bonds in an attempt to increase the supply of money in the economy.

a Explain what is meant by a recession. [3]

b The article states that 'higher tax rates do not work'.

i What does the article mean by this statement? [3]

ii Is there enough evidence in the article to justify this statement? [6]

c Discuss why the actions of the central banks mentioned in the article might have been expected to ease the recession. [8]

Source: Cambridge International AS and A Level Economics 9708 Paper 41 Q1 May/June 2011.

4 The main way a developing country could become a developed country is for government policy to concentrate on the protection of domestic industry and investment in infrastructure. Do you agree that this is the best policy? [25]

Source: Cambridge International AS and A Level Economics 9708 Paper 41 Q7 May/June 2011.

Chapter 10: Government macro intervention
A Level

Learning objectives

On completion of this chapter you should know:

- the aims of government macroeconomic policy
- the relationship between the internal and external value of money
- the relationship between the balance of payments and inflation
- the possible trade-off between inflation and unemployment
- what the Phillips curve and the expectations-augmented Phillips curve are
- the problems arising from conflicts between policy objectives
- the existence of government failure in macroeconomic policies
- how the Laffer curve illustrates the possible relationship between tax rates and tax revenue.

Introduction

The successful achievement of government macroeconomic aims may be hindered by the interconnectedness of problems and the resulting policy conflicts For instance, in seeking to reduce unemployment, government policy measures may increase the inflation rate. The Phillips curve shows a possible relationship between unemployment and inflation, although this relationship, in the long run, is challenged by the expectations-augmented Phillips curve.

The existence of policy conflicts can result in government failure, with government intervention resulting in greater inefficiency. An example of such possible government failure can be shown on the Laffer curve, where an increase in tax rates may actually reduce tax revenue.

The key concepts of choice, efficiency, progress and development are important in considering what economic policy measures a government selects to achieve its aims and in assessing the relative strengths of the different policy measures.

The aims of government macroeconomic policy

The aims of government macroeconomic policy were outlined in Chapter 5. Governments seek to achieve price stability. This actually means low and stable inflation. An increasing number of governments are setting an **inflation target** for their central banks to achieve. An inflation target makes the central bank more accountable and may reduce inflationary expectations if firms, householders and workers have confidence in the central bank's ability to meet the target.

KEY TERM

Inflation target: the rate a central bank is set to achieve.

Governments may have different aims for the balance of payments. Most governments do seek to achieve a balance on the current account of the balance of payments over time. In the short run, however, a government may welcome a current account deficit if it arises from the import of raw materials and capital goods. Alternatively, it may encourage a current account surplus in order to boost aggregate demand or to provide funds to repay external debt.

A government may also encourage a surplus on the financial account of the balance of payments by attracting foreign direct investment. The investment could increase output and employment in the country.

There are a range of aims a government may have for its exchange rate. A government will usually seek to prevent wide fluctuations in the value of a floating exchange rate because such fluctuations are destabilising. It may decide to operate a fixed exchange rate or a managed float. In these two cases, it may have to maintain the rate or may seek to alter its value. It may attempt to raise the external value of the currency in order to reduce inflationary pressure or it may seek to reduce its value to gain a competitive advantage.

A lower exchange rate may increase output and create jobs. Governments seek to achieve as low unemployment as possible. The nearer an economy is to full employment, the higher output will be and the higher the living standards people are likely to enjoy. Governments will be particularly anxious to reduce long-term unemployment as such unemployment can result in workers being discouraged and dropping out of the labour force.

A reduced labour force would lower potential output. Governments seek to increase both actual and potential output. They try to achieve sustained growth by matching the trend growth in potential output with increases in actual output. They also try to ensure that economic growth is sustainable so that future generations will be able to enjoy higher living standards. As well as trying to achieve economic growth, governments aim for economic development. They seek, for instance, to increase life expectancy and educational opportunities.

KEY CONCEPT LINK

Progress and development: Governments aim for both economic progress and economic development. It is easier to assess their performance in achieving economic progress as, for example, economic growth, unemployment, inflation and the balance on the current account position can be measured. There are measures of economic development, such as the Human Development Index, but no measure captures all the influences on economic development and some of the measures are hard to measure as they are subjective.

TOP TIP

Remember that a government is likely to prioritise its aims according to its current macroeconomic performance.

SELF-ASSESSMENT TASK 10.1

At the start of 2014 India was experiencing a decline in its economic growth rate, a rise in its inflation rate and a decline in its current account deficit. The IMF recommended that the Indian government and central bank should raise interest rates, reduce the budget deficit and improve bank supervision and invest more in infrastructure.

1 Explain why a decline in a country's economic growth rate might be expected to reduce rather than increase its inflation rate.
2 Explain whether increasing interest rates would suggest that economic growth or inflation is the top macroeconomic objective.
3 Discuss what effect an increase in government spending on the country's infrastructure may have on the budget deficit.

The relationship between the internal and external value of money

The internal value of a country's currency and its external value may be closely connected. The internal value will fall as a result of inflation. Each unit of the currency will buy less in the domestic market.

If the internal value of a country's money falls as a result of a rise in its inflation rate above that of rival countries, demand for its products will fall. As a result, demand for the country's currency will fall as foreigners buy fewer of the country's exports, while the supply of the currency on the foreign exchange market will rise as more imports are purchased. The reduced demand and higher supply of the currency will cause a depreciation, as shown in Figure 10.1

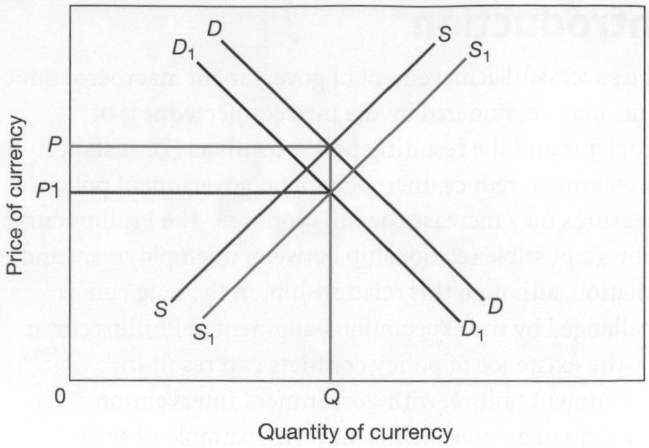

Figure 10.1 The effect of higher inflation on the external value of a currency

A change in the external value of the currency – the exchange rate – will, in turn, affect the internal purchasing power of a country's money. A fall in the exchange rate will raise the price of a country's imports in terms of the home currency. This will directly and indirectly reduce the value of the country's money. Each unit of the currency will now buy fewer of the now more expensive finished imported products. For example, originally US$1 may exchange for 8 Argentine pesos. If the value of the US dollar then falls to 6 Argentine pesos, an Argentine import priced at 480 Argentine pesos, will rise in price from US$60 to US$80. Purchasing power may also be reduced as a result of the increase in the price of imported raw materials and the reduction in competitive pressure, driving up the prices of domestically produced products. So the internal and external values of a country's money tend to be directly related, with a fall in the internal value leading to a fall in the external value and vice versa.

TOP TIP

Remember that, while the internal and external values of a currency are likely to be connected, this may not always be the case. For example, a country may experience inflation, but if it has a fixed exchange rate or if its inflation rate is below that of rival countries, its external value may not even fall. Indeed, it may rise.

The relationship between the balance of payments and inflation

As mentioned above, if a country's inflation rate rises above that of its main competitors, its price competitiveness will fall. Export revenue will decline while import expenditure rises and the current account balance will deteriorate.

An increase in a current account surplus may cause inflation as it will mean that net exports are making an increasing contribution to aggregate demand and more money will be flowing into the country than leaving it. This upward pressure on the domestic price level and so downward pressure on the internal value of the currency may, however, be short-lived. This is because an increasing current account surplus may cause a rise in the exchange rate. An appreciation may reduce the surplus and will tend to reduce the inflation rate as the price of imported products will fall and there will be more pressure on domestic firms to keep their prices low.

A net inflow on the financial account may reduce a country's inflation rate if MNCs bring in advanced technology and increase competitive pressure within the economy.

The relationship between unemployment and inflation

Economists have devoted considerable attention to the relationship between unemployment and inflation. The most famous study on the relationship was published in 1958 by Bill Phillips, a New Zealand economist based at the London School of Economics. He analysed historical data on the relationship between changes in unemployment and money wages (taken as an indicator of inflation) in the UK over the period 1861–1957. He found an inverse relationship, as shown in Figure 10.2.

A fall in unemployment may cause higher inflation due to extra aggregate demand and the possible upward pressure on wages.

The traditional **Phillips curve** suggests that a government can select its best combination of unemployment and inflation and can trade off the two. For example, if the current unemployment rate is 8% and its inflation rate is 4%, a government may seek to lower unemployment to 5% by implementing expansionary fiscal or monetary policy measures, while accepting this improvement may have to be bought at the cost of higher inflation.

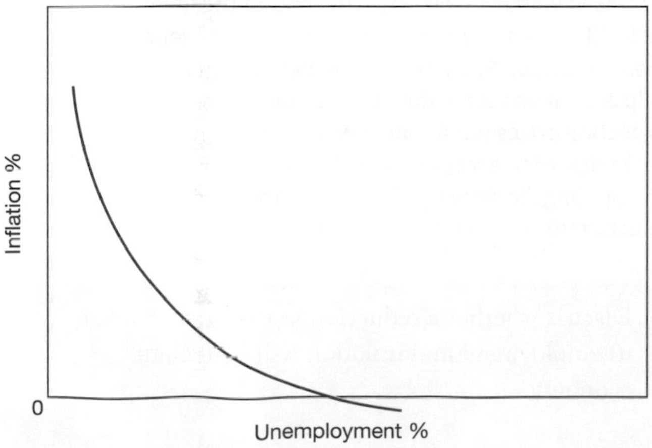

Figure 10.2 The Phillips curve

> **KEY TERM**
>
> **Phillips curve:** a curve that shows the relationship between the unemployment rate and the inflation rate over a period of time.

However, this interpretation supported by Keynesians is questioned by monetarists. They argue that, while there may be a short-run trade-off, in the long run government policy measures to increase aggregate demand will have no impact on unemployment but will only succeed in raising the inflation rate. To support this view, Milton Friedman developed the **expectations-augmented Phillips curve**, as shown by the vertical line in Figure 10.3. The position of this line is determined by the natural rate of unemployment.

> **KEY TERM**
>
> **Expectations-augmented Phillips curve:** a diagram that shows that while there may be a trade-off between unemployment and inflation in the short run, there is no trade-off in the long run.

Figure 10.3 shows that an increase in aggregate demand does succeed in reducing unemployment from the previous 8% to 4% but creates inflation of 5% and moves the economy on to a higher short-run Phillips curve. Firms expand their output and more people are attracted into the labour force as a result of the higher wages. However, when firms realise that their costs have risen and their real profits are unchanged, they will cut back on their output

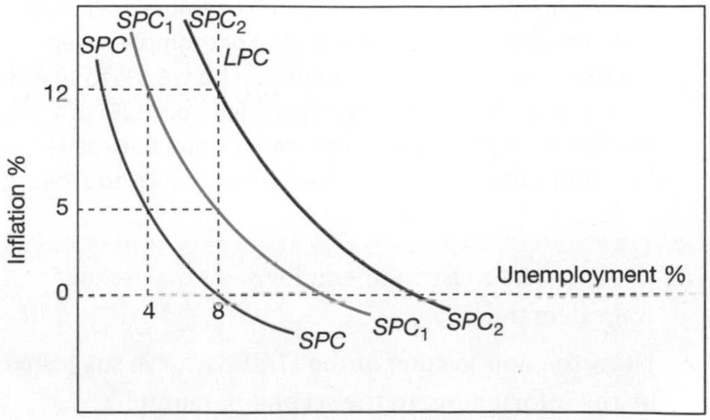

Figure 10.3 The expectations-augmented Phillips curve

and some workers, recognising that real wages have not risen, will leave the labour force. Unemployment returns to 8% in the long run but inflation of 5% has now been built into the system. Firms and workers will presume that inflation will continue at 5% when deciding on their prices and putting in their wage claims. Another attempt to reduce unemployment to 4% will now eventually move the economy to SPC2 and push up the inflation rate to 12%.

KEY CONCEPT LINK

Scarcity and choice, equilibrium and efficiency: Choice and efficiency are important concepts for a government when it is deciding its macroeconomic priorities and the policy measures it employs. Policy objectives may conflict in the short run but a government will seek to use policy measures that work as efficiently as possible and that avoid adverse side effects on other aims.

TOP TIP

To explain or evaluate the relationship between unemployment and inflation, it is useful to compare the views suggested by the traditional and the expectations-augmented Phillips curves.

SELF-ASSESSMENT TASK 10.2

Study Table 10.1 and then answer the questions that follow.

Year	Unemployment %	Inflation %
2008	6.1	2.8
2009	9.0	–0.3
2010	9.8	1.4
2011	7.9	2.6
2012	7.8	1.6
2013	7.8	0.6

Table 10.1 Unemployment and inflation rates in Sweden 2008–2013

1 Explain why changes in the unemployment rate and changes in the inflation rate may move in opposite directions.

2 Analyse whether the data above support this inverse relationship.

SELF-ASSESSMENT TASK 10.3

Read the feature below and then answer the questions that follow.

Unemployment and inflation

There is some evidence to suggest that the link between unemployment and inflation is weakening. Changes in unemployment in a number of countries appear to be having less influence on inflation. In the past, workers pressed for wage rises when unemployment fell, which pushed up the price level, and when unemployment rose they reduced their wage demands. For example, when the US unemployment rate increased from 6.3% to 10.8% from 1980 to 1982, the inflation rate fell from 12% to 4.5%. In contrast, a steeper rise in unemployment between 2007 and 2009 saw inflation fall from only 2.4% to 1.7%.

A new version of the Phillips curve may have developed, with inflation remaining stable as unemployment fluctuates. This may be because central banks have increased workers' and firms' belief that the inflation rate will remain stable and this belief has influenced their behaviour. Such a change in behaviour may also help economies avoid deflation during a recession. Expecting prices not to fall may mean that workers are reluctant to accept wage cuts and because of anticipating stable wage demands, firms may be reluctant to cut prices.

1 Explain why a rise in unemployment may reduce wage demands.

2 Draw the new version of the Phillips curve suggested by the information in the second paragraph.

3 Discuss whether a reduction in the link between unemployment and inflation will benefit an economy.

The problems arising from conflicts between policy objectives

Government reflationary fiscal and monetary policy measures designed to either reduce unemployment and/or increase the economic growth rate may, as indicated above, increase the rate of inflation. Similarly, if a government seeks to reduce demand-pull inflation by adopting deflationary fiscal and monetary policy measures, it may reduce the economic growth rate and increase the unemployment rate. A government may seek to avoid these policy conflicts by introducing supply side policy measures that may, in the long run, reduce the inflation and unemployment rates and increase the economic growth rate.

A conflict may also arise between the aims of low inflation and a reduction in a current account deficit. A central bank may raise the rate of interest. Such a move will not only increase unemployment; there will also be a knock-on effect on the balance of payments position and the exchange rate. A rise in the interest rate is likely to lead to an appreciation in the exchange rate. This could worsen the current account position but may attract hot money flows.

There may also be a conflict between creating greater income equality and stimulating economic growth. Making income tax rates more progressive and increasing benefits to low-income groups may discourage effort and enterprise and may reduce FDI. There is, however, the possibility that raising the living standards of the poor may improve the health and education of part of the labour force and so raise productivity. In addition, effort and enterprise may be more influenced by wage rates and profit levels than tax rates. Similarly, FDI may be attracted despite relatively high tax rates if, for instance, demand in the country is increasing and the country's workers are becoming more skilled.

To avoid conflicts between policy objectives, a government may employ a separate policy measure for each objective. Such an approach is said to be following **Tinbergen's rule**. For example, a government may cut income tax in order to reduce unemployment, while it may devalue the currency in a bid to improve the current account position. In practice governments use a combination of fiscal, monetary and supply side policy measures. For example, in 2013 the Brazilian government used a variety of measures in a bid to reduce inflation. These included raising the rate of interest and subsidising electricity and public transport.

KEY TERM

Tinbergen's rule: for every policy aim there must be at least one policy measure.

TOP TIP

In assessing the effectiveness of a particular policy measure in solving a particular economic problem, for example a high inflation rate, it is useful to consider the possible adverse effects it may have on other policy objectives.

Government failure in macroeconomic policy

There are a number of reasons for **government macroeconomic failure** – when government macroeconomic policy measures may actually cause a deterioration rather than an improvement in economic performance. For instance, if a government understates the size of the national income multiplier, it may increase its spending by too much. This may result in swapping one problem, a negative output gap, with another problem, a positive output gap.

KEY TERM

Government macroeconomic failure: government intervention reducing rather than increasing economic performance.

In the case of a number of policy measures there may be a series of time lags. For example, there may be a delay before a government recognises that inflationary pressure is building up – a recognition lag. There may then be an implementation lag – the time it takes to draw up and introduce a policy measure such as a rise in income tax. There is then the time it takes for the policy measure to influence the behaviour of households and firms – a behavioural lag.

By the time a policy measure does have an impact on economic behaviour, the level of economic activity may have changed, which may make the policy measure inappropriate. Indeed, governments may seek to use fiscal and monetary policy measures to offset the effects of the trade cycle, but these measures sometimes reinforce the trade cycle rather than acting **counter-cyclically**.

KEY TERM

Counter-cyclically: going against the fluctuations in economic activity.

As well as there being a delay before households, workers and firms react to policy measures, there is the possibility that they may not respond in the expected way. For example, during an economic boom a central bank may raise the rate of interest in the expectation that it will encourage saving and discourage borrowing. If, however, households and firms are optimistic about the future they may continue to borrow and spend.

Some elected governments may be tempted to introduce popular policy measures when elections are approaching. Measures such as an increase in government spending on pensions may win votes but may not necessarily improve economic performance. Government policy measures may also be influenced by powerful pressure groups and, as mentioned in the previous chapter, there is the possibility of government corruption. For instance, past attempts to reduce class sizes and increase resources in education and improve health care in Honduras were hindered by corrupt government officials who stole money from government budgets. This led to the country coming 140th out of 177 countries in the 2013 Corruption Perception Index. This index scores countries on a scale from 0 (highly corrupt) to 100 (very clean). Honduras scored 26.

KEY CONCEPT LINK

Equilibrium and efficiency: The key concept of efficiency is clearly linked to government failure. When a government implements a policy measure, it is seeking to improve economic efficiency but, as explained in this chapter, there are a number of reasons why the measures may worsen rather than improve the economy's performance.

SELF-ASSESSMENT TASK 10.4

Economic growth in Japan remained sluggish in the first quarter of 2014. A month later the Japanese government raised the country's sales tax from 5% to 8% to reduce the budget deficit. At the same time, export revenue was rising by less than import expenditure. Between April 2013 and March 2014 the value of the yen fell by 27% against the US dollar. Most Japanese exporters had reacted to the fall by increasing their profit margins rather than sales overseas. Some Japanese economists described the continuing increase in the trade deficit as a case of a missing J-curve effect. There are a number of explanations given for this phenomenon. One is that energy now accounts for a high proportion of Japanese imports. Another is the declining competitiveness of Japan's electronics industry and a steady outflow of manufacturing capacity to other countries.

1 Explain why seeking to reduce a budget deficit may conflict with the aim of increasing the country's economic growth rate.
2 What does the information suggest might have happened to the prices of Japanese exports between April 2013 and March 2014?
3 Explain one government macroeconomic aim which might benefit from a government reducing its budget deficit.
4 a What is meant by 'a missing J-curve effect'?
  b How may 'energy accounting for a high proportion of Japanese imports' explain a missing J-curve effect?
5 Discuss how the Japanese government could encourage its firms to keep more of their production in Japan.

The Laffer curve

The **Laffer curve** may be considered to be linked to government failure in two ways. One is that it shows that when tax rates are high, raising them further will be counterproductive.

> **KEY TERM**
>
> **Laffer curve:** a curve showing tax revenue rising at first as the tax rate is increasing and then falling beyond a certain rate.

The Laffer curve was first drawn by an American economist and advisor to President Ronald Reagan, Arthur Laffer, in the early 1970s. He drew it to support his view that a cut in tax rates may increase tax revenue by stimulating both total economic activity, because of the greater incentive effect, and declared economic activity. Figure 10.4 shows the Laffer curve.

At a tax rate of 0% there will obviously be no tax revenue. There will also be no tax revenue at a rate of 100% as workers will not be prepared to work if all their income goes in tax. The curve suggests there is a tax rate that will generate the most tax revenue. Raising the tax rate beyond this point would reduce tax revenue as it will discourage work and encourage tax evasion. Figure 10.4 indicates that a cut in the tax rate from 50% to 40% would increase tax revenue.

The curve also suggests that, apart from where tax revenue is maximised, tax revenue is associated with two

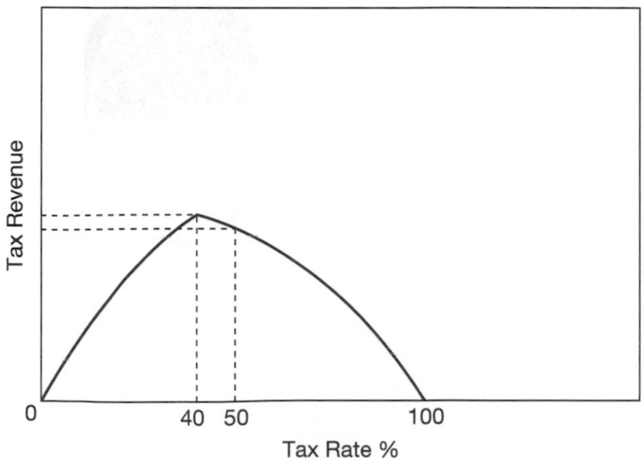

Figure 10.4 The Laffer curve

tax rates. Economists, however, question the usefulness and validity of the Laffer curve. They argue that it is debatable what the shape of the 'curve' actually is. They suggest it may be linear over part of its length and any shape is likely to vary over time and between countries.

Empirical evidence also suggests that belief in the Laffer curve can result in government failure. For example, soon after it was shown to Ronald Reagan, the American government introduced tax cuts that actually reduced tax revenue.

> **TOP TIP**
>
> Always indicate the 0% and 100% tax rates on a Laffer curve as well as the 'optimum' rate.

SELF-ASSESSMENT TASK 10.5

In 2014 the German government's economic policies came in for criticism from the president of its own central bank, Jens Weidmann. He claimed that the plan to phase in a minimum wage of €8.50 an hour by January 2017 and a cut in the retirement age of some workers would reduce the efficiency of the German labour market.

He also said that the government's willingness to stimulate consumption to reduce the country's current account surplus would penalise exporters just because they are more efficient than their rivals in producing relatively low-priced but high-quality products. In 2013 Germany had a current account surplus of €210 billion, which was 7.5% of GDP and a higher percentage than China's surplus.

1 Discuss whether introducing a minimum wage would reduce labour market efficiency.

2 Would increasing consumption necessarily reduce a current account surplus?

3 a Why may a government seek to reduce a current account surplus?

  b Explain how one policy measure may reduce a current account surplus and give one reason why such a measure may not be effective.

SUMMARY

In this chapter it has been shown that:

- Governments seek to achieve a low and stable inflation rate, usually a balance on the current account of the balance of payments, the avoidance of destabilising fluctuations in its exchange rate, full employment and sustained and sustainable economic growth.
- The internal value of a currency will fall if inflation occurs. The external value will fall if there is a depreciation or devaluation of the currency. The internal and external values of a currency tend to move in the same direction.
- A high rate of inflation is likely to have an adverse effect on the balance of payments.
- The Phillips curve suggests that a government can reduce the unemployment rate but at a cost of a higher inflation rate.
- The expectations-augmented Phillips curve suggests there is no long-run trade-off between unemployment and inflation.
- Conflicts between policy objectives provide challenges for governments, which have to use a range of policy measures to achieve their objectives.
- There is a risk because of lack of accurate information, time lags, unexpected responses, pressure groups and corruption but government intervention may not improve macroeconomic performance.
- The Laffer curve suggests that tax cuts may actually increase a government's tax revenue.

Exam-style questions

1 a Explain how the impact of the Keynesian multiplier process will change if a free-market closed economy becomes a mixed economy with foreign trade. [12]

b Analyse how a change in the equilibrium level of income resulting from the multiplier process might lead to unemployment or inflation. [13]

Source: Cambridge International AS and A Level Economics 9708 Paper 41 Q6 May/June 2011.

2 a Explain how economic growth can occur without the price level increasing. [12]

b Discuss what policy measures a government might use to increase the country's economic growth rate. [13]

Chapter 11: Preparing for examinations

Learning objectives

On completion of this chapter you should know:

- about the various skills and abilities that are assessed in the Cambridge International AS Level and A Level examinations
- how to plan your preparation for examinations in an effective way
- how to feel confident in tackling examination questions
- why some students do not succeed or perform to their true ability in written examinations.

Introduction

The assessment processes in this book are designed to test your ability to meet the aims of the Cambridge syllabus. These aims are to enable you to develop:

- an understanding of the factual knowledge of economics
- a facility for self-expression, not only in writing but also in using additional aids, such as statistics and diagrams where appropriate
- the habit of using works of reference as sources of data specific to economics
- the habit of reading critically to gain information about the changing economy we live in
- an appreciation of the methods of study used by the economist and of the most effective ways economic data may be analysed, correlated, discussed and presented.

The evidence on which this assessment of your skills and abilities in each chapter is based comes from your performance in two sets of written examination papers at Cambridge International AS Level and at A Level (see the Introduction for more details).

If you approach assessment in a positive and constructive way, then you should achieve the grade you are expecting, consistent with the time and effort you have devoted to your Economics studies. For some students, however, for all sorts of reasons, the final grade may be a disappointment.

So, what should you do to be successful? There is no magic formula but if you do the following, you will give yourself every chance of success:

- Read the relevant AS Level and A Level sections in this book and feel confident that you have understood the subject content.
- Complete all or most of the self-assessment tasks.
- Where possible, understand how the various problems, concepts, theories and policies might be applied to developing economics as well as to developed economies.
- Know what to expect and how best to tackle examination papers.
- Make sure to use the additional information that is provided on the Student's CD.

The seeds for success therefore are sown long before you enter the examination room. The key thing is to be prepared. It is worth remembering: 'If you fail to prepare, you are preparing to fail'. Why not put this on your wall? But if you do, remember to practise what it says.

Study and revision

Study is something you do from the first day of your course. This involves the gradual accumulation of the knowledge and skills of Economics. You should also see the regular review or revision of such knowledge and skills as part of this process. (This is where the self-assessment tasks in this book are a great help.) Revision therefore is not something that is only confined to the last week or so before an examination. So 'make study a habit; make revision a habit'.

Managing your time in an effective way is crucial. There should be regular periods in the week when you have spare blocks of time that you can devote to studying Economics. Even if it is only 30 minutes, if this is spent effectively, it will be of value to you. You should also try to have set places where you can study, ideally free from distractions such as loud music, talking, television noise and so on. This may not be easy but try to have set times and places for your study and stick to a routine.

A second important aspect of time management is *planning*. All students should try to do this by thinking ahead. This is particularly important where you are taking examinations on a staged basis. Time is therefore limited between the start of teaching and when you have to take your first examinations.

Here are a few simple suggestions that might help:

- Read through your class notes on a daily basis; follow this up by reading the relevant topic in this book.
- Make a weekly plan of what you will do; at the end of each week, go over the reading again and see if you can do the self-assessment tasks that are incorporated into the topic.
- When you have completed a block of topics, see if you can answer the examination questions at the end of each chapter and on the Student CD, ideally without referring to your notes or to the book.

Think and plan ahead. Find out when you might have to do a 'mock' examination and, above all, make sure you know when the actual examination will be taking place.

All of these simple things should help you feel relaxed and confident when you take examinations. So, remember: 'If you fail to prepare, you are preparing to fail'.

Adapted from an original drawing by Emily Bamford

A few hints on how to study effectively

Each of us has a preferred study environment where we can work in an effective and efficient way. For some it may be at home; for others it may be in a school or public library where the distractions going on around us can at least be shut off for an hour or two. The best time for study may also vary – much will depend upon your family circumstances and how you can arrange to study in relation to these and other commitments on your time.

Whatever the best time, the following advice should help you.

- Put yourself in a position where you can concentrate on your work. This is most unlikely to happen if your favourite television programme is on in the same room. The attention span of most people is 40–60 minutes. After such a period, have a drink and a rest, maybe do something else before studying for a further period.
- When reading from this book, make notes on what you have read and incorporate these into your class notes on a particular topic. You will also find it useful to do the self-assessment tasks. Writing and working in this way greatly enhances your understanding of a topic. Do not just read material on its own – the problem with this approach to study is that you will very quickly forget what you have read. The big advantage also of making notes is that they will be there for future revision when you need them.
- Once you have completed the study of a particular topic, condense your notes and write them on a revision card, which you will find invaluable for use shortly before examinations. An example of such notes is shown in Figure 11.1.

So, it is not so much how long you study but how effective you are in your studying. Make sure you use your time in such a way that you feel in control of your own learning experience.

Elasticity – responsiveness of quantity demanded to a change in price, income or prices of substitutes or complements

$$\text{PED} = \frac{\%\text{ change in qty demanded}}{\%\text{ change in price}}$$

elastic >1
inelastic <1
unitary =1
applies to all measures

$$\text{YED} = \frac{\%\text{ change in qty demanded}}{\%\text{ change in income}}$$

+ve – normal goods
–ve – inferior goods

$$\text{XED} = \frac{\%\text{ change in qty demanded, good A}}{\%\text{ change in price, good B}}$$

+ve – subsitutes
–ve – complements

Use and applications: prediction of effects of price changes on quantity demanded; forecast effects of a change in income on demand; pricing strategies for firms in competitive markets

Examples:
low PED – petrol, alcohol
normal goods – many consumer goods
inferior goods – cheap margarine, black and white TVs
substitutes – pork and chicken, car and bus travel
complements – petrol and car travel

Figure 11.1 Example of a revision card

Examination questions

Types of question

There are three main types of question in the Cambridge International AS Level and A Level Economics examinations. Examples of each can be found on the accompanying CD. These are:

1 multiple-choice questions
2 data-response questions
3 essay questions, including two-part structured questions.

Let us look at each type of question in turn, as various skills are being examined in each of these forms of question.

Multiple-choice questions

These are used to assess the extent to which you understand the full subject content of the Cambridge syllabus. Typically, they take the form of a 'stem' followed by four possible answers. You are required to identify which of these so-called 'keys' is the correct answer. In most questions, one key is clearly wrong, two seem temptingly correct, while one is the correct answer. So, beware! These questions are not as easy as they might appear.

With such questions, it is absolutely vital that you attempt all questions in the time available.

With multiple-choice questions, practice is essential. Below is a strategy that you may find helpful.

- Go through the question paper, answering those questions that you can answer quickly and with confidence that you know the correct answer.
- Leave any you find difficult or that require a lot of calculations.
- Go back and attempt those questions requiring calculations.
- Finally, return to those questions that you have found difficult.
- As the examination time runs out, make a guess at any questions you have not attempted.

If you take a 'mock' examination, find out all the correct answers – be sure you know how and why you got the right answer or why the answer you selected was wrong. It is very important that you do this so that you can better prepare for the real examination.

Data-response questions

Data-response questions are more varied. At AS Level, this type of question draws upon a relatively short, simple set of economic data with some text. For A Level, the questions are derived from more varied stimulus material, such as graphs, diagrams or text, which may contain data, as well as more detailed tables of data. The data-handling skills you need to feel confident when answering such questions are those contained in the Introduction.

When you come across a data-response question for the first time:

- look at the title as it may give some clues about its content
- read any table or column headings and see if you know what they mean
- see if you can pick out the main patterns in the data using the 'eyeballing' technique referred to in the Introduction
- pick out any notable features of a chart or diagram
- see if you can recognise the economic concept or concepts contained in the data.

Once you have done this you should feel comfortable with the information provided.

Data-response questions require short answers. These can take three forms:

1 Questions that require no more than interpretation of the data provided – answers to such questions might be no more than a word, a number or a short phrase.
2 Questions that require your understanding of an economic concept that is contained in the data.
3 Questions where you are required to discuss or comment on some aspect or concept in the data.

But do remember not to write more than you have to – the marks available should give some indication of how much is appropriate. This type of question is compulsory at AS Level and at A Level.

Essay questions

These questions require extended writing. Some of the questions are 'structured', i.e., they consist of related parts, usually two. Others may take the form of a single task. You may wish to spend around 45 minutes writing your answer to the essay question at AS Level; at A Level you may wish to spend a little longer on each answer, say 50 minutes. Make sure you consider how to allocate time proportionately to the marks in the paper, and ensure that you leave enough time to answer the essay questions.

General advice on how to write in an effective way is given in the Introduction – why not go back and refresh yourself on the main points?

The wording of questions

Examination questions are carefully written to test specific knowledge and skills. They never contain questions such as:

- Write all you know about . . .
- Write as much as you can remember about . . .

Unfortunately, students don't always appreciate this point!

Examination questions usually contain two very important instructions:

1 **Command or directive words** indicate what form the answer should take. For example, it could be in the form of a description, a discussion, an explanation or merely a statement. These words are there for a purpose, namely that they are intended as a guide to what skills should be used when you answer a particular question.

2 **Content words** are much more diverse in nature since they cover the whole of the subject area of the Cambridge syllabus. Their aim is to make clear what is the focus of the question and what you are required to write about.

Table 11.1 shows a list of key command words that are most likely to occur in examination questions. You should study these carefully and understand what each means.

Command word	What it means	Where you can expect it to be used
Calculate	Work out using the information provided	Usually in the early parts of data-response questions, multiple-choice questions and some structured essay questions.
Define	Give the exact meaning	"
Describe	Give a description of	"
Identify	Give an example or key point	"
Illustrate	Give examples or use a diagram	"
Outline	Describe the key point without detail	"
State	Make clear	"
Analyse	Set out the main points and show how they link and connect	Usually in the later parts of data-response questions and in the early parts of essay questions.
Compare	Explain similarities and differences	"
Explain	Give clear reasons or make clear	"
Consider	Give your thoughts about, with some justification	"
Assess	Show how important something is	Usually in the final part of data-response questions and in essay questions.
Comment upon	Give your reasoned opinions on, with some explanation	"
Criticise	Give an opinion, but support it with evidence	"
Discuss	Give the important arguments, for and against, ideally with a conclusion	"
Justify	Explain why the arguments for an opinion are stronger than the arguments against	"
Evaluate	Discuss the importance of, making some attempt to weight your opinions	"
To what extent	Give reasons for and against, come to a conclusion with a justification of which arguments are strongest and which are weakest	"

Table 11.1 Key command words

Source: Cambridge International AS and A Level Economics 9708 Syllabus.

You will then appreciate that the following instructions are not the same:

- Define price elasticity of demand.
- Explain what is meant by price elasticity of demand.
- Discuss the relevance of price elasticity of demand in business.

A simple method for interpreting essay questions

Consider the following typical example of an AS Level question:

1 a With the help of a diagram, explain how a production possibility curve can illustrate the concepts of opportunity cost and economic growth. [8]

b Discuss whether free market economies or centrally planned economies are more likely to make choices that will maximise the benefits for consumers. [12]

The subject content is in Chapter 1 of the book. Remember to divide your time for answering the question according to the number of marks available, so allow 15–20 minutes for part a and 25–30 minutes for part b.

Part a *must* contain a diagram of a PPC. You need to use this diagram to show how opportunity cost can be explained by a movement along the PPC; economic growth can be shown by an outward shift of the PPC. So put these two concepts (and identify them clearly) on your diagram and then write a few sentences to explain each.

Part b is more difficult. This is flagged up by the command word 'discuss', which means you should give arguments in your answer as to which type of economy is 'more likely to make choices that will maximise the benefits for consumers'. So, you need to analyse how choices are made in each. You may like to incorporate other diagrams in your answer but do ensure that you give a balanced explanation covering both types of economy. Finally, you should give a conclusion, based on the arguments that you have put forth in the body of your answer.

How to avoid common pitfalls

Let us start with a few typical comments on examination answers:

- Does not answer the question.
- Too vague.
- Misses point of question.
- No application.
- Descriptive. No analysis of issues.
- No discussion.
- Ignores second aspect of question.

These comments clearly indicate that the students have not done what was expected from them. So, the first way to produce successful answers is:

- **Answer the question:** In other words, produce an answer as directed by the question. The information above, in particular the simple method for interpreting examination questions, should help you to write your answer in a clear, well-structured manner as directed by the question. This point cannot be emphasised too much!

There are various other ways in which you might write a successful answer. For example:

- **Diagrams:** These are very important and a relevant means of economic explanation. Many of the topics you come across in Economics can be represented by a diagram or by means of an explanation supported by a diagram. You have only to glance at the topics in the book to see this. So, a relevant, correctly drawn diagram, used effectively *and referred to in your answer*, will strengthen your answer. An example of good technique is shown in Figure 11.2.

  Figure 11.2 shows how the price of tickets to watch cricket will be affected by the introduction of a subsidy. As this diagram indicates, the subsidy will lead to an increase in supply, shifting the supply curve downwards and to the right. The price which spectators will have to pay falls from P_1 to P_2 – it does not fall to P_3, as part of the subsidy (that shown between P_3 and P_2) will be retained by the ground owners to offset the higher costs incurred as a result of the increase in the number of spectators.
- **Current issues and problems:** One of the reasons for studying Economics is to help you understand some of the things that are taking place around you. So, when you get the opportunity to demonstrate your knowledge, do so! For example, if you are answering a question on the negative externalities associated with environmental pollution, you might refer to a local example that is known to you or something you have seen in a newspaper or magazine. Most of the topics in the Cambridge syllabus can be supported by additional up-to-date material that is not always found in textbooks.

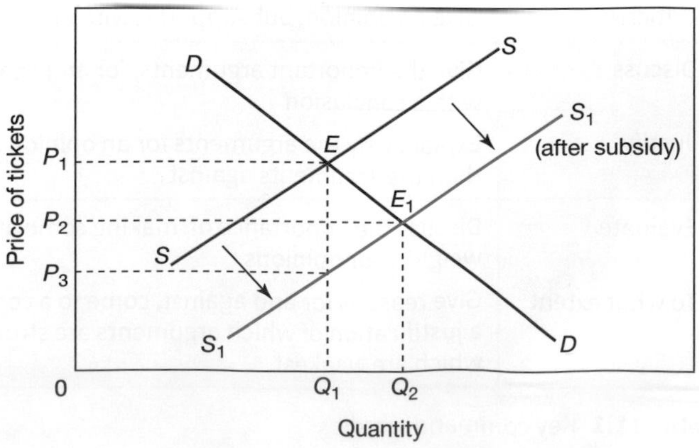

Figure 11.2 The effects of a subsidy on the price of tickets

- **Refer to things you have read:** It follows that there are instances where it would give more meaning to your answer if you referred to some material by name, such as a newspaper article, something from a website, an example from a textbook or the views of a particular economist.

Common mistakes made in Economics examinations

In addition to a failure to answer the question, the other main mistakes made by students are:

- a failure to allocate writing time in an appropriate way
- confusion over similar terms
- meaningless, wrongly drawn diagrams or diagrams that add nothing to an answer.

Let us conclude this section by looking at each in turn.

You must make sure you allocate your writing time in the examination in a meaningful way. Roughly speaking, allocate your writing time in direct proportion to the marks available for each question as referred to earlier.

- Do not exceed the time you have allocated for each question.
- If you cannot do a particular question, leave it and move on to the next one. (You can always return to it later on in the examination if time permits.) You will only get marks for the questions you answer – your script, however, will always be marked out of the total marks allocated.

A second problem is that, on occasions, students sometimes confuse terms that are similar (in terms of content) or that have similar names (but mean something different).

Table 11.2 contains a few common examples. Watch out also that you express formulae correctly – in particular elasticity formulae.

Finally, a common mistake that students often make is in the way in which they use diagrams in their answers. Common errors are:

- labelling axes incorrectly or not labelling them at all
- making diagrams too small
- drawing lines and curves incorrectly, usually through being wrongly sloping
- failure to use a diagram in an answer when asked for one to be included
- including a diagram when one is not needed and where it does not enhance an answer at all.

Topic	Often confused with
elastic demand	inelastic demand
allocative efficiency	productive efficiency
prices	costs
merit goods	public goods
direct taxation	indirect taxation
external costs/benefits	social costs/benefits
real income	nominal income
rate of interest	exchange rates
fiscal policy measures	monetary policy measures
aggregate demand	aggregate supply
balance of trade	balance of payments
income	wealth
monopoly	monopolistic competition

Table 11.2 Common errors over terms and topics in the Cambridge syllabus

SUMMARY

In this chapter it has been shown that:

- It is very important for you to be well-organised and to be able to plan ahead if you are to succeed.
- It is important to understand the type and style of questions that can be encountered in examination.
- Revision should be an ongoing process.
- Careful planning and making sure you understand the command words will help you in examination.
- There are three types of questions you are most likely to face in examination and how to go about answering each.

SELF-ASSESSMENT TASK 11.1

Below are examples of badly drawn diagrams. How many improvements can you make?

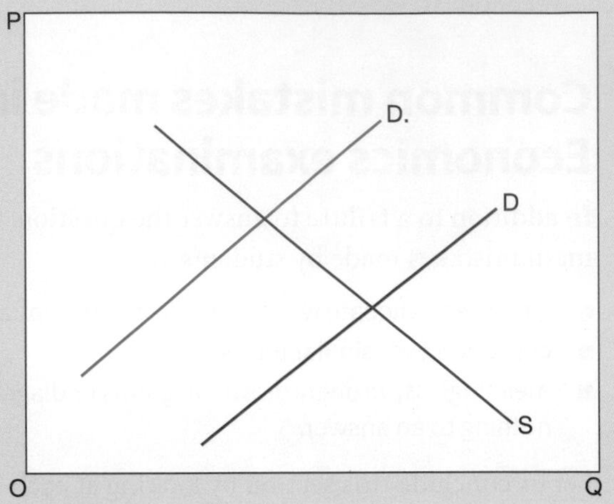

Figure 11.3 A reduction in the quantity demanded for a good

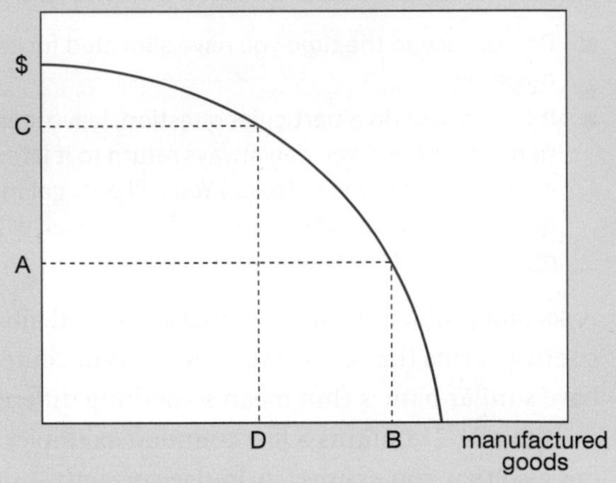

Figure 11.4 A PPC showing how the output of one good changes

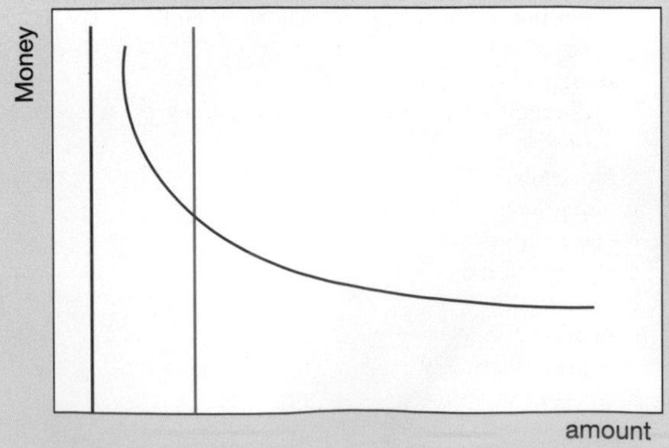

Figure 11.5 Figure showing an increase in the money supply

Index

Acknowledgements

The author and publishers acknowledge the following sources of copyright material and are grateful for the permissions granted. While every effort has been made, it has not always been possible to identify the sources of all the material used, or to trace all copyright holders. If any omissions are brought to our notice, we will be happy to include the appropriate acknowledgements on reprinting.

Text sources

Book

Reproduced by permission of Cambridge International Examinations: p66 Q1 Cambridge International AS and A Level Economics 9708 Paper 2 Q2 October/November 2007; p113 Q 1 Cambridge International AS and A Level Economics 9708 Paper 23 Q4 October/November 2012, Q2 Cambridge International AS and A Level Economics 9708 Paper 23 Q4 October/November 2012, Q3 Cambridge International AS and A Level Economics 9708 Paper 22 Q1 October/November 2011; p128 Q3 Cambridge International AS and A Level Economics 9708 Paper 21 Q1 May/June 2012; p215 Q3 Cambridge International AS and A Level Economics 9708 Paper 41 Q4 October/November 2012; p263 Q3 Cambridge International AS and A Level Economics 9708 Paper 41 Q1 May/June 2011, Q4 Cambridge International AS and A Level Economics 9708 Paper 41 Q7 May/June 2011; p272 Q1 Cambridge International AS and A Level Economics 9708 Paper 41 Q6 May/June 2011; p277 Table 11.1 Cambridge International AS and A Level Economics 9708 Syllabus.

p26 Daily Telegraph 16 Nov 2013; p39 Express Tribune 5 Sept 2013; p66 Q3 reproduced by permission of OCR; p70 The Standard Kenya 17 Sept 2011; p77 Asia News Network 3 January 2014; p198 The Express Tribune 30 July 2012 (Farooq Tirmiz); p210 The Guardian 8 August 2013 (J. Clay).

CD ROM

The two lakh car-just what India needs / The Independent 22 June 2007 and South China Morning Post 2010; Smog-weary Chinese vent / Daily Telegraph 26 February 2014.

Photography and Illustration permissions.

Cover SergeyP/Shutterstock; p12 © Blend Images/Alamy; p14 © DIZ München GmbH/Alamy; p21 moodboard/Thinkstock; p23 © travelpixs/Alamy; p24 huad262/Thinkstock; p 31 JanRoode/Thinkstock; p32 © Kumar Sriskandan/Alamy; p35 das-foto/shutterstock; p38 © myLAM/Alamy; p41 scanrail/Thinkstock; p42 Monkey Business Images/Thinkstock; p50 © Images of Africa Photobank/Alamy; p54 © epa european pressphoto agency b.v./Alamy; p55 tyler olson/Thinkstock; p59 © Peter Jones/Alamy; p67t hxdyl/Thinkstock; p67l gjp311/Thinkstock; p67r Ingram Publishing/Thinkstock; p77 © ZUMA Press, Inc./Alamy; p78 © Friedrich Stark/Alamy; p80 tcly/thinkstock; p85 © DWImages Northern Ireland/Alamy; p91 Kondor83/Thinkstock; p94 Danish Khan/Thinkstock; p98 © Alex Segre/Alamy; p103 Eric Gevaert/Thinkstock; p114 Adam Gault/Getty Images; p117 starekase/Thinkstock; p119 © GFC Collection/Alamy; p121 Bloomberg/Getty Images; p122 PORNCHAI KITTIWONGSAKUL/Staff/Getty Images; p126 TAGSTOCK1/Thinkstock; p129 © Imaginechina/Corbis; p133 Olga Serdyuk/Thinkstock; p135 © Global Warming Images/Alamy; p136 © Joerg Boethling/Alamy; p138 © travelib environment/Alamy; p140 hs2.org.uk; p141 © ANDY RAIN/epa/Corbis; p142 © Westend61 GmbH/Alamy; p144 © frans lemmens/Alamy; p145 tacar/Thinkstock; p150 © SCPhotos/Alamy; p156 MANPREET ROMANA/Stringer/Getty Images; p157l Gerard Koudenburg/Shutterstock; p157r Gordon Tipene/Thinkstock; p159 © Vijay Mathur/Reuters/Corbis; p162 © epa european pressphoto agency b.v./Alamy; p163 Fedor Selivanov/Shutterstock; p166t © ZOHRA BENSEMRA/Reuters/Corbis; p166b © Paul Chambers/Alamy; p168 Radu Bercan/Shutterstock; p177t Anne-Louise Quarfoth/Thinkstock; p177b Markus Mainka/Shutterstock; p190 © THOMAS MUKOYA/Reuters/Corbis; p194 Bloomberg/Contributor/Getty Images; p197 © Prisma Bildagentur AG/Alamy; p196 © JM LOPEZ/epa/Corbis; p200 © Horizons WWP/Alamy; p202 © Art Directors & TRIP/Alamy; p203t Natursports/Shutterstock; p203b cinemafestival/Shutterstock; p207 Dan Kitwood/Staff/Getty Images; p208 © 67photo/Alamy; p210 1000 Words/Shutterstock; p213 Jordan Tan/Shutterstock; p216-217 Liufuyu/Thinkstock; p224 Hindustan Times/Contributor/Getty Images; p229 enisu/Thinkstock; p237 RyanKing999/Thinkstock; p256t © Pictorial Press Ltd/Alamy; p256b © ZUMA Press, Inc./Alamy; p261 © B Christopher/Alamy; p264 © PjrStudio / Alamy; p266 © economic images/Alamy; p273 © OJO Images Ltd/Alamy; p270 © epa european pressphoto agency b.v./Alamy

Terms and conditions of use for the CD-ROM

This is End User License Agreement ('EULA') is a legal agreement between 'You' (which means the individual customer) and Cambridge University Press ('the Licensor') for *Cambridge International AS and A Level Economics Student's CD-ROM Third edition* ('the Product'). Please read this EULA carefully. By continuing to use the Product, You agree to the terms of this EULA. If You do not agree to this EULA, please do not use this Product and promptly return it to the place where you obtained it.

1 Licence

The Licensor grants You the right to use the Product under the terms of this EULA as follows:

- **a** You may only install one copy of this Product (i) on a single computer or secure network server for use by one or more people at different times, or (ii) on one or more computers for use by a single person (provided the Product is only used on one computer at one time and is only used by that single person).
- **b** You may only use the Product for non-profit, educational purposes.
- **c** You shall not and shall not permit anyone else to: (i) copy or authorise copying of the Product, (ii) translate the Product, (iii) reverse-engineer, disassemble or decompile the Product, or (iv) transfer, sell, assign or otherwise convey any portion of the Product.

2 Copyright

- **a** All content provided as part of the Product (including text, images and ancillary material) and all software, code, and metadata related to the Product is the copyright of the Licensor or has been licensed to the Licensor, and is protected by copyright and all other applicable intellectual property laws and international treaties.
- **b** You may not copy the Product except for making one copy of the Product solely for backup or archival purposes. You may not alter, remove or destroy any copyright notice or other material placed on or with this Product.
- **c** You may edit and make changes to any material provided in the Product in editable format ('Editable Material') and store copies of the resulting files ('Edited Files') for your own non-commercial, educational use, but You may not distribute Editable Materials or Edited Files to any third-party, or remove, alter, or destroy any copyright notices on Editable Materials or Edited Files, or copy any part of any Editable Material or Edited Files into any other file for any purpose whatsoever.

3 Liability

- **a** The Product is supplied 'as-is' with no express guarantee as to its suitability. To the extent permitted by applicable law, the Licensor is not liable for costs of procurement of substitute products, damages or losses of any kind whatsoever resulting from the use of this Product, or errors or faults therein, and in every case the Licensor's liability shall be limited to the suggested list price or the amount actually paid by You for the Product, whichever is lower.
- **b** You accept that the Licensor is not responsible for the persistency, accuracy or availability of any URLs of external or third-party internet websites referred to on the Product and does not guarantee that any content on such websites is, or will remain, accurate, appropriate or available. The Licensor shall not be liable for any content made available from any websites and URLs outside the Product or for the data collection or business practices of any third-party internet website or URL referenced by the Product.
- **c** You agree to indemnify the Licensor and to keep indemnified the Licensor from and against any loss, cost, damage or expense (including without limitation damages paid to a third party and any reasonable legal costs) incurred by the Licensor as a result of your breach of any of the terms of this EULA.

4 Termination

Without prejudice to any other rights, the Licensor may terminate this EULA if You fail to comply with any of its terms and conditions. In such event, You must destroy all copies of the Product in your possession.

5 Governing law

This agreement is governed by the laws of England and Wales, without regard to its conflict of laws provision, and each party irrevocably submits to the exclusive jurisdiction of the English courts. The parties disclaim the application of the United Nations Convention on the International Sale of Goods.